St Helenian English

Varieties of English Around the World (VEAW)

A companion monograph series devoted to sociolinguistic research, surveys and annotated text collections. The VEAW series is divided in two parts: a text series contains carefully selected specimens of Englishes documenting the coexistence of regional, social, stylistic and diachronic varieties in a particular region; and a general series which contains outstanding studies in the field, collections of papers devoted to one region or written by one scholar, bibliographies and other reference works.

General Series, Volume G37

St Helenian English. Origins, evolution and variation
by Daniel Schreier

St Helenian English

Origins, evolution and variation

Daniel Schreier
University of Zurich

John Benjamins Publishing Company
Amsterdam / Philadelphia

The paper used in this publication meets the minimum requirements of American National Standard for Information Sciences – Permanence of Paper for Printed Library Materials, ANSI z39.48-1984.

Library of Congress Cataloging-in-Publication Data

Schreier, Daniel, 1971-
St. Helenian English : origins, evolution, and variation / Daniel Schreier.
p. cm. (Varieties of English Around the World, ISSN 0172-7362 ; v. G37)
Includes bibliographical references and index.
1. English language--Saint Helena. 2. Saint Helena--Languages. 3. English language--Social aspects--Saint Helena. 4. English language--Dialects--Saint Helena. I. Title. II. Title: Saint Helenian English.
PE3330.S2S34 2008
427'.9973--dc22 2008031634
ISBN 978 90 272 4897 8 (Hb; alk. paper)

John Benjamins Publishing Co. · P.O. Box 36224 · 1020 ME Amsterdam · The Netherlands
John Benjamins North America · P.O. Box 27519 · Philadelphia PA 19118-0519 · USA

Contents

Maps, Table and Figures

List of Maps

List of Tables

List of Figures

Preface and acknowledgments

It is always good to keep notes; otherwise, I would probably have forgotten that I actually began writing this book more than seven years ago, on March 12, 2001, to be precise. I certainly remember that I first developed an interest in St Helena even earlier than that, sometime in autumn 1997, namely when I started my PhD on Tristan da Cunha English (TdCE). Preparing that project left no doubt that St Helenian English (StHE) had a considerable impact on the variety I set out to study and I was both surprised and disappointed to find there was practically no sociolinguistic information for St Helena, in contrast to the community's richly documented social history. I failed to understand why nobody had travelled to this beautiful island to document the oldest variety of southern Hemisphere English (though I have learnt in the meantime that Sheila Wilson, University of Cape Town, collected data in the mid-1990s) and decided to tackle this as soon as time and budget allowed.

The years went by, I finished my PhD on TdCE and then did a post-doc in New Zealand, carried out a "Habilitationsprojekt" on consonant variation and change in English at the University of Regensburg, Germany (custom in the German academic system, presumably to prove you are not discouraged with writing just one book and to demonstrate you still have life in you), and there were alternative projects and commitments here and there. Only in summer 2003 did the opportunity of carrying out fieldwork on St Helena finally open up; the end of the teaching semester and shipping schedules matched in miraculous ways, my boss did not mind me being away for almost three months (or, depending how you look at it, cherished the idea of having a quiet office for all that time) and my wife and I happily travelled to St Helena to collect first-hand recordings of the St Helenians. I returned with more than 25 hours of tape-recorded speech and hundreds of photocopies of historical documents to a piled-up desk, teaching responsibilities and all kinds of administrative duties (that, quite irritatingly, don't vanish into thin air when you are out of the office for three months). This meant that I had to leave the St Helena project lying, returning to it whenever I could. I then moved places, back to Switzerland, started a new position at the University of Bern, then another one at the University of Zurich, our family increased, days became longer and nights shorter, and all this did not enhance the progress of my writing at all. As a result, it all took much longer than I had anticipated (I think in my book proposal to Benjamins it says that I would hand in the complete manuscript by December 2005 at the very latest… here is a word of praise to publisher patience!).

So, all in all, it is a ten years' process from the initial decision to carry out such a project to the finished end-product in your hands. It was stop and go and writing was unconventional at times. Sections of this book were written in about a dozen countries on four continents, notes were taken on notepads, serviettes, handkerchiefs when no laptop was available, I wrote on board ships, in planes, buses and trains, while I was pretending to listen to people who should better not be named here, while waiting for what- and whoever was late (which turned out to be a bit of a problem in Switzerland, people start complaining here when a train is three minutes delayed), at faculty board meetings, exam supervisions, while baby-sitting our daughter (which she did not take to well at times, energetically rearranging our living room furniture or cheerfully unplugging my laptop to set priorities right), etc. Sometimes I would make excellent progress, then again there were months and months when I just could not make time.

Looking back now, I would not want to claim that I am ten years wiser (no-one who knows me would say anything as crazy as this!), but I have no hesitation to admit that, though the book still incorporates some of the intentions it set out with, it has taken quite a few twists and turns that I could not foresee at the time. These were so far-reaching that the 'St Helena book' is now, shall I say, distinctly different than from what I had envisaged in the late 1990s. It was a real journey of discovery in many ways; despite the fact that my impatience did not always cope well with the fact that I had to write 'piece meal' (and so it felt like), I am now under the impression that it has benefited quite a bit from the time I was forced to take.

It goes without saying that lots of people were somehow involved and I can only acknowledge those to whom I am particularly grateful, without whose help I feel the book would not be what it is. First of all, a huge thanks goes to my wife Karrie, human being (and fieldworker!) extraordinaire, who, as always, supported me all the way, this time even carrying out sociolinguistic research on St Helena with me; Walt Wolfram, for being Walt, putting everybody else first, going out of his way to support others and forgetting about himself occasionally, for his friendship, good-natured spirit and unfailing support in difficult times, and of course for making it possible that the William C Friday endowment fund of North Carolina State University granted me $4'000.-, which helped me finance the trip to the South Atlantic (and is gratefully acknowledged here); Edgar W. Schneider, who made it possible for me to return to Europe (though he may still think I never really arrived in Germany – und du hast wie eigentlich immer vielleicht fast ein bisschen recht, aber…), who let me go to St Helena and would always take time to discuss ideas with me when I was back, did not over-burden me with administration when I was his assistant, suggested I publish in the VEAW series, gave me much-needed advice, proof-read and commented on the entire manuscript, did all the extra work superb editors do, etc. etc. – this book would simply not be what it is without Edgar's input; Keith and Coral Yon, Kunjie Field, St Helena, givers not takers, who made us feel at home on St Helena and organised everything most efficiently for us; Ricky Fowler, archivist in Jamestown Castle on St Helena, who saw my despair in the face of thousands of leather-bound volumes of correspondence with the East India Company and directed my interest to documents needed for research on earlier forms of StHE (I would probably still be in the archives without his help); Basil George, "a dedicated Saint", for his interest in the project and for sharing his insider knowledge of StHE with me; audiences at conferences or invited guest lectures (at the Universities of Essex, Lausanne, and Heidelberg), for their interest and input and also for spotting what they spotted (I am doing what I can to avoid the terms 'inconsistency' or 'mistake' here); Kees Vaes, of John Benjamins Publishing Company, for giving me the opportunity to publish in this fine series and whose seemingly endless patience is evidenced by the fact that I have about half a dozen emails starting with "Dear Dani - Could you give me an update as to how you are progressing with the manuscript? I *urgently* need to know"; Patricia Leplae, also of John Benjamins Publishing Company, who checked the lay-out; Nicole Joho and Claudia Rathore, University of Zurich, two top-notch assistants, who read and commented on a draft version, convinced me how erratically variable my punctuation is, checked additional sources and found quite a few of what one might grudgingly call inconsistencies (of course they were unaware that I had carefully inserted mistakes to check how attentively they read…); Danielle Hickey, University of Zurich, who read several chapters and produced the index; and finally, a great number of colleagues who gave good advice over the years, in alphabetical order: Philip Baker, Dave Britain, Lyle Campbell, Elizabeth Gordon, Kirk Hazen, Magnus Huber, Alex Kautzsch, Paul Kerswill, Raj Mesthrie, Salikoko Mufwene, Peter Patrick, John R. Rickford, Edgar W. Schneider, Andrea Sudbury, Peter Trudgill, Richard J. Watts, Walt Wolfram, Laura Wright, and the farmer from Zimbabwe, whose name I long forgot, who fired the toughest questions about new-dialect formation at me on a memorable flight from Perth, Australia to Johannesburg (heck, I still can't answer some of them – but they sure made me think). No worries, all remaining errors are my own.

Last but not least, a heartfelt thank you goes to the 'Saints' who had a chat with us in summer 2003, thus providing the data without which this book would never have made it. Sadly, several of them did not live to see the publication they helped on the way, so the book is a tribute to them as well. You are not forgotten.

Daniel Schreier
Basel, Switzerland

July 2008

Das Buech mecht ych dr

Chiara Schreier (geboore 2006)

widme.

Fir our little Sunneschyyn isch ä jede Dialäggt 'new'.

1. Introduction

> The St. Helenian of to-day, however dark complexioned he may be, is English in thought, manners, and language – in fact the English tongue is spoken by him with greater purity than in most of our rural districts in England. (Robert Armitage Sterndale, Governor of St Helena, 1899)

> **St Helena Creole**: An English-based creole used on the island of St Helena; has some use as a pidgin. (David Crystal 1997: 341)

The spread and diffusion of English around the world has been widely discussed, both in the technical and the popular literature (to give but some references: Trudgill & Hannah 1982; McCrum, Cran & MacNeil 1992; Cheshire 1991; Crystal 1997; Graddol, Leith & Swann 1997; Jenkins 2003; Hickey 2004; Schneider 2007). One of the most unusual facts of the recent history of English is, beyond doubt, that one language was brought to so many locations outside its 'heartland', the British Isles, and that transplantation across the globe saw extreme diversification and the rise of distinctive 'new' varieties. In this sense, as Thomason & Kaufman (1988) point out, the 'export' of English offers fascinating perspectives for contact linguistics, since the embedding of English into a multitude of contact settings (with countless co-existing language systems) entailed an unprecedented amount of contact-induced language change. Needless to say, this challenged traditional taxonomies. New labels came into use, by experts and lay persons alike: *pidgins* and *creoles*, for offspring varieties of language contact scenarios; *koinés*, for varieties developing mainly through contact between mutually intelligible and structurally similar forms of one and the same language (dialects or sociolects); and more recently, varieties of English as a *Second Language* (ESL) and *Foreign Language* (EFL), that have gained in total number of speakers dramatically in the second half of the 20th century, now representing the majority of English speakers around the world (estimated at more than one billion; Crystal 1997). As useful as these labels are for descriptive purposes, they raise a major theoretical problem: how (and on what basis) are researchers justified to define 'new' varieties? For instance, what features does a koiné need to have in order to be classified as such? Are there checklists of features, against which we can measure the findings and produce a watertight classification, and which of them is most reliable? If not, how can we support our decision to label the 'new' variety the way we suggest and not otherwise?

The two initial quotes illustrate this dilemma; they come from different periods (one from the end of the 19th, one from the end of the 20th century), from two people who, though they have different backgrounds, are in some way qualified to make such statements: one of them being an authority on World English (who, however, has never visited St Helena), the other one a British civil servant who served on the island as an administrator to the Crown and stayed there from 1897-1902 (but had no training in linguistics). As different as their backgrounds are, both Crystal and Sterndale refer to the same variety, St Helenian English (StHE), one leaving no doubt that it is the equivalent of British dialects (though much 'purer', one of the most common myths about language), the other one classifying it as a creole, "with some use as a pidgin." No variety can be a regional dialect and a creole at the same time, so how are we to interpret these conflicting views? There is only one possibility, and that is turning to external history, finding out whether the community underwent far-reaching changes that redirected the evolution of StHE over the last hundred years. This turns out not to be the case at all. The 20th century was a period of reduced in-migration and sociodemographic stability, so the variety must have formed before 1900. So which of the two assessments is incorrect? And what selective criteria are/were these judgments based on in the first place?

The main aim of this book is to describe StHE as concisely as possible to answer (some of) these questions and define its status. Moreover, it discusses its relevance for various sub-fields of linguistics (most importantly the evolution of 'new' varieties), attempts to link present and past for an in-depth analysis of language change (namely by comparing and cross-evaluating historical and contemporary evidence), to look into the complex interplay of language-external (social history, migration patterns, global socio-demographic evolution, etc.) and -internal developments, i.e. to discuss the full complexity of contact-induced language change, and by doing so, to offer some hypotheses on the relevance of StHE for current theories on the formation of post-colonial Englishes (as discussed in Schneider 2007). Of course, the question that looms large here is the typological status of the variety and how we are to decide exactly what it is (or whether such a decision is possible at all). With reference to the two quotes above, it is certainly possible, as some colleagues have reminded me, that Sterndale may have acted on an impulse to defend the St Helenians, for personal or political reasons, and to emphasise their British heritage, whereas Crystal may have used faulty (or simply wrong) information about the variety in the absence of first-hand knowledge (which was practically not available at the time of writing, a notable exception being Hancock 1991). Since StHE ranks among the "lesser-known varieties of English" (cf. Schreier, Trudgill, Schneider & Williams fc.), a complete phonological and morpho-syntactic description has not been available so far, so all these claims are no more than personal judgments made in the absence of *prima facie* data. A well-founded typological assessment rests on taking into account a range of linguistic criteria, which means, among others, looking into sociolinguistic variation in StHE, i.e. regional variation, social stratification, concurring settlement patterns in various parts of the island, etc. The tasks of linguistic classification and historical reconstruction are extremely complicated, since first of all, we base our assessments on uncertain sources, and second, since we do not have a yardstick against which to measure the sociolinguistic status of 'new' varieties.

Consequently, this book covers a range of topics surrounding the history and status of StHE. It is based on ethnographic and sociolinguistic fieldwork carried out on the island of St Helena from July to September 2003. One of its major aims is to document a native-speaker variety of English that has found little interest to date and to describe the phonological, grammatical and lexical features of the variety as accurately as possible. The goal is to provide a descriptive profile of the oldest variety of Southern Hemisphere English (SHemE), thus closing a gap in the literature on English as a world language. On the other hand, the book takes a broader perspective in that it tackles a number of issues, by nature theoretical and methodological, that go beyond this particular variety only. From a general, theoretical, point of view, the focus is on the development of 'Englishes' in general, the similarities, differences, parallel developments and local innovations that characterise varieties of English around the world, on explanations that have been offered to account for them (substratist, universal, contact-specific, etc.) and their relevance for sociolinguistic theory, how transplanted language varieties develop and form and who is most instrumental in forming them (and for what reason). The bigger picture is how 'new' varieties evolve, and in what respect (social, linguistic, geographical, political, etc.) they are said to be 'new'. This means that I integrate all kinds of social and linguistic evidence available and discuss possible implications for the fields of historical and genetic linguistics, making frequent reference to variationist sociolinguistics and contact linguistics, most notably contact dialectology and pidgin and creole linguistics. The contact scenario on St Helena serves as an ideal microcosm for testing and evaluating a number of theories on general processes of language birth and language change (such as the founder principle, linguistic determinism, supraregionalisation, swamping, etc.).

The structure of the book is as follows. Ch. 2, "How St Helenian English could have formed: Some principles of contact linguistics", provides the theoretical backbone for the evaluative assessments and analyses that follow. It introduces general principles of contact linguistics, starting with accommodation theory and its permanent effects on the emergence of 'new' varieties. It continues with an investigation of the principal agents behind this process, i.e., whether it is children or adults that are more instrumental, and whether such varieties are more likely to thrive through second-language (L2) learning, accommodation to other dialects, or acquisition of a first (native) language (L1), particularly when norms and stable rules have not (yet) emerged in a contact setting that is heterogeneous and linguistically diffuse. Furthermore, ch. 2 identifies some major processes that underlie dialect contact and new-dialect formation: *mixing* of various inputs and feature selection, *levelling* of dialect differences and disappearance of individual features (social, regional, etc.), *regularisation*, the loss of irregular or abundant features that accompanies *focussing* and the emergence of norms, as well as a number of minor and less frequently attested processes. The chapter concludes with an overview of common processes in contact-induced language change, namely when language coexistence gives rise to jargons, pidgins and creoles (*simplification*, *reduction*, *expansion*, etc.). All these processes are illustrated with examples from English varieties around the world, from contact processes that manifested themselves in diverse sociolinguistic and sociodemographic settings. The aim is to set the ground for the later identification of change mechanisms that operated during the evolution phase of StHE, and to formulate some first hypotheses as to how the local variety may have originated and developed, which I then go on to test with a qualitative and quantitative analysis of StHE.

Ch. 3, "St Helenian English: Historical, sociodemographic and socio-linguistic background", looks into the social and historical context of the variety. Discovered in 1502 by the Portuguese, St Helena served as a secret landing and refreshment station for Portuguese vessels travelling from or to the Indian Ocean. The Portuguese never developed permanent settlements but did build a local infrastructure (a little village, gardens and fruit orchards, a church and a cemetery), which they used throughout the 16th century. The English and Dutch followed in their wake and contested possession of the island without formally claiming it. They explored and charted the island interior, a practice adopted by many visiting seafarers (as evidenced by Map 1.1, produced by the geographer H. Moll in 1732). It is only in the 1650s that we find the establishment of a permanent population and thus the foundations of an endemic variety. The East India Company had lost its possessions in the Table Bay area (taken by the Dutch) and along the West African coast (which were in Portuguese hands). The only place of strategic value left was St Helena, and the Company dispatched a group of army personnel and planters with their families to set up a permanent populace and to thus claim the island for the Empire in 1658. These efforts were strengthened after the Dutch briefly took control over the island and, as a result, St Helena became the most important stop-over in the South Atlantic Ocean. At one stage it was frequented by ships to such an extent that it was referred to as the 'punch bowl of the South Atlantic'. Ambitious settlement schemes were developed, and cheap labour was imported for the local industry. Accordingly, slaves were brought to the island from very early on, with origins as diverse as St Iago (on the Caboverde Islands), the West African Gold and Slave Coasts, India, various places throughout Asia and, most important of all, Madagascar. The early years of the colony saw massive fluctuations and population turnover (due to exoduses, rebellions, diseases, etc.), so that the sociodemographic situation stabilised by the mid-18th century only.

Map 1.1 An early map of the island of St Helena[1]

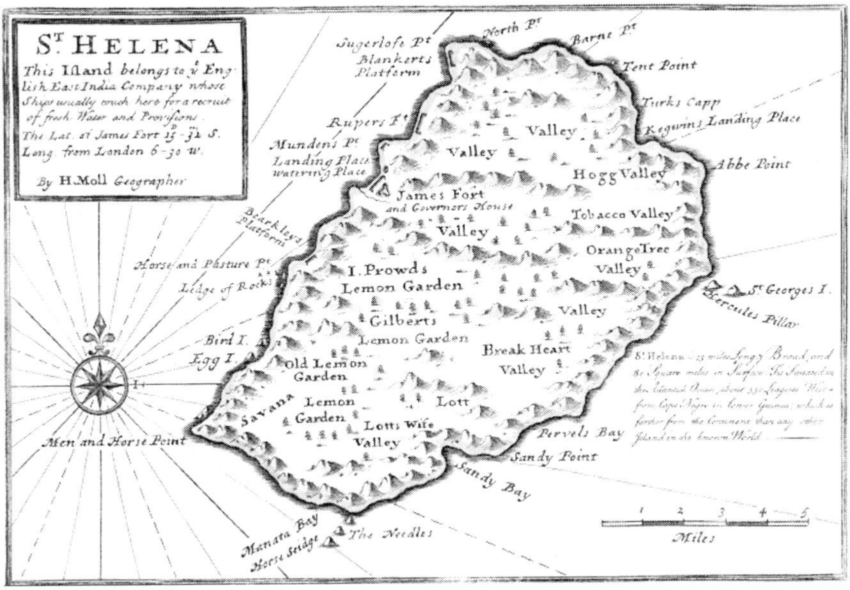

The abolishment of slavery coincided with the arrival of indentured labourers in the 19th century (mostly from China) and also with a period of rapid economic decline, namely when political control was transferred to the Crown and subsidies were cut dramatically. The last 150 years saw increasing poverty and out-migration (mostly to South Africa, in recent years to the UK), various business schemes to develop and maintain a local economy (whaling, the production and export of coffee, a local flax industry), and, as a most recent (and ultimately most threatening) development, the departure of many young families who left the island in search of more promising work opportunities in the UK. The chapter summarises the historical and social evolution of the local St Helena community, for convenience subdividing settlement history into four sections (1502-1673: Discovery of the island by the Portuguese, early British involvement and Dutch interregnum; 1673-1834: The reign of the East India Company; 1834-1981: Crown colony and Nationality Act; 1981-today: Nationality Act and British Dependent Territory). It concludes with a general assessment on the sociolinguistic evolution of StHE and offers some first

[1] Source: http://www.bweaver.nom.sh/maps/moll.htm

hypotheses as to how the social history of the community may have shaped the development of a local variety.

The linguistic analysis starts with ch. 4, "Earlier evidence of St Helenian English" (to be continued in chs. 5 and 6). The foundations of this variety were laid some 350 years ago (so StHE is considerably older than the major SHemE varieties); the aim is to locate and discuss material and observations that allow us to reconstruct earlier stages. Is there evidence of white speech so we can pinpoint the original inputs spoken by the British settlers of the community? Is there evidence of *prima facie* language contact on the island, as a result of which the community may have partaken in processes of pidginisation and creolisation? There are reliable reports that, by the end of the 19th century, English was the only language spoken on the island. Consequently, the aim of this chapter is to trace how long other languages were spoken, until when bi- or multilingualism persisted and by when language shift was completed. Moreover, it looks into the accessibility of English as a target language (i.e., how secure its status was as a *lingua franca* in the entire community) and whether – and if so, to what extent – contact-derived (or substratal) features were carried over and adopted when the variety formed. The material presented and evaluated in this chapter comes from a range of sources, namely verbatim speech samples from documents of the East India Company, court proceedings and transcripts of hearings, letters sent to the UK, observations by travellers and visitors to the island, accounts of direct speech in newspaper articles, short stories, and the like. The findings are presented in roughly chronological order and loosely ordered by reference group (white, black) and text type (newspaper, letter, court transcript, etc.). A final section summarises, cross-checks and evaluates the results, followed by a discussion of their historical significance for the origins and development of the variety (thus adding to the conclusions based on social history, ch. 3).

Chs. 5 and 6 present the analytical core of the book, and it is in these chapters where I present the findings and analysis of the data collected on the island in summer 2003. Great care was taken to document the variety as accurately as possible. Of course, a major problem is to choose what 'typical' features to report and to decide whose speech to portray. It is crucial to justify the choice as to which of the thousands of speakers of the variety should serve as role models for descriptive purposes, since any description is an abstraction and idealisation that, at its very worst, falls just short of stereotyping. The principal parameters of variation (individual, regional, and/or social) are often not taken into account and it is not always explicitly recognised that this poses a major problem for description and analysis. The question is how to recognise such variation and how to filter it into a general description. This is a serious challenge; the danger is that one presents a picture that is simply not accurate (for instance when one creates the impression that a feature that is infrequent, obsolete or idiolectal is characteristic of the variety as such). In order to be as concise as possible, wone should make every effort to provide quantitative information as well and say where a feature makes an appearance, how widespread it is, to what extent it is subject to variation and change, and, if at all possible, what language-internal factors condition its usage. The dilemma faced here is whether to provide a lot of general information about a barely documented variety, without looking into specific aspects of variation in depth, or whether to analyse a few selected variables in a most detailed way, an approach that would give insights into variation in and across the community but fails to provide a general overview of distinctive StHE features. The compromise adopted in this book is to provide a profile of the segmental phonology of StHE, based on the now common practice of Wells' (1982) lexical sets, and to give profiles for four individual speakers from various parts of the island. This allows me to address a number of issues qualitatively, most prominently whether StHE has focussed and developed its own endonormative features. The analysis of 20th century StHE is completed by an evaluative comparison of the most prominent morpho-syntactic characteristics, loosely ordered by grammatical categories.

Ch. 6 builds on this overview and addresses issues that cannot (or should not) be approached qualitatively. With this aim, I selected two variables, one phonological (consonant cluster reduction, or CCR) and one morpho-syntactic (copula absence), and subjected them to a quantitative variationist analysis. These two variables were chosen because they have been researched extensively in other contact-derived varieties, such as English-based creoles in the Caribbean. A set number of tokens were then extracted for each of a sub-sample of 14 speakers, and these data were subject to a more detailed analysis. This allows me to address a number of questions more directly, such as: Is there regional variation on the island? To what extent does StHE display contact-induced effects that manifest themselves elsewhere too? Can we trace the language-internal criteria that govern variation in StHE in other (and better-documented) varieties, which would allow us to trace potential donor varieties and founder effects, perhaps even an ancestral pedigree? Though space restrictions limit an in-depth analysis, a closer look at selected variables is helpful to explore socio-historical and qualitative-descriptive issues more precisely (which will be scrutinised in follow-up research and future studies on the variety). The aim of this two-fold analysis is to provide readers with an overview of StHE that is as complete and complementary as possible, that gives much-needed information on a barely documented variety of English and that at the same time offers perspectives for general issues of (socio)linguistic theory, such as its relevance for contact linguistics, language variation and change, regional diffusion, accommodation and language shift. Having said this, I would like to stress that the book was *not* written with the aim of 'proving' existing theories, for instance that StHE is an English-based creole. Adopting such an approach would be seriously misguided, since data are analysed with fixed expectations and subjective presuppositions. Instead, I will try to be as open-minded as I can, making every effort to integrate a variety of sources, observations and analyses into a theoretical framework that is as socio-historically coherent as possible, bouncing back and forth between qualitative and quantitative data, comparing synchronic and diachronic materials, etc.

Consequently, the main aim of this book is to provide a detailed analysis of the historical development and the phonological and morphosyntactic features of StHE. At the same time, it is hoped that the findings presented here – and the questions they raise – go beyond a simple and straightforward description of a hitherto neglected post-colonial variety of English. The accurate description of data is a most important tool for theoretical and taxonomic endeavours in linguistic research, yet reporting data is only the first step in gaining insights into general principles of contact linguistics. In this way, one can extrapolate from findings on one variety for more general issues of sociolinguistic theory and, if done right, show how much there is to be gained from a thorough analysis of a lesser-known variety of English. An ambitious aim, I know.

2. How St Helenian English could have formed: Basic principles of contact linguistics

Societies and communities, in Europe and elsewhere, are in a constant process of shift and flux, for a variety of social, political and economic reasons: crusades and war campaigns; climatic changes and natural disasters; famines; the transformation from largely rural and self-sufficient to urbanised and monetary-based economies; etc. The last four hundred years in particular have seen an unprecedented scale of population movements, both within Europe and from Europe to other continents. Many of these migratory movements take their roots in the Middle Ages and the Early Modern period: political expansionism following the discoveries of seafarers and adventurers (often in the service of governments, such as Sir Francis Drake, Fernão de Magalhães or Amerigo Vespucci); the opening of new economic markets and trade routes; technological innovations that made it possible for the first time to transport ever-increasing masses of people and cargo to far-away destinations; the establishment of official bodies to develop international trading schemes (such as the British *East India Company* or the Dutch *Vereenigde Oostindische Compagnie*; Lawson 1993); the rivalry of newly created nation states to take possession of overseas territories, etc. As a result, colonial powers struggled to expand their spheres of influence and gain a foothold in the 'new world', competing for the most promising and profitable possessions.

As a by-product, French, Spanish, Portuguese, German, and most of all English, were transported around the globe, initially by merchants, administrators, soldiers, planters, adventurers and many others, who arrived from different regions and came from distinct social classes in the British Isles. These pioneers found themselves in new and unfamiliar territories, where they came into contact with local communities and their languages. These encounters had all kinds of social, political, and linguistic consequences. Most importantly for our purpose, colonialism and expansionism ultimately lead to the emergence of 'new' varieties around the world, i.e., varieties that originated due to contact of languages and dialects spoken by the local and indigenous populations. The development of these varieties provides a showcase scenario for research on contact linguistics, challenging us to rethink social, political, ethnic, economic and linguistic facets of the relationship between language and space (Auer & Schmidt fc.). In terms of geographical space, migration and colonisation lead to an unprecedented extension into unknown territory; in terms of cultural/social space, there was a reshuffling and reorganisation of the local socio-ethnic landscape as well as the collapse, merging and consecutive redevelopment of social boundaries and networks in the colonial communities; and in terms of political and economic space, the creation of new nation states (often based on purely geographic and ethnically-ignorant conceptualisations of space, along topographic rather than socio-ethnic boundaries), and a complete transformation of local economic systems. Linguistically and sociolinguistically, the global diffusion and spatial expansion of language(s) would in time give rise to contact-based varieties, not only as a result of local and transplanted languages but also via contact between colonising languages (e.g. Italian/Spanish-based Cocoliche in Argentina or Dutch-based Afrikaans in South Africa, Roberge 2002) or dialect contact and koinéisation.

A most important question concerns the mechanisms of feature selection and retention that underlie external language change and ultimately account for the complexity of language evolution (see discussion in Mufwene 2001). New and challenging research questions were formulated, such as how contact between distinct linguistic systems and subsystems gives rise to distinctive local varieties, how these are shaped via extended language contact, how contact-induced mechanisms can in turn catalyse inherent changes, etc. New hypotheses and theoretical advances were developed with – and tested on – an ever-increasing amount of data from contact-derived varieties around the world. Island speech communities as diverse as Fiji (Siegel 1987), Tristan da Cunha (Schreier 2002b, 2003a), the Ogasawara/Bonin Islands (Long 2007) or the Falkland Islands (Sudbury 2000) have contributed considerably to our understanding of how 'new' varieties form and how they evolve through processes of pidginisation, creolisation and new dialect-formation.

Insular settings are particularly suitable for such research purposes indeed. They ideally lend themselves to *ab ovo* reconstruct the social history of a community (for instance when there exist extensive archives for territories controlled and administered by the East India Company, henceforth *EIC*). Socio-historical information can then be complemented and tested with diachronic and/or contemporary language data, enabling researchers to document and isolate the sociolinguistic mechanisms that operate(d). Put differently, insular communities offer ideal conditions for analysing the sociohistorical setting in which a contact variety develops, and this enables historical linguists to speculate on language genesis and evolution. If historical and sociolinguistic information is available, then it should in theory be possible to reconstruct the variants transplanted to the locale under investigation, to retrace the adopted features to their respective input varieties, and maybe even to explain why some features are selected whereas others fall out of usage and are dropped (and why). Ideally, this would allow for the precise modelling of a given feature pool with competing variants out of which new variants emerge and stabilise; in other words, to describe and theorise how a new variety *focuses*.

Unfortunately, ideal conditions (such as those found on the Falkland Islands) are rare and the potential for analytical pitfalls is immense. Explaining precisely how a language variety comes to have the properties it has is not the straightforward task we wish it to be, and the present study of StHE makes no exception. To name just a few of the most deep-rooted problems: Information on earlier stages is often sparse, incomplete or missing, so that it is unclear what the contributing donor varieties were in the first place. Even if such records exist, we cannot *strictu sensu* assume that place of origin equals input dialect from that area; inputs may have been modified prior to settlement due to accommodation or dialect shift. This means that, to take an extreme example, a native of Liverpool may have shifted to another variety after he left his native origins and before he settled in a new locale, so that a legacy of Liverpool English would be apparent only. This may seem perhaps a bit far-fetched but is a real issue in seafaring communities; in the case of the Bonin/Ogasawara islands, Pitcairn or Tristan da Cunha, we know for a fact that some of the settlement's founders spent decades at sea before they settled down, which might mean that they modified their speech patterns through long-term accommodation on board ship or elsewhere (Schreier 2003a, Long 2007; cf. Reinecke 1937 for the notion of *Ship* or *Nautical English*). Consequently, one possible explanation for the relative lack of Scottish features in early 20th century Tristan da Cunha English (TdCE) may have been that William Glass, the Scottish founder of that colony, had in fact shifted away from Scottish English (ScE) before arriving on the island. Another problem is that it is often difficult to establish a one-to-one relationship between features and donor varieties. A given feature is often present in more than one input, making a positive match impossible (which, in turn, may have influenced a feature's adoption chances in a competitive feature pool; this may explain why practically all the SHemE varieties are non-rhotic, the /r/-ful inputs being underrepresented in the overall dialect contact scenario; see below).

Moreover, to complicate matters, majority variants are not automatically selected. In fact, minority features can also win out and be adopted, for instance when they are openly emblemised as a marker of identity (see for instance the monophthongal variants for /ai/ in the American South, an originally South England feature, whose usage increased over the last century and is now commonly recognised as an emblem of Southern identity; Bailey 1997). Alternatively, non-majority features may undergo so-called *reallocation*, namely when they are reinterpreted as stylistically or socially marked variants (Trudgill 1986; Britain & Trudgill 1999; further discussion below). Another criterion, perhaps the most complicated and least predictable one, concerns dialect interaction: contact between distinct linguistic (sub-)systems may give rise to features not present in any of the inputs; the emergence of a feature may thus not reflect feature selection and retention but dynamic interaction of individual inputs, in which case it represents a so-called 'independent development' (Trudgill 1986). Consequently, we have to take into account not only how dialects mix and merge into a coherent endonormative system, but also how they interact and give rise to entirely 'new', i.e., hitherto undocumented, features.

Finally, contact-induced language change in general and the formation of new varieties in particular are fragile, 'vulnerable' processes. Changes in social demographics and consecutive population movements (most notably through in- and out-migration) affect the patterns and dynamics of linguistic contact at all times (for instance through *swamping*, Lass 1990: 267). Accordingly, pidginisation and new-dialect formation are in constant 'danger' of being redirected (or even arrested) by external events, such as catastrophic population loss or large-scale immigration. The sociodemographic dynamism is an ongoing one and social events may abruptly change the trajectory path and evolution of a newly developing variety: new settlers arrive while earlier ones leave, children are born while older community members pass away, etc., so the sociolinguistic set-up of the community really is in continuous transformation. As a consequence, contact-derived varieties are linguistically and socially determined and it is the interplay of these factors that makes up for the inherent dynamism under such conditions. Linguistic processes end abruptly with the dispersal or relocation of the community and this seriously challenges sociolinguistic analysis, making prediction virtually impossible.

These imponderables have stood in the way of formulating a coherent and unified theory of contact linguistics. Pidginisation, creolisation and new-dialect formation are complex processes; all 'new varieties', whatever their status, have both a linguistic and a social basis, and they must be approached with reference to the linguistic characteristics of the systems and sub-systems in contact and the social environments in which they were (and/or are) formed, i.e. social hierarchies and stratification of the founding populations, the formation of new social networks and communities in the earliest colonisation phases, etc. The task is thus not only to identify the original donor varieties and to determine in what proportions and by whom these were spoken in a newly-established community, but also what the founders' social relationships were, how they ranked in terms of prestige and status, and how a gradually emerging group hierarchy (in the form of emerging patterns of social stratification, communities of practice and social networks) influenced their development, ultimately determining why and how a 'new' variety became the way it is. The integration of social and linguistic factors is the ultimate challenge of any attempt at modelling or theorising the outcome of linguistic contact processes.

What does all this mean for the origins and evolution of English on the island of St Helena? The questions we must formulate, first and foremost, are the following: How exactly did StHE form, and who was instrumental in founding it? How can we use such information to determine the linguistic status of this variety, i.e., whether it is a Creole or the equivalent of an English regional dialect transplanted to the South Atlantic Ocean? (cf. ch. 1) What change mechanisms operated when StHE evolved, and how can we retrace them? Ch. 2 addresses these and related questions and provides the theoretical basis of contact linguistics that will be fleshed out with data from StHE in the following chapters. It begins with an outline of contact dialectology and a general discussion of linguistic mechanisms involved in new-dialect formation (2.1), continuing with an in-depth look at various scenarios of language contact, i.e. the processes that give rise to pidginisation and creolisation (2.2), with particular focus on agency, namely who is most influential in forming a 'new' variety and how processes such as accommodation, mixing and nativisation interact. A final section (2.3) brings together and evaluates some major approaches to contact-induced language change (founder effects vs. swamping, colonial lag, developmental continua, etc.).

Consequently, ch. 2 outlines the principal mechanisms that manifest themselves under contact conditions and discusses how sociodemographic and social factors underlie and influence mechanisms of contact linguistics. It provides the theoretical background for the present study of StHE, the framework against which I then go on to interpret the results from the descriptive and quantitative analyses in chs. 5 and 6.

2.1 Contact dialectology

Certainly one of the most important criteria to determine the outcome of sociolinguistic contact is the degree of differentiation between the varieties, and the functional aspect of language change is particularly important in this context (is convergence a *conditio sine qua non* for inter-group communication or not?). Chambers & Trudgill (1998) point out that the line between intelligibility and non-intelligibility is a fine one and that the ability to understand one another depends on a number of factors, such as: the will to communicate and to be understood; the degree, length and nature of exposure to another variety; the topic of the interaction; etc. The fact that people can communicate does of course not necessarily mean that they want to and will communicate. Nevertheless, we need to tackle how structurally and typologically distinct systems interact and whether contact between related varieties of one and the same language (regional dialects, sociolects) gives rise to processes that are different than those set off by contact between distinct systems. Are these different processes, and if so, which of them was more influential for the origins and development of StHE?

A look at the literature on the topic shows how widespread dialect contact is. Siegel (1985), for instance, lists the following varieties that have been studied and classified as contact-derived dialects: Arabic (Ferguson 1959), Lingala (Nida & Fehderau 1970), Fiji Hindustani (Siegel 1975), 14th century

Naples Italian (Samarin 1971), American Standard English (Dillard 1972), Trinidad Bhojpuri (Mohan 1978), Hebrew (Blanc 1968) and Canadian French (Gambhir 1981), and this attests to the geographical and historical dimensions of dialect contact and new-dialect formation. Notwithstanding, few writers (particularly Siegel 1985, 1987) have attempted to describe the properties of koinés in detail, and the following description relies heavily on his work.

This section focuses on contact scenarios that for the most part involve mutually intelligible and structurally related sub-systems of one and the same variety. It describes and exemplifies the major processes involved in dialect contact and new-dialect formation, starting with processes of accommodation and short-term adaptation.

2.1.1 Initial contact

Contact dialectology investigates mechanisms of language change in contexts of extensive, long-term contact. These processes have been researched in a variety of settings, many of which are characterised by high mobility and sociolinguistic heterogeneity, e.g. in Norway (Omdal 1977), Fiji (Siegel 1987), South Africa (Mesthrie 1993), Trinidad (Mohan 1978) or in the UK (e.g. the English Fens, Britain 1991, 1997, 2002; and New Towns such as Milton Keynes, Kerswill 1994, 1996; Kerswill & Williams 2000; and post-colonial varieties in New Zealand, Gordon et al. 2004, Tristan da Cunha, Schreier 2002b, or the Falkland Islands, Sudbury 2000, to name but a few). Following Trudgill (1986), research focused on the linguistic processes that underlie contact-induced language change and on the social contexts that favour or inhibit new-dialect formation. From a social point of view, the increase in mobility of individuals and groups is a crucial factor since groups of speakers engage in face-to-face interaction they did not have previously. Following Lass (1990) and Siegel (1985, 1987), the settings of contact scenarios may be *intra-* or *extraterritorial*, the latter one being more frequent since resettlement and out-migration often lead to contact situations and thus entail dialect contact. Extra-territorial dialect contact is mostly a product of political expansionism and colonisation (Falkland Islands English, FIE, Sudbury 2000, or New Zealand English, NZE, Gordon et al. 2004). Intra-territorial dialect contact, on the other hand, usually involves some sort of relocation of people from different regions to a new area within the same country and typically occurs as a result of increasing urbanisation (Payne 1976, 1980), New Town expansions (e.g. Milton Keynes in England, Kerswill 1996), or the gain of new territory for settlement (e.g. the draining of the English Fens, Britain 1991, or the Dutch Polders, Scholtmeijer 1992, 1997).

Importantly, many if not all new-dialect formation processes are triggered early on so that short-term accommodation is a necessary precondition (and may be particularly important for founder effects, see below). Social psychologists and language sociologists (Giles 1973; Giles, Taylor & Bourhis 1973; Bell 1984; Giles, Coupland & Coupland 1991) have investigated psychosocial and linguistic aspects of accommodation, both on intra- and inter-speaker levels (audience design, style- and topic-related switching, etc.). They showed that accommodation may lead to *convergence*,[1] for instance when a speaker assimilates her speech to that of another speaker for reasons such as gaining approval, making oneself understood, emphasising a common identity, avoiding regionally or socially stigmatised features, etc., or else to *divergence*, namely when differences are enhanced (to distance oneself from the interlocutor, to stress authority, etc.). Individual variation in *ad hoc* speech situations is thus a complex phenomenon and it raises three important questions. First of all, we need to ask exactly what motivates accommodation and convergence in the first place. Bell (1984: 197), for instance, views accommodation as a responsive process when he claims that "at all levels of language variability, people are responding primarily to other people." Others (Schilling-Estes 1998) have argued that style-shifting and accommodation are proactive instead, particularly when language variation is used creatively as a marker of speaker identity or to signal authority. Consequently, we need to differentiate between accommodation as an active or as a receptive/responsive process and this may change the outcome of initial dialect contact considerably. Furthermore, convergence may vary from case to case, determined by factors such as the social class of the addressee or the social significance of a variable (in the words of Bell 1984: 167, "A sociolinguistic variable which is differentiated by certain speaker characteristics (e.g., by class or gender or age) tends to be differentiated in speech to addressees with those same characteristics"), so these are factors one needs to take into consideration as well.

Second, some form of convergence must be operative for a new dialect to emerge; if not, then the input dialects would either be maintained for generations, or even diversify. If convergence through accommodation is a necessary prerequisite, then we must come up with an answer as to which of the competing variants should become targets for accommodation and how norms are recognised by and across the wider community. We will see below that this is a hotly debated issue and that there is no agreement as to whether this process is linguistically or socially motivated (or both).

Third, we need to tackle the question as to who is most instrumental and ask whether we can compare processes of accommodation in the wider population. Agency is an important issue here, since one of the most important considerations is exactly who comes into contact. Children, for instance, who are in the process of acquiring a first language, show maximum flexibility and

[1] This is not to be confused with the notion of convergence in language contact (see below).

are much quicker to accommodate or shift than adults. Research on dialect contact in New Zealand (Gordon et al. 2004) and in Milton Keynes, a new town in northern Buckinghamshire in the UK (Kerswill 1994, 1996), has shown that children pick and mix features available in adult speech around them and are thus paramount for the formation of a new variety (cf. also Trudgill 2004). Kerswill & Williams (2000) emphasise that contact between adults and/or post-adolescents leads to different processes than contact between children. As Trudgill (1994: 13) points out, "[i]n any examination of the effects of language contact, it is vital to distinguish between those situations where contact is between adult speakers only, and those where child language contact and bilingualism is involved."

One is thus well advised to distinguish between *language acquisition*, i.e., the processes by which children acquire their native language as L1, and *language learning,* the efforts of adolescents or adults to achieve competence in a second or subsequent language (L2). Even though both lead to an increase in linguistic competence, L1 acquisition and L2 learning differ for a number of reasons. Acquisition is a largely subconscious process, by which an L1 develops in the first years of a pre-adolescent, and the result is in almost all cases native-speaker competence. Learning, on the other hand, typically is a conscientious effort made after a first language is acquired, and its outcome is much less certain. The success of L2 learning depends on a variety of factors, such as the degree of difference between target language (i.e., the language to be learnt) and the learner's L1, the age, intelligence and motivation of the individual, as well as the exposure to the target language. The question as to whether native-like competence may be learnt by adolescents or adults with differential L1 competence is subject to much debate, but learning does generally not lead to total L2 mastery once the learner has reached a certain age (Goodluck 1991; Ritchie & Bathia 1999); indeed, a number of studies (e.g. Payne 1976, 1980; Chambers 1992) have argued in favour of a so-called 'critical period' of language (or, for that matter: dialect) acquisition, suggesting that phonology and grammar are roughly acquired by adolescence. Native-like competence is unusual after the 'critical threshold'; L1 competence as a result of L2 learning is the exception, not the rule. Consequently, some of the most important questions we must address in this context are: how do adults converge through accommodation, how do children select features in a diverse, multi-dialectal or even multilingual environment, to what extent do the parents' speech-ways influence their children, and how are we to filter in these processes for a model of new-dialect formation? These are important issues, not only for a study of StHE, but for contact linguistics in general.

We thus need to concentrate on accommodation when discussing new-dialect formation, both in its initial and advanced stages. However, it is important that we should focus on long-term patterns of accommodation in stable contact settings, as the stabilisation and crystallisation of new norms requires continuity and historical time depth (the precise length of which is disputed, however; discussion in Siegel 1985, 1987; Trudgill 1986; Kerswill 1994; Britain 1997). Face-to-face accommodation is thus an integral part of contact linguistics; somewhat paradoxically, though, it is too short-term to offer insights into permanent effects. Even though any theoretical account of new-dialect formation has to filter in accommodation effects, the emergence of new norms and the stabilisation of a contact-based dialect is a lengthy process that gives rise to alternative mechanisms.

2.1.2 Mixing

Several stages operate when koinéisation occurs. First of all, the total number of variants present in the contact scenario represents a pool out of which the first native speakers select features at an early stage of new-dialect formation (Mufwene 2001). None of the input varieties 'wins out' at this stage; were this the case, then all but one variety present in the contact scenario would disappear without a trace and the newly developing variety would represent the equivalent of one of its inputs. Riograndenser Hunsrückisch (RG), spoken in Southeast Brazil (Altenhofen 1996; Auer, Arnhold & Bueno Aniola 2005), would be no more than a transplanted (and systemically unaltered) form of a Rhineland-Palatinate German dialect, Québec French the equivalent of a regional variety found in France, Australian English (AusE) exported Cockney (as claimed by Hammarström 1980, 1985), etc. This is hardly ever the case, for reasons that are obvious. Dialects mix and interact as speakers accommodate to each other, which is why new-dialect formation (or koinéisation, two terms used interchangeably here) is particularly strong when children grow up in a multi-dialectal environment. The usual outcome is for the inputs to undergo a stage of *mixing*, which means that the inception phase of a new dialect displays mechanisms of feature selection and retention. According to Siegel (1985: 375-6),

> Koinéisation is the process which leads to the mixing of linguistic subsystems, that is, of language varieties which are either mutually intelligible or share the same genetically related superposed language. It occurs in the context of increased interaction or integration among speakers of these varieties.

Blanc (1968) argues that the formation of modern Hebrew was characterised by extensive feature selection and face-to-face accommodation: "usage [of Israeli Hebrew] had to be established by a gradual and complex process of selection and accommodation which is, in part, still going on, but which now has reached some degree of stabilisation" (1968: 239). As disputed as the process of new-dialect formation is (discussion in Schreier 2003a), there is consensus that mixing of several inputs is crucial. Ferguson (1959) examines the historical development of classical Arabic, arguing that it originated in the interaction of different dialects of Arabic with second language forms of Arabic: "the [Arabic] koiné came into existence through a complex process of mutual borrowing and levelling among various dialects and not as a result of diffusion from one single source" (1959: 619). Blanc (1968) argues that Hebrew developed from "a variety of literary dialects, several substrata, and several traditional pronunciations" (1968: 238), which is supported by Samarin (1971), who writes that "what characterises [koinés] linguistically is the incorporation of features from several regional varieties of a single language" (1971: 133).

Consequently, contact between linguistic systems triggers feature selection processes from several co-existing varieties (Kerswill 1996), and this may be influenced by factors such as total number of features present, salience, stigma and prestige of individual variables, sociodemographic characteristics and social mobility, etc. Fully-developed koinés, the end-product of *focusing* (LePage & Tabouret-Keller 1985; see below), have thus adopted features from at least two (very often, more) donors. Put differently, a crystallising contact-based variety combines a mixture of features (phonetic, grammatical, morphological, and/or lexical) that derive from some or all the dialects present in the original contact situation. One of the challenges of contact dialectology is to find exactly which of the features are adopted and what criteria enhance their chances at the expense of others.

2.1.3 Levelling

Tendencies towards regularity and transparency are in some way language-inherent, yet they seem to be particularly common in contact situations. Variants disappear from a diffuse mixture situation as other features are permanently selected, and this process is called *levelling* (Trudgill 1986; Siegel 1987, 1997; Britain 1997). The important question here, of course, is which features are most likely to undergo levelling and what reasons we can offer to account for the motivation behind this process. Most researchers would agree that criteria such as status (stigma or prestige of regional/social variants), social networks and sociodemographics as well as the frequency of competing variants in the contact scenario are all important here. This is born out by the fact that the surviving competitor is usually the one found in the majority of inputs (Mesthrie 1993; Siegel 1987), that variants with the widest social and geographical distribution have the highest chances of surviving the selection process (Trudgill 1986) and that regionally or socially *marked* features are usually not maintained.[2] This last point is stressed repeatedly in the literature:

> The usual result of dialect mixture is the loss of untypical elements, particularly in pronunciation. (Turner 1994: 283)

> As a result of continued contact ... one gathers experience as to which idiosyncrasies of one's own dialect are ill-communicative, mis-communicative, or non-communicative, and accordingly, one starts to shed the hardened localisms in one's speech, allowing one's speech to conform to another's to an ever-growing extent. (Gambhir 1981: 191)

These approaches are rather functional, implying that a definition of 'marking' be based on the fulfilment of communicative needs or on some alleged typicality of language features; however, the nature of "hardened localisms" or "untypical elements" is not further defined and no explanation is given as to why it should be exactly those features that are subject to adaptation (not even in what way they are considered to be "hardened" or "untypical" and who considers them as such). Nevertheless, the majority form usually (but not necessarily) has the highest chances of being selected (Mesthrie 1993; Siegel 1987), which is confirmed by Feagin's analysis of White Southern American English (WSAmE). She explains the selection of 'completive *done'* (e.g. 'we *done* got the other shell made') via founder principles (see below) and the fact that it occurred in several of the varieties in contact:

> It is possible to explain its occurrence [in WSAmE] as an inheritance from the Scotch-Irish ... I suggest that *done* was brought to Alabama by both the poorer settlers from Georgia and the Carolinas and the slaves who came with or were later sold to - the planters ... [*done*] is an archaic feature which was reinforced by the creole English of the Black slaves in the American South. Feagin (1991: 187-8)

Such observations have led Trudgill (2004) to adopt an extreme point of view, namely that new dialects are formed deterministically. He claims that frequency of features alone accounts for adoption and that social factors (such as prestige,

---

[2] *Markedness* is of course a controversial term. Here it is used with the meaning 'characteristic of a certain region, social class or speech style'. This contrasts somewhat with other uses in linguistic theory, such as the one of Crystal (1991), who classifies the 'values' of linguistic features as positive (marked), neutral or negative (unmarked). The *unmarked choice* would represent the neutral basic meaning. For example, the present tense is unmarked for English verbs; suffixation, on the contrary, entails marking (e.g. for past tense or progressive).

status, social network structures, etc.) are, with the notable exception of demography, simply irrelevant (see further discussion below).

SHemE varieties have undergone levelling to the extent that they are now characterised by extreme geographic uniformity, though they developed out of inputs that were regionally diverse and sociolinguistically distinct (AusE, for instance, had input of Irish English (IrE) and Southeastern English English (EnglE)). The lack of regional variation in AusE and NZE has been commented on frequently:

> Australians are for practical reasons almost completely unmarked by region within their speech community. (Bernard 1989: 255)

> [T]he overall picture [of Australia] must remain one of a continent across whose vast reaches there is comparatively little variation. (Collins & Blair 2001: 9)

> New Zealand, like Australia, is more remarkable for the absence of regional differences. (Gordon & Deverson 1998: 126)

> [T]he English of New Zealand is more noted for its uniformity than for its regional dialects. For whatever reason (and this might be grounds for a great deal of speculation) the regional dialects of the immigrants have not obviously given rise to corresponding regional dialects in New Zealand. (Bauer 2000: 41)

Importantly, the same claims have also been made for earlier stages of American English (AmE) and Canadian English (CanE), which Schneider (2007) considers as characteristic for the exonormative stabilisation phase of new varieties. According to Baugh & Cable (1951: 348):

> It has repeatedly been observed, in the past as well as at the present day, especially by travellers from abroad, that the English spoken in America shows a high degree of uniformity. Those who are familiar with the pronounced dialectal differences that mark the popular speech of different parts of England will know that there is nothing comparable to these differences in the United States.

One of the open questions is exactly where levelling occurs. In his explanation of AusE, Turner (1994: 278) maintains that "levelling of dialects had probably already taken place in England or at sea" and most "of the involuntary passengers had already left rural England for cities, accommodating their speech to their neighbours there" (p. 277). Similarly, Trudgill (2004) argues that salient regional features may undergo levelling on board ship already, which would explain apparent levelling in NZE (more on this below).

The case of NZE shows that levelling processes are to a large part shaped by the overall proportions of transplanted dialects in the local input scenario. Schreier et al. (2003) analysed the maintenance of voiceless labiovelar /hw-/ fricatives (minimal pairs *Wales* ~ *whales*, *witch* ~ *which*) in three regions of New Zealand (Otago/Southland, Canterbury, and the North Island) and found considerable regional variation in early 20th century NZE. Whereas New Zealanders from the North Island and Canterbury were predominantly using /w/ (so that the /hw/ ~ /w/ merger was practically completed by 1950), speakers from the Southland and Otago regions had high levels of /hw-/ well into the second half of the 20th century (Table 2.1).

Table 2.1 /hw- ~ w-/ variation in early 20th century New Zealand English

	/hw/	*/w/*	*per cent /hw/*
Southland	441	666	*40.0%* (441/1107)
Canterbury	51	596	*7.9%* (51/647)
North	21	369	*5.4%* (21/390)

The regional distribution of the variable was linked to population demographics and ancestral effects, thus reflecting the total input strength of /hw-/ retaining donor dialects. A high overall presence of /hw-/ variants in the inputs had an enhancing effect on adoption and maintenance, notwithstanding the fact that it was regionally marked. The strong presence of /hw-/ in the Otago/Southland dialect region was explained by high input frequency and the disproportionally high input of Scottish settlers, who made a distinction between /hw-/ and /w-/. In the other regions, however, /hw-/ was not adopted, simply because the social configuration and the local contact and mixture situations were different. The inputs were mainly from the South of England, where /hw-/ was a minority feature, and this enhanced levelling-out in the local forms of NZE (see also Trudgill, Lewis & Maclagan 2003).

2.1.4 *Simplification/regularisation*

A third process involved is what some have called *simplification* (e.g. Trudgill 1986), which others preferably consider as a manifestation of *regularisation* or simply *analogical language change*. I personally favour the latter since the outcome of new-dialect formation is not necessarily 'simpler' than any of the corresponding input forms. Rather, a given property of a variant X, no matter whether phonetic/phonological, lexical or grammatical, is subject to less variation than it originally was in the input varieties. For instance, Siegel (1987: 14) points out that simplification is not well understood and argues that such mechanisms should be investigated quantitatively rather than qualitatively (i.e., that one should with benefit adopt a variationist perspective to trace a putative decrease in variability). Simplification should thus preferably be investigated as a diachronic process, i.e. with reference to earlier evolutionary phases of a variety (or, if possible at all, of the input varieties). This problem is also recognised by Britain (1997: 141), who states that simplification represents "an increase in grammatical regularity and decrease in formal complexity", and Mühlhäusler (1997: 236), who claims that

> Simplification only refers to the form of the rules in which a language is encoded, indicating optimalisation of existing rules and the development of regularities for formerly irregular aspects, for example, grammaticalisation of the lexicon. Simplification is a dynamic concept. It expresses the fact that *as one moves along a developmental continuum, more and more regularities appear*. (Emphasis added, DS)

A good example for phonological regularisation in overseas varieties comes from devoicing of inter-vocalic alveolar plosives in Afrikaans (Booij 2002). In Dutch, voiceless alveolar plosives (/t/) are voiced in intervocalic environments:

/t/ > [d] / V_V

Table 2.2 Phonological simplification in Afrikaans

	singular	plural
Dutch: /t/ > [d] V_V	hoed /hut/ 'hat'	hoeden /ˈhudə/
	stad /stat/ 'city'	steden /ˈsteːdə/
	smit /smɪt/ 'smith'	smeden /ˈsmeːdə/
Afrikaans: /t/ > [t] V_V	hoed /hut/ 'hat'	hoeden /ˈhutə/
	stad /stat/ 'city'	statten /ˈstatə/
	smit /smɪt/ 'smith'	smitten /ˈsmɪtə/

Dutch plural formation commonly involves the affixation of an *-en* marker and changes the phonological environment from /-VC#/ to /-VCV#/. If a singular form ends in /d/, then the corresponding plural form maintains it. A voiceless /t/, however, assimilates to /d/, as in: *hoed* [hut] 'hat', *hoeden* [ˈhudə]. Afrikaans, in contrast, has regularised this assimilation rule so that the phonological environment has no effect on the alveolar plosive: *hoed* [hut] 'hat', *hoeden* [ˈhutə], *stad* [stat] 'city', *statten* [ˈstatə] (Table 2.2). Afrikaans is more regular than its ancestral variety Dutch in that it has reduced the number of phonological rules and does not make phonological contrasts in this particular environment (Booij 2002). Afrikaans is thus more regular than its ancestor Dutch in that it has reduced the number of phonological rules.

A case of morphosyntactic regularisation manifested itself on the island of Tristan da Cunha. As is well-known, the English past *be* paradigm stands out for its historically-inherited irregularity, with two allomorphs conditioned by grammatical environment (subject pronouns, singular vs. plural, existentials, etc.). In Tristan da Cunha English (TdCE), this paradigm underwent radical simplification: *were* disappeared (or, to be more precise, was levelled out) whereas *was* extended to all environments so that it is no longer context-sensitive. Table 2.3 (adapted from Schreier 2002a: 86-7) illustrates morpho-syntactic regularisation of past *be* and shows that *were* allomorphs were categorically absent from the speech of Tristanians born before WW II.[3] In other words, the special sociolinguistic scenario that gave rise to TdCE brought about an unprecedented regularisation of the past tense paradigm of *be* (with *was* as a pivot form, one of the "variables [that] appear to be primitives of vernacular dialects in the sense that they recur ubiquitously all over the world", Chambers 1995: 242). This was explained as a consequence of interacting language-external factors, such as new-colony formation, extreme geographical isolation, reduced in-migration after an initial founding period, dense social networks and practically no contact with a prestigious standard variety.

Table 2.3 Morphosyntactic regularisation in Tristan da Cunha English

		singular	plural
Standard pattern	1st	I was	We were
	2nd	You were	You were
	3rd	He/she/it was	They were
	NP	The cow was	The cows were
	Exist.	There was one cow	There were two cows
TdCE pattern	1st	I was	We *was*
	2nd	You *was*	Y'all *was*
	3rd	He/she/it was	They *was*
	NP	The cow was	The cows *was*
	Exist.	There was one cow	There *was* two cows

[3] One notes the interplay of simplification and regularisation. A past *be* paradigm that has undergone regularisation (we *was*, the fishermen *was*, etc.) is also in a way 'simpler'. Put differently, there is no process of simplification that does not also entail regularisation, which questions whether it is really necessary (or possible) to keep the two terms distinct.

2.1.5 Reallocation

A complicating factor is that majority features do not necessarily win out, so that an approach purely based on deterministic sociodemographic principles (as embraced by Trudgill 2004) fails to grasp the complexity of this process. For instance, several variants may survive the mixing and levelling stages and (initial) variability is not eliminated at all. In the words of Britain & Trudgill (1999: 247), "it is not always necessarily the case that the final outcome of the reduction process will be a single victorious variant. In some cases, even after koinéisation, a number of competing variants left over from an original mixture may survive." Though it is debated how often multiple selection occurs, minority forms may under certain conditions be adopted as well, often side by side with majority ones. Following Trudgill (1986), this is usually referred to as *reallocation*, defined as follows: "Reallocation occurs when two or more variants in the dialect mix survive the levelling process but are refunctionalised, evolving new social or linguistic functions in the new dialect" (Britain & Trudgill 1999: 245).

Domingue (1981) demonstrates multiple selection of variants in her study of Mauritius Bhojpuri (MB). She found that the total number of coexisting variants had not been reduced at all. In other words, the levelling of regional variants from the input varieties (Indian Bhojpuri is classified into the four subgroups eastern, western, central and Nagpurian) did simply not take place. Domingue adopted a social explanation for the maintenance of complexity and lack of regularisation/levelling (discussion in Trudgill 1986). On Mauritius, more than half of the local population (approximately one million) are native speakers of Bhojpuri/Hindi, but MB differs markedly from Indian varieties of Bhojpuri for several reasons (e.g. contact with other languages, such as a French-based Mauritian Creole). Dialect mixture of the original inputs was so extensive that present-day MB is comparatively homogeneous, with little regional variation (just like the major SHemE varieties, nota bene). The explanation offered by Domingue was that when MB formed, formerly regional variants were reanalysed as social and stylistic (rather than regional) indicators. If a newly developing colony undergoes social stratification, she argued, then variability from the original mixture situation may be maintained, not as an expression of geographical origins, but of group membership or affiliation to a social class. Reallocation, therefore, refers to the retention and reanalysis of regionally- or socially-marked features from the inputs and to the functional specialisation and redistribution of multiple features, either as social or stylistic variants, or as phonological variants in complementary environments. As a consequence, features from different inputs can also undergo a function change and express regional, social or stylistic variation.

David Britain's research on English Fens English (EFE) has provided ample evidence of reallocation. This area, located in the Wash, some 130 kilometres north of London, separates the East Midlands from Norfolk and has an extensive contact history. Until it was reclaimed in the mid-17th century, it was largely inaccessible and uninhabitable. As soon as the bogs and marshes had been drained, it attracted settlers from rural Norfolk and Suffolk as well as from the Midlands. Dialect contact between Midland and East Anglian English (EAE) gave rise to a distinctive local variety that emerged in the 17th and 18th centuries (Britain 1991). Today, EFE is increasingly influenced by a supra-regionalising form of London English, a trend that has accelerated due to the concerted planning of New Towns and London 'overspill' developments.

Britain (1997) found that several input features were adopted upon dialect contact in the Fens. Phonological reallocation manifested itself by the fact that EFE has both central and fully open onsets of PRICE diphthongs. The two features were present in roughly similar proportions in the inputs and underwent specialisation and refunctionalisation, so that they are now conditioned by the phonological environment exclusively (central onsets adopted for pre-voiceless environments and open onsets elsewhere; the *Canadian raising* pattern, Chambers 1973). EFE underwent morphosyntactic reallocation as well in that it has a past *be* paradigm that is exclusively polarity-based, at the expense of person and number (Britain 2002). Many of the input dialects alternated between *was*, *were* and *weren't* allomorphs, so that there were separate systems with individual patterns of internal conditioning: certainly the most widespread is *was* in the context of *were* (we *was*, the dogs *was* hungry, etc.; see the case of TdCE above, AusE, Eisikovits 1991, or Alabama English, Feagin 1979), but levelling to *were* is documented as well (for instance in Bolton; Shorrocks 1999: 168-9) and a third pattern involves levelling to *weren't* in clauses with negative polarity, independent of person concord (I *was* home, *weren't I*; reported in Reading, Cheshire 1982; York, Tagliamonte 1998, the BNC Corpus, Anderwald 2001, and various locations along the US North Carolina seaboard, Schilling-Estes 2002). Crucially, EFE has developed a past *be* paradigm that consists of two concomitant patterns, namely *was* and *weren't* levelling. *Was* is adopted for all positive environments and *weren't* for all negative ones (Table 2.4). Britain interprets the development of this system as reallocation, arguing that "given these factors, and given the robust evidence of both *was* and *weren't* as potential ingredient forms at earlier stages of these dialects' evolutions, reallocation is clearly the most plausible explanation for the development of a solely polarity-sensitive system over a person/number/ polarity-sensitive one" (Britain 2002: 37).

Table 2.4 Morphosyntactic reallocation in English Fens English

	Positive polarity		Negative polarity	
	Singular	Plural	Singular	Plural
1st person	I was	We was	I weren't	We weren't
2nd person	You was	You was	You weren't	You weren't
3rd person	He/she/it was	They was	He/she/it weren't	They weren't

Britain & Trudgill (1999) suggest a typology of reallocation, distinguishing two major subtypes. The first, *socio-stylistic reallocation*, refers to the refunctionalisation of formerly regional variants into social or stylistic ones, as illustrated by Domingue's work on BP. Similarly, Siegel (1997) demonstrates that Fiji Hindi (FH), a contact dialect that developed in the Hindi and Bhojpuri community on Fiji, retained both Bhojpuri /okar/ and Hindi /uske/ as 3rd person possessives, the former being used by lower-class rural communities and having a "rustic" and "country pumpkin" ring to it (Siegel 1997: 127). Another example comes from AusE, where words such as *dance*, *advantage*, or *chance* take the short TRAP vowel rather than DANCE. Britain & Trudgill (1999) explain this as simultaneous adoption of southern and northern EnglE features. At the time Australia was established in the late 18th century, the DANCE vowel was pre-eminent for this set of words in the south whereas TRAP was common in the north (this is a simplification, of course; there was considerable instability, as always when there is a change in progress). Even though AusE bears a striking example with southern EnglE (in that it is non-rhotic, has six short vowels rather than five, etc.), this is a case where both northern and southern variants survived the levelling process, simply because they were reanalysed into social and stylistic variants, /æ/ having lower social status than /a:/.

Phonological reallocation, on the other hand, refers to the refunctionalisation of regional variants into allophonic ones (as illustrated by the adoption of two onsets of PRICE in EFE; see above). Trudgill (1986) offers a similar explanation for the well-known feature of Canadian raising (see above), where onsets of PRICE are centralised in pre-voiceless environments (*night*, *write*, etc.) and open in other contexts. Diphthongs with central onsets were a legacy of Scottish inputs to CanE, whereas /ai/ was adopted from southern EngE dialects. The adoption of both is explained by specialisation and language-internal conditioning, since they were "reallocated a new function as positional allophonic variants" (Britain & Trudgill 1999: 251).

2.1.6 Independent developments and interdialect forms

The final process discussed here deals with dialect interaction and the potential for development of 'new' features. The process of new-dialect formation does not only involve picking and mixing, and feature selection and retention are not the only mechanisms to operate in long-term contact situations. New dialects affiliate with their inputs by drawing a vast number of features from them, but it would be simplistic to assume that they are linguistically predetermined by the systemic properties (and the frequency thereof!) of the varieties in contact. Contact-derived dialects are not mixed, levelled and regularised varieties that select *all* their phonological and structural properties from their donors. Furthermore, we must account for the fact that "contact between two [or more] dialects leads to the development of forms that actually originally occurred in neither dialect" (Trudgill 1986: 62). The role of accommodation is crucial here as well. Obviously, independent developments are most likely to occur when accommodation has not gone to completion, i.e., when a feature from an original input is not adopted in its original form.

Semi-rhoticity in Caribbean English provides a case in point here. As is well known, rhoticity is one of the most important criteria in English dialect typology, and one commonly distinguishes between rhotic accents and non-rhotic ones. In rhotic accents, such as ScE, IrE and most varieties of AmE, /r/ is pronounced in all environments, regardless whether it follows a vowel (*caress*) or a consonant (*cart*) or whether it is in word- or syllable-final position (*car*). Speakers with non-rhotic accents, in contrast, as in most of England and practically the entire Southern Hemisphere, pronounce /r/ in pre-vocalic environments only. This dichotomy holds by and large and is a useful criterion to distinguish varieties of English around the world. Jamaican English (JamE), in contrast, falls in-between these two categories in that it is semi-rhotic (Wells 1982: 76, 221). Pre-V /r/ is always present (just as in non-rhotic accents), while it variably features in pre-C and word-final positions. In other words, rhoticity in present-day JamE takes an intermediate position and is characterised by a considerable degree of context-dependent variability. Stress seems to be an important criterion here; whereas /r/ is dropped from unstressed syllables (*water*, *flower*, etc.) it is frequently (though not categorically) present in stressed syllables at the end of a word (*car*, *spare*, etc.). Semi-rhoticity can be explained as a consequence of incomplete accommodation in a diverse contact scenario, with additional effects or pidginisation and creolisation as well as second language learning. If this was the case, then accommodation to the (rhotic) varieties that were transplanted to Jamaica in the 16th and 17th centuries was incomplete.

An additional outcome of dialect contact is that variants appear that are absent from any of the input varieties, so-called "interdialect" variants "not actually present in any of the dialects contributing to the mixture but arise out of interaction between them" (Trudgill, Gordon, Lewis & Maclagan 2000: 106). Whereas semi-rhoticity in JamE can be explained as incomplete accommodation to a feature *present* in the inputs, dialect interaction may also give rise to features *unattested* in the donors. The case of *Veneziano* or *Common Veneto* (CoV), the contact dialect that developed in Venice in the late Middle Ages, provides a good example for this. CoV was formed when Venice urbanised and became an economic and political centre in the 14th century; there was massive immigration from the rural hinterlands of the Veneto as well as from northeastern and mid-central Italy. The path of koinéisation that gave rise to CoV is "best viewed as a more-or-less stable process by which mainland speakers have divested, or are divesting, their speech of its most markedly local, usually rural features in the direction of urban Venetian" (Ferguson 2003: 450). Ferguson (2003) analysed inter- and intra-textual variability in various *scripta* produced between the 12th and 15th centuries, i.e. official, legal, mercantile, epistolary and literary documents, which present the earliest evidence of the variety. He found that the documents "displayed exceptional levels of variability" (457), which is indicative of an early stage of new-dialect formation necessary for the emergence of a contact-derived variety (see above). Ferguson analysed a corpus of court proceedings and found strong evidence of dialect mixing ("rather than the reflex of a single mainland type, we seem to be in the presence of a stable koiné with diverse, mainly northern, inputs"; 458). Furthermore, he also found a number of interdialect forms that were not attested in any of the donor dialects. Nouns with an *–arium* suffix in Latin (*herbarium*, *aquarium*, etc.) took *–er* in northern dialects of the time and *–aro* in central-southern ones. Several scribes had intermediate writings, combining both forms into a new spelling *–ero*, which was unprecedented and did not occur in any of the inputs. Crucially, Ferguson found the very same interdialect form in other sources, and the fact that this interdialect variant made an appearance elsewhere shows that it was by no means idiosyncratic (though it did not survive when CoV formed).

Trudgill (1986) distinguishes between two types of interdialectalisms. First, features that are intermediate between the original dialect forms and thus indicative of incomplete, faulty or simply "intermediate" accommodation (such as *–ero* suffixes in 14th century CoV); and second, forms that originate in overgeneralisation or hyperadaptation (perhaps the most well-known case here is hypercorrection, which occurs when speakers misinterpret and incorrectly generalise rules by applying them to inappropriate contexts, e.g. when a learner of English inappropriately applies the CUP or BATH vowel in words that take TRAP, e.g. *grand* or *cancer*).

Therefore, mixing and levelling alone cannot explain why a newly developing variety has all the features it has. Whereas processes of feature selection and retention are crucial in new-dialect formation, multiple retention and interdialectalisms may manifest themselves as well, adding to the complexity of the process. Not all the features of a dialect can be traced to ancestral (donor) varieties and all dialects, whether old or new, have the potential for independent change. Any theory put forward to explain contact-induced language change has to leave room for patterns of independent innovation.

2.1.7 Summary: Dialect contact and new-dialect formation

Having discussed the major mechanisms involved in new-dialect formation, the question now is how we can retrace their interaction and model how a 'new' dialect is formed *ab ovo*. Two important concepts in this context are the *feature pool*, as suggested by Mufwene (2001), who argues that all the variants from the donor systems coexist in a pool, from which the new contact-derived variety draws its features. The second one is *focusing*, the emergence of stable endonormative features, as developed in and discussed by LePage & Tabouret-Keller (1985). Speakers of a fully focused variety are in agreement about normative structures and show an increasing awareness that their dialect differs from others on linguistic grounds. Focused varieties often have a 'proper' name and are accompanied by processes of standardisation and codification; these reinforce attitudes towards outsiders and foster a strong sense of a local identity on the part of speech community's members. In so-called *diffuse* communities, by contrast, speakers display considerable heterogeneity, having no (or little) consensus on linguistic norms and the status of the variety. Le Page & Tabouret-Keller (1985) illustrate this with the case of multilingual Belize, where English, Creole and Spanish coexist. There is a continuum between acro- and basilectal varieties, no consensus on the usage of high-standard norms, no clear delineation of the coexisting varieties and little (if any) agreement as to which of the varieties should be used in a given context or interaction. The maintenance of multiple varieties in a contact setting is therefore a crucial factor to determine whether a variety focuses or whether it remains diffuse, and this has implications for the development of overseas varieties in general. According to Kerswill & Williams (1992: 13), the initial stages of any dialect mixture situation are always characterised by extreme diffuseness. There is no agreement on shared norms in a newly founded community and language usage is characterised by the coexistence of a number of distinct variants. Variability may then be reduced when accommodation patterns between speakers in face-to-face interaction increase and as social networks are implemented. Network ties function as norm-enforcing mechanisms so that the focusing of new linguistic norms can manifest itself after a period of long-term accommodation.

Another important issue concerns the degree of mutual intelligibility. According to Siegel (1985: 375), this is a *conditio sine qua non* for koinéisation. Mohan (1978) agrees but makes a general distinction between koinés that developed out of dialects that share lexical and morphosyntactic properties and others that are based on varieties that are less typologically similar. She makes the claim that koinés of the second type, exemplified by TB, partake in more extensive levelling. This has wider socio-political consequences since the newly formed koiné undergoes a status change and is generally considered as a separate dialect with its own structural characteristics. Gambhir (1981) maintains that a koiné necessarily has its origins in contact between dialects of one and the same language and that these undergo structural simplification (without explaining the motivation, however).

In sum, there is consensus that a koiné is the linguistic outcome of a contact situation which involves at least two varieties that are typologically similar and (to some extent) mutually intelligible; moreover, all are in agreement that the koinéisation process necessarily involves processes of mixing and simplification (even though some are not explicit about the exact nature of these processes). However, there is no agreement at all as to whether or not koinés should function as *lingue franche* (see below) or regional languages (Nida & Fehderau 1970), or when and how they undergo nativisation and expansion (if at all). The following definition from Siegel (1985: 376) includes the principal aspects of new-dialect formation and, in my view, is the most helpful one in the literature:

> A koiné is [a] stabilised composite variety ... characterised by a mixture of features from the contributing varieties, and at an earlier stage of the development, it is often reduced or simplified in comparison to any of these varieties. Functionally ... [i]t also may become the primary language of amalgamated communities of these speakers.

The major task, then, is to model the processes that interact during new-dialect formation. Figure 2.1 incorporates Mufwene's concept of a feature pool at a first stage and the major mechanisms in a second one. The model is based on three inputs that co-exist in an early scenario of dialect contact, all of which feed variants into the feature pool from which the new dialect *could* adopt its features when it stabilises. The total number of variants competing for selection decreases as focusing progresses, i.e., while mixing, levelling and regularisation mechanisms are at work. The end product of this process reflects the adoption and stabilisation of so-called "endonormative" (Schneider 2007) features originally drawn from several donors. Such a model suggests clarity (as models usually do) and gives the impression that new-dialect formation is a nice and tidy process, and a chronologically ordered one on top. Nothing could be further from the truth, of course. Koinéisation, like all processes of contact-induced language change, is messy and far from straightforward. There complicating factors are numerous: Processes may co-occur and influence each other, interdependent developments are impossible to predict, social factors may intervene at all times, changing the outcome, etc. The unpredictability of koinéisation is born out by the fact that focussing did not occur in settings that seemed to offer ideal conditions for new-dialect formation (insularity, stability, etc.), most notably in FIE (Sudbury 2000; see below). Nevertheless, such a model illustrates the processes at work and combines several approaches.

Figure 2.1 A schematic model of new-dialect formation

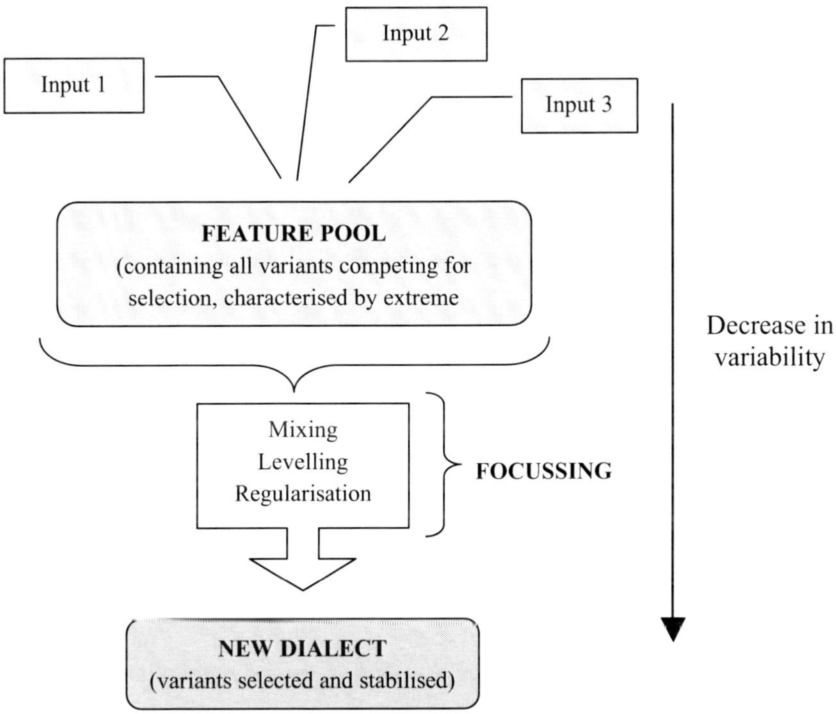

A far-reaching question is how long it should take for new norms to emerge. How much time would it take the first generations to drive koinéisation forward and by when is it completed? The fundamental question is exactly when initial variability gives way to more regularised and structured patterns. What is the cut-off point for the evolution of new dialects, and when can we say that stabilisation and crystallisation are completed? Trudgill (2004) argues that accommodation plays a crucial role among both the first generation of immigrants and the native-born generation of children. The latter are more important since they are instrumental in forming a more stable variety out of all the inputs. Trudgill proposes a basic 3-step model, adult immigrants representing Stage I, which he documents by looking into the formation phase of NZE. Although there is no direct evidence of the immigrants' speech (who were born in the UK), he does not rule out that they underwent rudimentary levelling before arriving in New Zealand, e.g. that they dropped marked or salient features through accommodation. The first native-born generation would represent Stage II; these children pick and mix features from their parents' speech, which means that they display an unusual amount of inter- and intra-individual variability (though we would have to compare this with communities that have no recent contact history, of course). Trudgill (2004) argues that the speech of the adults has great influence at this stage since there is no common peer-group dialect (yet). Instead, children select variants from different dialects "at will" (103) like in "a kind of supermarket" (108). The great variability suggests that these speakers did not "indulge in long-term accommodation to one another" (ibid.), mixing features around them instead. Stage III, finally, the second generation, i.e., the children of the first locally-born children, sees the formation of a focused, stable new dialect, drawing from the initial feature pool of the Stage I input, filtered through the Stage II speakers, who develop the koiné via the sociolinguistic processes discussed (levelling, reallocation, etc.). Consequently, Trudgill suggests that the whole process may be completed within three generations.

One of the major issues here concerns variability, or rather: the decrease of variability and diffuseness. The problem is of course that variation is language-inherent and that invariant monolithic dialects do not exist. The question we are consequently facing is by what stage we can confidently claim that variability has decreased to the extent that an endonormative dialect that *still* displays some amount of variation has emerged. Clearly, the outcome must still display some sort of variation, no matter what the conditioning factors are. Taken to extremes, one might even suggest that new-dialect formation is never finished since the offspring varieties are in a constant state of variation and change, making it impossible to decide when norms have stabilised. This point is crucial and has not always deserved the attention it should have. I fully agree with Siegel, Mühlhäusler and Britian that the most promising (perhaps even only) method to show decreasing variation and emerging stabilisation in contact dialectology is a quantitative analysis; empirical information is crucial to decide whether new-dialect formation is progressing or not. I will return to this point in ch. 6 below.

In any case, it should be stressed that 'pure' dialect contact scenarios are the exception rather than the norm. Linguistic contact comes in many shapes and sizes and I now discuss the possible outcomes of a different contact setting, i.e., when there is interaction between speakers whose native languages are *not* mutually intelligible, and look into an altogether different type of contact-induced change: language contact.

2.2 Language contact

Language contact occurs when speakers of structurally distinct, mutually unintelligible varieties interact, either short- or long-term. The basic principles of accommodation (as discussed above) apply here as well, with one important difference: some modifications *have* to be made to render communication possible. Otherwise, one of the essential goals of face-to-face interaction, i.e. the transmission of information in the form of requests, orders, etc. cannot be successful, unless the interacting individuals resort to other techniques (such as sign or body language). Put differently, immigrants from various regions of England have no essential need to accommodate upon relocation in a colony (such as in South Africa or on the Bahamas). This changes when a common language is lacking, for instance when they find themselves in the presence of languages other than English (indigenous or other European ones, as in Australia, North America or in the Pacific, nearly in the entire former British Empire).

There are various strategies to communicate in multilingual contact scenarios. One is to adopt some form of one of the languages present. This typically is the one spoken by the colonising power, which serves as a *lingua franca* or language of wider communication and is "a common language but one which is native only to some of its speakers" (Sebba 1997: 16). However, complete accommodation and ensuing langue shift is extremely unlikely in such scenarios, for a number of reasons: access to the target, cognitive limits on language learning by adults, etc. To the contrary, speakers create a 'makeshift' language by drawing elements from at least two of the varieties in contact. If this occurs, then one of the languages (the transplanted non-local superstrate) commonly contributes most of the lexicon (and serves as a *lexifier*), whereas the (local) substrate languages (spoken by the indigenous populations that hold a socially subordinate position) exert considerable morphosyntactic influence. Consequently, when speakers of different languages interact closely over lengthy periods of time, then the makeshift language that is to be the community's lingua franca shows influence from several linguistic systems. Though complete language shift via several generations is by no means uncommon (as witnessed by the catastrophic rate of language death in the 20th and 21st centuries, particularly in North America and Australia, where indigenous communities have abandoned their languages and shifted to English or other languages), contact usually gives rise to processes such as jargonisation and borrowing at an early stage of the contact scenario, and pidginisation and (perhaps) creolisation or alternative processes, such as mixed languages and creoloidisation, at subsequent ones. This section briefly discusses some of the major processes in language contact, but I would like to emphasise that such a brief account can in no way do justice to the complexity of the phenomenon (see recent introductory textbooks: Holm 2000, 2004; Thomason 2001; Winford

2003). I can do no more than look at the essentials and provide some examples that are of relevance for the purpose of this book.

2.2.1 Early stages: Jargonisation and borrowing

The early stages of language contact witness the development of a functionally restricted *jargon*, which effectively does no more than cover the most basic needs of communication (usually for purposes such as bartering or trade). Jargons represent the most rudimentary form of contact-induced language change and are defined as "linguistically the least structured stage of pidgin development; at the same time, it has the most limited range of functions and is used in the most restricted of social situations" (Sebba 1997: 102).

They are the product of idiosyncratic strategies developed by individuals who are in spontaneous need of communicating in a multilingual environment (tourists, traders, travellers, etc.). Jargons are formed for a specific purpose, one that it is clear to all the participants, and they are extremely dynamic and unstable, being shaped on the spot and dying out when there is no more need for using them. Moreover, they are developed *ad hoc* by adults and very often not transmitted from one generation to the next (which means that in all likelihood they are not acquired as a native language by children).[4] The colonisers' language typically takes the role of the lexifier. The social status of groups and speakers is an important criterion here as well, since prestige and power of the communities affect the amount, frequency and direction of lexical transfer (Winford 2003). The status of individual groups is thus evident at this early stage, in that the impact of the languages present, i.e. their contribution (mostly of lexical items) to the jargon, reflects the social relationships of the groups in contact. When speakers are in *super-/substratal* relationships and of unequal power and prestige, then borrowing typically proceeds from the superstratal to the substratal language (exemplified by contact between Spanish and Meso-American languages, Aboriginal languages and English in Australia, Norman French and Middle English, etc.). Borrowing from the local languages is typically restricted: "lexical items selected from indigenous languages stem from a small number of specific semantic domains and are taken over at characteristic evolutionary phases, namely, in turn, toponyms, terms for flora and fauna, and words for culturally distinctive items and customs" (Schneider 2007: 79).

This is different in situations when the social hierarchy is more balanced. Borrowing tends to be more or less bidirectional in *adstratal* contexts, when speakers of the two languages consider themselves of equal prestige (Old Norse

---

[4] Chinook Jargon, which developed as a trade language in the north-western USA in the 18th and early 19th century, is a typical example here (Thomason 2001).

and Old English, for instance). This affects jargons as well. Russenorsk ('Russian-Norwegian', Broch & Jahr 1984) was a trade jargon spoken along the Arctic coast of northern Norway between the 18th and early 20th centuries, mainly by Norwegian fishermen and Russian sailors and merchants. The evidence we have suggests that there must have been some codified stable form of this jargon, which is remarkable since it was only used in the short summer trading season (unless it was created on the spot every year, which seems unlikely). Holm (1989: 621) emphasises that this particular jargon did not develop in a typical colonial setting: the two groups were not socially stratified and had more or less identical status. This had linguistic consequences: the lexicon is derived from both languages in approximately equal proportions (according to Fox 1983, 39 per cent of the vocabulary is Russian in origin and 47 per cent Norwegian), so that there was no lexifier language *per se* (in sharp contrast to jargons elsewhere, where more than 90 per cent of the words used are drawn from the superstrate).

Sociolinguistically speaking, interaction strategies are individualistic and *ad hoc* so that jargons have very few (if any) fixed norms (Mühlhäusler 1997). They are characterised by a comparatively simple sound system, one- or two-word utterances, a relative lack of grammatical complexity (such as word-order inversion, embedding, etc.) and small – typically specialised – lexicons. Under special conditions (namely when the scenario contact persists and perhaps even intensifies, the population remains stable, and none of the languages present is adopted as the *lingua franca*), the jargon may undergo expansion so as to fulfil many of the communicative purposes it previously lacked. If this is the case, then a jargon is said to represent the first stage in the life-cycle of a *pidgin*.

2.2.2 *Pidginisation*

The agents behind *pidginisation* are adults who need a language for the basic needs of permanent inter-group communication and who (for whatever reason) do not adopt any of the (superstrate or substrate) varieties as a target. They consequently face the task of developing a makeshift variety that is not (or only in a very limited way) available as a role model. It is crucial that pidgin speakers already have native-like competence in a variety *other* than the pidgin, which means that they develop, learn and speak the pidgin as a second language. This means that pidgins to some extent resemble the formation of an *interlanguage*, displaying strategies typically employed in language learning. Pidgins are never the first language of a given community and have no native speakers. Holm (1988: 4) offers the following definition:

> A *pidgin* is a reduced language that results from extended contact between groups of people with no language in common; it evolves when they need

> some means of verbal communication, perhaps for trade, but no group learns the native language of any other group for social reasons.

A pidgin is consequently a contact-derived variety that is reduced to fulfil minimal purposes of face-to-face interaction (Romaine 1988; Sebba 1997). At their most basic, pidgins are "stripped of everything but the bare essentials necessary for communication" (Romaine 1988: 24), which makes it somewhat difficult to keep them distinct from jargons. At an early stage, pidgins are *reduced* in that their vocabularies are small and limited, that they have few grammatical constraints and that there is no stylistic variation (Romaine 1988). Moreover, their range of social functions is limited (Holm 1988; Mühlhäusler 1997).

What, then, are the linguistic mechanisms that operate during pidginisation? First of all, pidgins undergo simplification (see above), which (in my view) is a more adequate term in language contact, simply because it can be demonstrated much less controversially in what way the phonological and structural systems of pidgins are less complex than those of their respective donor languages (Holm 1988; Sebba 1997). The domains of phonology, semantics and morphosyntax provide good examples. Phonologically, for example, pidgins have a strong tendency to avoid marked[5] phonemes, preferring sounds that occur in the phonemic inventories of all or most its donors. Fanagalo (Pidgin Zulu), for instance, provides an excellent example (Mesthrie 1989). Fanagalo developed in the South African gold and diamond mines and was spoken as a lingua franca by workers from across southern and central Africa and also had some use in the English and Afrikaans-speaking communities (Adendorff 2002). This pidgin is unusual in that it draws heavily from an African lexifier (taking some 70 per cent of its vocabulary from Zulu, ca. 25 per cent words from English, and some words from Afrikaans and Portuguese as well). Interestingly, one of the most salient characteristics of Zulu, click sounds, is entirely absent in Fanagalo. Clicks are typologically unusual, regionally confined (to south and central African languages; Sands & Güldemann fc.) and thus highly marked. Fanagalo, though formed with substantial input from Zulu, replaced these phonemes with unmarked ones (namely velar plosives [k]), which featured in the other inputs. Similarly, French-based pidgins tend to replace rounded front vowel (/y/ and /œ/), which are marked, with more common unrounded ones (/i:/ and /e:/; Corne 1999). Simplification is also at work when phonological contrasts are no longer made, the consequence of which is an increase in mergers and a decrease in phonemic inventories. Tok Pisin (TP) in Papua New Guinea displays extensive phonological mergers. The English phonemes /s/, /ʃ/ and /tʃ/ are all merged to

[5] Marked is used here in the sense that they occur in only a minority of the world's languages and that they are acquired at a late stage in the child's language acquisition process.

[s] (Smith 2003) and /f/ and /p/ have merged to [p] (*pinis* 'finish'; Mühlhäusler 1997: 139). Pidgins tend to have symmetric systems of five or seven vowels /i e a ɛ o u/, plus on occasion nasal vowels (mostly in French-based creoles). Simplification manifests itself in the domain of phonotactics as well, since pidgins have strong preference towards CV syllable structures and employ a number of strategies to avoid consonant clusters (which are unusual typologically and highly marked). These strategies include the deletion of word-initial consonants (English *stand* > Sranan *tan*) or vowels (Portuguese *ocupar* > Príncipe Crioullo Portuguese *kupa*), the deletion of consonants in clusters (English sis*t*er > Sranan *sisa*), vowel epenthesis (Portuguese *alma* > Príncipe Crioullo Portuguese *álima* 'soul') or the addition of word-final vowel (English *dog* > Saramaccan Creole English *dágu*; discussion in Schreier 2005).

Simplification is at work in the area of morphosyntax as well. Pidgins have a strong tendency towards analytic morphology, i.e., they have few (if any) bound inflectional morphemes so that lexical items tend to be mono-morphemic. According to Sebba (1997: 46), "[t]he preference for isolating and agglutinating morphology can probably be explained in terms of the need for pidgins to be easily learnable: for example, learners of the pidgin will not be confronted with more than one form for any verb." Inflectional morphology entails irregular verb paradigms and (mostly) redundant word endings (of course, redundant only when person-number concord is expressed by pronouns also, as in English), and learning irregular patterns carries a particularly high memory load for language learners (and pidgin speakers). Due to simplification, complex structures of this kind are done away with, so that the target is more 'learner-friendly'. TP, for instance, one of the official languages of Papua New Guinea, has no morphosyntactically overt gender distinctions, as in the object pronoun *em* 'him, her, it', and prefers circumlocutions in place of inflections, e.g. 'haus bilong John' instead of 'John's house' (Smith 2003). Similarly, Fanagalo lacks the complex system of Zulu inflectional morphology and has English SVO word order (Adendorff 2002). Moreover, pidgins lack morphological markers to indicate plurality, possession or object function. In plural formation, the noun generally does not change in form since there is no affixation; instead, the plural is inferred by context, or else indicated by a quantifier (such as TP *ol* from English 'all', Holm 1988) or postponed *dem*. Similarly, verbs typically have reduced inflection: tense is often inferred from the immediate context of the verb (Sebba 1997) or alternatively indicated by free morphemes or preverbal markers (such as *done* or *been*). The lack of inflection also leads to a decrease of agreement in syntax, for instance in TP *Sikspela man i kom* 'Six people are coming' and *Wanpela man i kom* 'A man is coming', where the numeral is the only means to indicate a meaning change (in this case: on plurality). On a semantic level, finally, pidgins favour 'transparent' words, i.e. words whose meaning can be inferred from its component morphemes (such as Sranan Tongo *wrokosani* 'tool', which is made up of the two free morphemes *wroko* 'work' and *sani* 'thing', Sebba 1981: 107).

Consequently, pidgins are characterised by reduced vocabularies and simplified grammars, and the structural and phonological properties of contact languages reflect the learning processes of adults. Pidgins can remain stable for more than a generation, namely when they maintain their function in a multilingual environment. However, all contact scenarios are dynamic and can change quickly. The pidgins can cease to be spoken because the community disperses, it can undergo *depidginisation* (namely when there is a shift to another lingua franca) or else it can undergo further development and extension when its function enhances.

> Pidgins, like other communication systems, are dynamic, responding to the needs of the situation, or rather to the needs of the speakers in that situation. As the complexity of social interaction increases, so the demands on the pidgin increase, and it will evolve into a linguistic system of greater complexity, with a greater range of functions. Sometimes the reverse will happen: a pidgin, brought into being to met a particular set of communicative needs, may die out when there is no further need for it. (Sebba 1997: 101)

Consequently, as the community continues to use a pidgin as a vehicle of communication, it may extend it to more and more domains and contexts so that the pidgin's functional range and social role increases subsequently. In other words, the pidgin is remodelled to fulfil the needs of its speakers. This means that the state of variability found in jargons and early pidgins is reduced further, that norms emerge, that the lexicon increases in size and that the (formerly basic) makeshift language is used in more social domains. Lexical and grammatical conventions are established and become fixed (such as patterns of new-word formation or grammatical rules) and borrowing from sub- and superstrates continues on a larger scale, being not only lexical but also *structural-systemic* (of morphological and syntactic features) and *phonological* (of individual phonemes). Contact intensity is an important factor here (Thomason & Kaufman 1988). Lexical borrowing may occur when there is low intensity contact; structural borrowing, on the other hand, usually requires heavy contact and is particularly common in communities where there is sustained bi- or multilingualism, namely when permanent effects of contact-induced language change are most likely. As a result, the social role and prestige of the contact variety changes drastically ("An extended pidgin … proves vitally important in a multilingual area … Because of its usefulness [it] is extended and used beyond the original limited function which caused it to come into being"; Todd 1990: 5). The pidgin becomes the main variety in a multilingual setting though it still has the status of a second language and despite the fact that it is not spoken natively. As Sebba (1997: 105) points out, "the speakers target is now the pidgin, not the lexifier language."

2.2.3 *Creolisation*

Pidgins may be extended if (and only if) their social roles increase and if the multilingual community selects them as a vehicle of communication for everyday purposes. Creolisation is less frequent than pidginisation, for the simple reason that the requirements for this process are more extensive (sociodemographic stability, sociolinguistic continuity). A traditionally held belief, as expressed in the following quote, is that jargons develop into pidgins that in turn develop into creoles:

> [C]reole languages are pidgins that have acquired native speakers. In linguistically mixed communities where a pidgin is used as the lingua franca, children may acquire it as their native language, particularly if their parents normally communicate in the pidgin. When this occurs the language will re-acquire all the characteristics of a full, non-pidgin language. As spoken by an adult native speaker the language will have, when compared to the original pidgin, an expanded vocabulary, a wider range of syntactic possibilities, and an increased stylistic repertoire. It will also, of course, be used for all purposes in a full range of social situations. That is, the reduction that occurred during pidginisation will be repaired, although the simplification and admixture remain. (Trudgill 1995: 160)

The point taken her is that adults in need of a *lingua franca* are the main agents of pidginisation. Children growing up in such an environment may adopt the pidgin as a major vehicle of communication (so that it undergoes *nativisation*). A pidgin is thus extended so as to meet the needs of native speakers (lexis, grammar, etc.). The earlier reduction and simplification processes are "repaired" and according to Trudgill, the variety gains in complexity, eventually emerging as a "full, non-pidgin language".

This view has been contested on account of being too simplistic and idealistic and of not doing justice to the full complexity of language contact. Though such claims are still found in recent work (e.g. Myers-Scotton 2002: 272: "The general view probably still is that creoles develop from pidgins"), a growing body of research on pidgins and creoles with different lexifiers around the world brings to light several major problems. These are so far-reaching that Thomason (2001: 175) doubts whether such a view is plausible at all (or whether one should even try finding one):

> I believe that some, perhaps many or even most, of the controversies surrounding the topic of pidgin and creole genesis will vanish if we recognise that the common assumption of a single developmental route to creole genesis - which is the main locus of the controversies - is unmotivated.

There are many problems indeed, and the task is not made easier by the fact that exceptions seem to spring up whenever a rule is proposed. The major points of controversy are the following. First of all, there is no agreement as to whether creoles really are nativised pidgins or whether they require a prior pidgin stage. The question is whether a creole presupposes a prior pidgin stage out of which it evolves, or whether creolisation can occur *ab ovo*. Mühlhäusler (1997) claims that it is "abundantly clear … that there are numerous difficulties with this simple formula." He distinguishes between two types of questions: "1. What are the linguistic correlates of initial creolization? 2. What are the sources for subsequent structural expansion?" (p. 186). He thus shifts the focus on sources of expansion, i.e. on the varieties in contact that contribute to the feature pool. This would not invalidate the (jargon >) pidgin > creole development, of course, but emphasise that other evolutionary paths exist and that these be analysed by looking into the linguistic development of creoles. Thomason (2001: 160) sums this up succinctly:

> In fact, some creoles are nativised pidgins. Such a creole was originally a pidgin which later became the main language of a speech community, learned as a first language by children and used for general community activities; its linguistic resources expanded with the expansion in its spheres of usage. Other creoles seem never to have gone through a pidgin stage at all, but to have developed gradually by increasing divergence from the lexifier language, and still others apparently arose abruptly, also without going through a well-defined pidgin stage.

In fact, whereas a prototypical creole development is attested (for instance in Torres Strait Creole (TStrCr) or TP; Siegel 1985), other contact varieties were shaped by what has been labelled "abrupt creolisation" (Thomason & Kaufman 1988: 148). Under special sociolinguistic conditions, they argue, such as rapid in-migration or importation of large groups of speakers from diverse linguistic backgrounds (as in plantation slavery), the need for a lingua franca in the transplanted community is so pressing that adults have to act as agents of creolisation. For instance, it has been argued that JamCrE originated in a complex process involving brief pidginisation and abrupt creolisation. Substrate languages continued to be used for a long time, coexisting with the expanded pidgin from which a creole emerged. In contrast, the development of TP is one of gradual creolisation, i.e., expansion of a fully developed pidgin (Arends & Bruyn 1995: 111). However, TP seems to have expanded without, or at least before, it was acquired as a first language (Smith 2003), which poses another challenge to the definition offered by Trudgill above. If TP expanded into all spheres of public life before it underwent nativisation, then it must have creolised before it was spoken natively. Consequently, the prime agents of expansion and stabilisation here are adults, not children. Subsequent creolisation by children is then accompanied by few linguistic changes, which makes it difficult to keep it distinct from an expanded and elaborated pidgin.

The concept of *nativisation* deserves a further mention here. A pidgin, which is no one's native language, is said to undergo nativisation when children acquire it as an L1 in a multilingual community. Older generations, on the other hand, continue using their native (substrate) languages with family and peers and the pidgin as a *lingua franca* with community members from distinct sociolinguistic backgrounds. When children acquire an expanded pidgin and set off nativisation, then the resulting situation becomes extraordinarily diverse since the pidgin is still used by their grandparents and parents (who may expand it). In other words, a contact variety may function both as a pidgin and a creole for different groups in the very same community. We bear in mind, consequently, that nativisation is not necessarily a prerequisite for creolisation (Thomason & Kaufman 1988) and that pidginisation and creolisation may readily co-occur within the same community. This has led some creolists (e.g. Mufwene 2001) to argue that expansion without nativisation depends on the social circumstances and the linguistic ecology of the community (see below).

Time depth is another crucial issue. How long would creolisation processes take until the creole becomes sociolinguistically distinct from the pidgin out of which it evolved (if it did)? Gradual creolisation takes considerably longer than the generation or two suggested for abrupt creolisation. Creole genesis is considered as an interruption of inter-generational transmission of language and a challenge to the family-tree model (Sebba 1997; Mühlhäusler 1997). Creoles develop "by some historical process other than normal transmission", which is to say "complete and successful transmissions, by native speakers to child or adult learners, of an entire language, i.e., a complex interlocking set of phonological, morphological, syntactic, semantic, and lexical systems" (Thomason 2001: 74, 75). This was most evident in large-scale contact scenarios that involved the transplantation of tens of thousands of slaves for work on plantations, as was common in the Caribbean or Hawai'i.

> The plantation system is crucial because it was unique in creating a catastrophic break in linguistic tradition that is unparalleled. It is difficult to conceive of another situation where people arrived with such a variety of native languages; where they were so cut off from their native language groups; where the size of no language group was enough to ensure its survival; where no second language was shared by enough people to serve as a useful vehicle of intercommunication; and where the legitimate language was inaccessible to almost everyone. (Sankoff 1979: 24)

It is in contexts of a "catastrophic break" that pidginisation and creolisation are most likely to occur, fostering abrupt creolisation in particular. If there is sociodemographic stability, by contrast, the transition stage between pidginisation and creolisation is not necessarily abrupt at all. TP, for instance, saw a lengthy phase of extension before it creolised (Smith 2003). Similarly, French-based creoles (such as Mauritian Creole) appear to have evolved via gradual creolisation of an expanded pidgin that had already served as a lingua franca for several generations (e.g. Baker 1995; Corne 1999). Under these circumstances, children and adults would have been simultaneously involved in the gradual process of transforming the pidgin into a creole. Corne (1999: 167) proposes a generational model that bears striking similarities with the one suggested for new-dialect formation (discussed above). Corne speculates that a first generation would consist of slaves speaking various L1s and pidgin French as L2, along with the French colonisers providing access to the superstrate (in this case: French). Language usage in the second generation would be characterised by bilingualism in the ancestral languages and the developing creole whereas the third generation would see the first monolingual creole speakers, for whom the emerging creole serves as an L1. In other words, just as in the scenario sketched above, a creole may emerge through gradual creolisation within three generations, in exceptional circumstances within the first 50 years of settlement history.

Still others argue that the social embedding of language contact is crucial for the ultimate length and outcome of the process. Mufwene (2001: 8ff.) takes the position that the contact environments that give rise to pidgins are sociodemographically and sociolinguistically different than those that give rise to creoles, questioning both the role of nativisation and the conventional evolutionary pidgin > creole path. Creoles primarily develop in settlement and planter colonies where there is "regular and intimate" contact (Mufwene 2001: 9) between the colonising and the colonised populations, i.e. slaves and/or indentured labourers. Pidgins, on the other hand, emerge as basic tools of communication in trade scenarios that are transient and unstable. If the colony, perhaps following an initial contact and the usage of a jargon, is primarily "commercial", then the pidgin is most likely to stabilise and expand, which does not mean that it might not nativise and creolise at a later stage. Following this line of thinking, the difference between pidginisation and creolisation is predominantly a socio-historical one. A very similar point of view is expressed by Singler (1988: 47): "The dichotomy between extended pidgin and creole correlates with differences in social history; the creole scenario … leads to a break with the substrate, but the extended pidgin scenario need not."

Regardless of whether creolisation is a social or a linguistic process (Mufwene 2001; McWhorter 1998, 2005), the social ecology into which the community is embedded will in some way influence the outcome of the process. Accordingly, Arends, Muysken & Smith (1995: 15) use external history to distinguish between four types of creoles: plantation creoles, fort creoles, maroon creoles, and creolised pidgins. They claim that the result is influenced by a number of factors. The *degree of access* to the target language is paramount. A more or less equal proportion of superstrate to substrate speakers in a community will favour extensive incorporation of items from the target language (in terms of lexis, but also grammar and phonology). This is evidenced by the case of Réunion in the Indian Ocean, where French colonisers outnumbered the slaves, vis-à-vis Mauritius were there were fewer speakers of French present when Isle de France Créole developed. Réunion Creole displays a significantly higher number of French grammatical categories than Isle de France Créole, and overall population statistics, integration of the colonised groups as well as accessibility to the target are a most plausible explanation for this. Similar contrasts exist between the Bahamas and Jamaica (lexifier: English) or Cabo Verde and São Tomé (lexifier: Portuguese; Holm 1988). A second point concerns the *diversity and typological properties of the substrate(s)*. A (comparatively) homogenous substrate is likely to have greater influence on the emerging creole than a diverse and multilingual scenario involving several substrates (as outlined by Sankoff 1979: 24). When the Gulf of Guinea creoles emerged with inputs from Bini (Kwa) and KiKongo (western Bantu), the creole adopted a negative construction with one negative particle before the verb and another at the end of the sentence, which is similar in KiKongo (Holm 1988). Typically, high diversity leads to extreme social heterogeneity and diffuseness, so the feature pool is more sizeable and there is more competition of potentially selected variants. Few substrate items may become incorporated because no individual substrate language is numerically dominant.

No matter what the local impact of these criteria is, we must focus on the linguistic and sociolinguistic processes that underlie pidgin expansion and (gradual) creolisation. What happens when a language system increases in complexity, for whatever reason and by whatever evolutionary path? The development of a contact language from a highly limited and variable jargon to a fully fledged creole is accompanied by changes in the subsystems of phonology, morphology, syntax and lexicon (Mühlhäusler 1997). First, the pidgin stabilises further, i.e., the (formerly) high degree of diffuse variability decreases continuously. The extension of pidgins into new spheres of communication entails an increase in vocabulary and phonemic inventory: "Once stabilisation of the pidgin has begun, the effect of substrate languages diminishes, as the pidgin acquires its own norms" (Sebba 1997: 108). There are new developments in derivational morphology: TP distinguishes transitive verbs by the suffix *-im* and develops a plural and adjective marking suffix *-pela* (< English *fella*; Smith 2003). The changes in inflectional morphology are less far-reaching, however: "Most Creoles, it appears, still have not acquired any significant inflectional categories and those that have, like some Portuguese-based ones, may have acquired them some time after creolization, in which case their change from isolating to inflectional languages is comparable with that in other full languages" (Mühlhäusler 1997: 194). These changes are accompanied by growing syntactic complexity: word order stabilises further (with a strong preference for SVO order) and the grammatical system increases in complexity through the emergence of relative and embedded clauses. In Sierra Leone Krio, for instance (as in other Atlantic creoles), *se* 'say' is reanalysed as a complementiser 'that' (*A no se yu bisi* 'I know that you're busy'; Holm 1988). It is also common for invariant preverbal particles to express negation, tense, mood and aspect. In Sranan, *ben* indicates past tense, *sa* future and *e* continuous aspect (Plag 1993). In the words of Thomason (2001: 159), "[t]he grammar of a creole, like the grammar of a pidgin, is a crosslanguage compromise of the languages of its creators, who may or may not include native speakers of the lexifier language." The emergence of new syntactic categories often sees the beginnings of stylistic and social variation as well.

2.2.4 Mixed languages, creoloids and semi-creoles

The discussion of language contact is completed with less common scenarios: *language mixing*, *creoloidisation* and *semi-creolisation*. The first term refers to languages that come into stable long-term contact, undergoing mixing and merging into a new system while at all times retaining their synthetic and analytical complexity. According to Bakker (1994), for example, a prime example of language mixing is Michif, spoken by the Métis people of Canada and the northern United States, who are the descendants of Amerindian women (mainly Cree, Nakota and Ojibwe) and fur trade workers of European ancestry (mainly French Canadians but also some Ulster Scots):

> Michif is a language with French nouns, numerals, articles and adjectives, Cree verbs, demonstratives, postpositions, question words and personal pronouns, and further possessives, prepositions and negative elements from both languages. Not only is there a fairly neat distribution of the two languages across the two categories, both languages lost little or nothing about their complexities. (Bakker & Papen 1996: 1174)

Michif is unusual (quite possibly unique) in that, rather than drawing its lexicon from the superstrate and showing heavy substrate influence on its grammar (common in pidginisation and creolisation), it incorporated most complex synthetic elements of the two donors in contact and blended them into a distinctive system. Michif combines Cree and Métis French (Bakker 1997: 85), with some additional borrowing from English and Amerinidan languages such as Ojibwe and Assiniboine. French-origin noun phrases retain grammatical gender and agreement; Cree-origin verbs retain much of their polysynthetic structure. Michif word order is basically that of Cree (relatively free), the verb phrase is that of Plains Cree-origin with little reduction, nouns are almost always accompanied by a French-origin determiner or a possessive, adjectives are French-origin (Cree has no adjectives) and as in French they are either pre- or postnominal. As for the lexicon, about 90% of the nouns are of French origin; by contrast, it is estimated that 88-99% of verbs are drawn from Cree. In terms of phonological mixing, Michif combines two separate systems: one for French- and one for Cree-origin items. For instance, /y/, /l/, /r/ and /f/ exist only in French words, whereas preaspirated stops exist only in Cree words (Papen 2003).

In any case, phenomena of language mixing with full maintenance of input complexity are rare since the vast majority of contact-derived languages are (at least in the first stages) characterised by 'minimalisation' and reduction at all levels (see above). Contact varieties typically have a fairly limited number of grammatical categories (few tenses, no grammatical gender, no morphological plural), reduced morphological complexity (no inflections) and semantic transparency. The adoption and merger of complex and marked structures that occurred in Michif is thus the consequence of close and intimate contact between two speech communities, both of which contribute in equal terms to the newly developing contact variety.

Creoloidisation presents quite a different scenario. *Creoloids* resemble creoles though they have developed in quite distinct social settings (and do not have a prior pidgin stage). Creoloids have taken part in processes of admixture and simplification despite the fact that they have at all times been spoken natively. Such varieties have been labelled creoloids by Platt (1975), who, in his discussion of Singapore English (SingE), states that "some of the same processes involved in creolisation can take place in a multilingual society like Singapore, where English acts as a superstrate language and a continuum of varieties develops between it and more 'basilectal' varieties which reflect influence from the speakers' mother-tongue(s)" (Platt 1975, in Romaine 1988: 160) and a creoloid is defined by Trudgill (2000: 182) as

> a language which demonstrates a certain amount of simplification and admixture, relative to some source language, but which has never been a pidgin or a creole in the sense that it has always had speakers who spoke a variety which was not subject to reduction.

Trudgill (1996) further distinguishes between 1) what he labels 'creoloids proper' like Afrikaans, and 2) non-native creoloids, as exemplified by SingE:

> A non-native creoloid may develop when, as in pidgin formation, a pidginised variety of a source language becomes focussed and acquires stability as a result of being employed as a lingua franca ... The difference between a non-native creoloid and a pidgin lies in the degree of pidginisation which it has undergone ... simplification and admixture [in Singapore English, DS] have never been extreme, and its use as a primary (as opposed to first) language by many speakers in Singapore means that the reduction is also relatively slight. (Trudgill 1996: 8)

Learning and fossilisation play a role here too: "A 'creoloid' can arise, it is claimed, through fossilization of inadequately learnt languages (at school or work); the degree of stability would here be lower than with stable pidgins (assuming that the standard is available to speakers of the creoloid and is accepted for at least some domains – the sociolinguistic situation being similar to a post-creole continuum)" (Görlach 1986: 332). Crucially, due to a continuous native-speaker tradition, creoloids are not subject to large-scale reduction.

Perhaps one of the most well-known creoloid varieties is Afrikaans, the language that derived from varieties of Dutch transplanted to the (then) Dutch colonies in South Africa. Afrikaans has undergone grammatical simplification (as discussed above) that is characteristic of pidgin and creole formation also: "verbal paradigms are reduced and regularised, noun cases (which were still present in seventeenth century Dutch, though being lost) are absent, and grammatical gender in nouns (still present in Dutch) is missing" (Sebba 1997: 161). Such simplification and admixture is most plausibly explained as the result of language contact, imperfect learning and transfer; however, Afrikaans was continuously spoken as a native language and therefore never underwent reduction or relexification, which distinguishes it from pidgins.

By the same token, *semi-creoles* are "pre-creoles, those that haven't quite made it – varieties that have originated in areas and under circumstances that might have led o the creation of a creole but did not go all the way" (Schneider 1990: 83). The idea that some contact-based fall in-between the rigid taxonomies of creoles vs. non-creoles was formulated in the 19th century already, for instance in Hesseling's (1897) study of Afrikaans: "the Dutch on the Cape was on the way to becoming some sort of creole … this process was not completed" (1979 translation, p. 12; quoted by Holm 2004: 7). Reinecke was one of the first to use the term "semi-creole", which he explained by the fact that "the plantation creole dialects that had begun to form never crystallized, never got beyond the makeshift stage" (1937: 61). The idea of a continuum (or to use Schneider's 1990 term: a "cline of creoleness") is also taken by Markey (1982: 204) who asserts that Afrikaans be positioned "on a continuum somewhere between creole and non-creole." Thomason & Kaufman (1988) use this term in their discussion of contact-derived varieties that never have completed full creolisation, such as Afrikaans and Schneider (1990) discusses three putative semi-creoles in the Caribbean, Bay Islands English, Caymanian and Bajan (Barbados), all of which have but a handful features typically associated with creoles (completive *don*, habitual *does*, copula deletion, etc.), explained by the sociodemographic peculiarities of the communities (e.g. a comparatively high proportion of whites).

One thing that is not clear at all is whether this stage of incompletion is the result of decreolisation, i.e. the moving away from a fully-fledged creole, or alternatively, the failure to complete the process that was triggered by initial contact (and continued perhaps via pidginisation). Put differently, are semi-creoles 'semi' because they move away from the creole state they used to have or because they failed to reach that stage in the first place? Also, it is subject to debate what a 'semi' status means for feature adoption and inheritance, i.e. which features (or better: what combination of features) a semi-creole needs to have to be classified as such. Are some domains (e.g. pronouns or the verb phrase) more indicative than others? These uncertainties have led to scepticism whether these terms should be used at all, cf. the discussion in Holm (2004), who prefers discussing them as "partially restructured" varieties.

In any case, it seems undisputed that some contact-derived varieties fall in between the two extremes of creole and non-creole and that classification is not straightforward at all. Creoloids and semi-creoles blur the developmental continuum of pidgins and creoles for two reasons. First, contact with a creolised variety can result in the 'importation' of creole-like features, which means that features were adopted from a creole yet did not originate via direct language contact. Second, the creolisation process may be interrupted (or else redirected or even reverted), so that the outcome falls short of a fully-developed creole. In any case, varieties such as Afrikaans, SingE or Bajan resemble creoles without having a typical creole history, and this renders the task if asserting the status of contact-derived varieties considerably more complex. As a result, the term 'creole' is not a monolithic concept at all (Mufwene 2001) and there exist various degrees of restructuring (Schneider 1990; Neumann-Holzschuh & Schneider 2000).

2.3 *Conclusion and some theory-building*

We are now left with bringing together and assessing the theoretical framework of contact linguistics. For instance, processes involved in dialect and language contact were discussed separately for the sake of clarity. Several mechanisms were identified and discussed in both (e.g. simplification/regularisation, levelling, etc.). A central question we must address in such an overview is whether a strict separation is justified or whether the parallels between the two scenarios are strong enough so as to justify viewing it as a similar process, which would speak in favour of a unified theory. In this context, it is important to ask whether koinés, pidgins and creoles follow similar evolutionary paths. A second question concerns factors that influence and determine the outcome; as mentioned, this has been vividly discussed in recent approaches to creolisation (McWhorter 1998; Mufwene 2001), a debate that has also sprung up in koinéisation (Trudgill 2004). The issue is whether 'new' contact-derived varieties are primarily a product of linguistic or social factors, or of both. Third, we need to look at possible impacts of topography and the nature of the setting. To what extent is the outcome shaped by the eco-linguistic environments of the speech community and how does this affect the evolution of language change? These are the questions addressed here.

2.3.1 Dialect vs. language contact: One theory or two?

From a strictly functional perspective, dialect and language contact seem to involve different processes. The rationale is that accommodation and mixing processes in face-to-face interaction are simply not a matter of communicative necessity when two or more varieties are mutually intelligible. Modifications and change mechanisms brought about via accommodation by speakers of regionally or socially different varieties are quite likely different than those that arise due to sheer necessity to communicate. This may also influence how long it takes the contact-derived variety to stabilise and focus: whereas koinéisation takes time, jargonisation and pidginisation are ad hoc and necessarily short-term. Consequently, we must ask whether and to what extent processes of dialect and language contact differ, since this is relevant for any diachronic analysis. Does simplification operate distinctly in koinéisation than in language contact and pidginisation? If so, is it justified to keep the two distinct? (as the above discussion would imply). If not, then it would be preferrable to look at levelling as a general and isolated process that is independent of the nature of the linguistic systems in contact.

Contact linguists have indeed speculated as to whether the two contact processes are similar enough so that the term koinéisation can be extended to all types of linguistic mixing and hybridisation. For instance, it has been suggested that this term be used with reference to contact varieties in multilingual contact settings as well. Mohan (1978), to take but one example, argues that mere typological similarity of the input varieties leads to koinéisation:

> [Koinéisation is] a convergence and levelling between language varieties which are either closely related genetically or typologically very much alike (p. 21)

Mohan makes a general distinction between multidialectal koinés, such as TB (discussed above), and multilingual koinés, such as Koiné Swahili. She argues that contact of mutually intelligible varieties (i.e. dialects) results in levelling at the lexical and morphosyntactic level. On the other hand, she suggests that in the case of contact between typologically similar varieties (i.e. closely related languages), levelling takes place only on morphosyntactic and grammatical levels as one of the input varieties functions as a lexifier (which would account for the directionality of lexical change). Similarly, Gambhir (1981: 180) argues that colloquial urban Hindi is a "koiné [that developed] out of the confluence of two distinct languages", namely English and Hindi. Koinéisation, accordingly, can be used for language contact as well. Hymes (1971) takes an opposing point of view when he classifies new-dialect formation as a sub-branch of pidginisation and creolisation. He claims that koinés and pidgins undergo identical processes of simplification and reduction: "the most important point … is the relation between creolisation and the processes by which standard languages and koinés are sometimes formed. Expansion in content, admixture, and expansion in role as a primary language occur in both" (p. 78-9).

Many others insist that one should distinguish between koinés and pidgins. Nida & Fehderau (1970) claim that pidgins and koinés are distinct not because their origins and development are different but simply because they undergo similar processes to a different extent. This, they argue, is most visible in the operation of simplification, which seems more radical and deep-rooted in pidgins than in koinés. In the words of Gambhir (1981: 185), koinés "exhibit structural continuity with the language from which they issue"; pidgins, on the other hand, are "structurally discontinuous from their linguistic parents." A second difference concerns the feature pool. Mohan (1978) emphasises that the social context of pidgins and koinés is far from similar and that (sharp) social stratification in multilingual contact scenarios does not foster feature selection from all languages in contact: "the superstrate speakers do not themselves change their language, nor do they actively fraternise with the sub-strate speakers" (p. 2). New-dialect formation, in contrast, results in the modification of all input varieties since the koiné is likely to draw its features from all of them (a controversial point; see below). A third consideration is the amount of time these two processes take. Pidginisation, by necessity, is a rapid process, 'designed' for ad hoc communication between adults with no native language in common; koinéisation, on the other hand, is a gradual process and modifications only surface after extensive periods of stable interaction.

Could it be, then, that the difference between koinéisation and pidginisation is one of degree, not of rank? As pointed out above, relying on mutual intelligibility alone is risky. After all, the problem how to distinguish between dialects and languages is among the most notoriously difficult ones in sociolinguistic theory. To take an extreme example, it may be more difficult for a Londoner to understand working class Glaswegian English or for an American to understand Broad SAfrE than it is for a Norwegian to understand Swedish or Danish. So the borderline between the two is by no means clear-cut. A contact scenario with languages that have higher mutual intelligibility than dialects is by no means inconceivable. By the same token, a strict separation between dialect and language contact obscures the fact that the two often co-occur. 'Pure' dialect contact scenarios are exceedingly rare and there is nearly always concomitant language contact as well (see above). We must therefore carefully assess global statements, for instance that "there are probably more similarities than dissimilarities between dialect contact and language contact" (Trudgill 1994), and analyse the outcome of contact for each setting individually and with due caution. Only a detailed feature analysis allows us to find out from where the newly emerging variety (whether koiné or pidgin) drew its structures and to thus reconstruct the processes that gave rise to it.

2.3.2 Socially- or linguistically-determined? (or both?)

The above discussion has made it clear that contact settings differ for linguistic, sociolinguistic and demographic reasons. Consequently, then, which of these criteria is most important in determining the evolutionary path of koinéisation and/or pidginisation? What is the main motivation and driving force behind this process?

Perhaps the most important question of all is why the gradually emerging local dialect would select features from input A and not input B, develop structure X at the expense of structure Y, etc. The idea has been around for some time that the linguistic properties of the varieties in contact are a decisive factor here, e.g. by Bernard (1981: 20), who claimed that "the ingredients of the mixing bowl [in AusE and NZE] were very much the same, and at different times and in different places the same process was carried out and the same end point achieved." In their discussion of the formation of NZE, Trudgill, Gordon, Lewis & Maclagan (2000) argue in favour of a deterministic model, suggesting that the eventual outcome of koinéisation is determined by the inputs that contribute to the new dialect:

> [D]ialect mixture and new-dialect formation are not haphazard processes. We demonstrate that, given sufficient linguistic information about the dialects which contribute to the mixture, and sufficient demographic information about the proportions of the different dialects, it is possible to make predictions about what the outcome of the mixture will be. (Trudgill, Gordon, Lewis & Maclagan 2000: 299)

Accordingly, a koiné is 'preconditioned' by its ancestral varieties to the extent that it reflects the proportions of the input mixture. Trudgill et al. argue that new-formation mechanisms are linguistically driven and/or motivated, even that they can be predicted on condition that sufficient demographic information is available on the overall proportions of transplanted donor varieties. In this view, the directionality of koinéisation is exclusively governed by social demography and feature frequency. This claim is made in extremis by Trudgill (2001: 44), when he says that "[w]e have not found it at all necessary to call on social features 'prestige' or 'stigma' as explanatory factors, nor have we had to have recourse to notions such as 'identity'." Social factors thus play no role at all except among the original adult immigrants, who, however, are not instrumental in new-dialect formation. Following such a view, one would have to exclude the impact of social factors (with the exception of sociodemographics, of course), an extreme position Trudgill has modified subsequently:

> Linguistic change in general, of course, is not deterministic ... a theory of linguistic change cannot be genuinely deterministic in the sense that it is impossible for a theory to predict "that a change will occur, which change will occur, when a change will occur" (Harris and Campbell 1995: 321). I concur wholeheartedly with this point of view ... I do not even suggest that the outcomes of language contact and dialect contact are normally deterministic. My claim about determinism is made solely with respect to the unusual type of situation in which colonial varieties develop, in tabula rasa environments, out of dialect mixtures. (Trudgill 2004: 26-7)

All in all, though, Trudgill claims that the evolution of NZE is predictable given that there is reliable information on the demographic mix of the English, Scottish and Irish immigrants in the early colonial period from 1840 to the 1870s. Predicting the outcome (contemporary NZE) depends on finding out where the settlers came from, what dialects they spoke, and in what proportions they settled in the newly set-up colonies.

These views have not gone unchallenged. Several scholars have argued that it is erroneous to exclusively focus on feature frequency in the input varieties. One problem with such a hypothesis is that it cannot account for reallocation, when more than one original variant survives the levelling process (pointed out by Trudgill 1986 and discussed above). If levelling was solely driven by the frequency with which a feature occurs in the dialects in contact, then it would be impossible to explain why minority features can survive the selection process or how independent developments should arise in general. Others take issue with the alleged insignificance of identity and nation-building. Domingue (1981: 150) states that dialect differences may be levelled out as a result of "the need for unification among speakers of different speakers of different dialects in a new environment." By the same token, Siegel (1985) focuses on social criteria when studying the outcome of dialect contact in North Malaitans migrating to Fiji. In their places of origin, they spoke mutually intelligible varieties (i.e. regional dialects). Upon emigration to Fiji, however, levelling and koinéisation occurred side-by-side with social restructuring, a new sense of identity sprung up and the linguistic outcome of these socio-cultural changes saw the development of the koiné Wai. In earlier work, Trudgill (e.g. 1986) stressed that contact between speech communities with similar dialects lead to koinéisation only if certain social conditions are met. In Scandinavia, for instance, typologically related varieties with a high degree of mutual intelligibility have been in contact for centuries and koinéisation has not taken place on a general level which would stress the impact of non-linguistic factors, by nature social, sociopsychological, political, economic, cultural and demographic. A social motivation can also account for reallocation since there is a social motivation to functionally redistribute minority features as socially or stylistically distinctive variants. This has been documented by Domingue (1981) in MB, where the total number of coexisting variants was not reduced since former regional variants of Hindi became reinterpreted as indicators of formality and style (see above).

Mufwene (2001) emphasises that the social relationships between individual ethnic groups have consequences for the directionality and future development of a pidgin. He takes the position that the predominance of lexical input from the superstrate language (in this case, English) is a linguistic reflection of the unequal balance between different ethnic groups present in the mix, stressing the influence and high prestige of the lexifier language. This explains why English or French were most important for lexical selection in places where they were spoken by a minority of the general population only (Mauritius, Jamaica, etc.). Processes of feature selection in pidgins thus reflect the asymmetrical power relationships between the contact groups; the less influential groups (i.e., the speakers of substrate varieties) accommodate more extensively than more powerful members of the community (i.e., the speakers of superstrate languages). Social criteria (prestige, access to target, stratification, etc.) are paramount in pidginisation, a point also made by Thomason & Kaufman (1988: 35), who emphasise the importance of extra-linguistic factors.

> It is the sociolinguistic history of the speakers, and not the structure of their language, that is the primary determinant of the linguistic outcome of language contact. Purely linguistic considerations are relevant but strictly secondary overall.

Hickey (2003) subscribes to this point of view. He accepts that numerical proportions between colonisers are an important factor in the eventual crystallisation of new norms, while at the same time rejecting the idea that the social embedding of new-dialect formation should not matter at all. Hickey sees a shortcoming in Trudgill's claims that status and prestige of individual colonisers as well as social standing of colonising populations should be irrelevant. Documenting the chronology of Irish settlements in New Zealand, he suggests that the earliest forms of settlements may well have been socially stratified. He argues in favour of a social approach to koinéisation and suggests that the distinct prestige patterns attributed to donor dialects had a decisive impact on the future development of new-dialect formation. Among others, this would explain why IrE, though arriving early and being socio-demographically prominent in large settlements such as Auckland, disappeared without making an impact, the social stigma of its speakers being too burdening.

Hickey explains norm-emergence and stabilisation by what he refers to as *supraregionalisation*: "[D]ialect speakers progressively adopt more and more features of a non-regional variety which they are in contact with. There does not have to be direct speaker contact" (2003: 236). With regard to the second generation, i.e., the children of the first locally-born children, who are instrumental in forming a focused, stable new dialect, Hickey says that the new variety can "be seen as a product of unconscious choices made across a broad front in a new society to create a distinct linguistic identity" (Hickey 2003: 215), thus strongly rejecting Trudgill's argument against identity factors at stages II and III (cf. also Schneider 2007, discussed below). A supraregional form of NZE, according to Hickey, would have emerged in the melting pot settlements, which had mixed populations of high density and size, and then spread to rural settlements that subsequently became dialectally distinctive.

To complicate matters, dialect and language contact do not automatically lead to the formation of a stable contact-based variety (whether this be a pidgin or a koiné). The stabilisation and expansion of pidgins, for instance, depends on factors such as sociodemographic stability and limited access to the target language. Increasing mobility rates, as a result of renewed or ongoing colonialism, trade, emigration or political expansion, affect the outcome at all times, altering its evolutionary path or causing it to disappear. Sociodemographic dynamics are practically always ongoing; new settlers or colonists arrive (see the discussion of *swamping* below) and earlier ones leave, so that the community's linguistic and social configuration is continuously transformed so that it stays in a state of social flux. This, needless to say, poses problems for research and challenges sociolinguistic analyses. The new-dialect formation process ends abruptly when the community in which a koiné develops disperses or relocates. More complicated still, there is not even a way to predict whether focussing will occur or not. Norm-emergence and stabilisation may not even operate when the setting seems ideal, i.e. in communities that have sufficient time depth, that are self-contained and not swamped by waves of immigrants.

The Norwegian Arctic territory of Spitsbergen (Svalbard), for instance, has not developed a koiné though it has existed for over a century now (Mæhlum 1992). The reason is that families stay only for ten years on average, which means that the locally-born children move away before focussing can occur. Children have an "unclear dialect identity" (Mæhlum 1992: 123), identifying both with "home" in Norway and with Spitsbergen. Though the initial stage (Trudgill's Stage I) may be triggered (young children are reported to have much influence from their parents' speech and to be more heterogeneous as well as internally inconsistent) they are not given sufficient time to drive forward Stages II and III. Mæhlum argues that they use code-switching, dialect mixing, and a version of standard East (Oslo) Norwegian as "strategies of neutrality" instead. The Dutch polders, to give another example, did not see the development of a locally distinctive stable variety though the conditions meet all these criteria; Scholtmeijer (1992, 1997) explains this as a consequence of high mobility and extensive contacts outside the community. By the same token, Sudbury (2000: 368) found in her pioneering research on Falklands Islands English (FIE) that "the Falklands accent has not yet focused … FIE has not become a fully focused variety like the rest of the southern hemisphere Englishes." This deals a heavy blow to Trudgill's (2004) speculations about new-dialect formation under *tabula rasa* conditions. The Falkland Islands come as close as possible to such a scenario, since there was no permanent population when colonised by the British in the 1840s. The fact that focussing did not occur (Sudbury 2000, 2001) shows how unpredictable theses processes are. FIE is a case where new-dialect formation was not triggered even though the conditions were ideal; dialect contact, insularity, sociodemographic stability and a time depth of more than a century and a half.

Following Kerswill (2001), successful koinéisation depends on three criteria. First of all, the trajectory and tempo of koinéisation is influenced by "the kind and level of social integration of the new community" (Kerswill 2001: 695). Social homogeneity favours stabilisation whereas heterogeneity and social stratification have an impeding effect. Second, "children's access to peer groups is crucial" (Kerswill 2001: ibid.). Koinéisation depends on loose and open social networks so that children interact freely with other and that older children or adolescents can serve as role models in the absence of stable norms in the speech of adults. Compulsory schooling may also have an effect (Britain 1997: 165, though this has been contested in Gordon et al. 2004). The third point singled out by Kerswill is the one I discussed in detail above: "the degree of difference between the input varieties will affect the amount of accommodation that individuals have to engage in" (Kerswill 2001: ibid.). It is thus crucial how distinct they are systemically and structurally and what the degree of mutual intelligibility is. Consequently, Kerswill (2001) emphasises that the social embedding of a community (i.e. its networks and emerging communities of practice, social stratification, in-group prestige, etc.) is an important factor to set off koinéisation, either speeding it up or slowing it down. As for language contact (pidginisation and creolisation), social criteria are undisputed anyway.

To conclude, contact-induced change depends on a number of external factors, duration and intensity of the contact scenario being most important, and is shaped in a complex interplay of sociodemographic, socio-psychological as well as language-internal and structural-systemic criteria. My own view is that contact varieties are ultimately shaped by their social histories; the selection and evolution of structural properties reflects not only the properties and proportions of the input varieties (though they are certainly essential) but also the social characteristics of the community.

2.3.3 Feature inheritance and the nature of the setting

An important factor is the setting where a community comes in contact. As has repeatedly been pointed out (Wolfram & Schilling-Estes 1996, 2004; Wolfram, Hazen & Schilling-Estes 1999; Schreier 2003a) insular localities are particularly suitable for an examination of feature selection and mixing. The common belief is that the location at a geographical and sociocultural periphery affects koinéisation so that isolation slows down language change and leads to linguistic conservatism (discussed in Montgomery 1998). Isolated speakers are generally believed to be slow, backward and old-fashioned; by analogy, isolated dialects are regarded as archaic, even 'pure', relics of earlier language forms (Montgomery 1998, 2000). The investigation of isolated speech communities reflects the belief that enclave communities are more resistant toward the adoption of changes dispersing throughout the wider population (Poplack & Tagliamonte 1989, 1991; Wolfram & Thomas 2002). This is the so-called 'relic hypothesis' (Andersen 1988), i.e., the widespread assumption that isolated dialects are to a certain extent conservative with respect to language change. Isolation is a crucial factor for the examination of contact-induced language change in that it inhibits mobility and sociodemographic movement. In the words of Schilling-Estes (2002: 64):

> It is often assumed in studies of language and dialect contact that isolated communities necessarily must be linguistically conservative and homogeneous, since residents of such communities come into little contact with outside varieties from which to adopt novel forms, and since the close network ties that we often find in such communities should serve as powerful enforcers of linguistic and cultural norms.

These views have been put into perspective (Montgomery 2000; Wolfram et al. 1999; Schilling-Estes 2002; Schreier 2003a), for a number of reasons. First of all, isolation is not an 'either-or phenomenon' and no dialect exists in a sociohistorical vacuum. Though quite a few dialects have formed on islands, no dialect is an island *per se*. Second, Andersen (1988), Wolfram & Schilling-Estes (1996), Schilling-Estes (2002) and others have stressed that isolated communities have innovative potential and that they may undergo independent developments. Andersen (1988), for instance, claims that insular varieties have the "ability to sustain exorbitant phonetic developments" (70) and Schreier (2003b) documents the emergence of preterit forms instead of infinitives (e.g. 'we used to *went* there all the time' ' What did you *saw* there?') in TdCE, a feature not documented in other nativised varieties of English. Andersen (1988) goes on to make an important distinction between what he calls open vs. closed and endocentric vs. exocentric community types. The former distinction refers to the degree of interaction with other communities, the latter to whether an enclave community focuses more on its own 'internal' or on outside norms.

Andersen stresses that communities may continue to be inward-looking (i.e., maintain their endocentricity) while at the same time opening up to the outside world; at the same time, comparatively 'closed' communities may be exocentric (i.e., attitudinally open). This has important linguistic consequences as "residents of formerly closed communities set up psychological - and, often, linguistic - barriers against the encroachment of the outside world" (Wolfram & Thomas 2002: 18).

These conflicting forces have been documented in island communities. Certainly one of the most seminal studies on language change in the light of external changes in insular communities is Labov's (1972 [1963]) landmark analysis of the social significance of raised onsets in /ai/ and /au/ diphthongs on the island of Martha's Vineyard, Massachusetts. The onsets of these diphthongs are commonly realised as mid-central variants when followed by voiceless consonants and as fully open /a/ in other environments (the Canadian raising pattern). As Labov points out, this realisation is a reflex of earlier forms of English rather than an innovation since "the first element of the diphthong /ay/ was a mid-central vowel in 16th- and 17th- century English" (Labov 1972: 10). Complementing his own findings with results from the *Linguistic Atlas of New England* (*LANE*), Labov found that the usage of centralised onsets was on the decline historically and that islanders had a strong tendency to accommodate to mainlanders by using more open onsets of /ai/. Then, however, the trend reversed and islanders born around and after WW II began to use significantly higher levels of centralised variants. Labov's in-depth quantitative analysis revealed that this linguistic change had a social motivation. The trend towards centralised variants was led by the local fishermen, who represented traditional values and were held in high esteem by other Vineyarders, also by the comparatively more urban population groups on the island. Labov argued that the reversal of this language change, which in effect saw the revival or *intensification* of a feature that was in the process of dying out, was to be explained by the fact that raised /ay/ diphthongs became socially significant: "It is apparent that the immediate meaning of this phonetic feature is 'Vineyarder.' When a man says [rəɪt] or [həus], he is unconsciously establishing the fact that he belongs to the island: that he is one of the natives to whom the island really belongs" (Labov 1972: 36). The intensification of Canadian raising on Martha's Vineyard is thus a direct consequence of an increase in tourists spending their summer holidays on Martha's Vineyard and mainlanders buying up property on the island (which led to antipathy and scepticism in the local population, as epitomised by an islander's claim that 'You can cross the island from one end to the other without stepping on anything but No Trespassing signs', quoted in Labov 1972: 28). The more the local Vineyarders felt threatened by outsiders, the more they oriented themselves towards local values and symbolically embrace local language features as an expression of solidarity and group membership.

Another case of dialect intensification comes from Smith Island, Maryland (as documented in Schilling-Estes 2002; Wolfram & Schilling-Estes 2003), situated in the Chesapeake Bay, southwest of Washington DC. The island population is declining rapidly, from about 700 residents in the early 1960s to 364 in the (2000) census. Local employment opportunities have decreased in recent decades since the island-based crabbing and oystering industry has lost its importance continuously. The decline of a local job market forced islanders to leave their homes and to look for employment elsewhere. Moreover, some areas of Smith Island may soon become uninhabitable as a result of soil erosion, and there is some speculation that the island may be physically sinking into Chesapeake Bay. The departure of the local workforce is not made up for by an influx in residents coming to live on the island. Even though these conditions might favour the thinning-out, and eventually the loss, of the community's traditional dialect features, as they have in locales such as Ocracoke, North Carolina, Schilling-Estes (2002) and Schilling-Estes & Wolfram (1999) document an opposite scenario, namely a rapid increase in the usage of local features. Levelling to *weren't* increases to an extent that it "is near-categorical for the younger generations of speakers" (Wolfram & Schilling-Estes 2003: 140), and younger Smith Islanders intensify the local realizations of /ai/ and /au/ diphthongs to [əɪ ~ ɛɪ] and [aø ~ aɛ], respectively. They thus use local dialect features more often as a symbolic reaction against economic threats and the island's uncertain future. The breaking-up of the community thus leads to an increased usage of local features, which, similar to the situation on Martha's Vineyard, has a socio-psychological motivation.

Observations such as these have led Trudgill (2001) to argue that the speed of language change correlates with the degree of insularity. Since "the rate of linguistic change is not constant chronologically" (Trudgill 2001: 342) the phonological and grammatical properties of enclave communities may be a reflection of their isolation and thus their reduced contact histories. Trudgill (2001) offers a three-way distinction between communities and their dialects, namely: (1) 'high-contact language communities where contact is stable, long term and involves child bilingualism'. Communities of this type would tend to have complex grammatical structures and comparatively large phonological inventories. (2) 'high-contact language communities where contact is short-term and/or involves imperfect learning by adults'. These communities would have smaller phonological inventories and grammatical reduction that is characteristic of pidginisation. And finally type (3): 'isolated low-contact communities', which would have small phonological inventories but are more likely to retain 'deictic and allophonic complexity'. The investigation of parallels in linguistic and social structures of isolated communities is still in its infancy, and further research is necessary to gain insight into this exciting area of research. However, the locality at the periphery of mainstream varieties and the insular status of these areas may be a decisive factor in explaining why these varieties are the way they are.

This raises a question that is important in this context: Does dialect transplantation lead to linguistic conservatism (at least in its initial stages) or does it speed up the rate of language change? Discussing the evolution of transported varieties of colonial English, for instance, Marckwardt (1958) has coined the term *colonial lag* and devoted it an entire chapter in his "American English" (1958). His basic claim was that AmE was linguistically conservative since American society was socially conservative. There are many claims about the alleged conservativeness of AmE indeed, in particular that it has preserved patterns of pronunciation and lexis now obsolete in the British Isles. For Preston & Shuy (1979), contemporary "AmE is just as close to 17th century BE as Modern BE is – perhaps closer" and Baugh & Cable (1951: 351) write that a "quality often attributed to American English is archaism, the preservation of old features of the language which have gone out of use in the standard speech of England. Our pronunciation as compared with that of England is somewhat old-fashioned. It has qualities that were characteristic of English in the seventeenth and eighteenth centuries." Marckwardt himself defines the concept of 'colonial lag' as follows:

> These post-colonial survivals of earlier phases of mother-country culture, taken in conjunction with the retention of earlier linguistic features, have made what I should like to call a colonial lag. I mean to suggest by this term nothing more than that in a transplanted civilisation, such as ours undeniably is, certain features which it originally possesses remain static over a period of time. Transplanting usually results in a time lag before the organism, be it a geranium or a brook trout, becomes adapted to its new environment. There is no reason why the same principle should not apply to a people, their language, and their culture. (Marckwardt 1958: 80)

SHemE presents a forum for discussion here as well. Discussing the development of AusE, for instance, Hammarström (1985: 369) makes the claim that "[t]he language of immigrants usually changes very slowly. Consequently, it becomes 'archaic' … it takes time for a new feature to gain a whole language area. Often the older feature remains for hundreds, or thousands, of years in some parts of the area." As for NZE, Trudgill (1999: 227) claims that

> 'colonial lag' is, or at least in certain situations can be, *a demonstrable linguistic reality* … that can indeed be explained in terms of the transplantation of colonial societies … I use the term here … to refer to a lag or delay in the normal progression and development of linguistic change that lasts for about one generation and arises solely as an automatic consequence of the fact that there is often no common peer-group dialect for children to acquire in first-generation colonial situations involving dialect mixture. (emphasis added, DS)

According to Görlach (1987), however, "there are at least as many innovations in the pronunciation of AE as there are retentions" and "the great majority of lexical divergences is owing to innovation rather than survival ... the fact that Americans vociferously claimed to be the preservers of undefiled Elisabethan English can probably be explained as a defensive measure directed against those who argued that 'America will be the death of English'." Hickey (2004: 9) sums the situation up by saying that

> a closer look at allegedly conservative dialects reveals that they are not simply preserved versions of earlier forms of the language on the mainland but have themselves gone through processes of their own. Such processes can be inherited, i.e. overseas varieties continue processes initiated at their historical source ... This is clearly the case with the raising of short front vowels in varieties of English in the southern hemisphere.

Consequently, dialects formed in isolated or insular settings may indeed have conservative tendencies. 'Vineyarders' maintained central onsets in PRICE and MOUTH (which disappeared in mainland Massachusetts), Smith Islanders commonly have leveling to *weren't* for negative polarity of past *be*, intrusive /h/ has survived on Tristan da Cunha, etc. On the other hand, the very same communities may undergo independent developments that are not attested elsewhere, which sets them apart linguistically. On Martha's Vineyard, a feature that was in the process of dying out was revived since it came to function as an emblem of local identity and island pride (which has now been adopted throughout the community; Blake & Josey 2003). To sum up, we have to leave room for topographic effects on contact-induced language change and closely examine the features for their potential of conservatism or dynamism.

Another point that must be mentioned in this context is the overall directionality of contact-induced language change. Ongoing change in transplant varieties may be explained by the continuation of a change in progress, so that parallel developments in colonial varieties (e.g. the SHemE varieties) go back to an inheritance of changes in progress in the British Isles at the time of colonisation. Contact-derived varieties often share a set of similar features, as noted by Mesthrie in his discussion of Bhojpuri Hindi in South Africa (1993: 27):

> Although each colony developed its own koiné, the parallel processes involved resulted in their probably being more similar to each other than of their parent Indic varieties.

Why should dialects with origins in dynamic mixture situations in different locales share a set of given properties and continue similar paths of change? It has been suggested that "the structure of a language appears to constrain the types of (non-contact-induced) changes it may undergo, making some changes more likely than others" (Hartman Keiser 2001). This idea was first developed by Edward Sapir (1949), who attributed these phenomena to linguistic *drift*:

> If individual variations "on a flat" were the only kind of variability in language, I believe we should be at a loss to explain why and how dialects arise, why it is that a linguistic prototype gradually breaks up into a number of mutually unintelligible languages. But language is not merely something that is spread out in space, as it were - a series of reflections in individual minds of one and the same timeless picture. Language moves down time in a current of its own making. It has a drift. If there were no breaking up of a language into dialects, if each language continued as a firm, self-contained unity, it would still be constantly moving away from any assignable norm, developing new features unceasingly and gradually transforming itself into a language so different from its starting point as to be in effect a new language.

Related to this is the question as to whether and to what extent the settlement founders leave a legacy, as a result of which structures are directly retained from the input varieties. Mufwene (1996, 1999), in his detailed analyses of linguistic-ecological principles of pidgins and creoles, has introduced the term 'founder effect' principle.[6] He argues that the linguistic impact of the first colonisers is maximal and that the founders of any community have a tremendous impact on the directionality of koinéisation.

> Structural features of creoles have been determined to a large extent (but not exclusively!) by characteristics of the vernaculars spoken by the populations that founded the colonies in which they developed. (Mufwene 1996: 84)

The structural properties of a given dialect are (at least to a certain extent) predetermined by the input varieties that were transplanted to the region by the first settlers. Limited social mobility and extensive interaction patterns with other communities, then, may have a retentive effect on features and structures present in the original founding situation. A combination of the founder principle and the relic assumption underlies much of the theoretical framework of dialect research in enclave communities. An important qualification here is of course that extensive population movements subsequent to the founding period may have a significant effect on the direction of new-dialect formation. If the founding population is outnumbered by subsequent waves of settlers, then the local variety might take an entirely different trajectory. The founder's linguistic legacy is *swamped* (Lass 1990: 267) and the founder effect is minimised, perhaps eradicated.

---

[6] Mufwene originally applied the term to pidgins and creoles but the principle certainly is applicable to new-dialect formation as well.

2.3.4 Life-cycles and evolution

The final point is whether the contact varieties' show similarities in their life-cycles and general developments. Siegel (1985) stresses that koinés and pidgins represent stages along a developmental continuum and show parallels in their evolution (Table 2.5, adapted from Siegel 1985). As discussed above, *jargons* evolve into a more stable and developed pidgin when there is a social need for it, and focussing is highly relevant. The contact variety gains phonological, semantic and grammatical *stability*, although variable usage and diffuseness continue to exist. In an *expansion* stage, the former variability gives rise to increasing regularity and elaboration, as interactive purposes intensify and interaction of social interaction becomes more complex (Holm 1988). These are reinforced upon nativisation and creolisation.

Table 2.5 Developmental continua of pidgins and creoles

	Stage of development	
	Pidginisation	*Koinéisation*
Stage 1: *Initial contact*	jargon	pre-koiné
Stage 2: *Stabilisation*	stabilised pidgin	stabilised koiné
Stage 3: *Expansion*	expanded pidgin	expanded koiné
Stage 4: *Nativisation*	creole	nativised koiné

Siegel (1987) applies this continuum to varieties issued from dialect contact and suggests an identical typology in the development of koinés. First, in a *pre-koiné* stage, there is extreme variability and diffuseness: even though mixing and levelling may occur to some extent, norms have not emerged yet. In the next stage, what Siegel labels the *stabilised koiné* stage, some stabilisation has taken place, accompanied by simplification and reduction: "lexical, phonological, and morphological norms have been distilled from the various subsystems in contact, and a new compromise system has emerged" (Siegel 1985: 373). This continues when the koiné is diffused to other speech communities during the *expanded koiné* stage. The geographical spread of a koiné generally entails linguistic expansion, resulting in increasing morphosyntactic complexity and stylistic variability. Finally, the koiné may acquire native speakers and serve as a community's L1. The *nativised koiné* stage represents the continuation of linguistic expansion; it may undergo internally motivated independent developments that cannot be the legacy of the inputs. The developmental continuum outlined by Siegel is strikingly similar for both dialect and language contact and the fact that pidgins and koinés can undergo the same evolutionary path fuels the discussion as to whether these processes are similar or not.

Another remarkable similarity is that neither pidgins nor koinés necessarily need to follow all stages of the continuum. As discussed above, Thomason & Kaufman (1988) argue that nativisation can occur after any of the stages 1-3, thus jump the stabilisation and expansion stages. Consequently, a jargon may creolise without necessarily becoming a pidgin first (via abrupt creolisation; Table 2.6). By the same token, neither stabilisation nor expansion is necessary for the formation of a stabilised and focussed new dialect, so that a pre-koiné may nativise as well (Table 2.7). This is what happened in Fiji Hindustani (Siegel 1987) and Trinidad (Mohan 1978). The Hindustani dialects spoken by indentured labourers from India koinéised rapidly, i.e. within one or two generations, and Trinidad Bhojpuri emerged. Mohan (1978: 13) concluded that "the Bhojpuri of the first generation Trinidad Indians is much more homogeneous than that brought by the immigrant generation, *to the extent that it constitutes a single system incorporating residual dialectal variation*" (emphasis added, DS). The development of TB is therefore on a par with Hawaiian Creole in that it evolved directly from an unstabilised jargon (cf. also Bickerton 1981).

Table 2.6 Three evolutionary paths of varieties derived from language contact

<table>
<tr><th></th><th>Type 1</th><th>Type 2</th><th>Type 3</th></tr>
<tr><td>Development</td><td>Jargon
|
|
|
|
|
Creole</td><td>Jargon
|
Stabilised pidgin
|
|
|
Creole</td><td>Jargon
|
Stabilised pidgin
|
Expanded pidgin
|
Creole</td></tr>
<tr><td>Example</td><td>West Indian English Creole</td><td>Torres Strait Creole</td><td>Tok Pisin</td></tr>
</table>

It goes without saying that contact varieties do not evolve along the same trajectory and may disappear at every stage of the continuum. *Dekoinéisation*, by analogy with depidginisation or decreolisation, occurs when the contact variety comes into extensive contact with its lexifier or when the community disperses. By the same token, the development of contact varieties is not as homogeneous as the above models suggest (Thomason & Kaufman 1988). For example, a koiné may undergo parallel development, as a result of which some speakers or communities are at a more advanced stage of the continuum than others. More recent immigrants would speak a pre-koiné, settled immigrants or the colony's founders a stabilised or expanded one and their children may already be in the process of nativising the koiné. The same, of course, may apply in the case of language contact, namely when older members of a community speak a pidgin whereas their children and grandchildren have already creolised it.

Table 2.7 Three evolutionary paths of contact-derived dialects

	Type 1	Type 2	Type 3
Development	Pre-koiné | | | | | Nativised koiné	Pre-koiné | Stabilised koiné | | | Nativised koiné	Pre-koiné | Stabilised koiné | Expanded koiné | Nativised koiné
Example	Trinidad Bhojpuri	Guyanese Bhojpuri	Greek Koiné

A final complication is that pidginisation and koinéisation processes may readily co-occur (for instance when Dutch colonisers in South Africa interact with each other, other colonisers (English and French) and with the indigenous populations). New-dialect formation and pidginisation are therefore by no means mutually exclusive. To quote Siegel again,

> Pidginisation may occur with speakers of one dialect trying to learn another very different dialect. Even more likely, it may occur with speakers of other languages becoming part of the koinéising community and learning the koinéising language. These pidginised varieties can also be thrown into the koinéisation melting pot, and they may be responsible for certain pidgin-like features of the resultant koiné. (Siegel 1985: 372).

This has to be taken into consideration as well.

Schneider (2007), finally, builds on all these criteria when developing his life-cycle model of the evolution of post-colonial Englishes (PCEs). His main point is that, notwithstanding the fact that English develops in heterogeneous multilingual contexts around the world (see above) and

> despite all obvious dissimilarities, a fundamentally uniform developmental process, shaped by consistent socio-linguistic and language-contact conditions, has operated in the individual instances or relocating and re-rooting the

> English language in another territory, and therefore it is possible to present the individual histories of PCEs as instantiations of the same underlying process (Schneider 2007: 5).

His model rests on five characteristic stages that may overlap or occur simultaneously: (1) foundation, (2) exonormative stabilisation, (3) nativisation, (4) endonormative stabilisation, and (5) differentiation. Each of these stages sees developments in a number of parameters, by nature extralinguistic (external history), identity-building, sociolinguistic and contact-induced (including attitudinal factors), as well as language-internal (structural-systemic). Phase 1 (*foundation*) is characterised by the transplantation of an English variety, which comes to be used alongside other indigenous varieties. This entails dialect contact and initial language contact, triggering linguistic processes such as koinéisation, jargonisation, early stages of pidginisation, as well as toponymic borrowing. An *exonormative stabilisation* phase (2) witnesses continuing ties with the British Isles and the permanent establishment of a colony. Identity construction hinges on the orientation towards the 'homeland', the settlers often considering themselves as an outpost of the Empire (what Schneider 2007: 37 refers to as a "British-cum-local" type of identity). This is accompanied by an increase in bilingualism as well as a gradually arising awareness of social differentiation in the co-existing varieties, which leads to incipient convergence and is the "kick-off phase for the process which is linguistically the most important and interesting one, viz. structural nativization, the emergence of structures which are distinctive to the newly evolving variety" (39-40). This intensifies during the *nativisation* stage (3); it is typically an era of conflicting loyalties and calls for political independence, when economic, socio-cultural and personal ties with the homeland weaken. The result is a kind of "semi-autonomy", a sense of double identity accompanied by the continuing decrease of social differentiation between immigrant and indigenous population groups. One commonly observes discourses of linguistic independence vis-à-vis complaints about deteriorating and corrupted usage of English in the colony, which is set against the 'correct' ancestral variety in the mother country (the classic 'complaint tradition', as documented by Milroy & Milroy 1985). The linguistic mechanisms at work here are large-scale lexical borrowing in all domains, continuing koinéisation and focussing, phonological transfer from indigenous languages, as well as instances of morphosyntactic change, sped up by "the fact that the gap between erstwhile first-language and second-language forms of language diminishes gradually" (45). Phase 4, *endonormative stabilisation*, is one of political independence, either via peaceful or violent means, which goes hand in hand with cultural self-reliance and the establishment of a distinctive local identity. The inhabitants view themselves as members of a newly-born or young nation and as different from their country of origin. The linguistic correlate is that local forms of English are adopted as an emblem of local identity and independence, that the variety is considered as homogeneous and free of variation, which is of course indicative of an advanced stage of focussing as well. Phase 5, finally, *differentiation*, operates in a context of political and socio-cultural self-dependence where “the focus of an individual’s identity construction narrows down, from the national to the immediate community scale” (53). The strong sense of national identity fragments up into smaller, sociolinguistically characteristic communities, forming their own feeling of group belonging. ‘New varieties’ of the new variety emerge, correlating with extralinguistic parameters such as regionality, social class, ethnicity, etc. catalysed by the strengthening of social networks and the emergence of permanent communities of practice (which is the phase when reallocation is most likely to occur, see above).

Schneider (2007) illustrates the 5-step life cycle of PCEs in minute detail, drawing on examples from English in North America, Asia and throughout the Southern Hemisphere, from inner, outer and expanding circles, and he takes great care to incorporate processes of dialect and language contact. Indeed, his model reconciles many of the conflicting views discussed above and goes quite some way toward bridging the gap between koinéisation and pidginisation and/or creolisation, incorporating both into a coherent evolutionary model of the mergence of new Englishes. It is to be emphasised that the major force behind the formation process as advocated by Schneider is an extralinguistic one since “to a considerable extent the emergence of PCEs is *an identity-driven process of linguistic convergence*” (30; emphasis added, DS). This view is thus almost an antithesis to Trudgill’s (2004) model of new-dialect formation, which excludes sociolinguistic factors such as identity, concentrating on population demographics exclusively (discussion above).

2.4 ... *and the relevance for St Helenian English?*

How are we to interpret all this for our analysis of StHE? Contact-induced language change is an intricately interwoven process and the diachronic and synchronic development of a contact-derived variety depends on the interplay of linguistic, sociolinguistic, sociopsychological and demographic factors. As each contact setting has its own history, interaction of all these factors is multifaceted and in each case individual; their combination ultimately accounts for the linguistic outcome of language/dialect transplantation and contact.

First of all, we have to reconstruct the social history as concisely as possible in order to gain insights into the social, economic and socio-demographic development of the community, the locus in which the variety evolved. Second, donor identification is highly relevant for a reconstruction of the original input scenario. We need to check for origins of the settlers and slaves, find out how long they stayed on the island and where they settled and established their villages. Further, we need to accurately describe the variety, both in terms of phonological inventory and morphosyntactic system. How many phonemes does StHE have and how complex are its grammatical properties? This allows us to compare the variety with others that are better documented and researched. The ultimate goal is applying these insights for a thorough feature analysis, i.e., pinpointing the features to the putative donors that contributed to the mix and thus reconstructing the historical evolution of StHE. Special emphasis must be given to contact issues; how did the inputs interact upon their transplantation, and to what extent can we make use of feature selection to explain the mutual influence of donor varieties and founder effects? We thus need to consider the interplay of social and linguistic factors, focussing not only on the individual inputs but also on the social roles of the settlers themselves. What was their function in the community, and how was their position to influence the formation of a local dialect?

The only means of addressing these complex issues is to sight as much earlier evidence as possible to gain glimpses of the past. What did the settlers speak like and how competent were the slaves in English? How long did it take the non-English-speaking settlers to shift and until when did languages other than English survive? Is there evidence of sustained bi- and multilingualism on St Helena? Was the rate of local reproduction high enough for the variety to nativise? Is StHE primarily a product of dialect or language contact or both, and by when did a focussed stable form emerge, if at all? These are the topics of the next two chapters.

3. Historical, sociodemographic and sociolinguistic background

This chapter provides an overview of the external history of St Helena, looking into a range of factors, topographical, geophysical, historical, sociocultural and demographic, that are in some way instrumental in influencing the evolutionary path of StHE. I begin with the island's topography and geography (important since they affected settlement patterns and may have given rise to regional variation on the island; ch. 6) and go on with the community's social history, starting with the discovery by the Portuguese in 1502, with particular emphasis on the first century and a half of British colonisation. The chapter concludes with some first sociolinguistic assessments (founders, population stability, etc.), which will subsequently be tested against samples of earlier StHE (ch. 4).

I should add that this chapter draws on a number of sources. These consist of detailed social histories of St Helena (Brooke 1808; Beatson 1816; Anon. (F. Duncan?) 1805; Melliss 1875; Gosse 1938), visitors' reports and diaries (Cavendish's account in Hakluyt 1600; Gargen 1665; Beeckman 1718: Darwin 1839), logbooks (by William Dampier, Joseph Banks, Edmond Halley, Father Fernandez Navarette), as well as letters, court cases and other records produced for the East India Company (EIC) that I located in the Castle archives of Jamestown, St Helena (see ch. 4). Some of these sources have not been studied before, at least not to my knowledge. The archive in Jamestown hosts the complete set of the *St Helena Consultations*, the EIC' minutes of the councils and all correspondence with the local administration, running to more than a thousand volumes, some of which have more than a hundred pages. Fortunately, Ralph Hudson Janisch, the first native-born governor of St Helena, published an abbreviated version of this massive collection; upon his retirement, he selected (what he considered) the most important and memorable events in the community's history. Consequently, the *St Helena Records* (henceforth *StHR*; Janisch 1885) consist of selected entries from the complete body of correspondence with the Company's headquarters in London. Even though there certainly is a personal bias (after all, Janisch only collected what he considered to be relevant, and this ranges from missing lifeboats to death penalties and quarrels over stolen apples), the 700-page collection is an extremely important document for our purpose (simply because it was impossible to sight the entire correspondence with the EIC. All the quotes labelled *Consultations*, *Company Instructions*, *Letter*, etc. are taken from the StHR.

Another useful source of information was the "St Helena Virtual Library and Archive", created and maintained by Barry Weaver, a website that is updated regularly and that hosts a wealth of materials (books, descriptions, maps, photographs) on the island and its population.[1] There I found at least a dozen manuscripts that were long out of print and impossible to obtain. These materials were immensely valuable for the summary of St Helena's social history; moreover, they had the advantage that keywords could be searched for electronically (for instance of island localities). One disadvantage, however, was that the manuscripts were scanned without their original page numbers. This information is therefore lacking, and I had to omit the page reference when quoting directly from these sources. Last but not least, oral history was an important source of information as well. I relied on the recollections of interviewees for the history of St Helena in the 20th century, which made many of the interviews truly memorable (more on fieldwork in ch. 5).

3.1 St Helena: Topography and geography

St Helena is situated in the mid-South Atlantic Ocean, latitude 5°43' West and 15°56' South, some 1,200 miles (ca 2,000 km) off the south-west coast of Angola and some 1,800 miles (2,900 km) off the coast of Brazil. The nearest land mass is Ascension Island, 703 miles (1,125 km) to the north-west. The island is the deeply eroded summit of a composite volcano, formed perhaps as early as 50 million years ago, when a gigantic volcano erupted in the mid-Atlantic ridge and rose to a height of almost 5,000 metres from the sea floor (Weaver 1990). Today, the volcano is extinct and it is estimated that the last major eruption occurred some 7 million years ago. There are practically no beaches on the island due to heavy erosion; most of the coastline is characterised by steep cliffs, rising up to 300 m in height. These precipices, together with the constant swell and the danger of sharp rocks hidden below the surface, restrict landing sites to the few places where valleys reach the sea. The leeward areas in the north are relatively calm; in contrast, the southern (windward) parts of the island are exposed to constant gales and waves, making landing (or even sailing close) extremely hazardous.

St Helena's topography owes its characteristics to the fact that there were not one but several volcanic eruptions. The island was shaped by the coalescence of lava streams from at least three volcanoes, with two major centres of activity in the north-east (near Deadwood Plain), in the south-west at Sandy Bay, and a minor one in the eastern part of the island (near Stone Top Ridge). The volcanic activities in the southern part of the island occurred later than those in the north-east. Eruptions occurred predominantly along fissures, and both major centres were transgressed by dyke swarms (Weaver 1990). Those were eventually carved out and thus shaped into a number of long and

[1] The website is: http://www.bweaver.nom.sh/; accessed Jan 18 2008.

narrow valleys that radiate away from the higher points of the island and breach the steep coastline (see map 3.1).

Map 3.1A topographic map of St Helena

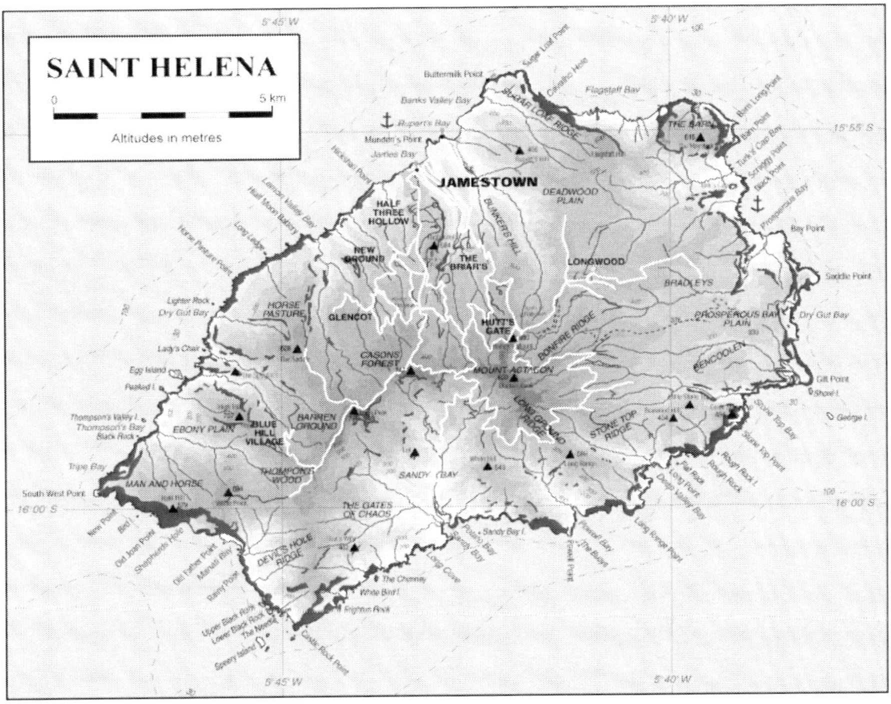

Today, the island is roughly rectangular in shape, covering an area of approximately 122 square kilometres (47 square miles). It is some 16 kilometres long and 10 kilometres wide, elongated in a northeast-southwest direction. A high central ridge occupies the major axis, prominently towering above and cutting off the Sandy Bay area from the rest of the island. The highest point, Mount Actaeon, rises to 823 meters above sea level. Deep gorge-like valleys, such as Thompson's, Fisher's, Sharks, Lemon or Deep Valley, some of which are up to 300 metres deep, cut across the island. As a consequence, there are very few level areas, the exception being Deadwood Plain (where the Boer War prisoners were housed, see below) and Prosperous Bay Plain in the arid north-east (where the local golf course is situated). Most valleys are dry in all but the winter season; only James Valley, in which Jamestown is built, has a permanent stream of water.

Because of the cool South Atlantic trade winds, St Helena's climate is oceanic and temperate, with warm summers and slightly cooler winters. The annual rainfall is 8 inches (200 mm) at sea level and more than 30 inches (760 mm) in higher regions. As a consequence, St Helena has several climate zones and the local vegetation can be divided into three categories: a rocky, barren coastal region with a desert-like flora, extending inland about 1.5 kilometres; a middle zone, extending another 0.5 to 1.5 kilometres inland, featuring grassy hill slopes and gorse, willows, poplars, and Scotch pines; and the central zone, about 4.5 kilometres long and 3 kilometres wide, which is sub-tropical and hosts most of the island's indigenous vegetation as well as imported oak trees, cedars, eucalypti, bamboo, and banana plants. However, the island's ecosystem has undergone drastic change as a result of human settlement, deforestation and clearance for pasture land, and imported animals (most notably wild goats) have caused major environmental damage. Therefore, whereas the topographical properties continue to influence the social life and human expansion on the island, colonisation and settlement in turn have had an impact on the local environment, as will become clear in the next section.

3.2 Social history

The social history of St Helena stretches over more than five centuries, which for convenience are separated into four main periods:

- 1502-1673: Discovery of the island by the Portuguese, early British involvement and Dutch interregnum
- 1673-1834: The reign of the East India Company
- 1834-1981: Crown colony and Nationality Act
- 1981-today: Nationality Act and British Dependent Territory

These periods are discussed in turn. Special focus is given to the 1673-1834 period, which was without doubt the single most important phase for the formation and development of the community.

3.2.1 1502-1673: From discovery to Dutch interregnum

The island was first discovered by João de Nova Castella, a Spanish admiral in the service of the Portuguese. He was on a return voyage from India and sighted the island in the early hours of 21 May 1502, which in the Eastern Church is the feast day of St Helena, mother of the Roman emperor Constantine the Great (Brooke 1808). Logbook entries indicate that the Portuguese landed and explored the island, finding it uninhabited. de Nova Castella reported that the climate was fertile and that the local fauna was plentiful (the abundance of lemon trees was particularly important in seafaring days, so as to avoid the risk of scurvy), so that the island offered ideal conditions to refresh a crew after a long and strenuous journey and to fix the boats for the final leg of the homeward trip. The island's strategic value was immediately recognised by the authorities and St Helena makes an appearance in Portuguese sea maps produced throughout the 16th century. The first boats left behind goats, donkeys and hogs to serve as food provisions for the following fleets, but the authorities developed no plans to settle the island permanently. Instead, St Helena was used as a transitory port of call and refreshment station in the remainder of the 16th century. The Portuguese built huts and a church for sick or injured sailors, who were in ill health and unlikely to survive the return journey to Portugal (in the valley where Jamestown is situated now). The first permanent settler was a certain Dom Fernandez Lopez, a Portuguese prisoner who fell into disgrace in the East African colonies and opted to remain on the island with a few runaway slaves in 1513, rather than to return to Europe. Melliss (1875: 3) reports that Lopez was removed four years later (i.e., in 1517).

The island remained a well-kept Portuguese secret for almost a century. It was only on June 8 1588 that the EIC became aware of St Helena, namely when Captain Cavendish discovered it on a return trip from India. He reported signs of civilisation and found a little village in the island's main valley, complete with a church and well-kept fruit orchards. Melliss (1875: 4) writes that Captain Cavendish "does not seem to have molested the St. Helenians", who, according to Brooke (1808), consisted of a handful of runaway slaves only:

> We found in the houses, at our coming, three slaves, who were Negroes, and one who was born in the island of Java, who told us that the East Indian fleet ... were gone from the said island of St. Helena but twenty days before we came hither. (Captain Cavendish's report, as quoted in Brooke 1808)

The English renewed their interest after two detailed reports by Captain Lancaster, who visited the island twice, on April 3 1593 and on June 16 1603, and reported the island to be uninhabited. Around the turn of the century, St Helena served as a resort to Dutch, English and Spanish vessels. The Portuguese, on the other hand, had not developed colonial interests and in fact stopped calling at the island altogether (they simply had no need to – the strategically eminent possessions in West Africa allowed them to use the safer sailing routes along the coast). Consequently, the island was used by the major seafaring nations and during the first half of the 17th century, it became a port of call for hundreds of ships en route between Europe and the African and Asian colonies. The Dutch formally took possession of the island in 1633 and retained it until 1651, without ever attempting to occupy it. Consequently, then, not one seafaring power made permanent settlement plans for almost 150 years. This meant that all populations in this period were stationary and transitory, consisting mostly of injured or sick sailors who were left behind to recover or die (Gosse 1938: 43).

Political events forced the EIC to reassess the option of colonisation. By the mid-17th century, most of the important port regions on the West African coast were in Portuguese hands (Fort Cormantine, one of the last English strongholds on the Slave coast, was lost in 1662; Huber 1999). By the same token, the passage around the Cape of Good Hope was no longer safe after the Dutch had colonised the Table Bay region in 1652. The EIC found itself in a quandary. The return journeys from East Africa were long and strenuous and privateers and mutineers posed a constant danger to the exhausted crews and their fully laden and slowly manoeuvring ships. Consequently, the Company's authorities focused their attention on alternative places that would allow their ships' crews to recover and safely procure fresh water and provisions. In 1649, orders were issued that all vessels bound for England from India or the Far East should remain at St Helena and from 1656 onwards the EIC annually petitioned a man-of-war to sail to St Helena and convoy the Company's ships home (Gosse 1938: 44). It was in this period that the Company's authorities recognised how important it was to make St Helena a permanent possession. This is evidenced by the following entry in the *StHR*, dated December 15 1658:

> The Court having several tymes very lately taken into their consideration the great conveniencing and concernment that it might prove, both to the Company and to this nation, for to fortify the island of St. Helena, whereon (it is believed) many good plantations may in tyme be made, did again this day reassume the serious consideration of that business. And finding so much reason to engage them in this work, as well as encouragement, after a long debate of the whole business, resolved, by a general election of hands, to send 400 men with all expedition to remayne on the island, with conveniences to fortifie and begin a plantation there.

This official resolution was immensely important for the social history of the island: it effectively marked the beginning of British involvement on St Helena. Preparations were made to send out a garrison and planters and Captain Alexander Dutton was charged with organising an advance party of soldiers and planters to start a colony on the island. He received specific instructions to "settle, fortifie, and plant upon the island of St. Helena … where when it shall please the Allmightie to arrive you, we hereby impower, authorize, and require you that, forthwith after your coming to anchor in the roade, you, with the commanders and as many English as convenientlie may be spared from aboard the ships, do repaire on shoare" (StHR, January 11 1659). Brooke (1808) noted that

> the English East India Company settled on it in the same year … they were also empowered to send thither any persons desirous of becoming settlers …

> The offers held out upon this occasion were accepted by many; who, on their arrival, had lands allotted them. Additional supplies of black cattle were procured from Madagascar; yams were introduced from the same quarter. Some slaves were likewise imported from thence, to work in the plantations; and, after the year 1666, the island received a considerable increase of inhabitants by the dreadful fire in London, which ruined so many families.

Dutton's fleet arrived on May 5 1659. Efforts were made to assist the colonists in every possible way. As early as January 1659, the EIC sent out instructions that ships returning from Surat (southwest India) were to deliver a ton of rice as well as trees and other useful plants when calling at St Helena. Soon afterwards, all calling ships were instructed to support the garrison and settlers during the early stages of colonisation; orders were given that each passing ship was to deliver goods and provisions for Company representatives and planters.

Support came from England as well. When the man-of-war *Success* arrived in October 1659 to convoy the returning fleets from India, it brought out supplies and more settlers. By the same token, the *Truro*, bound from England to Madras in June 1659, was instructed to call at St Iago (one of the Cape Verde Islands) with the purpose of acquiring "all manner of plants, roots, grains, and all other things necessarie of plantation there to be had or procured, but more espetially in those which are to be esteemed your most certaine provisions, as planton rootes, Cassandra sticks, large yams, potatoes and bonavist, pease, gravances, and beans of all sorts, oranges and lemons ... In case at St. Iago you can procure five or six blacks or Negroes, able men and women, we desire you to buy them, provided they may be had at or under 40 dollars per poll" (*Company Instructions*, quoted in Gosse 1938: 46-7). Consequently, the plan to set up a plantation system based on slave labour was made early; Captains were instructed to acquire slaves in West Africa or, if possible, in Portuguese colonies in the Atlantic Ocean.

Given this support, it is strange to find that in the very same period, the Company made decisions that seriously thwarted its own colonisation efforts. In December 1660, for instance, Captain Dutton received instructions to leave for Bantam immediately and to hand charge over to Captain Stringer. Moreover, he was ordered to take with him all the settlers who were willing to leave (Melliss 1875). 25 men accepted the offer and left, and as only 11 new planters came out in the *Africa* shortly after, Governor Stringer found himself with no more than 30 settlers. The situation eased somewhat when more settlers came in the mid-1660s (after the Great Fire of London), though out-migration was still common:

> The *Constantinople* brought out twenty-six men in 1663, and the *Charles* another thirty or perhaps more, victims of the Great Fire of London, four years later, but these and other reinforcements were largely countered by those others returning to England or went to the East. (Gosse 1938: 51)

Similarly, Jackson (1903: 13) writes that "this year [1666] saw the great fire of London, and many ruined families sought refuge in St. Helena."

A big problem was that planters could not become free settlers or landholders. The early social history of St Helena was characterised by quasi-feudal relationships between the Company and the planters, who were in fact nothing else than indentured labourers. In return for rights to till the land they were allocated, planters had to deliver a set amount of their produce to the Company, to assist in maintaining the fortifications and organise themselves in militias, to man watch posts along the coast, etc. Most of the planters were dissatisfied with these conditions and left the island on the first occasion. The Company realised that this scheme was altogether unfavourable towards attracting planters to St Helena and that it was practically impossible to keep a permanent stock of settlers there. Consequently, the EIC sent instructions to free all those remaining on the island and to allot a share of land to each. Stringer divided up the island into one hundred and fifty parts, reserving fifteen for the Company, five for himself and giving one share to each planter and their families (Brooke 1808).

The social situation on St Helena is documented by an eye-witness account by Henry Gargen, who resided there from 1661 to 1665. Gargen wrote a short yet highly insightful account of the island's population in the earliest phase of colonisation:

> Now I shall enbold my selfe to give you account of ye inhabitants and there [sic] habitations. Firstly Mr Robert Stringer and his family which is his wife and his sonnen and sonne in law. And his two daughters 2 maid servants and one man servant and 4 blacks. Mr Butler second: with his wife and his childe and one servant: now for ye rest: John Coulson His wife and childe, John Wood His wife and childe; William Young Steward His wife and childe; John Evans Militiaman His wife and childe; Thomas Harper His wife and childe; John Waily His wife and childe; William His wife and sonne in law; Thomas Holton and his wife; Now for ye rest as are single persons: William Rogers: William Fox: William Gates: Richard Price: Frances Mold: James Hastings: Thomas Evans: Edward Carre: James Codner: John Young: Thomas How: John Greentree: Henry (Pride) … William Goy … Thomas Collins: Richard Swally Thomas Hallicross staied in my birth: Mr Charles Higginson; … now as for ye rest of ye Englishmen there is 3 that run away … Now I will sattisfie you of ye freemen and there [sic] plantation and hoe they lie there 4 of them in all. John Coulson; John Wood; Thomas Harper; John Waily. (Gargen 1665)

The total number of white planters in the mid-1660s therefore amounted to 53 (30 men, 13 women, and 10 children) and that of the slaves to 21 ("Then of ye Blackes 17 men and women 4 children of which"). Economic disparities become evident by Gargen's observation that a total of 17 slaves (81 per cent) belonged to the Company or to the Governor and just four to a single planter, Charles Higginson. Consequently, practically none of the earliest settlers were in the possession of slaves. Unfortunately for our purpose, Gargen says nothing about the origins of the slaves. However, Captain Dutton was instructed to acquire slaves in St Iago and on the Guinea Coast, which points to these origins (and has sociolinguistic implications, see below).

Another important account of the colony's early social history comes from Sylvain de Rennefort, a Frenchman who visited in spring 1666 and noted his impressions of the island's inhabitants as follows:

> We were half a league off shore, when we sighted in a little bay, an important looking English building ... A long boat having approached with pistol shot, they hailed us in English, asking from whence came the ship ... The dinner was most cleanly served and consisted of dishes, half of which were French and half English. The ladies sat at a table with us and we were free and easy as if we had been in France. The only thing which shocked Rennefort was that when healths were proposed, they were drunk by everyone out of the same glass ... The inhabitants numbered fifty English and twenty women ... Most of the English had houses about the Island and came in turn to the fort to guard and keep watch. There were a few negroes for the heavier labour ... Mr Stringer had about twenty-four cows, looked after by his Negroes, while four women milked and made the butter. (quoted in Gosse 1938: 52-5)

In 1670, Governor Stringer requested to leave the island. He was replaced by Captain Cony, who soon upon his arrival sent unfavourable reports to London; among others, he complained that the settlers drank too much arrack that was imported and sold cheaply on the island. Perhaps these social tensions were intensified by the fact that the late 1660s were a period of heavy traffic in the South Atlantic Ocean and that the island was frequented by ships from all seafaring powers. Robert Barlow, a visiting sailor, reported that Portuguese ships bound from Angola to Brazil frequently called at the island in the 1670s and that there were also numerous French ships and English privateers who transported slave cargoes from the Guinea Coast and Madagascar (Brooke 1808). This worried the Company's representatives and they reacted by dispatching an additional 80 soldiers to the island, and this caused further civil unrest and tensions among the planters.

3.2.2 1673-1834: The reign of the East India Company

Following King Charles II's declaration of war on Holland in 1672, a Dutch fleet, led by Jacob de Gens, set sail from the Cape and arrived at St Helena in December 1672. The first attempts to land on the rocky coast and to invade the island were unsuccessful. Despite a lack of troops and poor fortifications, the English used the island's topography to their advantage and fought back all attacks. The situation changed when the Dutch managed a landing at Bennetts Point, close to Swanley Valley, on the island's northwestern coast. They were aided by a settler by the name of William Coxe, who, accompanied by his slave, had lit a fire and then agreed to guide the Dutch invasion forces up the precipitous cliffs. The entire local population was trapped in Jamestown Valley and had to abandon the island in haste (Melliss 1875). Led by Governor Beale, they sailed en bloc across the Atlantic Ocean and replenished their stocks in Brazil, only to return and warn English vessels; just before arriving at St Helena they had the incredibly good fortune to meet up with an English fleet, commanded by Captain Richard Munden and en route to the island. Munden had been unaware of the capture of St Helena. He decided to attempt a recapture immediately, without waiting for specific orders from the Company (Gosse 1938).

It so happened that on board the ship there was a planter by the name of Coulson and his family. One of his slaves, Black Oliver, had an excellent knowledge of the island and volunteered to guide the troops. He accompanied a party of soldiers that landed in Prosperous Bay, on the western coast, in order to attack the fort from the hills above Jamestown. By the time the forces had arrived at James Fort, however, the Dutch had already succumbed to naval bombardment and on May 15 1673, the English formally repossessed the island. In order to disturb the social continuity of the island population as little as possible and to thus facilitate recolonisation, the Company decided to accept all the planters who wished to return. The *Governor's Commission and Instructions*, dispatched on December 19 1673, include the following order:

> [A]ll the old planters formerly settled on the said Island, & now bound thither, shall be repossest of their severall houses & plantations w'ch formerly they enjoyed, in the condicon [sic] they shall be found at the arrival of these shipps, and that all new planters, shall upon their arrivall have twenty Acres of Land rough & plaine, sett out unto them, by the Gov' & Councell for each family to build and plant upon it, and that all the plantaicons [sic], both to the old, and new planters, be con[veyed] to them, their heirs, and assignes for ever ... That besides the said porcon [sic] of land, each family shall have two Cowes.

All the settlers who had held land before the Dutch interregnum thus had their properties and land restored. As a reward for his help, Black Oliver was allowed the same amount of land and cattle as an English planter; he thus became the island's first black freeman. The Dutch attack made the EIC acutely realise how valuable (and, by implication, how vulnerable) the island was and that it was in their best interest to intensify colonisation efforts.

The Company had apparently learnt their lesson from previous mistakes. Colonists wishing to settle on the island were guaranteed free land, animals, seeds, plants, and provisions for the first year of their stay. Accordingly, there was an unprecedented influx of settlers in 1673; two ships, the *European* and *John and Alexander*, brought a total of 94 whites and 16 blacks (see Appendix 1 for a detailed list of the passengers on board the two ships) and another 160 settlers arrived in December of the same year. This abrupt population increase had a number of consequences. First of all, the land-holding rights had to be reorganised as all settlers had the right to cultivate land; instructions were given for "any of the Inhabitants … to be allowed on their request ground sufficient to build a house in any valley" (Janisch 1885). This effectively meant that the population dispersed over the entire island. Second, the influx of new planters intensified the social problems between Company representatives and planters. Gosse (1938) speculates that these tensions were caused by the fact that most newcomers came from the lower strata of British society. We do not know how justified claims of this kind are, but is noteworthy that all the sources agree that a) the majority of the planters had working class origins, and b) the Company recruited many of its soldiers (and settlers as well, for that matter) from among the unemployed in England (Gosse 1938: 72). This was a period of social unrest, not only between planters and army personnel but also among the soldiers themselves. The 1670s and '80s saw a number of rebellions, organised by soldiers dissatisfied with their conditions. One of the worst uprisings occurred in 1674, when Governor Richard Keigwin was attacked by some of his own soldiers and held hostage for three days (Brooke 1808). The ringleaders of the mutiny, among them a Scottish sergeant by the name of Taylor, were arrested and executed or deported to other colonies. The Company directors reacted by reducing the total number of forces on the island:

> Wee therefore order that you keep only in pay 75 of the oldest civillest and best soldiers and for the remainder that you propose, to them the Company's terms for their staying there as free planters, which if they will not accept send them home. (*StHR*, Letter from London, April 10 1674)

The island's militia was reinforced to replace the leaving soldiers and to strengthen the defences. Ships brought out more settlers while the Company withdrew army personnel, and the garrison was reduced to 50 men by December 1674. It was at this time that plans were made to construct a proper town near the main fort, Jamestown, complete with church and free market, which was to serve as a centre for the island's commercial life. English development schemes were set out as a role model:

> In the contriving of the market place and the building for increasing of the ffort Towne, We would have you use all possible regard to the uniformity & regularity of the Streetes & buildings after the manner they are now in London since the ffire. (*Company Instructions*, March 1682)

It is not clear how many of the settlers arriving in this period came from London, but there is some speculation that the Great Fire of 1666 enticed Londoners who had lost all their possessions to start a new life on St Helena (see the quotes above). Dickson (1973: 209), for instance, speculates that the name of the island's capital, originally James Town, may have been a tribute of

Londoners to the Duke of York, later James II, who superintended the fire fights and may have been instrumental in granting travel assistance to the families who had lost all their possessions.[2]

This period was particularly important in that it saw first attempts to integrate the black population and to enhance their standard of living. Slaves who converted to Christianity were to become freemen after a period of seven years, so that they could enjoy the same privileges as white planters. As a result, the island population, both black and white, increased quickly, rising to 357 in 1675 and to 390 in the following year, while the number of officers and soldiers under pay dwindled, numbering 39 and 27, respectively (Gosse 1938: 74).

When Major John Blackmore took office as Governor in 1678, he reorganised the administration and instated a more transparent democratic government (island or parish officers, for instance, were now elected by free planters and their heirs) and a rigorous legal system, namely a Court of Judicature assisted by a jury trial. He also laid the foundations of a semi-feudal system: any planter with more than twenty acres of land by law had to maintain two cows and house two English persons aged 16 years or more, one of which had to serve in the military forces upon request. Every planter, workman and slave had to work in the public services (i.e., on the public highways) for one day a year.

Blackmore's ambitious plans were hindered by social unrest in the black population. Slaves ran away repeatedly and fled to remote areas of the island, often hiding away for months; moreover, rumours of slaves attempting to poison their masters caused serious concern, and fears grew that the blacks were secretly plotting a rebellion or concerted attacks against the white settlers. As a consequence, a number of regulations were introduced to enforce social control and to restrict the rights of the black population. Slaves were not allowed to absent themselves from their master's house without permission and were severely punished if they did. The import of slaves was forbidden in this period. In the words of Brooke (1808),

> The introduction of slavery appears to have been coeval with the first settlement of the island, or very soon after. In the year 1679, restrictions were laid upon the further importation of slaves, from an apprehension of danger, should their number, which was then about eighty, exceed, in any considerable degree, that of the Europeans.

---

[2] In contrast, the website http://website.lineone.net/~sthelena/settlersslaves.htm (accessed March 14 2005) states: "However important a myth in debates on St Helenian identity, there is no truth in the claim that in 1667 the number of settlers was increased by the arrival of thirty emigrants left homeless after the Great Fire of London." Unfortunately, the authors make no attempt to justify their views and provide no alternative explanation whatsoever.

Upon reconsideration, however, the Company's directors realised that similar situations in other colonies (particularly in the Caribbean) had not led to social unrest at all and that these restrictions were in fact only hindering the development of the local economy. Accordingly, they sent "a system of the laws and customs of Barbadoes – remember its absolutely necessary you should hold our Negroes to the rigour of the Barbadoes discipline without which your owne lives nor our Island can be safe" (*Letter from Court of Directors*, 25 April 1684). The ban on the import of slaves was stopped, evidently to raise revenues for the local administration:

> In regard this ship comes with a Commission from His Majesty to take all interlopers and ye commander is such as will be sure to doe what is enjoined him by his Superiors you will do well to sett upon producing so many yams, &c. as you can because if any Madagascar ships fall in while these ships are about the Island the Blacks will be sold upon the Island one halfe for the King and the other halfe for the Company. (*Letter from the Court of Directors*, August 1 1683)

Slaves were imported again, though not in numbers sufficient to work all the local plantations. This time it had nothing to do with official Company orders, though; rather, it had become more difficult and dangerous to procure slaves in Africa and Asia. For instance, a request to import slaves from western India was turned down by the local administration: "We cannot procure any slaves. Here is no such thing. There is but one way to have them viz – to take them by force off some parts on the sea coast and that we dare not attempt" (quoted in Janisch 1885). Gosse (1938: 81) points out that English ships trading to Madagascar were required to leave one slave, male or female, on the island, selected by the Governor himself for the service of the Company: "As taxes, every English ship trading to Madagascar has to leave a negro slave on the island also to pay a duty of 2s. 6d. for every ton measurement" (Jackson 1903: 24; apparently, though this could not be verified in the sources consulted, Governors were instructed to choose slaves who had at least some command of English). It is in this period that we also find some adventurous expansion schemes, such as colonisation plans for the island of Tristan da Cunha, situated some 2,200 kilometres to the south:

> Upon further consideration of the great advantage that may accrue to us if there prove to be a harbor at the Island Tristan de'Acunha we think fit upon Capt. Knox arrival from Madagascar in case you find encouragement by the acct you shall have from Capt. Knox you doe put on board Capt. Knox some intelligent person by the name of Governor at the salary of £30 per ann: 5 soldiers at 14/ per mouth besides their dyett – *3 or 4 of the Company's oldest negroes that speak English with their wives &c.* and what animals, plants or seeds Capt. Knox can conveniently carry all which wee would have him land

> in his pasaage for India. (*Letter from the Court of Directors*, April 25 1684; emphasis added, DS)

This is the first reference to English-speaking slaves on St Helena.

One problem at the time concerned the housing of the army personnel. The fort and barracks were too small to provide sufficient room for all the soldiers. Consequently, planters were paid to accommodate members of the garrison, an opportunity that was taken up with pleasure as it provided a steady income in insecure times. However, the majority of the soldiers were dissatisfied with their conditions. Residence in planters' houses allowed them to voice their disillusions freely, to exchange ideas with others who shared their feelings and to clandestinely plot escape attempts and uprisings.

Not surprisingly, then, there were concerted rebellions from the 1670s on, some jointly organised by soldiers and planters. A successful rebellion in 1684 claimed the lives of several civilians, among them Black Oliver (who enjoyed a mere decade of freedom). Another meticulously planned uprising was carried out in 1693. Governor Johnson was mortally wounded by his own soldiers, who then proceeded to plunder the stores, seize a ship and flee the island. Following this particularly daring endeavour, the Company implanted a policy of strict discipline and zero tolerance. Soldiers were to be housed in barracks instead of in planters' homes and orders were given to squash all attempted rebellions with utmost brutality. This was to have particularly severe consequences for the black population. The 1680s and '90s saw a series of public trials and brutal corporal punishment, often for shockingly trivial (and unproven) crimes (such as allegedly plotting to run away with a company boat). Slaves had no civil rights whatsoever and were often tortured until they confessed to their alleged crimes. Several of these trials were reported verbatim in the *StHR*, which thus represent an invaluable source of information on earlier StHE also (see ch. 4).

It was in this period that the Company devised yet another scheme to make the colony a profitable undertaking. To date, all projects (the establishment of sugar cane plantations, cotton, indigo, and tobacco) had failed and ended in disaster. Following the anti-Huguenot movements in France, French Protestants were hired to cultivate grapes for the production of wine and spirits on St Helena:

> After divers attempts to make some profitable productions upon the Island we have at length fixed upon the planting of vines and the making of Wine and Brandy … We have agreed with Capt. Poiryer upon termes contained in his instructions. He is an honest man and lived formerly in great plenty upon his own land in France … But being a Protestant was driven from all he had in France by that violent persecution ... All the Vineroons that goe with him are likewise French protestants … M. Poirier as you will see our instructions is for his great reputation to have place at our Council when he is at the Fort and to have the appealacon [sic] of Captain though under the pay of a Sergeant. He

> speaks little English yet, but we hope he may learn more in his passage and that by the time he comes to St. Helena his sons may be perfect in our language. (*Letter from the Court of Directors*, April 5 1689)

A party of 20 French Huguenots arrived in 1690 on the *Benjamin*, en route to Surat. It is unclear how their business scheme developed (though the contribution of French to the formation of a local dialect was not substantial; see below), but the *StHR* indicate that several of them remained on the island for lengthy periods. In fact, the Huguenots seem to have gained considerable prestige on the island as Captain Stéphane Poirier later even became Governor of St Helena. On the other hand, there were anti-foreigner sentiments as well. Some planters objected to the presence of the Huguenots, as evidenced in a court case from 1697, when a minister insulted Matthew Bazett by calling him a "nasty French Fellow" (Gosse 1938: 115).

A valuable description of social life on the island came from William Dampier, who visited St Helena in 1691:

> There is a small English town within the great bay, standing in a little valley, between two high steep mountains. There may be 20 to 30 small houses whose walls are built with rough stones; the inside furniture very mean. The Governor hath a pretty tolerable handsome low house, by the Fort; where he commonly lives, having a few soldiers to attend him, and to guard the fort. But the houses in the town, before mentioned, stand empty, save only when ships arrive here; for the owners all have plantations farther in the island, where they constantly employ themselves. But when the ships arrive, they all flock to the town, where they live all the time that the ships lie here; for then is their fair or market, to buy such necessaries as they want, and to sell off the product of their plantations … We stayed here 5 or 6 days; all which time the islanders lived at the town, to entertain the seamen; who constantly flock ashore, to enjoy themselves among their country people … They are most of them very poor … While we stay'd there, many of the seamen got sweet-hearts. One young man belonging to the *James and Mary*, was married, and brought his wife to England with him. Another brought his sweetheart to England, they being engaged by bonds to marry at their arrival in England; and several other of our men, were over head and ears in love with the St Hellena [sic] maids, who tho' they were born there, yet very earnestly desired to be released from that prison, which they have no other way to compass, but by marrying seamen, or passengers that touch here. The young women born here, are but one removed from English, being the daughters of such. (Quoted in Gosse 1938: 102-4)

The closing years of the 17th century saw an important project for the entire community. Instigated by Governor Kelinge, plans were made to renovate the local infrastructure and to extend the local transport systems; Kelinge gave orders to construct footpaths and cattle 'drift-ways' so that all the houses and plantations on the island were connected and accessible from Jamestown. This plan was vigorously pursued by Captain Poirier, who followed as Governor in 1697. He renewed administrative efforts and it is in this time that we find the first complete census of the island population. A 1698 census, undertaken to devise a fair work scheme for the maintenance of the local infrastructure, indicated that the total number of men on the island (exclusive of 23 soldiers and all the slaves who were property of the Company) amounted to 163, 71 planters and 92 slaves. In other words, the total number of slaves had surpassed that of the adult white male population by the end of the 17th century. Nevertheless, if we consider the planters' families as well, the whites still outnumbered the blacks. Notwithstanding, the sociodemographic development of the community was changing quickly.

The early years of the 18th century saw considerable socio-economic challenges. Following a long-term drought, the production of agricultural goods could barely meet the demand of the local market, let alone those of export or sale to visiting ships. I found an entry in the *StHR* that most of the planters were planting potatoes at the time. The drought caused considerable damage, not only to the potato crops but also to the yams originally imported by slaves from the Guinea Coast and cultivated as a main food-stock for the slaves. Notwithstanding, the local population continued to grow; the 1708 census indicated an increase in total numbers so that the two ethnic groups were now about equal in size. The *Consultations* of May 25 1708 read:

> Two years head money due to the Church from the inhabitants being computed after the rate of sixpence per head for all whites and blacks over 16 years of age. List shows 180 whites and 177 blacks–men and women–soldiers of Garrison and Company's slaves excepted.

Melliss (1875: 13) says that in the early 1700s, the total population amounted to 832, "in about equal proportions of whites and blacks, and it went on steadily increasing at the rate of about forty-five or fifty each year."

This increase is to be explained by two major events in island history. First of all, the 'discovery' of gold and copper in Breakneck Valley in 1708, as a result of which "every able-bodied man, white or black, who could wield a pick or handle a shovel, was out prospecting" (Gosse 1938: 124), only to find that the alleged gold nuggets were iron pyrite. Second, an ambitious development scheme was planned for an area immediately below the Governor's house on the northern coast: 'New Ground'. Governor Roberts devised a visionary plan to reroute the irrigation patterns of Plantation Valley and to build canals and water runs for an area as large as 350 acres. The newly developed land was to be cultivated for yams as food for the slaves, sugar cane and Indian corn for export and sale as well as for vineyards for wine and brandy production to increase revenues for the local Government (Janisch 1885). Additional manpower was needed to carry out the Company's works and plantations, and it was decided that 200 slaves should be imported from Madagascar with immediate effect. One of the first population censuses, providing general information on all the groups, was conducted in 1714 and reported as follows in Janisch (1885):

> Whites 405, officers and soldiers 125, total 530 of which 91 women and 247 children – Blacks 302 exclusive of Companies slaves – Cattle total 964 – owned by 71 planters. The largest proprietors Powell, Carne, Coales and Doveton – 89 – 46 – 43 and 40 head respectively – 26 families had no cattle. The Blacks owned by 65 persons, the largest proprietors Powell and Carne 17 each.

We note that the number of slaves increased at a constant rate and also that the ratio of slaves per planter shifted considerably. Whereas there was almost a 1:1 ratio twenty years earlier, slave ownership now was on a bigger scale, two planters possessing 17 slaves each. One reason is that the Company effectively subsidised the importation of slaves and that inhabitants could derive a considerable income from letting out their slaves as labourers to the Company, earning up to one shilling and six pence per day (Brooke 1808). In due course, the expense for hiring blacks amounted to the astronomical sum of about £2,250 a year. As a result,

> 200 or 300 Blacks more are wanted by the Government. The planters knowing we have not hands sufficient and must come to them they'll not let them under 18d. per day which makes all your work come out very dear. This is not the worst for by letting their Blacks many of their own Plantations are neglected. A small vessel from Madagascar would effectually do our business and they are the best blacks for our purpose. The next best to them are the Gold Coast Slaves of Guinea and the Slaves that are sometimes in great plenty in Bengal. (*Letter to Court of Directors*, January 20 1716)

An interesting eyewitness account comes from Captain Daniel Beeckman, who visited the island on June 9 1715. He wrote that all the white inhabitants were "English" and that they owned a large number of slaves. Moreover, it struck him that the local feeling was very much one of dependence on the mother country and one of a colonial outpost rather than of an independent colony: "They all have a great desire to see England, which they call home, though many of them never saw it, nor can have any true idea thereof" (quoted in Gosse 1938: 139). Beeckman also reported that Jamestown had expanded to a size of 70 to 80 houses, which, however, still were only inhabited during the visit of ships.

The arrival of a new wave of slaves affected the entire community. The effects of the drought lingered and diseases ravaged the island. To make matters worse, some of the slaves who arrived from Madagascar in 1717 suffered from chicken pox. 30 planters died in the first half of 1718 alone and there were a good number of victims in the black population. Mortality rates in this period were exceptionally high indeed. An entry in the *Consultations* from 26 May 1719 reads that "We usually decrease here among the white people five in a hundred per annum – but in each of the two last years not lesser than 10 per 100!!". This affected the slaves as well and Brooke (1808) comments on the slaves' high mortality rates in the first half of the 18th century as follows:

> Even in healthy seasons, according to Governor Pyke's calculation, the annual decrease in the number of blacks newly imported was two in fifteen, and amongst those inured to the climate, one in ten.

The result was that many planter families requested to leave the island (and it goes without saying that there were serious tensions when these were turned down by the Government) and there are also numerous reports of slaves attempting to escape on stolen boats (some of them being so desperate that they left without rudder, sails and oars). There is evidence that some of them wanted to return home and a *Consultations* entry (dated June 10 1718) is particularly instructive here:

> Four blacks missing and widow Carne's boat which was a small yawl – one of them said for some time before he knew how to find his countrey out for it was a great way off upon the waters where the Sun rose for he had often observed the Sun to rise over a great mountain which is on Madagascar.

The 1720 census returns yielded the information that the total population (excluding army personnel) amounted to 826: 391 whites (58 men, 77 women, 6 youths, 41 maidens, 92 boys, 117 girls) and 435 blacks (8 freemen, 194 men, 65 women, 110 boys, 58 girls). Notwithstanding escape attempts and higher mortality rates, the black population still outweighed the white one, though only by a slight margin (ca. 54 per cent). Three years later the number of free blacks rose to 20 and this caused growing concern among the planters. The situation escalated when John Coulson, a planter, agreed to sell a slave to "Town Collier a free black"; planters immediately complained and argued that this posed a serious threat to the white population. They reacted by sending an official petition to the Governor, asking him to put an end to this practice. Accordingly, the Board of Directors discussed the matter and resolved that "Free Blacks are not to be allowed to have any Slaves and if any master enfranchize a Black for good conduct then such Black must be obliged to leave the Island by the first shipping" (*Letter from England*, February 12 1725). This affected the free blacks severely as they were banned from hiring or acquiring labourers; it became effectively impossible for them to increase their economic productivity and to enhance their social standing in the community.

Moreover, strict laws were introduced to regulate the status of children of free blacks and slaves. A number of court cases reported in the *StHR* indicate that unlawful sexual relationships between blacks and whites (involving army personnel, free planters and slaves) had become frequent by the late 1730s. It is somewhat ironic that this was to the interest of the Company: it allowed them to punish free blacks and by doing so to increase the total number of Company's slaves. In the mid-1730s, a court case ruled that children born to parents of mixed ethnicities were to be sold as slaves, as was the practice in the West Indies. Similarly, it was decided that if free black women had a child with soldiers then they lost their status and privileges; both woman and child were to serve as Company slaves for an indefinite period of time. In 1736, a soldier by the name of Thomas Swindle was on trial for having a child by a free black woman. He was found guilty and sentenced to ride the wooden horse for two hours with a blackened face. The free black woman, in contrast, was publicly whipped and enslaved by the Company.

In the same year, Mary Gurling, the widow of a planter, had a child with a black man. She was punished and imprisoned till she forfeited the identity of the father of her child. Upon confessing, she received 39 lashes and the slave was castrated. Cruel punishment and social injustice of this kind enticed numerous slaves to flee the island. Toward the end of the 18th century, we find frequent reports of escapes, both of Company and planters' slaves, and there was also an increase in suicides and murders. Some slaves set up truly adventurous escape plans. In 1760, for instance, two Company slaves hid on a ship and travelled all the way to England. One of them, Grewer, was described as "a stonelayer and a very useful man but an artful notorious villain" (*Letters to England*, December 18 1760). He was returned to the island on the next ship. The Governor expressed his gratitude and reasons for growing concern as follows:

> We are obliged to you for returning Grewer to us. Although he is a serviceable man he is very artful and designing and as you thought proper to forgive him he has not been punished, we were in great hopes he would have been sent hither in irons and to be punished in order to deter others from the like villanys. This fellow boasts of the indulgence he received from you and industriously spreads among his brethren a notion of the great liberty allowed in England. Says it was in his option whether to have returned to the Island or not, withal having the assurance to appear upon his first landing in a dress very unbecoming to a slave and which no gentleman would have thought beneath him to wear. All precautions are adopted. (*Letter to England*, May 26 1761)

Reports of this kind obviously enticed other slaves to escape from their miserable conditions and to start a new life in England. Though runaway slaves were severely punished, the exodus continued throughout the 1740s and '50s. Only adult and able-bodied men left the island (I have not found a single report of escaping women or children) and this affected the labour situation considerably. There was an acute lack of manpower and the Governor felt compelled to dispatch two ships to Madagascar to procure slaves, "able-bodied men under 25 or well-grown boys". The Captains took a local slave by the name of Cupidore as an interpreter to Madagascar (which is an indication that he was bilingual in English and Malagasy; see below). The mission was successful but the return journey became a total disaster:

> *Mercury* and *Fly* returned from Madagascar with 16 men slaves and 2 boys, 107 cwt. rice, 32 cwt. paddy. An insurrection occurred among the slaves 29th Nov. 1764 8 days after leaving Madagascar on board the *Mercury* at two in the morning – Captain mortally wounded with five stabs and mate's scull fractured. The slaves were fired upon killing two and wounding three. Cupidore a slave sent from St. Helena as interpreter speaking the language of the natives of Madagascar alleged to have excited the revolt "by filling their heads with shocking notions of their wretched fate as slaves." Cupidore and Winchester one of the slaves were tried after arrival at St. Helena for the above, and executed for murder. (*Consultations*, January 25 1765)

The 1765 population census (exclusive of 284 army personnel) returned a total of 649 white inhabitants (248 men, 154 women, 156 boys, 91 girls) whereas Governor Walker's *Minute on the Progress of the Population* indicated that the number of blacks in 1769 amounted to 976 (60 per cent of the total population).

The second half of the 18th century saw far-reaching social changes. For one, there is evidence of increasing stratification in the black population. First reports of black overseers appear in the late 1760s:

> Four Madagascar slaves attempt to run off in Sam Alexander's Fishing Boat in Sandy Bay – not knowing how to manage a boat the sea drove them on shore on the beach. Their excuse they did not like to be under *a Black* overseer. (*Consultations*, April 18, 1768; emphasis in original)

Moreover, the importance of Jamestown as a commercial, social and cultural centre of the island increased and larger population groups urbanised, leaving the rural hinterlands and moving to town permanently. Captain Cook called at St Helena on the return legs of his first two world voyages. His first visit was in May 1771. Joseph Banks, chief botanist and naturalist on the ship, reported his impressions of the island as follows:

> As the fleet was to sail immediately and our ship to accompany it, it became necessary to make as much of a short time as possible, so this whole day was employd in riding about the Island … In sailing along the shore ships come uncommonly near it so that the huge Clifts [sic] seem almost to overhand and threaten destruction ... in this manner they sail till they open Chappel Valley where stands the town ... very small and except a few houses ill built ... All kinds of Labour is here performed by Man, indeed he is the only animal that works except a few Saddle Horses … the simple contrivance of Wheelbarrows

> would Doubtless be far preferable to carrying burthens upon the head, and yet even that expedient was never tried.[3]

Banks' observations indicate that Jamestown now had a permanent population. Urbanisation increased steadily and by 1802, "the number of handsome residences ... went up every year in the town, while the number of dwellings in the country did not alter. The occupants of these town houses required domestic servants, shopmen, porters, fishermen, hewers of wood and drawers of water, and thus more labour was withdrawn from the farm. Whenever slaves were to be sold, the rich townsman was able to outbid the countryman and the difficulties of the latter were made so great that many, who would have preferred to remain farmers, were induced to leave their farms and migrate to Jamestown and enter into trade" (Gosse 1938: 230). According to Brooke (1808), the five-year period from 1801 to 1805 had an average of 165 ships calling at St Helena annually. An anonymous visitor (thought to be Francis Duncan) described the situation in the early 19th century as follows:

> The arrival of the homeward–bound Indiamen is the greatest event of the year. It fills the whole settlement with alacrity and joy. They quit their gardens, flock to JAMESTOWN, open their houses for the accommodation of the passengers, and entertain them with plays, dances, and concerts. These gay assemblies are enlivened by the presence of many agreeable and handsome young women, natives of the place, who, amid the general festivity, seem to feel a peculiar interest in what is going forward; probably, not without some throbbing expectations of being taken from a scene.

These developments had drastic consequences. For one, they intensified social divisions and stratification on the island (thus widening the gap between middle and working classes). On the other hand, urbanisation also seems to have led to segregation. It is interesting to note that the *Consultations* of January 24 1780 reported a total of 1,161 slaves on the island, including some 80 or 90 free blacks, all of whom "live chiefly in the country where there are very few white men not above 40 in number." The late 18th century thus saw the beginnings of town life on St Helena; until then, Jamestown was only inhabited when ships called in order to barter or trade or when slaves were sold on the market. This meant that a new social class emerged, which consisted mostly of whites taking up residence in urban Jamestown. This is also reflected in the rise of class-consciousness in this period (according to the *Consultations*, dated April 15 1816, a Mr Boys refused to take the corpse of a deceased person to church since he considered this a privilege for the upper classes only). The influence of the rural population dwindled rapidly, both economically and

---

[3] Quote taken from the website http://www.captaincooksociety.com/ccsu414.htm, accessed March 11 2005.

socially. Social stratification in the white community further intensified in the early 1800s when the decrease in labour forced planters to hire impoverished whites (usually discharged soldiers), who often found themselves in the rural plantations working side by side with slaves.

The late 1700s were again a period of brutal punishments of blacks, often by planters who took matters into their hands and did not consult with the Court of Magistrates. The *Consultations* (December 13 1779) report that "Woodberry a slave complains of inhuman punishment from his master who ran fish hooks through his ears and burnt his hands by putting greased wick between his fingers so as to destroy the nerves of one of the hands." In 1792, Governor Robert Brooke instated a penal code for the protection of slaves and restricted the owners' authority while at the same time considerably extending that of the magistrate (Gosse 1938: 219). The legal status of blacks was enhanced when evidence provided by blacks against whites was officially allowed in court. Moreover, blacks were given equal rights when the island's defences were restructured in 1796. The plan was to secure the island by organising the male population into a militia (before that, no more than 30 or 40 white planters assisted the garrison). Brooke hired discharged soldiers from England to settle on the island and set up a local defence corps; two companies of blacks were embodied and the whole militia was subsequently organised into a joint and desegrated corps. As a result of all these developments, it came as no surprise when the import of slaves was officially ended in 1789.

The early 19th century again was a period of misery and poverty. Infectious diseases introduced from the Cape quickly spread across the island and affected the entire population. A total of 160 St Helenians died of measles in March and April 1807 and the situation became truly alarming:

> The Register of Burials from 1st March to 1st May exhibited a list of 102 Blacks and 58 Whites, but many more blacks have been carried off the exact number of whom has not yet been ascertained as they had not been Christened and their burials of course not registered in the Church Books. (*Letter to England*, May 3 1807)

As before, the increase in mortality affected the labour situation. For one, slave prices increased by almost 400 per cent (Melliss 1875: 18). The majority of the population was impoverished so that Governor Wilks founded a Benevolent Society in 1814 to provide education to "the children of slaves, free blacks and the poorer classes of the community" (Janisch 1885). To fill the urgent demand for cheap labour, Governor Beatson lobbied for a relocation of farmhands from England to St Helena; when this was not successful, he made arrangements to hire indentured labourers from China instead. Accordingly, a few hundred workers arrived from Canton in May 1810 and July 1811. The Company initially offered them three-year contracts, with the possibility of an extension for a period up to five years. There were several immigration waves of Chinese workers. Gosse (1938: 246) estimates that some 650 Chinese labourers may have taken the opportunity to work on St Helena. The most complete census at the time, conducted in 1814, gives a total number of 247, that continued to rise rapidly (a population census conducted in October 1817 listed 618). It remains somewhat unclear when and how many Chinese labourers arrived but all reports agree that practically all of them left the island again and that they did not integrate themselves into the local community. Melliss (1875: 18), who resided on the island at the time, writes that the last Chinese labourer died in the early 1870s: "It is much to be regretted that such industrious men have quite disappeared. A year or two ago the last remaining Chinaman died at a good old age, and … the only records of their time exist in the Chinese cemetery, at a spot called New Ground." The same source indicates that in 1815 the island population amounted to 3,587. The number of white settlers was 694 (110 men, 201 women, 173 boys, and 210 girls; plus 933 civil and military) and that of the black population 1710 (420 free blacks, 93 Company slaves, 342 male slaves, 245 women, 329 boys, and 281 girls). In other words, blacks now outnumbered whites by almost three to one, representing some 70 per cent of the population.

Then, in 1815, the island was put on the world map once and for all. On Sunday, the 15th of October, H.M. *Northumberland* arrived from England, transporting Napoleon Bonaparte to his South Atlantic exile. The military and army personnel were increased to prevent escape attempts of Napoleon and his allies, and the St Helena population doubled overnight. This had economic and political consequences. During Napoleon's exile the island was placed under the jurisdiction of the British crown. Governor Wilks was replaced by a British Government appointee, Lieutenant-General Sir Hudson Lowe. The strong presence of government, administration and army meant that more money came to the island. Though staying on St Helena for a relatively short while only (until Bonaparte's death in May 1821, to be precise), Lowe played an eminent role in local history, since he was one of the main instigators of the abolition of slavery. Following an incident when a slave owner was fined a statutory £2 for crudely whipping a young slave girl, Lowe lobbied in favour of abolishing slavery on the island once and for all.

In accordance, the *Consultations* of August 24 1818 state that a "Public Meeting of Inhabitants resolved that from the 25th December 1818 all children born of Slaves be considered free." Slave owners were also in charge of enforcing the attendance of free-born children at church and Sunday schools. This had legal complications and caused considerable confusion. We note from the *Book of Judicial Consultations* that in the early 1820s there were

> [n]umerous cases of slaves claiming freedom on the ground that they had been kidnapped, &c. Toby, Mr. Balcombe's slave, one of the cases. He was brought to the Island by Capt. Frazer and sold or given to Mr. Wrangham. His claim to

> freedom not entertained on the ground that he had been brought to the Island prior to the date when the importation of Slaves was prohibited … Several of the Slaves claimed freedom on the ground of their having been in England, and their claim was referred to decision of the Company.

A *Singular on the Progress of the Population* (conducted in 1824) documents an increase in the total number of blacks in the late 18th century, from 976 in 1769 to 1030 (1785) and 1208 (1803), not including more than 300 free blacks. This must have been due to local reproduction since slaves were no longer imported. Walker's census also indicates that the black population underwent massive changes in the 1820s. Between 1810 and 1824, the number of free blacks increased by more than 250 per cent (amounting to 1,066 in 1824) and blacks were increasingly listed on the Company's payroll. In 1830, for instance, the crew of the *St Helena*, a Company schooner, was manned with sailors and deckhands of both groups (who jointly met with a sad fate: seven white and four black crew members were massacred by pirates off the Sierra Leone coast; Gosse 1938: 299). In 1828 finally, the Governor received instructions that within five years' time all slaves were to be set free with the help of Company loans. Slavery officially ended in 1832:

> Slavery to be abolished as soon as possible. 869 Slaves valued £37639. Since 19th December 1826 124 Slaves had been freed for £5550 pf which upwards £ 1300 had been repaid. Number of Slaves by return to 30th Sept. 1830 – 272 men, 160 women, 107 boys, 88 girls; Total 627. Slaves to be divided into classes and one–fifth to be liberated every year. Purchase money to be considered as a Loan to the Slave. (*Consultations*, January 26 1832)

Few realised that these decisions foreshadowed far-reaching socio-political changes. Under the India Act, St Helena was no longer ruled by the Honourable East India Company. On April 22 1834, His Majesty's Government took control of the island and the transfer of powers dealt a serious blow to the local economy, heavily influencing the community's social life.

3.2.3 1834-1981: Crown colony and Nationality Act

The decision to transfer the control and administrative powers over St Helena dealt a crushing blow to island life. The annual budget of the Company amounted to £90,000 (Gosse 1938); now that St Helena was a crown colony, financial support and monetary aids were cut by about 75 per cent. The garrison dispersed quasi over night and most of the army personnel were disbanded or removed. Some soldiers were pensioned, receiving a lump sum of money for their services, while others were employed under the new Government; most of the civil establishments and offices were broken up, the benevolent societies and governmentally-subsidised bodies were no longer operative and many islanders found themselves in extreme poverty: "So hard did the Company's treatment of their servants press upon many of them, that twenty years after this event officers of high rank might be seen digging the soil side by side with their own negro servant in the struggle to support their families" (Melliss 1875: 29). The economic situation was desperate; many left the island in search of work. In the late 1830s, dozens of families and over a hundred young men saw no prospect of improvement and went to South Africa. A particularly insightful account of life on the island at that time comes from Charles Darwin, who spent a few days ashore when the *Beagle* called on their tour around the world in 1836. He described the social situation on St Helena as follows:

> The English, or rather Welsh character of the scenery, is kept up by the numerous cottages and small white houses; some buried at the bottom of the deepest valleys, and others mounted on the crests of the lofty hills ... There is so little level or useful land, that it seems surprising how so many people, about 5000, can subsist here. The lower orders, or the emancipated slaves, are I believe extremely poor: they complain of the want of work. From the reduction in the number of public servants owing to the island having been given up by the East Indian Company, and the consequent emigration of many of the richer people, the poverty probably will increase. The chief food of the working class is rice with a little salt meat; as neither of these articles are the products of the island, but must be purchased with money, the low wages toll heavily on the poor people.

A slight economic recovery set in from the 1830s onwards, namely when St Helena became one of the main centres of the South Atlantic whaling industry. As many as a thousand ships called at the island each year and the United States and Norway installed resident consuls to control their interests. Another source of revenue opened up when the Government established a Vice-Admiralty Court for the trial of privateers engaged in illegal slave trade. Large numbers of ships were captured off the West African coast and brought to St Helena in the 1840s. The ships were to be sold or broken up and the slaves were clothed and nourished at a Liberated African Depot established in Ruperts Valley. This brought financial relief and employment opportunities to the local population; on the other hand, termites came to the island on an infested ship and this ruined many inhabitants.

As in the case of the indentured labourers from China (see above), the Africans were not integrated into the community and many left at the first opportunity. Only few of the estimated 10,000 liberated Africans stayed behind. Archbishop Gray, who visited the island in 1850, noted that there were only about 600 people in the depot (quoted in Gosse 1938: 320). Upon recovery, most accepted a passage to the West Indies or to British Guyana and worked as labourers there; only few remained as servants or as public workers on St

Helena. There was open sentiment against them, and Melliss (1875: 31) reported that "the introduction of a new race of people … after some years, developed into a poverty-stricken, dependent portion of the population" and wrote that "the negroes, which could have been best spared, still remain." The depot was finally closed in 1874.

St Helena became increasingly isolated towards the end of the 19th century, for a number of reasons. First of all, the Suez Canal opened in 1869. This led to a decrease in ship traffic in the Atlantic Ocean, on which the local economy depended. Moreover, steam ships had more storage space and allowed for more efficient transport so that captains were not forced to call at St Helena for fresh water and provisions. St Helena thus was cut off from communication channels with England, and local enterprises had to provide work. Jacob's Ladder, a 700 step long path connecting Jamestown with the Half Tree Hollow area, was constructed by royal engineers and a local workforce in 1871. There was a project to start a local flax industry in the 1870s: "a Company, called the Foreign Fibre Company, was formed for the purpose of preparing the fibre … But after five years incessant work the Company ceased its operations; thus many men and boys were thrown out of employment" (Grant 1881: 13). A main reason for the failure was that a central flax mill was built in Jamestown, which caused transport problems from the plantations in the countryside. Other work schemes included the establishment of a local whaling and fishing enterprise; a whale ship was built and manned by islanders, many of whom had worked on the American whalers that used the island as a base (Gosse 1938: 330-1). However, whaling in the South Atlantic was in decline by this time and the project failed as well. All this led to further out-migration. The island population peaked at 5,838 in 1871 but dramatically decreased when more than 2,000 Saint Helenians left for the Cape area and Natal in the 1870s and 1880s.[4] The contrast between country and town intensified during this period. Melliss (1875: 38, 43) writes that

> [w]ith its immediate neighbourhood [Jamestown] numbers about 290 houses ... including two churches, a chapel, two hospitals, a markethall, and at least six schools … The population of the town is somewhat more than one–half that of the whole island, or about 3500 persons … There are in the country 266 distinct properties, with about 200 houses.

St Helena continued to serve as an important place of imprisonment and exile. The Zulu chief Dinizulu was banished to the island with his family and allies in the 1890s and an estimated six thousand South African Boers, taken as POWs during the South African War (1899-1902), were sent to St Helena and held in concentration camps, the principal one being on Deadwood Plain. A

---

[4] http://website.lineone.net/~sthelena/settlersslaves.htm, accessed March 14 2005.

temporary wave of economic improvement came to the island (revenues of £10,000 a year); the population reached an all-time record of 9,850 only to decline abruptly with the repatriation of practically all the South African prisoners. In 1907, the troops of the West India regiment stationed on St Helena were officially withdrawn and all the volunteers and militia were disbanded.

Governor Gallwey took office in 1903 and introduced some important changes, such as the reorganisation of the education system (Evans 1994). After much debate, compulsory education was introduced for all children up to the age of 14 years. This applied to all schools, no matter whether run by the Government or by independent societies. Moreover, the moribund flax industry was re-established and lace making was introduced to boost export and sales. This time experts were sent out to assist the islanders in their economic endeavours. A government mill was started at Longwood in 1907 (not in Jamestown, as the lesson had been learnt from the failure of the first enterprise). In the 1920s, the flax industry employed some 300 people. This was insufficient and a number of St Helenians were forced to search for jobs off the island, such as contract work on the American-run army base on Ascension Island (which would increase during and after WWII with the construction of a modern telecommunications centre) and also in South Africa. Furthermore, there was steady emigration to the United Kingdom (e.g. the so-called group of "The Hundred Men", who left to work as agricultural workers in the UK in 1945). It was estimated that in the early 1960s, about 150 Saint Helenians relocated to England each year. This trend was reinforced after the British Post Office decided to use synthetic fibres to tie its mail bags. The local flax mills were closed once and for all in 1965.

3.2.4 1981-today:Nationality Act and British Dependent Territory

The 1981 Nationality Act came into effect on January 1 1983 as "an Act to make fresh provision about citizenship and nationality ... as regards the right of abode in the United Kingdom." This deeply affected the Crown Colonies, the main consequence being that all persons born outside the UK after that date were to have British Citizenship only by descent or if, at the time of birth, their father or mother was a British Citizen. As a result, the St Helenians had no longer right of abode in the UK and lost their rights and privileges as British citizens. This halted emigration somewhat, and the 1987 census returned a population of 5,644, a total of 1,302 of whom (amounting to 23.7 per cent) resided in Jamestown. The situation changed in 1999 when the St Helenians received full British citizenship; the newly gained freedom catalysed emigration and an estimated 20-25 per cent of the population have left the island in the meantime, mostly young families. It remains to be seen how this affects the future development of the island.

Today, St Helena has the status of a British Dependent Territory. The island is administered by a governor and expatriate British magistrates. Education is compulsory and free for children aged between 5 and 15 years. St Helena's main income is the export of fish. St Helena coffee is of a very high quality but the production is too small to compete with international markets. There is some limited tourism, which comes to the island on the RMS *St Helena*, and this also provides jobs to the islanders. St Helena receives a substantial annual grant-in-aid from the United Kingdom in the form of subsidies; the remainder is mostly raised from the sale of postage stamps and philatelic items.

3.3 Sociodemographic background

Every attempt to reconstruct an earlier contact scenario, and thus the origins and evolution of a variety, depends on what we know about – and how we interpret! – the community's social history. The previous section detailed the socio-historical development of the St Helenian community at great length, focussing particularly on the 18th and 19th centuries, which, I argue, are most important for the development of the local variety. This background knowledge now allows us to take a further step in our analysis, namely to raise some first hypotheses as to how the sociodemographic formation of the community (may have) affected the linguistic mechanisms that gave rise to StHE. Put differently, we can now speculate on how the island's *external* history triggered the linguistic and sociolinguistic processes that underlie the formation of a distinctive local variety. Based on the information provided above, I now go into more detail, especially in terms of the local living conditions (and what these mean for contact linguistics) and the sociolinguistic significance of interaction patterns, both within and across communities on the island. The following questions are paramount for this purpose:

- What were the origins of the settlers and when did they arrive? Is it likely that there was a founder effect?
- How stable was the population?
- What were the patterns of in-, out- and cross-migration?
- Where did the colonists settle on the island and how did they interact? Did they form their own little sub-communities?
- What was the amount of social stratification in the white community?
- What was the amount of segregation of the black community?

The following sections discuss them in turn.

3.3.1 Where did the settlers come from?

A first and most important question concerns the origins of the people who came to St Helena. This allows us to address the potential for *founder effects* (as discussed in ch. 2) and to offer some first hypotheses on the origins of StHE (or put differently, to identify who was instrumental in forming it). The social history, as outlined in the previous section, indicated that there were four principal groups: (1) the British settlers; (2) the slaves from Africa, Madagascar and various parts of Asia; (3) the settlers from continental Europe; and (4) the indentured labourers from China. The input and contributions of these four groups are discussed subsequently.

Unfortunately, the sources do not provide precise information as to the exact origins of the British settlers, even though the (Greater?) London area seems a likely place of origin for many of them. Perhaps the main reason for uncertainty and confusion is that "English" is often used as a generic term (as in the original orders given to Captain Dutton: "with the commanders and as many English as convenientlie may be spared"). This is also evident in first eyewitness reports that make reference to the "Englishmen" on St Helena (Henry Gargen 1665; Sylvain de Rennefort 1688). Similarly, Captain William Dampier emphasises that the "young women born here, are but one removed from English, being the daughters of such" when he visited the island in 1691, and as late as 1808, Brooke reported that the local population was subject to the following types of regulation in the early settlement period:

> In the year 1679 it was ordained, that when a soldier desired to become a free planter, if he married a planter's widow, and became entitled to her deceased husband's land, he should further be allowed ten acres and one cow from the Company, and, in the event of his marrying a farmer's daughter, or a young woman sent out from *England*, who had no land, he was in such case to have twenty acres and two cows. Every unmarried man, sent out from *England* as a settler, was to have ten acres of land and one cow; and ten acres more, and another cow, on his marrying a planter's daughter, or an *English* woman. If a planter's son married an *English* woman, during his father's life-time, he became entitled to twenty acres and two cows … For every ten acres of land the holder was obliged to maintain an *Englishman*, on the premises. (emphasis added, DS)

The only area specified in the sources is London, and there are several reports of immigration after the disastrous 1666 fire (though at least one source strongly rejects this, see above). By the same token, it is striking to find that there are practically no references to settlers from areas other than England. In the entire *StHR*, for instance, we find only one reference each to a Scotsman and to a Welshman, both of whom resided on the island in the early 1700s. Even Scottish visitors (e.g. Gill 1878) only refer to the "English"; they would almost certainly have commented on settlers from their own region. In the absence of direct historical evidence, we have to turn to other criteria. At the risk of being somewhat speculative, it would appear that the majority of the settlers came from the South of England. For one, similar developments in other colonies indicate that this area provided a most influential founder stock elsewhere (e.g., in the Caribbean and later in the Southern Hemisphere).[5] Another piece of evidence comes from the settlers' family names. A *Consultation* entry in 1709 provides the names of the principal planter families. These are instructive:

> The Extract of all Laws being prepared it was found that some of them were proper for the Govr and Council only and some not in force being since repealed. A Digest was therefore prepared and resolved to summon 36 of the principal inhabitants to the Church by Plantation to read and receive them … viz:—Thomas Cason, Thomas Southen, Joshua Johnson, Gabriel Powell, Robert Addis, Hugh Bodley, James Draper, Richard Gurling, Charles Steward, Richard Alexander, Richard Swallow, Thomas Perkins, Benjamin Sich, John Twaits, Stephen Lufkins, John Robinson, William Seale, William Marsh, Thomas Harper, Henry Coales, Sutton Isaac, John Nichols, Thomas Swallow, Ripon Wills, Matthew Bazett, Thomas Gargen, Henry Francis, James Greentree, Jonathan Doveton, John Coles, Orlando Bagley, James Vesey, Robert Leach, Robert Bell, Thomas Burnham, and Francis Wrangham.

Dickson (1973) states that many of the English colonists who arrived in the 17th and 18th centuries had traditional southern names (Banks, Bennett, Cason, Swain, Coles, Francis, Hunt, Powell, etc.), and her careful analysis of place names on St Helena leads her to conclude that "most of the British immigrants were from southern England, so *Peak Dale*, a northern name, is unusual" (Dickson 1973: 208; see below).

Finally, there is evidence that many settlers came (or were recruited) from the lower strata of English society. Some of the visitors mention this explicitly (which testifies to the planters' origins as well as to the visitor's snobbery and social prejudice). Ms Ovington, for instance, who arrived in 1690 en route from Surat, described her impressions as follows:

> The minds of the inhabitants are generally as Uncultivated as the neglected Soil, their Intellects as ordinary as their Qualities, but what was infinitely worse, the pravity of their Manners compares them with the rankest soil, productive of nothing but noxious herbs, untractable to all the Arts of Husbandry and Improvement. (quoted in Gosse 1938: 99)

---

[5] A word of caution: even if this had been the case, it would not necessarily mean that they were Londoners and native speakers of London English. They may have grown up elsewhere and moved to the city at a later stage in their lives (namely when London underwent urbanisation; cf. ch. 2).

Similarly, we know that the Company typically recruited personnel from the working classes (not only on St Helena, but also elsewhere), which invites the implication that many of the soldiers were illiterate (trained soldiers would have been sent to more important and financially viable colonies). This is made explicit in several reports:

> On 31st Jan. six soldiers deserted in the night taking two Boats ... The deserters were illiterate men of bad character and only a few days provisions and must inevitably perish at sea. (*Consultations*, February 2 1774)

All this suggests that the core of the British founders of the community most likely originated and hailed from the South of England, and there is strong evidence that many of them had a working class background.

Let us turn to another influential group, namely that of the slaves. Fortunately, we have more detailed information here. From very early on, reports of travellers and visiting Captains indicate the origins of slaves and we also have numerous reports and requests in the correspondence between the local Government and the Company. The picture that emerges is a complex one as it appears that slaves were imported from at least a dozen different locations. The first slaves were acquired by Dutton's convoy on their voyage to St Helena (i.e., prior to colonisation). Instructions were given to buy slaves on St Iago (held by the Portuguese) and British strongholds along the Slave and Gold Coasts (i.e., what at the time was Lower Guinea). Gargen's (1665) account mentions some 20 slaves on the island, most of them being Company property, and this must mean that Dutton's mission was successful. A much later entry in the *Consultations* (dated May 8 1717) indicates that some of the slaves came from Guinea indeed, as "There are but twelve out of 42 Guinea Blacks now living yet more dyed from want of care or victuals." The fact that these areas were colonised by the Portuguese could have influenced the early contact scenario; it is striking that some of the slaves had Portuguese names (e.g. Mingoe, from Domingo) and it is certainly plausible that the first slaves spoke Portuguese or a Portuguese-based pidgin/creole, that may then have been reinforced at a later stage:

> Portuguese shipp arrived bound to Angolo [sic]. The Captain sick and wishes to remain till his ship returns. Resolved – The Portuguese are our allies and most necessary confederates with the great alliance of Europe against France– and the ship may do some considerable service by leaving at their return some slaves greatly wanted on this Island. (*Consultations*, September 10, 1706)

From very early on, slaves came from India as well, and these formed another influential group. All the ships travelling to England from Surat called at St Helena to procure refreshments or to wait for other vessels so as to form a safe convoy. Instructions were given that these ships were to provide food and livestock for St Helena, and slaves were imported as well. This is evidenced by Father Fernandez Navarette, a professor of philosophy at the college of Saint Gregory at Valladolid, who visited St Helena in December 1673. He reported the following:

> The place where the English were is a small valley … In that place there is a little town of the English, who till the ground, sow rice, make butter and cheese … there I found some blacks of Madrastapan, for whom I was concern'd, because they had bin Catholicks at home, and were hereticks there; there were also two Frenchmen in the same way. (quoted in Janisch 1885)

The *Consultations* repeatedly make reference to slaves from western India. There are references to single slaves (as to "Antony a Maccausa man had been on the Island for some years sent here from Madras", in 1712) and also to larger groups of Indian slaves who arrived throughout the late 17th and first half of the 18th century:

> Complaints that several Blacks guilty of notorious crimes had been sent here from India and requests the President at Fort George[6] that no more should be sent. We send some of them in this ship to Bencoolen according to our Honourable Masters orders. (*Consultations*, July 16, 1724)

> Nine of the Company's slaves men, women and children who we received this year from Bombay were enticed by a fellow named Drake to make their escape in the Long Boat which they effected by cutting her from her moorings in the dead of the night. (*Consultations*, September 11, 1739)

A less substantial group of slaves came from other places in Africa (i.e., other than Lower Guinea): Calabar (southeastern Nigeria) and quite likely southern Africa. The usage of generic terms makes it difficult to pinpoint exact origins. Some slaves are simply referred to as "Coffrey blacks", and this does not give any indication where they were from (perhaps even from Madagascar?). This problem is apparent in the following entry from the *Consultations*:

> Eleven slaves (all Madagascar or Coffrey Blacks) reserved for tryal. Four of them that consented not but did not discover what they knew to be severely slashed at the Flagstaffe. The rest all dismist. (*Consultations*, December 2, 1695)

---

[6] Fort St George, in Chennai, West India, was originally built in 1640 and served as a British military garrison and place of trade.

On the other hand, entries such as this one indicate how important Madagascar was as a resource of cheap labour. In fact, requests were made to obtain slaves from there exclusively (for instance for the ambitious New Ground development project) and we need to focus on Madagascar in more detail to gain insights into one of the most important founding populations.

Originally settled by the French, Madagascar was soon visited by Dutch, Portuguese, English, and French vessels, mostly en route to or on their home voyage from India. The increasing trade attracted large numbers of buccaneers to the Indian Ocean and these posed a constant threat: "In the absence of a significant naval power in waters remote from Europe, privateer vessels attacked ships of many nations … Madagascar was a popular hiding place where crews could recuperate and replenish supplies for another attack."[7] Madagascar soon became a popular source of slaves, particularly so since the local kingdoms were stratified into societies of nobles, commoners and slaves. Captains and crew members of trading ships could thus easily acquire slaves instead of risking their lives hunting them. As a consequence, "[t]he towns became centers of trade where cattle and slaves, taken in war, were exchanged with European merchants for guns and other manufactured goods."

We know from the *StHR* that slaves from Madagascar were brought to St Helena as early as the 1680s and 1690s. Indeed, their labour and discipline was held in such high esteem that Governors specifically asked for slaves from this island. Consequently, slave ships arriving from Madagascar were required to leave one slave behind as a poll tax when calling at the island (Gosse 1938). Slaves from Madagascar were also ordered to undertake the New Ground project (see above): "200 or 300 Blacks more are wanted by the Government … A small vessel from Madagascar would effectually do our business and they are the best blacks for our purpose" (*Letter to Court of Directors*, January 20, 1716). Accordingly, almost 100 slaves were imported from Madagascar in early 1717:

> Capt. William Mackett ship *Drake* 40 days from Madagascar delivered 12 slaves for the Company and sold 55 at an outcry to the Planters who averaged £ 2160. (*Letter to Directors*, January 12, 1717)

> We have received thirty Blacks out of the *Mercury*: If your Honors think fitt to lycence any more ships from Madagascar we pray that one article of the agreement may be that we may have liberty to choose out the best. We know the voyage is very profitable and even better termes than those we desire may be very well afforded. (*Consultations*, May 8, 1717)

[7] This quote is taken from the website http://countrystudies.us/madagascar/, which is the on-line version of a book previously published in hard copy by the Federal Research Division of the US Library of Congress; accessed January 18 2008.

This increased the slave population by about 30 per cent and significantly changed the sociolinguistic set-up of the island community.

Apart from these major areas, we also find references to smaller groups of slaves from elsewhere, such as Indonesia ("John Batavia a Slave of the Company aged 30" is mentioned in 1716, and a group of "Bencoolen slaves" fled the island in 1747) or the Maldives ("Capt. Polly of the *Drake* at the distance of 150 leagues from land took up a Boat with ten Blacks of the Maldive Islands who were drove out to Sea and near perishing – three died on board, 5 men, 1 woman and 1 boy landed here"; *Consultations*, March 17 1735). However, slaves from these areas were insignificant in number and certainly not in a position to exert much influence.

What about white settlers from areas other than England? The socio-historical account revealed that a variety of population groups came to the island, thus considerably diversifying the local scenario. First of all, one should mention the *French Huguenots*, led by Captain Poirier, who were hired by the Government in the 1680s to start wine and spirit production. The French group was quite substantial in size (about 20 members) but they still represented a minority of the white population at the time (which amounted to more than 100). Consequently, though it would be sociodemographically plausible that they could have shaped and influenced the evolution of early StHE, all the sources consulted are in agreement that the Huguenots, rather than maintaining their own lifestyles and speech ways, accommodated and acculturated to the local population. It is ubiquitously stressed that they were keen to integrate and that they did so quickly; Captain Poirier, for instance, became Governor after being on the island for seven years only. He conducted his administrative duties and wrote his business correspondence in English. He had thus mastered a foreign language and was used to English as a medium of every-day communication in the community (however, it is certainly plausible that he continued to speak French with other Huguenots, which would have lead to bilingualism). Consequently, the French Huguenots were small in number and quick to integrate themselves. Though staying on the island for lengthy periods of time, it is unlikely that they had a lasting input on the local population. The same goes for isolated individuals, such as "Nicholas Matthews a Lieflander by nation", who resided on the island in the late 1670s.[8]

The indentured labourers from China and the South African Boer prisoners provide us with a different scenario. These groups were larger in size, in fact so numerous that they almost equalled the local population. Both the

[8] This is quite obviously a case where any social or linguistic impact was minimised by the individual's unpopularity with the locals. Matthews was "imprisoned and to be sent off the Island for saying that for 1000 guilders he would conduct the French Admiral and shew him a place he had found where he might unseen land what men he would—and that the English were as bad as Turks" (*Consultations*, September 27 1680).

Boer POWs, held captive during the 1898-1902 South African War, and the indentured labourers from Canton/China, brought to the island in the early 19th century, arrived in numbers large enough to influence the local variety (or to swamp StHE). However, this was unlikely in both cases: the two groups stayed on the island for short periods of time only and did not mix with the local community (either they were segregated in concentration camps or they preferred to live in self-chosen isolation). Moreover, most of them left at the earliest occasion. The situation is less clear in the case of the freed African slaves, but the fact that they were isolated in a Depot in Rupert's Valley (and that Melliss reports that most of them had left in the 1870s) invites similar implications. None of these groups was likely to leave a social or linguistic legacy.

To sum up, the sociodemographic account suggests that the groups most sizeable and likely to influence the social development of the St Helenian community came from the English South, West Africa, India and particularly from Madagascar.

3.3.2 Where did the planters settle?

Origins are one important aspect for the reconstruction of St Helena's early settlement history. However, identifying where the settlers came from is insufficient for studying the microcosm of local contact patterns via which the local variety formed. Of equal significance is exactly where the colonists settled on the island: In close proximity or in relative isolation? Did they reside in villages, hamlets or isolated farmhouses? (This, needless to say, is a crucial criterion since it influenced the interaction patterns between groups and subgroups; see below). Consequently, it is important to determine settlement movements and development schemes across the island.

The settlers' family names have already provided evidence that many of the community's founders came from the English South. Evidence from these sources is important for the present purpose as well; place names indicate where the first buildings and human dwellings were erected on the island and provide evidence of the locations of the earliest farming activities. The *William and Thomas*, a ship that arrived in 1673 and brought a total of 37 settlers to the island, had Richard Alexander, Henry Francis, and Mathew Pouncey (and their families) on the passenger list. Dickson (1973) found that these names appear in the local toponymy very early on. Since farmsteads, as was the practice in many places, were named after their founders, the respective passengers and their families must have fanned out immediately and built farms and plantations soon after their arrival. Dickson (1973: 205) states:

> Because of the remarkable conservationism which the islanders have displayed in their retention of place-names, the island's history is written on its map … Even some sixteenth century place-names survive and seventeenth century names are particularly tenacious ... St Helena has preserved a very full record of her past and … the origin of many place-names is known.

Place names given at the whim of the owner are of no importance for sociohistorical analysis. However, those places named after settlers, such as Francis Plain, Wranghams, Casons, Lufkin, Seale or Pounceys, make it possible to reconstruct early settler movements on the island. This yields a regional pattern. The northeastern part of the island was non-arable and heavily forested (in fact not settled until the 18th century); the names of settlements in this area are topographically derived (Longwood, Deadwood, etc.), which contrasts with the practice employed in the western part of the island where houses were commonly named after individuals.

Jamestown Valley, having the advantages of a steady water supply and easy sea access, was a prime location for the first settlers (and for the Company that claimed the best property for its own usage). Given that this area was limited in size, however, planters arriving at successive stages would have been forced to move on, either into the island interior (where we find Francis Plain) or "up country" along the north-western coast (where we find Pounceys, Luffkins or Wranghams).[9] At the time, the settlers would have lived in relative isolation; they were pioneers who ventured into uncultivated land. However, and this is a crucial point, they continuously depended on Jamestown as a market and trading place. Every visitor comments on the settlers flocking to town when ships lay at anchor, when foreign goods were bartered, slaves sold, or when entertainment was sought. This in turn suggests that the earliest planters lived in close proximity to Jamestown (and that they quickly received word when a ship called).

The Dutch invasion and interregnum had little effect since the island was recaptured immediately and most of the families returned to their former property. However, the Company's renewed efforts to colonise the island and entice settlers to move to St Helena soon affected the influx of planters. As a consequence, there was a shortage of arable land, government regulations were lifted and the newly arriving planters were allowed to settle anywhere on the island. The most fertile areas in Sandy Bay (which had a more temperate climate, due to their windward location on the south-western coast) were settled

---

[9] Place names give us additional information on the distribution of land. To give but one example: Pounds were places where animals grazing on company land were counted on a regular basis (as evidenced by places called Sheep Pound Gulch, Goat Pound Ridge or Wild Cattle Pound). However, this is of minor importance for the present analysis and not pursued in detail here (see Dickson 1973 for more information).

in the early 1680s, as evidenced in the following *Consultations* entry from 1682:

> 8th May.—Sundry families settled in Sandy Bay and other windward vallies [sic] at a great distance from the Alarm Guns—ordered the Guns to be removed to "*Hawley's Mount*" and to be fired by any person discerning a ship.

Due to its fertile climate and good soil conditions, Sandy Bay soon became one of the most sought-after areas on St Helena. In 1689, for instance, there was a sugar cane plantation and a lime kiln, which was of vital importance for the local economy. Throughout the 1690s, Sandy Bay was successively connected with the rest of the island and a local infrastructure was built up; paths and so-called "cattle driftways" were constructed so as to allow safe passage and transport of goods over the precipitous Sandy Bay Ridge. Farming was profitable here; vegetables and fruit grew in abundance and (comparatively) big farms were soon established. The excellent climate meant that the local planters were soon in demand of cheap labour to cultivate the land and harvest the crops, which again meant that they were instrumental in lobbying for cheap slave labour.

Consequently, the earliest streams of settlers radiated from Jamestown outwards. First south, up Jamestown valley, and when all these areas were claimed, into the island interior and along the north-western coast in direction of today's Blue Hill and Sandy Bay areas (most likely via both the northern and interior routes). The Company developed an interest in these areas as well; New Ground, for instance, was to be established on the western coast. The Governor had his mansion there and councillors met in Plantation House to discuss political matters. Halftree Hollow was one of the first villages of importance. The first church outside Jamestown (St Paul's Cathedral) and one of the most eminently strategic fortifications were built here.

What happened from the early 1700s onwards is not entirely clear. We know that there was large-scale deforestation throughout the first half of the 18th century and the most seriously affected areas were Deadwood, Longwood and Prosperous Bay Plain. Firewood was needed for heating and cooking and also for local arrack production (which caused concern to the local authorities; see above). Documents show that in the 1740s Colonel David Dunbar experimented on Longwood Plain with the cultivation of oats, barley and wheat (Gosse 1938: 184). The barn he built was later converted into a rural mansion inhabited by the resident Lieutenant-Governor (and was ultimately to become the place of exile for Napoleon some 60 years later). The clearing of land allowed farmers to establish new plantations in these areas, for instance Longwood Farm. This area was economically important since it produced goods for the growing demands of the Jamestown market. Gill (1878) gives the following account:

> ... Longwood Farm, which we had already admired from Diana's Peak ... Having previously received a kind intimation that the farmer would gladly show whatever might be of interest to us, we now took advantage of this proffer to ride across the fields with him, and see the different agricultural operations that were going on. From this and the neighbouring farm, "Teutonic Hall," come the chief supplies of James Town. This is due to the energy and skill of two English farmers, who, with their families, have turned to good account the rich soil of decomposed lava, which is ready and willing to yield food for man and beast.

The economic success and increasing demand for agricultural products meant that smaller farms sprang up throughout the 1800s. Longwood, one of the island's biggest settlements today, was established in the 19th century, drawing settlers from other (rural) parts of the island. Levelwood, situated in the island's south, half-way between Longwood and Sandy Bay, was settled around this time as well.

3.3.3 How did the population increase?

The third point of interest concerns the global development of the St Helena population, particularly issues related to the growth and stability of the local community. Since contact-induced change such as creolisation or koinéisation take time and are to a large part determined by social factors, it goes without saying that sociodemographic stability is a prerequisite for the emergence of a "new", i.e., endonormative, variety. Put differently, founder effects cannot operate when the founders move away or if they are in some way decimated or outnumbered. "Catastrophic" events and high population turnovers (due to natural disasters, diseases, drastic in- or out-migration, etc.) hinder focussing and impede the crystallisation of new linguistic norms (ch. 2). In this context we need to address the evolution of the populace as a whole; was it linear and regular or "catastrophic", characterised by all kinds of fluctuations?

The sociohistorical account indicates that the island community was far from stable. Unlike other British settlements in the South Atlantic, e.g. Tristan da Cunha or the Falkland Islands, the population on St Helena was at all times subject to massive fluctuation, particularly so during the first two centuries of settlement. There exist no reliable census data or population statistics for the 17th century, and we have already seen that any reconstruction of the first 30 years of settlement history is necessarily speculative. Nevertheless, there is little doubt that practically all of the first planters were short-term residents only, many leaving at the first occasion. When comparing the list of planters who arrived in the early 1670s (Appendix I) with a complete list of inhabitants in the 1709 census, for instance, it is striking to find that with one exception, Orlando Bagley and his family, all of the earliest settlers had left the island again (we know that they stayed on the island for some time since their presence is confirmed by places named after them). The fact that only one planter was still registered as residing or holding possessions on the island in the early 1800s means that the entire (British) founding population had moved on within four decades. The explanation is simple; social inequalities and favouritism practiced by Government representatives were appalling and just short of an official plan to control the white planter population. For instance, the import and possession of slaves was controlled by the EIC and the Governor had exclusive buying rights when slaves were sold on the market. The official explanation given was that large numbers of slaves would endanger the safety of the island:

> Wee have formerly prohibited free planters from bringing any negroes upon this reason viz. least the number of negroes upon the Island exceeding the whites should become formidable and dangerous to the Inhabitants and the security of the Island. (*Letter from Court of Directors*, August 1 1683)

Consequently, most of the settlers in this period were poor; so poor in fact that even when markets became free they did not have the money to buy land. Mass poverty, coupled with the scarcity of fertile and arable land, meant that private property was not on a large scale; the Company's business scheme of cultivating crops and other goods for export existed on paper only. The *Consultations* state that in 1714 "Plantations and pastures private, 3089 acres. The greatest landowners Powell, Carne and Doveton—owning 255—111—and 151 acres respectively." Most families had barely enough ground to be self-sufficient. The situation changed somewhat when the island was recaptured from the Dutch. Both old and new settlers arrived, and Government regulations were adjusted (see above). However, the harsh living conditions and political problems continued. Most planters saved whatever they had so that they could leave the island for good, and some soldiers even gave up their land rights and privileges in exchange for a free passage to England or Surat.

> The good ship *Johannah* is lately returned from Bantum preparing to return to England in some few days, but having lost many of his seamen this voyage and brought several sick to this Island and needing some of the soldiers who have been seamen to supply their roome – ordered – that some soldiers who came hither with Sir Richard Munden about six years since when this Island was recovered out of the hands of the Dutch have leave to shipp themselves and return to England. (*Consultations*; June 16 1679)

There are also cases of planters who left the island secretly, fully conscious that they would lose their entire property by doing so:

> George Hoskison on 6th July 1708 clandestinely left the Island. It was ordered that his Estates seven in number containing 268 acres be forfeited to the Company for breach of the law requiring that two English persons should be

> maintained on every 20 acres for the defence of the Island. (*Council Proceedings*, January 7 1710)

The situation could not continue like this. The EIC realised that an unstable colony had no chances of survival. A reassessment of the political situation was followed by a subsequent implementation of deregulation practices, and this meant that larger numbers of slaves were imported and that these became available to larger sections of the white population. The total number of slave owners increased and an entry in the *Consultations*, dated October 6 1702, states that "The Toll for compensation to the owners shows there were 71 owners of slaves, 111 men slaves and 37 women slaves exclusive of the Company's." Moreover, local governors pursued an at times excessively active settlement policy and enticed practically all newcomers to take residence on the island. This was taken to extremes. Even pirates, captured in the Indian Ocean and shipped to England for trial, were pardoned and allowed to settle on St Helena:

> About 20 Pyrates who had accepted the King's pardon through Commodore Warren arrive in the "*Pink*". Four allowed to remain for a while and hope it will prove some considerable profit to the inhabitants. (*Consultations*, February 13 1699)

Most importantly though, there was a sudden increase in ship traffic. Trade routes changed and trade opportunities opened up, money was to be made with whaling in the South Atlantic Ocean, and thousands of ships frequented St Helena with sailors in search of food, drink, and entertainment. The island was soon nicknamed "the punch bowl of the South Atlantic" and locals could make good money by selling local produce.

Unfortunately, the late 17th and early 18th centuries is one of the darkest periods of St Helenian history, but if we compare estimates from the 1670s with data provided in later censuses (such as the one conducted in 1714), then it is obvious that the population grew considerably, amounting to more than 700 inhabitants in total. In fact, it grew so much that there were even fears of overpopulation (which, in hindsight, turned out to be quite irrational; the island at times housed more than 6,000 inhabitants). For instance, we find the following suggestion in a *Letter to Directors* sent on February 19 1715:

> We hear that the fruitful Island called Mauritius that was lately left by the Dutch is yett uninhabited and has not had any dearth upon it but abounds plentifully … First that we have several young people here more than we can supply with plantations.

However, these plans soon became futile. The local population was ravaged by diseases (imported via slaves from Madagascar). A mysterious epidemic claimed white and black victims alike and the general populace decreased, only to pick up again from the 1750s onwards.

This period is remarkable for another reason: this was the first time that the black population outnumbered the whites. The arrival of more than 100 slaves to start off the New Ground project meant that slaves represented the majority of the (permanent) population from about 1722 onwards, though many fled the island to escape the harsh punishment and living conditions. In 1742, an epidemic ravaged the island, perhaps imported via fleas as "constantly ships were arriving at St Helena from plague-infected ports in India" (Gosse 1938: 181). The consequences were dramatic:

> We have had abundance of mortality in this Island, The inhabitants has been seized with a violent distemper very little inferior to the Plague that hath carried off abundance of them. (*Letter*, April 6 1743)

> The disease chiefly amongst the Company's Slaves. What's worse of all they prove to be our very best working fellows that drop off. (*Council Proceedings*, 1743)

Consequently, the first half of the century witnessed a decrease in the total population. It was only in the 1750s that numbers began to rise again; the slaves' living conditions improved in the advent of emancipation, and this manifested itself in a significant rise in the local black population. This sociodemographic development is particularly important since it was not the result of immigration and/or importation (which, as we saw above, came practically to a halt in that period). Consequently, this was the first time in island history that the local population remained stable and that it reproduced at a steady rate. A *Letter from England*, dated February 29 1792, expresses the Company's Authorities' astonishment that "the Slaves belonging to the Inhabitants had increased while those belonging to the Company had decreased. We commence in 1765 because there has been no importation since that period for the Company and as to the Planters, we understand there has not been above 3 or 4 a year left as domestic servants." The net increase is most evident by the fact that the total amount of children and adolescents in the populace was high. The 1779 census, for instance, indicated that 372 out of 918 blacks (40.5%) and 202 out of 334 whites (60.5%) were children.

Figure 3.1 and Table 3.1 show the sociodemographic development on St Helena from 1665-1817. One has to bear in mind that the situation is not as clear-cut as one would wish. For instance, it is extremely fortunate that the EIC conducted such detailed censuses; on the other hand, it is a great pity that there are periods for which we have no official counts or estimates whatsoever. The 1714-23 and 1765-1815 periods are particularly well recorded (in fact, two censuses were carried out in 1716 alone!). For other periods we rely on selected and less representative estimates (mostly from the StHR) and have to approximate population statistics and general demographic trends from secondary reports (such as diseases, flights or mutinies, etc.).

Figure 3.1 Demographic development of the black and white populations, 1665-1815

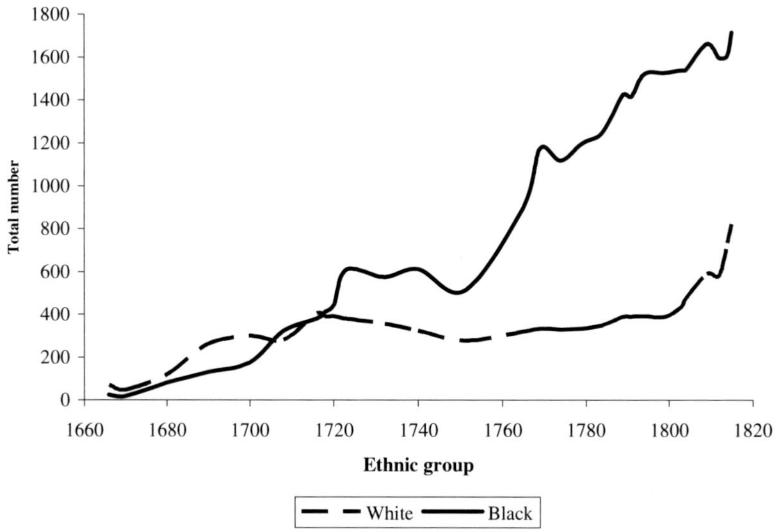

3.3.4 *How did the ethnic groups interact?*

A final question concerns the extent to which blacks and whites interacted on the island. There is no doubt that many of the slaves had very little (if any) command of English, most of them being native speakers of Malagasy. Determining how integrated they were in the local population yields insights into how long they were likely to maintain their native language and how much time it took them to adopt and shift to English. Consequently, then, it is crucial to look into the extent to which the ethnic groups interacted and how accessible English was as a mode of everyday communication in the community.

The situation is far from clear-cut. The social history and sociodemographic development of the community gave rise to a complex interplay of social stratification and racial segregation. For one, there were constant tensions between white settlers and Company representatives. We know from Henry Gargen's report that the white settlers in the mid-1660s were indentured labourers and not freemen. There are numerous references to tensions between working class planters and soldiers and middle-class army personnel or bureaucratic staff. The white population was thus socially stratified from very early on. It is more than likely that the same applied to the black population. From the beginnings of the colony, blacks were allowed to have their own land and to grow their own crops. Some blacks had more extensive rights and possibilities than others. To quote Gargen (1665) again:

> Some of ye beans being greene and moist with all and bruised they began bitter and not fitt to eate: nor to plant butt some of them was planted butt nott any came to any proportion as I see them and them that were planted they were beholding to ye freemen and to the Blacks that hath a small plantation of their owne making

This contrasted with the slaves who were imported to serve as labour for the local population. This caused social tensions and vehement reactions from the planters (particularly when black freemen wanted to buy their own slaves, which by implication meant that they earned money by selling their produce). Consequently, both ethnic groups witnessed social inequalities and differential access to economic opportunities.

To start with the most important question, we need to find out how many of the white planters possessed slaves in the first place, and if they did, how many slaves they had. Slave ownership never was on a large scale; in 1714, for instance, the two wealthiest planters had 17 slaves each. The 1815 census, though conducted a century later, provides excellent data and yields detailed information on the settler-slave ratio, particularly the number of slaves per family. The results of the 1815 census are summarised in Figure 3.2. Slave ownership was small scale: out of a total of 222 settlers, 136 had no slaves at all (61.3 per cent); 56 had between one and ten slaves (25.2 per cent); only 30 (13.5 per cent) are registered as having 11 slaves or more, two planters possessing a total of 35 slaves each. The plantation scenario is thus very different from those that gave rise to creoles in the Caribbean, for two main reasons: 1) the total number of slaves was low by comparison and ownership was concentrated in the hands of a minority of settlers; and 2) slaves were commonly integrated into family life, working alongside their white owners in the fields.

Table 3.1 Sociodemographic development of the St Helena population, 1665-1817

	White				*Black*				*Army*	*Free blacks*	*Company slaves*	*Pop. total*
	Men	Women	Children	Total	Men	Women	Children	Total				
1665	30	13	10	53		17	4	21				74
1666				70				"a few"				70+
1670				48				18				66+
1679								80				
1689												"below 500"
1698	71				92							
1708				180				177				832
1714	67	91	247	405				302				855
1716	55	70	280	405	136	54	117	310				715
1716	58	71	287	416	143	58	126	327				743
1720	58	77	256	391	194	65	168	443		8		842
1723	50	79	251	380	186	67	153	406	120	18	186	1,110
1765					248	154	247	649			284	
1769	53	93	188	334	271	170	280	721		255		
1774	46	87	197	330	284	177	358	819				
1779	41	91	202	334	346	200	372	918		80		
1784	54	96	199	350	377	207	417	1,001		90	134	1,575
1789	56	97	235	388	451	278	496	1,225				
1791					439	230	430	1,099		190	228	
1794	48	102	242	392	439	272	519	1,230				
1799	48	104	236	388	405	268	584	1,257				
1803	73	108	255	436	383	220	524	1,127	892	227	185	2,867
1804	87	121	268	476	386	213	541	1,140		331		
1809	100	153	338	591	386	277	536	1,199		404		
1812	110	152	320	582	337	239	574	1,150				
1815	109	202	383	694	342	245	610	1,197	933	420	98	3,342
1817				821				1,514	2647	500		6,150

(Data adapted and supplemented from http://www.bweaver.nom.sh/beatson/F1#F1, accessed January 6 2006).

Figure 3.2 Total of slaves per St Helenian household in 1815 (n=222)

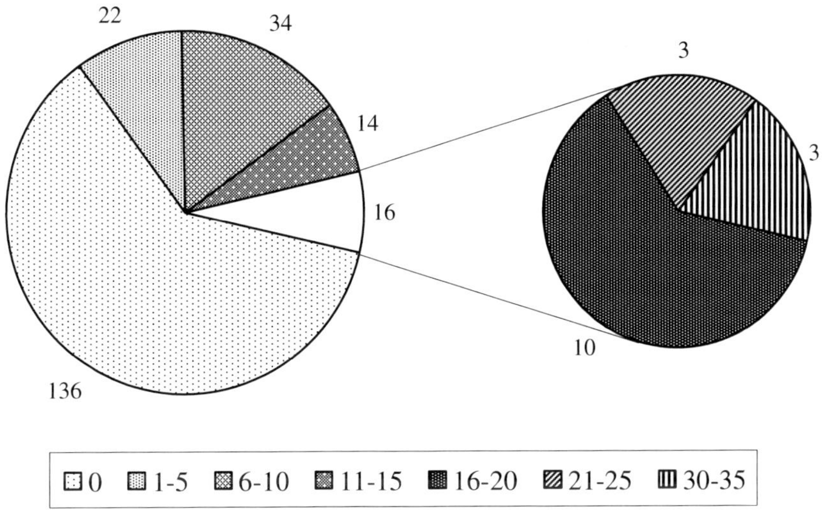

This raises the question as to whether the black population was segregated or not. The rationale is that strict segregation and independent housing, as was common in large plantations in the Caribbean, for instance, would have favoured the maintenance of the slaves' native language(s) and impeded accommodation to - or even L2 acquisition of - the varieties of English spoken by the planters from the British Isles. The evidence available suggests that St Helena cannot be *strictu sensu* compared with scenarios in other British colonies, for four reasons. First of all, there are frequent reports of blacks and whites collaborating in small groups for the benefit of the entire community. Official orders were given (both from the London EIC Authorities and from the local representatives) that white planters and black slaves were to cooperate in the construction and maintenance of roads and cattle paths:

> Provision for repairs of the Highways of the Island for the year 1698. Mr. Thomas Dixon and Mr. William Doveton appointed overseers of Highways for the year – a list given them of the names of all the white inhabitants excepting such as are in the Company's service and of negroes and Blackmen that any persons hath excepting the Company's slaves: – and a Warrant to the Overseers to cause all persons both Whites and Blacks to work one day and no

> more in mending making and repairing of such Highways as seemeth best in your judgment, so as all and every the White Inhabitants and their Blacks do worke at the said highways this present year one day and no more as aforesaid. (*Consultations*, May 16 1698)

Second, the local government did not pursue a policy of housing large numbers of slaves together and was not in favour of isolating them from whites as much as possible.[10] In my research in the archives in Jamestown, St Helena, I found several maps of houses and planter cottages from the 18th and 19th centuries. It was quite striking that only few of the settlers seem to have arranged separate housing facilities for the plantation slaves, perhaps with the exception of a few farmsteads in Sandy Bay. Whites and blacks must have lived under the same roof and maybe even took their meals at the same table. As for house slaves, I have not found reliable sources as to how many there were, but there is ample evidence that they were held in this function from very early on (see above). There is evidence from testimonials (see ch. 4) that slaves in Jamestown had a separate room in their master's house. Governor Johnson, for instance, who died in the 1693 mutiny, was carried away by his wife and two "Negro women" employed in his household, and one of the alleged slave rebellions was betrayed by an Indian house slave named Annah. By the same token, we learn from a *Letter from the Directors* that "We have been informed whilst Mr. Hoskison lived he affected so much pomp that he had always three or four of our blacks to wait upon him" (March 30, 1712). Having said this, there is no doubt that house slaves were held by the more wealthy population and by Company representatives only. Planters were simply too poor to afford the luxury of house slaves, and if they could buy slaves at all, they would have acquired them for labour work in their orchards and plantations, certainly not for housework. Consequently, the function and integration of slaves (and, by implication, their exposure to English) in a way reflected the social stratification within the white community. As for the question of integration vs. segregation, perhaps the most important point, all sources consulted suggest that the slaves were housed with their white owners, and that they lived and worked in close proximity to them. English was thus accessible to the slave population.

Thirdly, the black population on St Helena seems to have been better integrated than elsewhere. A *Letter from London*, dated December 19 1673, thus very early on in settlement history, shows that the children of blacks (at least those who converted) were to be given a school education. Official instructions were given that slave children were to be taught basic reading and writing skills:

---

[10] The following entry from the *StHR* is exceptional: "Capt. Mashborne reports that the hard winds on Sunday night blew down the Old Blacks house in the Country, but neither killed nor hurt any of the Blacks, they running out so soon as it began to crack." (May 29, 1711).

> We have entertained Mr. William Swindle a Minister of the Gospel of whom we have received a very good character to preach once and catechize every Lord's Day and to teach or direct the teaching of children as their Schoolmaster and also as many of the Negro children as are capable of learning … We also order that all Negroes both men and women living in the said Island that shall make profession of the Christian faith and be baptized shall within seven years after be free planters and enjoy the privileges of free planters both of land and cattle.

Evans (1994) found that these plans were implemented and that some slave children did receive schooling indeed, at least until the early 18th century. Blacks were also trained on the job and acquired skills, to the extent that they received work training. This, however, met with resistance from the white planters, as pointed out above:

> Some Blacks we have taught to lay stones, but joynery or carpentery we cannot have them taught, the Europeans will not show them, they talk among themselves that teaching a Black is a hindrance to their trades and that they shall be less depended on if they show the Blacks their art. (*Consultations*, May 8 1717).

Skilled slaves were sought-after and much valued. The case of Grewer, "a stonelayer and a very useful man", discussed above, shows that requests were made for runaway slaves to be pardoned and returned to the island, because they were extremely skilled workers and of value to the Company.

A final point to consider is the amount of exchange of slaves on the island, which seems unusual when compared with other colonial settings. The limitations imposed on slave import were deregulated towards the end of the 17th century. This meant that planters could acquire slaves for their own purposes more freely; many took the opportunity to hire out their blacks to the Company, as this provided a steady and reliable source of income. Slaves were thus frequently interchanged, working for several masters; not only were they collaborating closely with their owners on the farms and plantations up country, but they also worked jointly (and in constantly changing groups) for the Company. A similar practice affected the children of Company slaves, who were not in the workforce and thus of little use to the Authorities. These children were often hired by planters. Indeed, Wright (2004) reported that it was common practice to "let out" Company slaves to planters for limited and contractually fixed periods of time. In January 1711, for instance, there was a public notice on behalf of the Governor and Council of St Helena:

> These are to give Notice to all the Inhabitants that the Governour and Councill design to sett Out the black Children belonging to the Honble Company from Three Years of Age to any that will take them for the Term of seven Years Or till they Attain to the Age of Ten Years, Maintaining them Onely for their

> service, but with this Caution not to Vse them Barbarously or Ill. Wherefore any person that has a minde to take any of the Aforesaid Children may Repair to the plantation house and Conferr with Cap^{tn} Hoskison about the same.

This opportunity was taken up readily and immediately:

> Mr Tovey According to an Order of Council of the 26th July last further Reports that he has taken Account of the Hon: Companys Blacks Lett out to the severall Persons following (vizt) To Doctor Thomlinson a black fellow called Will aged about 18. years, had him for no Certain time Mr French a black Girle called Sarah aged ab^{t} Eleven years, had her for 3 years of which above one is Expired. Doctor Porteous. One wench Named Margarett aged 16 years. had her for no Certain time, but upon his Petition he being sickly, she is to live wth him One year longer. John Bagley one Girle called Ellin aged Ten years. had her for no Certain time. John Robinson a black boy Named Harry aged about Ten years. had him for no Certain time. (MS G/32/5, October 11 1715; both reports from Wright 2004)

Consequently, we find a scenario where pre-adolescent Company slaves were hired by planters in the country and where adult slaves, belonging to the settlers, were frequently employed by the Company. This meant that they worked all over the island but were housed in Jamestown or New Ground, near the authorities' headquarters. The slave population was thus constantly fluctuating; needless to say, this had an impact on face-to-face accommodation and affected the accessibility of English even further.

To sum up the complex situation: the social conditions on St Helena cannot be compared with large-scale multilingual plantation scenarios in places such as Hawai'i, in the Caribbean or elsewhere. The island was too small in size to support thousands of slaves; the various business schemes were unsuccessful and the revenues derived from exportation or direct sales of local goods were low; slave ownership was small by comparison, whites and blacks commonly working side by side (either in the house or in the field) and practically always living in the same building; slaves, though belonging to single owners or to the Company, were in the habit of working for several people, either for community service or when hired by others; there were official instructions that slaves who chose to convert to Christianity should receive a school education; and slave children, of no use to the Company, were very often "let out" to individual planter families until they reached adolescence. The slave population has therefore at all times been comparatively small (numbering no more than 2,000 when slavery was abolished); nevertheless, it represented the majority of the population from the 1720s onwards. It was unstable and fluctuated to a high degree (diseases, poor sanity conditions, escapes, etc.) and, in the early years, constantly transformed via import of new slaves. On the island, the slaves were likely to be mobile, being interchanged or "lett out." Families were broken apart when children were sold or hired out. Consequently, there is ample evidence that the slave populations on St Helena did not live in sociodemographically stable conditions, that they worked in an English-speaking environment, which means that they were likely to develop some rudimentary competence quickly (if they did not have any prior to their arrival on the island, this is). This is extremely significant for the early sociolinguistic evolution of the local variety and discussed in more detail in the next chapter.

Before moving on, though, it must be emphasised that the historical sources provide further clues on the development of the population; comparing documents from various periods yields fairly concise information as to when the ethnic groups began to mingle on a regular basis and by when mixed relationships became commonplace. From the 1730s onwards the *Consultations* make reference to severe punishments of soldiers and freemen who were found guilty of having sexual intercourse with members of the other ethnic group; blacks and whites, planters and soldiers alike were cruelly punished for this felony. There is thus no doubt that efforts were made to segregate the two groups in the early 18th century. However, as we saw above, mixed relationships became more frequent from the 1760s onwards.[11] It cannot be ascertained how many children were born to parents with distinct ethnicities throughout the late 18th and early 19th centuries, but population mixing must have been extensive. The *Consultations*, dated August 26 1824, read:

> The Vestry having recommended a Tax on Free Blacks the Governor points out that they cannot recognise any distinction of Colour in legislation and that *in the case of hundreds of individuals it would not be an easy matter to determine whether they ought to be classed as Whites or Blacks*. The Law recognise three classes only: The Military governed by Articles of War, Slaves by a special Code, and the rest of the Inhabitants who do not come within these two descriptions. (Emphasis added, DS)

Charles Darwin, visiting the island in 1836, commented on the appearance of his local guide as follows:

> My guide was an elderly man, who had been a goatherd when a boy, and knew every step amongst the rocks. He was of a race many times crossed, and although with a dusky skin, he had not the disagreeable expression of a mulatto.[12]

[11] However, the possibility of double standards certainly exists. Whereas there was tight social control in and near the fort and the seat of the Government, i.e., in Jamestown and Plantation House, one can only speculate about the situation in the country. It is certainly possible that, in the absence of authority, population mixing began much earlier there.

[12] Darwin's reports can be accessed online (website accessed March 14 2005: http://www.online-literature.com/darwin/voyage_beagle/21/).

The extent of racial and ethnic mixing progressed and former distinctions soon became blurred, eventually disappearing altogether. Governor Charles Elliot remarked in 1868 that "there can be no position on the face of the earth where it would be more difficult to discriminate between the various strains of blood of which the body of the population is composed than here in St. Helena." In other words, the St Helena population underwent ethnic mixing in the second half of the 18th century; whereas interethnic relationships were forbidden and harshly punished in the 1730s, local administrators found it impossible to distinguish between ethnic groups in the 1860s, considering the St Helenians as one single community with African, Asian and European roots. Consequently, the population changed from a bi-ethnic and by and large separated one to a mixed and fully integrated one within the space of a century and a half, or within six to seven generations. It goes without saying that ethnic mixing would have favoured sociolinguistic mixing also, which supports previously made claims that 1730-1800 was the most instrumental period in the formation of StHE.

3.4 Some first sociolinguistic implications

Historical, social and demographic evidence provide important clues for reconstructing the evolution of StHE. Such information is crucial for assessing the descriptive accounts and quantitative analyses that follow in chs. 4-6, even though it means that the speculations put forward on socio-historical assumptions here may not necessarily be supported by linguistic evidence later on. Consequently, we have to be flexible and continuously weigh social against linguistic evidence and assess their importance for our goal to understand when, how and by whom StHE was formed and why it took the particular developmental trajectory it did.

What are the major insights and main findings from this chapter? Perhaps most importantly, settlement history underwent several phases, not all of which were of equal relevance. The first century and a half following the island's discovery was unimportant; residence was transitory, and those who stayed on were sick or injured seamen waiting for the next ship. Upon colonisation, we have to separate the population into permanent, semi-permanent and non-permanent sections, the former being of course the most influential one for the social and sociolinguistic development of the community. This chapter has shown that the situation did not change much in the early years of the colony, i.e., from the late 1650s onwards. When comparing the first passenger lists and a complete population census carried out in 1714, we find that only one planter family remained on the island for the first forty years. The others stayed for shorter periods of time and attempted to make a living (hence their legacy in island toponymy), but they left by the early 18th century at the very latest. As for the other groups, it is striking that the first 60 years or so were characterised by an exceptionally high population turnover throughout. This had several reasons: high mortality rates, out-migration due to economic uncertainty, rebellions, harsh living conditions and imported diseases, constant escape attempts, etc. The loss of (both black and white) manpower was compensated by bringing in more people, and the Company followed the practice of recruiting settlers from England or elsewhere (i.e., passengers on transit from India) or by granting land and work permits to whoever showed an interest (even pirates!). These conditions persisted well into the 18th century and practically all the white colonists, regardless of whether they were Company representatives, army personnel or planters, fell into the non- or semi-permanent population groups, having little influence. If founders are constantly on the move and replaced (or "swamped") by others, then it is impossible for them to leave a legacy. Table 3.1 evidences this clearly. The population had risen from 48 in 1670 to 405 in 1714 and perhaps more than 100 slaves arrived from Madagascar in 1717 alone; if we take into consideration that many of the island names were not reported before, there is absolutely no doubt that the community was ever-fluctuating and dynamic at that time. Consequently, the early settlement period was characterised by extreme sociodemographic fluctuations and we can rule out sociolinguistic founder effects on St Helena.

When did the situation change, i.e., at what stage did the population stabilise and begin to grow through internal reproduction rather than through (external) import? Immigration slowed down from the 1720s onwards yet the population continued to grow steadily. This must be interpreted as an indication that natural losses were compensated by high birth rates and an increase in total family size. Those most likely to leave the island at that time were male black slaves (as evidenced by the numerous flight attempts reported from the 1730s onwards). This is the period where there are first indications that the locally-born population had begun to outnumber the foreign-born one. In the *Consultations* (dated July 7 1715), for instance, we read:

> If your Honours would please to send English farthings and halfe pence they would certainly doe much better than Pice and have been more agreeable to the English people, for all the St. Helenians account themselves so, though three quarters of them never saw England.

Consequently, the community thrived through local reproduction rather than in-migration, and these conditions would have had an impact on the sociolinguistic landscape on the island, favouring the emergence and adoption of distinctive local norms (ch. 2). It is noteworthy that this trend continued throughout the 18th century, so that the state of permanent flux gradually came to an end as the population (both black and white) gained stability. Consequently, the period from the 1720s-1800 seems to be most important since it saw an increase in the total population and trends toward ethnic mixing and this strongly implies that the 18th century was a crucial period for the development of StHE.

Consequently then, how did the sociolinguistic landscape on St Helena look like in the 17th and 18th centuries and what was the feature pool from which the variety drew its distinctive features? Put differently, what socio-linguistic implications can we draw from the historical observations? There is no doubt that the contact history on St Helena was multifaceted and complex, multidialectal and at the same time multilingual. It is clear that the development of StHE took place in a context that involved both dialect and language contact. To start with the dialect situation: though the scenario is a bit sketchy, everything points to southern (or perhaps even south-eastern) varieties, perhaps with considerable input by settlers from the city of London and its surroundings. However, the sources unfortunately do not reveal their exact whereabouts. It is unlikely that a substantial portion of the British settlers came from outside the English South but we simply do not know whether (and how many) English planters came from adjacent areas (such as East Anglia, the Midlands, Sussex, or even the English Southwest) and we have to wait for the results of the linguistic analysis to clarify this issue further.

The language contact situation is much clearer and we have more specific information here. Up to a dozen different varieties co-existed on the island at various stages: they were brought to the island from Europe (English, Dutch, Portuguese, French; including Dutch-derived Afrikaans), Africa (unspecified, though from the Gold Coast, Nigeria and southern Africa), and Asian (mostly Cantonese, various West-Indian languages), and, if this can be included here, Malagasy. Not all of these varieties were of equal importance. Some groups were numerically small (the slaves from Nigeria, Angola or the Maldives, or the Huguenots from France), whereas others were not integrated into the community to the extent that they could have transmitted their language features to the newly developing variety (here we can include the indentured labourers from Canton, the Boer prisoners or the liberated slaves from West Africa). The latter groups arrived in numbers large enough to swamp the local community; however, their segregation in camps and their short stay on the island thwarted their numerical advantage. Accordingly, we can discard the potential impact of a good number of varieties brought to the island, such as French, Afrikaans, or Cantonese, on account of the fact that speakers of these languages were insignificant in number, that they arrived too late to have an impact, or that they were simply not integrated in the community, leaving at the first occasion.

Consequently, we are now in a position to reconstruct the European, African and Asian background of StHE. Figure 3.3 pinpoints the varieties transported to the island, i.e., it identifies the donors that fed into the feature pool and that were most important (at least on sociodemographic grounds) for the development of a local variety. We see that from the entire set of donors that fit the outlined criteria and that could have had an impact on the ultimate sociolinguistic outcome, i.e., the contemporary form of StHE, two inputs are especially influential: non-standard southern EngE and Malagasy.

Figure 3.3 The feature pool of St Helenian English

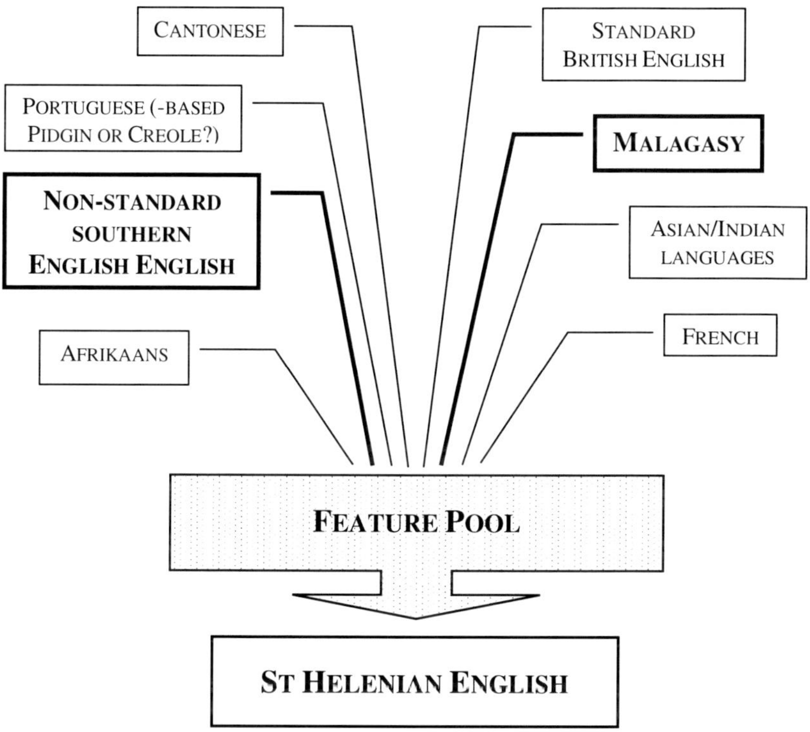

By the same token, it would be simplistic to argue that StHE originated due to mixture (or convergence) of English and Malagasy only. Saying that these were the most influential donors does not necessarily mean that all the other inputs disappeared without a trace. It is more than likely, particularly at a lexical level, that varieties such as Afrikaans, Javanese or Cantonese in some way contributed to the ultimate shape of StHE and the descriptive/quantitative analysis will go some way towards identifying whether this was the case or not. Based on the evidence presented here, however, there can be no doubt that these two donors were most influential; moreover, English was the most important input of them all and Malagasy disappeared in due course, being no longer spoken by the end of the 19th century at the latest. In 1879, the population was fully mixed and English-speaking; whatever linguistic diversity there may have existed on the island at earlier stages had disappeared. This is confirmed by Benjamin Grant, a native and resident of St Helena:

> The Inhabitants, who are of European, Asiatic and African origin, and whose only language is English, are peaceable and kind, and are as independent as their white brethren, with whom they intermarry (Hence the many pretty–coloured girls and boys which are to be met with in one's travels through the island). (Grant 1879: 10–11)

The question, then, is how much (substratal) influence Malagasy had, i.e., how it would have affected the trajectory of English in this setting.

Finally, there must have existed large-scale variation on an individual level. We have every reason to assume that the early inhabitants of St Helena displayed a wide spectrum of linguistic competence. First of all, the local variety was in an early stage of evolution, so that there were no linguistic norms for children and pre-adolescents. Moreover, the amount of social stratification meant that the English population included poor working class labourers with manual jobs, illiterate soldiers, educated transcribers, book keepers and other Company representatives, who served in the local administration and were responsible for all correspondence with other colonies and the London headquarters, and well-trained Governors and other authorities, who were most likely from middle middle or even upper middle class backgrounds. They thus represented all stages on a lectal continuum, ranging from highly basilectal to more or less acrolectal. The same goes for the black population. Some slaves may have had a good command of English very early on whereas others did not speak it at all. We can hypothesise that some of the slaves were fluent in English; Black Oliver, who was instrumental in guiding the English troops on their rescue mission and helped recapture the island from the Dutch, enjoyed full privileges and his family was held in high esteem by the white community. There is some evidence to suggest that many slaves who came before 1715 had a rudimentary knowledge of English. During the time when it was common practice to extract slaves as a human toll fee from passing ships, the Governors on St Helena were instructed to choose individuals who spoke English:

> [E]very Madagascar ship that touched for refreshment, was obliged to leave one Negro, a man or a woman, at the Governor's election, for the service of the Company's plantations … Besides the Negro which every English vessel trading to Madagascar was obliged to leave on the island, each ship paid a duty of two shillings and six pence for every ton of her admeasurement. (Brooke 1808)

We still have to ascertain whether the slaves had learnt English in other colonies or whether they spoke an English-based jargon used on board the ships that brought them to St Helena (i.e., *nautical* or *ship English*; see ch. 2). The fact that English was accessible to all sections of the community and that planters used it as a medium of communication with their slaves legitimises speculations that it was quickly adopted as a *lingua franca* across the island.

This concludes our discussion of the social and sociodemographic conditions of a distinctive variety on St Helena. The basis for the linguistic analysis is thus laid and we can now go on and put the remaining puzzle pieces together, looking into historical and contemporary evidence of StHE. What linguistic evidence is there of the language varieties on the island and how did this socio-ethnic melting pot affect the development of a local variety (or local varieties)? It is with this aim that we turn to an analysis of historical attestations of earlier StHE.

4. Diachrony: Evidence of earlier St Helenian English

This chapter is perhaps the most problematic one of this book, for an obvious reason. Its aim is to collect and evaluate linguistic evidence of earlier StHE and thus to throw light on the evolution and development of the community and its variety (or perhaps: varieties). In the absence of direct speech samples from the first two centuries and a half, we have to refer to insights gained indirectly, i.e., from letters, reports sent by island representatives to the London headquarters of the EIC, verbatim protocols of court cases, short stories or the like, hoping that these can provide us with information on (some of) the characteristic features of earlier StHE. Of course, the material presented here raises a number of analytical problems, since there is no way of assessing whether the sources used are representative and reliable. Consequently, one must be extremely careful and rethink or challenge conclusions and interpretations; as Montgomery, Fuller & DeMarse (1993: 345, quoted in Schneider 2002: 90) remind us, the analysis of historical documents and written samples represent

> potential pitfalls for linguists. Assessing the degree of their vernacularity is a crucial issue that must always be addressed, though it is very often slighted by linguists. Written documents inevitably conceal some, perhaps many, of the speech patterns of their authors and can never be taken at face value as the equivalent of transcripts, especially for phonological purposes.

Space is limited here and I simply cannot go into a detailed discussion of all the problems one faces when analysing written documents (see Montgomery et al. 1993; Campbell 1998, ch. 10; Gordon 1998; or Schneider 2002 for excellent discussions of critical issues in historical linguistic analysis). For the present purpose, it suffices to point out some of the most problematic issues and to assess their relevance *in situ* below. First of all, it is often unclear whether the sources are reliable and trustworthy: who wrote the documents we base our hypotheses on, for what purpose were they produced and how accurate are they? Did reported features really make an appearance in StHE or are they just attributed? (Creole features in ghost stories, for example, may be stylistic devices and purely fictional, or else borrowed from thematically similar sources; see below). To render the situation more complex, in case reports are trustworthy and accurate, there is very often no information as to where the feature in question occurred – in the speech of small groups, across the island community or in single speakers' idiolects only? Plus, we must not forget that written evidence is selective and often anecdotal or stereotypical, and that it hardly ever yields information on the frequency and salience of specific features (making a quantitative analysis impossible, for instance). This means that individual samples are not representative of the population as a whole, nor that they yield information on how widespread the features of interest were in periods for which no sources are available (i.e., 'dark ages' when documents were lost, incomplete or simply non-existent). Finally, most authors remain anonymous and we also lack background information on the individual/s whose speech is documented (in fact, in some cases it is not even known whether they were really natives of the island and familiar with the local variety at all). As a result, any historical interpretation of linguistic features (in our particular case: all that we can infer about earlier StHE) is limited by the amount and nature of documents available to us, and how we decide to weigh and evaluate them. As is often the case, the interpretation of historical sources is open to debate, and it is sad but true that they often raise new questions instead of answering old ones, as one would hope.

Notwithstanding these limitations, researchers have to make every effort they can to locate and consider every shred of evidence that may be of help, and there is simply no other option than collecting what we can and working with what we have. If it is letters, reports, etc. that can put us in a position to retrace and reconstruct the evolution of StHE, then we should try locating them (while of course being aware of – and constantly pointing to – problematic issues about significance and interpretation). My personal view is that it is better working with problem-laden data (and, of course, properly assess the difficulties and making carefully justified claims) rather than opting for the easy way out, i.e., not to make the effort or ignore them.

Consequently, this chapter draws on my personal research in the Castle Archives in Jamestown, St Helena, on features of direct speech (or at least, what I believe to be just that) from a variety of sources, the analysis of letters, newspapers and short stories, etc. They include court cases, short stories, letters by semi-literate writers, official documents from the London archives of the EIC (discussed in Wright 2004), and anecdotal eye-witness reports by travellers, visitors, or office personnel. The sources discussed in this chapter cover the period from the 1670s to the late 20th century, i.e., more than three centuries of island history. The approach adopted is to introduce and discuss the various sources (when were they written, by whom and for what purpose?), then to reproduce the text (in excerpts, if it is a lengthy one) and to point out features of interest. The documents are discussed separately, and I adopted the practice of loosely ordering them chronologically and classifying them by text genre (short stories, newspapers, letters, etc.) wherever possible. A final section summarises and evaluates the major findings, comparing the text types throughout the formation phase of StHE. Chs. 5 and 6 build on and complement the data presented here, providing descriptive and quantitative evidence of early 20th

century StHE, i.e., the result of my own sociolinguistic and ethnographic fieldwork on the island.

4.1 *The St Helena Records (17th and 18th centuries)*

The diachronic investigation begins with the most copious and reliable account of St Helena's social history: the *StHR* (Janisch 1885), referred to and extensively drawn upon in the socio-historical chapter above. The historical information is invaluable, but the document can also be used for the purpose of historical linguistics. Though few and far-between, the *StHR* contain some verbatim reports of direct speech samples. Many of them are of little use for the present purpose, being formulaic, stylistically conservative and/or highly formal. The following passage, for instance, taken from a trial against a Mr Buttler, charged with illegally wedding a couple in December 1685, illustrates this well. We read in the *StHR* that the accused

> was ordered "to give under his hand a catalogue of all the Christennings, Burialls and Mariages by him officiated on the Island since the coming of the said shipp to-morrow morning by nine of the Clock and when so done yt ye said Mr. Buttler shall be presently carried on board of ye said shipp and there remain without coming on shore any more at this place".

The quotation marks (as well as deictic time reference) indicate that this is meant to render spoken language closely (most likely by the judge or foreman of the jury), but the passage, even if it was produced like this, is of little value. The formality of the context, the register-type restrictions as well as common practices in court recording render the "degree of vernacularity" (Montgomery et al. 1993: 345) of such a passage practically nil (it is even possible that the court recorder transcribed the reading aloud of the verdict). Consequently, many passages of the *StHR* abound in formulaic expressions and technical formalities; most of this material is highly stylised or formal and simply non-authentic und of little value for our purpose. Samples such as these are not representative of the dialect(s) spoken on the island in the earliest colonisation phases, even if the scribes intended them to be so. Needless to say, many of the earliest documents (and most of the *StHR*) are marred by these problems.

Occasionally, though, we find specimens that allow us to trace more diagnostic features, particularly when the direct speech of white soldiers and planters is reported. Court cases are particularly important here; the scribes had to render the exact wording because the testimonials were sent with the general reports to the Company's headquarters in London, where punishment and indictment were assessed and approved (or, though this hardly ever occurred, rejected). An additional source of information comes from islanders' letters sent to the UK (some of which were reproduced in the *StHR* as well), either to families or relatives in England or to the EIC directly. Consider for instance the following passages (emphasis added):

> Taylor complains that "Parrum's cow is an *unlawful beast* for she hath bin seen to leap over a wall *above six foot high* and over *a ditch nine foot wide* and *eight foot deep*." (*StHR*; January 21 1687)

> Mr. Coxe late Member of Council accused of employing the Company's blacks on Various and numerous occasions for his own benefit and advantage—also "keeping one Black when ships were in the road continually shooting of Patrages and Ginny hens for presents to commanders and *when shipps was not here* to kill him wild goats which he presented as he pleased and sent nor spent any of them to ye Govr" (*StHR*; April 26 1688)

> I remember *you was some years past very uneasy* wth Mr. Beale (Letter from Josiah Child; *StHR* February 20 1689)

> Complaint against Jonathan Mudge that he whipt Sarah Sinsemig's son while picking green tobacco on the Common. Mudge says yes he did because she and her son used to call to him as loud as they could in a jeering way as he went by her house "Goe home Boy, Goe home Boy, *Red cards is trumps*." (*StHR*; April 19 1697)

> *Mr. Humphrey is come here* and would faine extenuate ye crimes (Letter; *StHR* April 16 1701)

> Edmonds answered what for running away I believe *the Governor and Field is agreed* (*StHR*; September 29, 1702)

> Again last night he came drunk into my private room putting many impertinent questions chiefly why did I not order a guard to wait on him ashoar being a gentleman, when I myself rather than to weaken our guards *I won't use none*, or very seldom (*StHR*; October 27, 1703)

> Anthony the Prisoner of the Bar, Juba and he *eat* some Rice together about Nine of the Clock, that same night, after *they had eat* the Rice, the Prisoner bid them a good Night. (*StHR*; 1762)

With the exception of the last sample, these passages come from documents produced between 1687 and 1703, thus very early on in settlement history. They contain a number of insightful features:

- no plural *–s* with nouns of measurement ("a ditch nine foot wide")
- past *be* levelling with pivot form *was* ("when shipps was not here")
- bare root extension (i.e., usage of infinitives as preterits and past participles: "they had *eat* the Rice",[1] also found in Thomas Goodwin's report of the Jackson Conspiracy: "When they weighed anchor and set sail and *run* two leagues off")
- present tense *be* concord with *is*, particularly with plural NPs and conjoined subjects ("Red cards *is* trumps", "the Governor and Field *is* agreed")
- perfective be ("Mr. Humphrey *is* come here")
- multiple negation ("I wo*n't* use *none*")

The "degree of vernacularity" seems more reliable in these samples and spoken and written language is likely to match more closely here. As for the diagnostic value of these features, however, one cannot help but notice that they are attested in many (if not all) non-standard varieties of BrE. In fact, most of them are so wide-spread that they are not regionally confined (such as no plural with nouns of measurement, or multiple negation, or past *be* regularisation, the latter two representing "vernacular universals" (Chambers 2004), i.e. features that make an appearance in English varieties all over the world). If they are of any value for our search of the original inputs and the successive development of StHE, then the presence of these features is evidence of a working or lower middle class background of the planters and soldiers, which ties in well with the socio-historical information provided above. Only some of these features are regionally distinctive, in the sense that they allow us to trace potential donor varieties. Features here include present *be* regularisation, which is particularly common in the North, or perfective *be*, found in the English South and South-East, which is also in agreement with the hypotheses formulated on sociodemographic principles above.

In any case, whereas we may not gain much information about the regional origins of the settlers, it is noteworthy that the above features, though sporadic, correspond with claims from visitors and travellers, namely that the majority of the white population had a working class background (see ch. 3). These observations are a first linguistic indication that a high percentage of white settlers spoke non-standard varieties.

---

[1] Unless this spelling represents a past participle form after all, as Dave Britain points out to me (p.c. February 9, 2006).

4.2 Court cases and testimonies (17th and 18th centuries)

The next point of interest concerns the slaves; their speech-ways are of particular importance since they formed the biggest group on the island from the 1720s onwards. When attempting to reconstruct the evolution of StHE, it is paramount to find out 1) whether, upon their arrival on St Helena, the slaves spoke (some form of) English and/or other languages (Portuguese, Malagasy, Niger-Congo languages, etc.), and 2) whether (and if so, for how long) other languages were maintained and used alongside English in the non-white community. What was the slaves' proficiency in English when they arrived on the island (proficient or rudimentary, or none at all?) and how quickly did they shift to English? We know for a fact that by the end of the 19th century, languages other than English were no longer used and that the community was entirely Anglophone by then. However, languages other than English may have been spoken for generations (which would have entailed individual bilingualism, which is attested, or even small-scale societal bilingualism). This would have influenced the evolution of StHE, particularly if bilingualism was still common in the crucial 1750-1800 period. Consequently, we need to ask whether there is any evidence of sustained bi- or multilingualism that would have fostered substrate influence, maybe even to the extent that the local variety underwent pidginisation or creolisation.

Direct speech from trials and court cases involving blacks goes some way toward answering these questions. Ch. 3 showed that the late 1680s saw continuous uprisings and revolts (which persisted until the mid-18th century). Slaves were accused of plotting conspiracies against whites on numerous occasions, and they also had to defend themselves in court against charges of robbery, rape, murder or witchcraft. All slaves accused had to face trial on St Helena. The court cases were transcribed verbatim and sent to the EIC in London. Importantly, the exact wording of judges and plaintiffs had to be recorded as closely as possible, so that the London authorities could follow the proceedings and confirm the verdicts. Consequently, these documents are particularly inclined to report the slaves' speech directly.

One of the first references dates from November 3 1679. A white planter by the name of John Boston claimed that one of his slaves, Sattoe, had physically attacked and attempted to kill him. The *StHR* state that

> Sattoe being examined confesseth that upon his said master beating him and threatening to do it a second time he took his knife and wounded him in the arm and legge. That he received the knife from Rowland Mr. Swallows Black about ten days before who said *when your master beat or strike you then doe you beat him again and kill with this knife* (emphasis added).

The emphasised passage is a report of spoken speech; though short, it contains several linguistic features of interest:

- 3rd person singular present tense zero (“your master beatØ or strikeØ you”)
- periphrastic or emphatic *do* (“then *doe* you beat him”)
- PRO drop (“you beat him again and kill Ø with this knife”)

We need to cross-check whether these features make an appearance elsewhere, of course, but this short excerpt shows that even a small sample can yield qualitative insights to be used as a piece of the puzzle for our research task (but which, needless to say, can only be interpreted with confidence once we find that this feature makes an appearance in unrelated sources as well). More importantly, we gain another type of insight into the local sociolinguistic scenario. It is striking that Sattoe defended himself in English, and he was by far not the only one to do so. In fact, all the slaves who appeared in court in the 17th century were judged to be proficient in English so that they could face trial and answer the Governor’s examination and/or the jury’s questions. Moreover, it seems that the administrators and magistrates of the island implicitly assumed that the slaves would use English to plot the rebellions, which allows no other interpretation than that it was commonly recognised that English served as a *lingua franca* in a multilingual environment from very early on.

The only exception I could find is the case of Hary, accused of conspiring in the 1695 uprising. When defending himself in court, Hary claimed that he was innocent and wrongly accused, simply because his English was not good enough to partake in the planning of a rebellion, and that he spoke a rudimentary form of English only (which is supported by the fact that the court recorder often refers to indirect speech). The *StHR* read as follows:

> Hary Madam Johnsons slave Examined saith: y^{t} ab^{t} a month agoe: Hemp cam<> To him in the plantation as he was at worke: and told him y^{t} Powells Jack sent him to aske him: if he wold make one to help to kill the white people to which he rep<> *how can y^{t} be done: wheare must I then live: noe not I wont make one*: then said to him *what is the matter Jack sent to me: me noe save speake English*. (*Consultations*; MS G/32/2, December 1695; from Wright 2004; emphasis added)

The strategy was ultimately successful. The Governor believed that Hary’s English was not proficient enough and found him not guilty (in contrast to the other slaves, who were punished with utmost cruelty). Consequently, we may interpret this as evidence that at least some of the slaves spoke a type of jargon, which allowed for rudimentary interaction only. However, Hary’s case is exceptional. Leaving aside for a moment whether their words are rendered accurately or not, and what liberties the court recorders took in their transcriptions, we can safely assume that the first generations of slaves on St Helena had at least some command of English.

Following the putative slave revolt in 1695, more than a dozen male slaves were charged with conspiracy and high treason. Rumours of alleged plots gave the Company representatives and local authorities reason for concern (evidenced by the fact that import and sale of slaves was strictly regulated in the 1780s). Several male slaves appeared in court, where they were charged with plotting to murder white planters and to escape from the island. Their examinations are recorded in full detail, luckily by a transcriber who took great care to report the trial as accurately as possible.[2] Here are the reports of two slaves named Hemp and Jack:

> Hemp Examined saith that he never was made aquainted wth the s^{d} designe untill last Fryday nor never spoake to madam Johnsons Hary for saith he *though Jack and I live together he wold not trust me*: *for I allwayse tell talles of him to my Master: and Jack noe such foole to trust such a boy as I* … Jack speaking to hemp saide *you saucy Rouge: how can you denye before the Gove^{rs} that you noe savy this thing before last fryday: I noe tell you a great while agoe: and sent you to hary: and you told me Hary said he wold goe wth all his hart.* (*St Helena Consultations*; MS G/32/2; December 2 1695; from Wright 2004: 3; emphasis added)

Just as above, this document leaves no doubt that the language officially used in court was English. The sample contains features indicative of language contact and pidginisation (see below); nevertheless, the impression is given that the two slaves appear had a sufficient command of English.

It is of relevance that the slaves in all these examples were plantation slaves, who would presumably have had a more restricted access to English. House slaves, as discussed in ch. 2, were more involved with the white community and thus more firmly embedded in an English-speaking environment. The following passage contains verbatim reports of Hannah, a house slave (apparently of Indian origin), who reports her conversation with Will, a male slave, as follows:

> Hannah a slave of Mr Thos Goodwins: Examined saith: that Beivans Will told her last thursday night: that he wod doe something: said shee *What will you doe Oh* said Will *you will see by an by*: soe she urged and prayed him to tell her: … that he with gargens: alias Jo^{n} Gurlings Jack: firebrass and severall others: … wold kill all the white people on this Island upon which she Replyed y^{t} she thougt the whites weare to strong: for ye Blackes: Oh saide Will *wee will venter y^{t}: for we will kill them at night* (*Consultations*, MS G/32/2, Monday 2 December 1695; from Wright 2004; emphasis added)

[2] The following four samples are taken from Wright (2004).

Unfortunately, most of this testimony is rendered indirectly. It is clear that slaves were communicating in English, which again backs speculations that it served as a *lingua franca* for slaves from different places of origin (Africa, Asia, Madagascar) and would have ensured the strong position of English as a superstrate and catalysed language shift. What is noteworthy here is that the direct samples from slave speech contain two future markers: *will* ("wee will venter y^{t}: for we will kill them at night") and *by and by* ("you will see by and by"). The coexistence of distinct patterns is perhaps indicative of an early pre-focussed stage of StHE, which may have witnessed mixing and coexistence of various systems.

The next passage is linguistically informative as well. Three slaves, Garret, Will and Fortune, were accused of being responsible for the preparation of the 1695 rebellion:

> Garret a slave of Elizth Gurling who dwelles at Mr Goodwins: Examined saith That ye 28th of 9ber last past Fortune a slaue of Sam^{ll} Taylers: and will A slave of Owen Beivans weare a tallking to gether: and in theare discourse the Laughed: soe the s^{d} Garrett saide to them: *whats you laugh at: cannot you tell me: no* replyed will *you are a Rogue: you haue no good hart and I cannot trust you*: soe Garrett asked ye s^{d} fortune: *what twas thatt will had told him: well* said Fortune *Ile tell you to Morrow:* who accordingly did: Will being then in company though seemingly dubious: of him: this *night if youle be a good boy and not tell noe body Ile tell you:* soe Told him that they wold kill all the white people: and asked him if he cold deale wth his M^{r}: yeas sayd Garrett *I can deale wth him well enough: well* saide will *and Ile deale wth My M^{r} and M^{rs} well enough:* but said he to Garr<> *If you think you cannot deale wth yor M^{r} you shall haue some body to help you:* and saith will *after wee haue don that: wee will goe to Lemmon Valley: kill the two sold^{rs} thear:* and take what amuniton and gunns They cold find thear: And soe become Masters of this Island: and y^{t} Beivans Black will was to be Gouern^{r}: and Jacob a slave that run away from Capt Nynns shipp: and now by his order dwells wth Mad- Johnson and Gargens Jack weare to be two of the head: and that he shold find hand enough to assist them: and named 2 slaves of Thos Allissons: and one of Mad^{m} Johnsons & one of Boxes: and y^{t} Fryday ye 29th of 9^{ber} was ye day the designe was to be executed: and y^{t} Gargens house and Madam Johnsons: weare to be theare Randezvouse: all which he told to hannah A slave of ye a afores^{d} Thos Goodwin: In order that shee might Make her Mistres aquainted wth it: the which she did In his presence (*St Helena Consultations*, MS G/32/2, Monday 2 December 1695; from Wright 2004; emphasis added)

First of all, this passage may provide us with insights into the court recorder's own speech, as he uses the following features in his writing:

- *a*-prefixing ("weare *a* tallking to gether")
- bare root extension ("Jacob a slave that *run* away from Capt Nynns ship")
- absence of plural marking ("he shold find handØ enough to assist them")

Figure 4.2 Facsimile excerpt from the court records of the 1690 trial against John Oliver

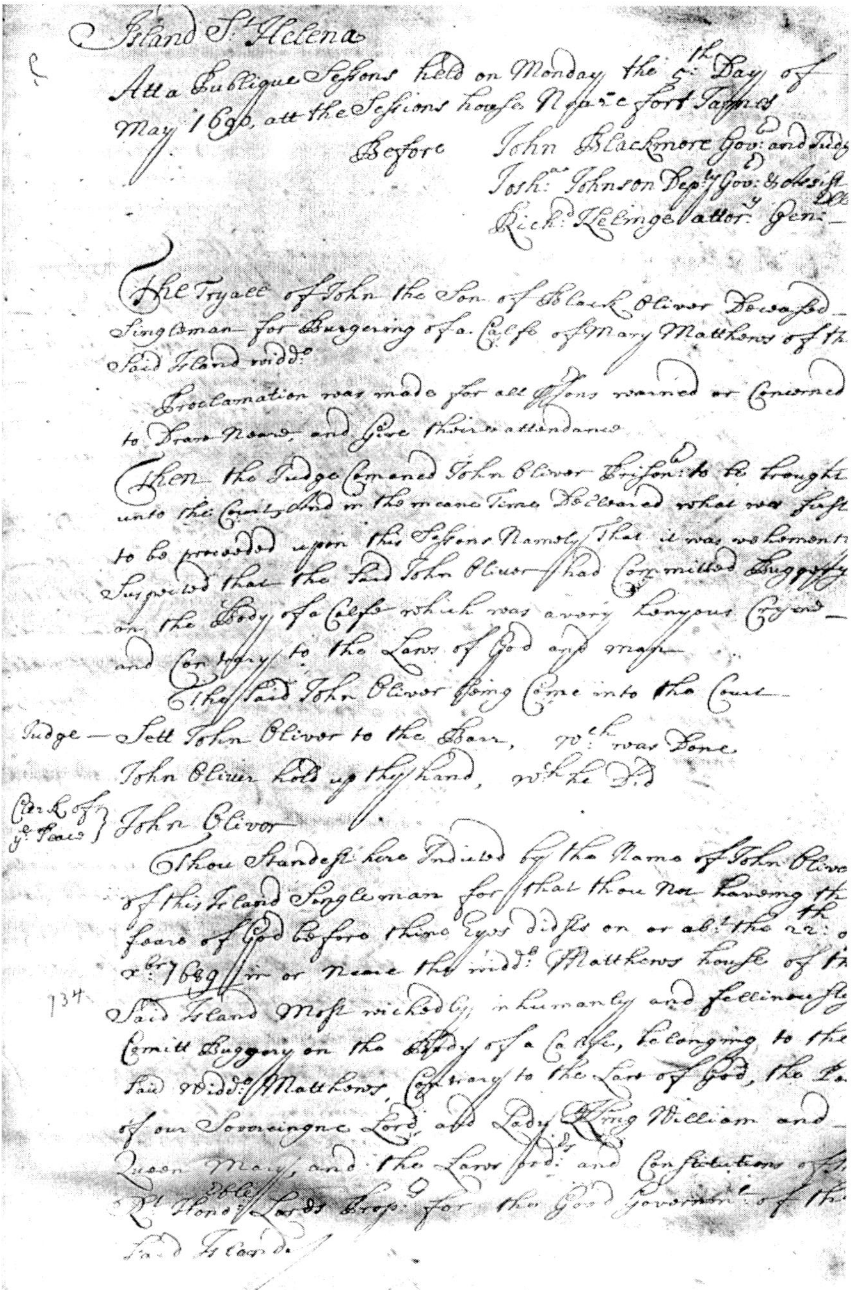

Island St Helena

Att a Publique Sessions held on Monday the 5th Day of May 1690, att the Sessions house Neare fort James

Before John Blackmore Gov: and Judge
Josh: Johnson Depty Gov: & Assist.
Richd: Kelinge Attor: Gen:

The Tryall of John the Son of Black Oliver Deceased Singleman for Buggering of a Calfe of Mary Matthews of the Said Island widd:

Proclamation was made for all persons warned or Concerned to Draw Neare, and Give their attendance

Then the Judge Comanded John Oliver Prison: to be brought unto the Court, and in the meane Time Declared what was first to be proceeded upon this Sessions Namely That it was vehemently Suspected that the said John Oliver had Committed Buggery on the Body of a Calfe which was a very heynous Crime and Contrary to the Laws of God and man

The said John Oliver being Come into the Court

Judge — Sett John Oliver to the Barr, wch was Done

John Oliver hold up thy hand, wch he did

Clerk of ye Peace } John Oliver

Thou Standest here Indicted by the Name of John Oliver of this Island Singleman for that thou not having the feare of God before thine eyes didst on or abt the 22th of 8br 1689 in or neare the widd: Matthews house of the

134 Said Island Most wickedly inhumanly and felloniously Comitt Buggery on the Body of a Calfe, belonging to the Said widd: Matthews, Contrary to the Law of God, the La[w] of our Soveraigne Lord and Lady King William and Queen Mary, and the Laws ord: and Constitutions of the Rt Honoble Lords Prop: for the Good Governmt of the said Island.

Of special interest here, however, is the slaves' direct speech. All three of them spoke English proficiently. For instance, futurity is expressed by the combination of will (sometimes contracted with the pronoun) and a main verb ("Ile tell you to Morrow", "wee will goe to Lemmon Valley"); even modals are reported: "you shall haue some body". Garret is also reported as using a perfect ("after wee haue don that") and a past perfect construction ("what twas thatt will had told him"), which does not seem indicative of a simplified or restructured TMA system at all (see below).

To complicate matters further still, some members of the black community seem to have spoken English excellently. This is borne out by the transcripts of a trial involving John, one of Black Oliver's sons (the first black freeman on the island; ch. 3). The background is the following: In May 1690, two white planters accused John of homosexuality and brought him to court. He eloquently denied all the charges brought against him and pledged innocence, claiming that this was a deliberate plot to extract money from him and to hurt his integrity and status in the community. John had to stand trial before a jury and was interrogated by Governor John Blackmore, the acting judge. The court case was fully documented and the records are now stored in the Castle archives in Jamestown (an excerpt is reprinted in Figure 4.1). Following the practice of jurisdiction, John was not allowed to have a lawyer or legal counsel and had to defend himself alone without legal advice. A passage from the transcripts (reprinted in Figure 4.2) contains one of several exchanges between the judge and John ("The Prisoner"), transcribed as follows:

Figure 4.2 Facsimile excerpt from John Oliver's statement

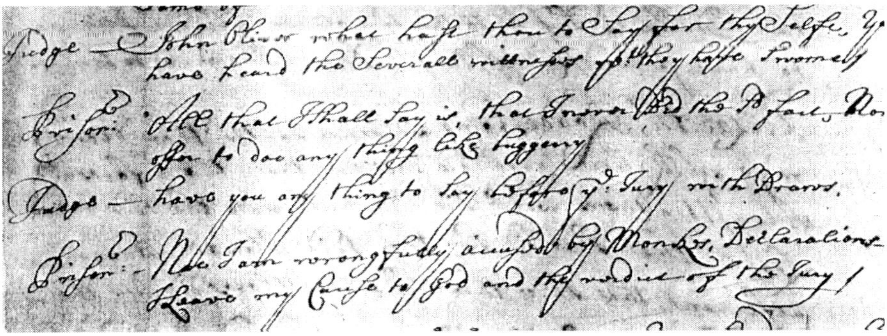

Judge: John Oliver what hast thou to Say for thyselfe you have heard the several witnesses and (?) they have sworne

Prisoner: All that I shall say is that I never did the said fact, nor offer to do anything like buggary

Judge: Have you one thing to say before the jury withdraws

Prisoner: No I am wrongfully accused by Monks declarations. I leave my cause to God and the verdict of the jury

The authenticity of this document is strengthened by the fact that others are recorded also, most importantly the plaintiffs Monk and Matthews, both of whom are white. The court recorder rendered their speech using non-standard features (e.g., past *be* regularisation to *was*). The verbatim transcripts suggest that John is more eloquent and versed in legal terms than those who accuse him. Moreover, they imply that John's command of English was more acrolectal than that of the two white planters interrogated. This contrasts sharply with other reports of slaves' speech discussed and is a first indication of sociolinguistic diversity within the black community.

Consequently, we can make two important assumptions about the function and early development of English on St Helena:

1) In the period from the 1660s till about 1720, there is not a single report of slaves who did not speak English. Only one slave self-reported that he spoke little or rudimentary English, which may be indicative of a jargon or pidgin. Notwithstanding, it is paramount to stress that *all* the slaves who appeared in court defended themselves in English.
2) We have every reason to assume that the black population, just as the white one, was linguistically heterogeneous. Some of the first generations of blacks on the island (here: members of Black Oliver's family) were highly proficient in English.

Consequently, then, it is misguided to consider the black community as linguistically homogeneous. Quite the contrary, the slaves' language backgrounds and repertoires must have been diverse, taking all positions on the lectal continuum and thus certainly equalling the sociolinguistic situation that manifested itself in the white community.

What about the maintenance of languages other than English? Again, we have evidence that the slave population was multilingual and that languages other than English survived for quite some time, most notably Portuguese (or Portuguese Creole), Indian and African languages, and also Malagasy. Ch. 3 discussed the case of Cupidore, who was bilingual in Malagasy and English and who was employed as an interpreter on slave ships. Documents from around 1700 indicate that other languages were used by the slave community as well. Records of the putative 1705/6 uprising indicate that some of the blacks spoke Portuguese (or a Portuguese-based Creole):

> Caesar Henry Francis black says he was at M^{r} We<>leys, where Mingo said in Portugeeze he would break open the Powder Room … Caesar says Tobey told

> him so, Tobey says he Never di<> and that Caesar and Mingo talkt Portugeeze about half an hour Together … In the Kitchin, at .9. at Night a Monday she says that .3. blacks Viz^{ll} Clause, Phill, and Tobey, went out and talk'd portugeeze together (*St Helena Consultations*, MS G/32/3, January 1706; from Wright 2004).

The following passage indicates that other languages were spoken as well (though, unfortunately, the term "country langua" is unspecified here):

> Sarrah Gurling a seruant of Mr Thos Goodwin: saith that ab^{t} a day or 2 before this designe was discouered: Jo^{n} Gurlings Jack: Bivans: Will: and Roger Mr Thos Goodwins slave: weare tallking together In there one country langua Laughing and pointing severall wayse: ye s^{d} Sarrah saide unto a slave of ye Afores^{d} Goodwins y^{t} was an Indian black: *I doe not understand what they say: nor I* saide the other: *no* s^{d} Gurlings Jack *dont you understand us: Noe* replyed they *Then y^{t} Is very good* said he (*St Helena Consultations*; MS G/32/2, December 12 1695; from Wright 2004; emphasis added)

I find it hard to interpret this. One might speculate that this was not Portuguese, since that language was known in the community and could have been identified quickly. It quite certainly is not an Indian language (otherwise it would have been identified by Goodwins' "Indian black"). Were they perhaps speaking an African language? We do not know and have no means of fidning out. In any case, it is noteworthy that Jack addresses Sarah Gurling in English, that he is bilingual and that he used a language other than English deliberately with his companions so that bystanders and eaves-droppers could not overhear them – which made the bilingual slaves highly suspicious, of course; English, it seems, provided the vehicle of communication for slaves with different linguistic backgrounds. Slaves reported that they could not understand Portuguese, communicating in English instead.

To conclude, the transcripts cited here contain several reports of slave speech. We simply do not know whether the court recorders documented the slaves' testimonies faithfully or not, but it is striking that they contain several features commonly found in pidgins or creoles, such as:

- negator *no* ("Jack noe such foole to trust", "me noe save speake English")
- serial verbs (*know tell*, "I noe tell you a great while agoe")
- article absence ("you haue Ø no good hart")
- copula absence ("Jack Ø noe such foole")
- multiple negation ("noe not I wont make one", "and not tell noe body")
- *sassy* adj. ("you saucy Rouge")
- *no good* adj. 'bad' ("you haue no good hart")
- *save/savvy* v. 'know' ("me noe save speake English", "you noe savy this thing before last fryday")

To sum up the major findings concerning the slaves' inputs until the mid-18th century: the population was multilingual (we know that Portuguese and Malagasy were spoken, along with Indian and perhaps also West African languages). Moreover, there was language diversity within the early black population, which was almost certainly the consequence of social status and function in the community: black freemen (such as Black Oliver and his family), plantation and house slaves.

4.3 Newspapers (19th century)

We now move on to the 19th century and another source of information: local newspapers and gazettes. The 1850s saw a rise in local newspapers and these can give us quite a few insights into the local speech patterns as well. Short stories, jokes, articles and letters to the editor are particularly promising in this context. However, what was said above applies here as well: we have to take great care when interpreting these documents. It would be misleading to assume that they represent 19th StHE at face value. For one, we do not know how adequately direct speech is rendered, if at all. The authors of short stories may overuse local features and stereotype them (which often happens for humorous purposes), or they may not use local features or may reproduce speech patterns they came across elsewhere.

In my research in the Castle archives in Jamestown, I came across two letters written in a highly local and non-standard style, featuring an abundance of interesting features. Both letters appeared in *The Advocate, or St Helena Weekly News*, in No 2 and 3 of Volume 1, published on May 15 and 22 1851. The motivation for this exchange is unclear; the first letter could have been a serious concern by a semiliterate Saint (who describes himself as somebody "vot aint ad no heddykashen" and prefers to remain anonymous, signing the letter "A OULD YAMSTOCK"), whereas the second one could be William Jinkens' irate reply. Authorship could not be verified in both cases. It is not clear whether a man by that name resided on St Helena: neither was there a reference to him in any of the sources I consulted, nor is a Jinkens (or Jenkins?) family mentioned in the 1815 census (the *StHR* mention Governor Robert Jenkins in the 1740s, but, having lived a century earlier, he cannot have been the addressee of the first letter). Perhaps it was a visiting Englishman or a local low-rank administrator? We will never know. Alternatively, and perhaps ultimately the most plausible explanation for me, the two documents are made-up mock letters, produced for humorous purposes and general amusement (e.g. to attract readership for a newly established newspaper). What is clear is that the two letters abound in non-standard features; if these are in any way representative of 19th century StHE, then they provide a veritable treasure chest for our present purpose (regardless of questions relating to authorship and authenticity).

Consequently, they are reproduced in full here (from *The Advocate, Or St. Helena Weekly News*, May 15 1851):

> Mr. HEDDITOR, I is but a ould Yamstok, but Bil Jinkens wot is a Hinglishman sais, as ou u is the proprest wun to rite to bout evree ting ; and Bill noes a kow's tale from a jak-ass as well as any man vot hever I seed; and ven he fus cum'd to de hiland Bill knowed a yam from a tater drekly – by instink as he kalls hit. So I takes Bills adwice, and if so be has I his rong, u musint be hangry. Vot I wants to no is the rites of dis ere ; vy. they maks us pore fellers pa for everee ting as day dus. – If ve vonts to go a fishen it ar 30 shillens for a bote licens everee yare, an' 3 poun for a passeg bote, an one poun for everee tun if it ar a luggedge bote–wich don't luke rite an jonnak; cos ve mus git as vell as udder fokes vot is gut mor munny den ve is. An nou day maks us pa werry hi for de vine vot ve drinks by risin de dooty, an it vornt so werry little afore needer. Nou do it be werry fine for em to sa as ou day vonts us not to drink, stil it don't luke natril like not to drink nuthin. Bil sais as ou in Hinglend day drinks a mortel lot o' beare, but ere ve aint a gut nothinels nor vine nor sperrets; an taint as ou I kares bout it meself, cos I only drink sperrets, an day aint bin rising de dooty on dat, doe it be deer enuff areddy. But mi ould oomin do like a drop o' vine for dinner, and I likes to av a drop for a fren cos sperrets is werry deer to giv awai. Nou I aint a goin to sa nuthin for dem fellers vot drinks so 'ard, an gits so beestlee toksikated, but doe I sa it myself I is a onnest man vot tries to git a onnest liven, and don't oe no vun nuthin as I noes on, an I never gets toksikated, but I dus like a little sperret sumtimes. It's all werry vell for the grate fokes to tauk so much bout it, but I'd like to no iff that aint so good nor all thare borls and partees and fine close, and nor all thare moonshine. And asides vot kan a pore feller be spected to do vot aint ad no heddykashen, ven them as as, arnt no better as I sees. But I fansies if day tink as on the hi prose vill keep fokes from drinkin day arnt a acten jonnak, cos day only vonts the munny, an nuthin' moor; els we wudnt day giv us a little moor larnin den day dus. now it aint so much mat–er [sic] to me, cos as I sed afor I drinks sperrets, an my ould oomin' arnt in luv bout the "Coleysun," but I dus pittee them as has too grate a hinclynashon for it; cos dem is the fokes vot vil du it at no prise, an' dem vot as got a ould oomin vot drinks is ard put to it, cos taint no use a lokking the kubbord–the wimmen is so wishus ven day taks it into thare heds, and is so kunnin day can put a spel on it, an git it enny way day liks, an den de moor vot day as to pa the wuss it be for de ould man an de children vot as to be fed, an git coles asides. So I opes as ou u vil se de rites of dis ere kase, an du sum gude for us as too pa so mutch.
>
> I is, Mr. Hedditor, Yours specfully, A OULD YAMSTOK
>
> P.S. –I rites agin to sa as ou Bil as bin an seed vot I as rote; an Bil sais ar rite bout the wimmin speshaly, cos day is like hosses, witch ven day is hosses u ken du as u likes long em ; but ven day is mairs or fillees u never noes ven day

is a goin' to kik, an day isn't to be trusted no ou votsumever, vitch is I tink werry clever of Bil a-sa-ing.

This passage contains numerous phonological and morphosyntactic features of interest, which are listed here separately and exemplified with specimens from the text. To start with phonology:

- hypercorrect /h/ ("Bil Jinkens wot is a Hinglishman", "u musint be hangry ", "has too grate a hinclynashon")
- /h/ dropping ("dem fellers vot drinks so 'ard", "So I opes ou u vil se de rites of dis ere kase")
- /v~w/ interchange, both towards /w/ ("I takes Bills adwice") and /v/ ("a drop o' vine for dinner"), sometimes in both directions and in the same sentence ("the wimmen is so wishus ven day taks it into thare heds", "nou day maks us pa werry hi for de vine vot ve drinks")
- consonant cluster reduction ("ven he fus cum'd", "a drop for a fren")
- jod dropping ("by risin de dooty")
- TH stopping ("vitch is I tink werry clever", "the rites of dis ere")
- alveolar /n/ for *–ing* ("to git a onnest liven", "keep fokes from drinkin", "giv us a little moor larnin den day dus")
- HAPPY tensing ("pa for everee ting", "I dus pittee them")
- STRUT for NURSE ("ven he fus cum'd", "de moor vot day as to pa the wuss it be for de ould man")
- KIT rather than DRESS ("an git it enny way day liks", "I rites agin")
- clipping of unstressed initial syllables ("from a Øtater", "vot kan a pore feller be Øspected to do", "Yours Øspecfully")
- monophthongal /iː/ in *neither* ("so werry little afore needer")

The list of morphosyntactic features is equally extensive:

- present tense *be* concord with pivot form *is* ("I is but a ould Yamstok", "the wimmen is so wishus")
- present tense *be* concord with pivot form *are* ("it ar 30 shillens for a bote licens")
- *weren't* levelling with negative past tense *be* ("it vornt so werry little afore needer")
- *aren't* levelling with negative present tense *be* ("my ould oomin' arnt in luv")
- present tense *–s* agreement with all persons ("vy. they maks us pore fellers pa for everee ting as day dus", "fellers vot drinks so 'ard, an gits so beestlee toksikated")

- *–ed* affixation with strong verbs for past tense ("any man vot hever I seed", "Bill knowed a yam from a tater drekly", "he fus cum'd to de hiland")
- multiple negation ("don't oe no vun nuthin", "like not to drink nuthin", "vot aint ad no heddykashen")
- *a*-prefixing with progressives ("If ve vonts to go a fishen", "taint no use a lokking the kubbord", "I aint a goin to sa nuthin for dem fellers")
- 3rd person singular present tense zero ("wich doØn't luke rite")
- *be got* for possessive *have* ("fokes vot is gut mor munny")
- negator *ain't* ("day aint bin rising de dooty on dat")
- demonstrative *them* ("to sa nuthin for dem fellers")
- relative marker *what* ("dem is the fokes vot vil du it", "dem fellers vot drinks so 'ard")
- pre-predicate *do* ("gits so beestlee toksikated, but doe I sa it myself I is a onnest man", "day aint bin rising de dooty on dat, doe it be deer enuff areddy")
- existential *it* ("cos taint no use")
- invariant *be* ("de moor vot day as to pa the wuss it be for de ould man")

A sequel (or Mr Jinkens' alleged reply, depending on how we interpret this exchange) followed in the next issue of the newspaper, just one week later (*The Advocate, or St. Helena Weekly News*, May 22 1851):

> Mr. HEDITOR : I once knowed a werry respectable indiwidual, as I alvays thought, but I decline now in considerashiun of the feelins that once gloed in my buzum, to diwulge that ere indiwidual's name. Wen a man so forgets himselfe as to hold up a gentilmin to the public hie, in such a course and vulgar vay, and to translate the sentimens and hidears vot has passed tveen him and that gentilmin, I obeys the feelins of my art, and cuts that man without no manner of ezitashiun wotsomever. Not as I am ashamed of the name of W. Jinkens ; it is none vot has never bin in a court yet, and vot never will be, with the consent of its owner ; but ven I wos unfoldin of my sentimens and my hidears to a hunsofistikated spooney. I little thought as they vould be diwulged to the hies of the vorld, and my name so vulgarly set up by a feller, for he is nothing else, a callin his-self by the werry helegant happilashun of "a ould yamstok." What I has said to that man in the priwate conwiviality of soshal hintercourse, I never could have hexpected to be asseminated as he has done ; for a man what has had a movin art, and has unfolded his-self for the hinformashiun of such a feller to have the trouble to be obliged for to come torrard in a public paper, is aggrawaitn, rather ; but I feels it is my due to let the vorld know that I ain't to be looked on no longer as the fren of that ere feller. I has told my opinions freely, and I aint ashamed of them now, now that these ere Ilanders aint like us in Hingland ; and that the poor has to bare a grate expense of taxes, and don't git no hedikashun nor anything else for what they pays, all vich is werry clearly contrary to every principal of our glorious Constitushun, and tha Magny carter ; but they takes it all quite cool, and

> doesnt seem to mind in vay votsomever, only gremlin on ard times, and vishing the ould times vas back agin ; though I thinks by thare own showin thay vas no times for a hindependent Briton to hold up his hed and for any man vot aint like a dog, or vat has got in his nob a hidear more than eatin or drinkin. As for his sayin in that I vas the orther of that ere corse and wulgar joke about the wimmin, it is a downright lie. I am awerse to let my feelins git the better of vat is due to myselfe as a gentilmin, but ven it is insivated that W. Jinkens vat has had a esq. tacked to his name afore today; and vat vas looked on as a real nobby cove in Lunnun, and a dewoted servant to the ladies, could make so coarse and unproper a joke, vy, I agin hasserts, that it is a lie, a villfil lie, and is reddy to giv him the satisfacshun of a gnetilin venhever he vants his luvly and hinteresting phisog warigated with a pare of black hies.
>
> I am. &c. William Jinkens

This letter has fewer dialect features than the first one, mostly phonological ones, which is interesting, and it seems to be stylistically different as well (sentences are generally longer and more complex), which suggests that it was written by a different author (most likely from England, since he says that "these ere Ilanders aint like us in Hingland"). Prominent features in this text include:

- /h/ insertion ("for a hindependent Briton", "the public hie")
- /h/ dropping ("no manner of ezitashiun", "only gremlin on ard times")
- /v-w/ interchange, bidirectional ("a werry respectable indiwidual", "such a course and vulgar vay"), /w/ being much more frequent
- alveolar /n/ for *–ing* ("the feelins")
- consonant cluster reduction ("as the fren of that")
- KIT for DRESS ("my feelins git the better")
- relative marker *what* ("sentimens and hidears vot has passed")
- present tense *-s* agreement with pronouns ("I obeys the feelins of my art, and cuts that man", "they takes it all quite cool")
- negator *ain't* ("I ain't to be looked on", "and I aint ashamed")
- *a*-prefixing with progressives ("by a feller, for he is nothing else, a callin his-self by the werry helegant happilashun")
- *–ed* affixation with strong verbs for past tense ("I once knowed")
- multiple negation ("is none vot has never bin in a court yet")

All of these occur in the letter written by the "ould Yamstok" as well, which is interesting *if* the two letters were indeed written by two different people. The question we need to address here (as everywhere in socio-historical linguistics) is how representative these samples are. If the author(s?) had a Dickensian talent for picking up local features and using them for all sorts of literary purposes, then the two letters to the "Mr Heditor" are a real treasure chest, giving us plenty of evidence on the phonology and morphosyntax of 19th century StHE. If these are made-up mock letters, however, written for the amusement of well-educated newspaper readers, then we are rather dealing with an old curiosity shop filled with all kinds of non-standard features (needless to say, not necessarily local ones).

My personal opinion is that we are dealing with two writers who were familiar with St Helena to some extent, having spent quite some time in the local community (which is made clear by detailed references to the community and allusions to local people and events; perhaps they were even natives), and this would strongly suggest that many of these features were characteristic of the local vernacular indeed. However, this is not to say that Saints spoke like this; if the anonymous editors exaggerated and overused local features (just as Dickens did in his work), then we would be mistaken to take this as evidence of direct speech. Rather, they may represent a collection of localisms (blown out of proportion and thus of little quantitative value), whose usage is overemphasised and stereotyped for humorous purposes.

4.4 *Short stories (19th century)*

The *Monthly Critic and Flashlight*, first published in January 1892, featured a series of short stories. One of them, "The Secret of Mount Eternity", written by an author who prefers to remain anonymous, is a fictional first-person narrative by a surgeon employed on St Helena. In three sequels, the narrator recounts some of his experiences with St Helenians and liberated slaves from the Depot in Rupert's Valley. The main part of the story consists of the search for a hidden treasure on the island, which was first mentioned to the narrator by a dying slave. One character in this short story is Jake,

> who had come as a lad to St Helena … He knew the country well, as regarded the finding of game, and his stories of the amount killed by "Ole Massa Brooke"[3] and "de Gin'ral" … bordered on the marvellous. He had other tales, however, equally marvellous to tell, of hidden treasure … To hear him talk, one would have supposed him versed in all the mysteries of "obi" and negro witchcraft.

The following is an accident told by Jake in direct speech:

> Ye see dis powd'-horn Massa? Well, one day that ere cork in de small end done stuck fas', and I 'magines all day in my kop how I get him out. Not like knock him in fear I split de horn, so I dinks I jus' burn him out shua! So I put my ramming rod in the fiah, and when he jus' nice and read, I stick de cold end of de rod inter de ground … I done forget dat de horn full ob powder, and

[3] Perhaps this is a reference to Governor Brooke, who served as governor on the island in the late 18th century.

> when de rod burn troo de cork, it go kerslick inter that powder. And de powder explode … I clar to the Lord, Massa, it take three doctors to cut it out, and it leave mark all around my eye you see. Surgeon-Major say 'Jake, you berry long-headed man, and you head jus' thick as it long; dat what save you.'"

In addition to the usual interpretation problems, Jake may not have been a speaker of StHE at all since he came to the island in his youth (notice the word *kop* 'head', which is of Afrikaans origins). Nevertheless, he lived on the island long enough to contribute to the local feature pool and the above passage displays quite a few interesting features:

- completive *done* ("that ere cork in de small end done stuck fas'", "I done forget dat")
- *–s* agreement with pronouns ("and I 'magines all day", which could also represent historical present)
- consonant cluster reduction ("stuck fasØ", "dat what saveØ you")
- non-rhoticity ("rod in the fiah", "I jus' burn him out shua")
- TH stopping ("so I dinks", "de rod burn troo de cork")
- /v/ stopping ([b]) ("full ob powder", "you berry long-headed man")
- bare root extension (infinitive forms as preterits: "it take three doctors to cut it out", "I stick de cold end of the rod", "and it leave Ø mark")
- clipping of unstressed syllables ("I 'magines")
- copula absence ("you head jus' thick as it long", "when he jus' nice and read")
- absence of articles ("it leave Ø mark all around")
- animate pronouns ("I split de horn, so I dinks I jus' burn him out")

In a later sequel to the story, the author recounts a local dance event and uses direct speech for various characters. Ebenezer Green, for instance, an "island dandy", is arguing over a young girl with Pompey, a freed African slave temporarily housed in the Depot in Rupert's Valley: "What fo' you heel stick out so people tink am toeas?" The local president of the Ball Committee, a respected Saint, feels the need to interfere:

> You not African genelmen, you ornery black niggahs, and if you behaves as sich out you goes … You, Pompey, not know nuffin yet, you's excuse, but you Ebenezer Green, if you not pollygize right away I takes you name off the Ball Committee and p'raps off the Ball list all'gether."

In a later passage, an elderly woman makes fun of Jake always telling ghost stories: "Hyah yon Jake, you much too sassy, what you know 'bout ghosses? You nebber see nutting but deam Dutch spooks and den run 'way."

The most insightful passage is the final part of the sequel. During the treasure hunt and denouement, Jake is quoted as saying

> I tink if we work around Mt. Ternity, dat red hill over there, we get few more rabbits … Dar's where de treasure is if you can read that writin', an expoun' it, you want nuffin moah … You nebber find no black niggahs 'bout here dis time of night, dey too much 'fraid, and you and me, massah, we know dere ain't no such tings as spooks.

Finally, the entire ghost story is told by a character called Chloe, an elderly slave who is said to have spent all her life on St Helena. Her account is reported here in full.

> Ah' I tell you so dat Jake no good–you set down right I tell you all about the treasure … When I was 'bout fourteen years ole, I live with ole Massa Bagster away out behind High Peak and me and two or three udder gals work in the house and we all mighty 'fraid of her, she so strick, but she berry kind to me because I always listen to her." Dis was before de "Mancipation" and some of the slaves was a bad lot and 'feared of nothin' but de whip. Well, one afternoon, Missus she come into de kitchen quite scared like and she say "three of our hands have run away and hide themselves, I very much feared they up to mischief, your Massah and most of de men gone off to look for 'em and I tink dey know this and perhaps they come back here tonight and steal. One of them knows where I keep my jewels and I don't like keep it in the house: here it is Diana you hide it for me." Well, just afore sun down Diana she go out above the house and she look roun' and when she come in she say "some ob dem runaways is in the gumtrees top of de peak I got to go and see 'em and keep 'em from coming to de house and I got to hide dis box too, Idon't [sic] rightly know what to do," den she sit down in a chair and she put her apron over her head and she sit there for ten minutes or mo' and rock backwards and forwards. Den sudden she sit up and she say "You got to come with me a bit of the way. You wait here till I come back." Den she go out up de peak and in half an hour she come back, when de moon rise and she put on a white shawl and tell me put on a grey one and she take the box that missis give her and out we goes. When we gets round below de peak, where de bushes is high she say "Quick, honey gib me you shawl and take my white one, and now she says, you run along the road to Bevin's where you fadder working. Dose wicked devils followin' me to get de box and when dey see de white shawl they tink it me dey followin'." Well, I run along and when I get to Casons gate I look back and see two men come along steady like and den I turn down de road a bit towards Bevin's and presently I hear de pit pat ob dere feet on the road behind me : den I run like I nebber run before straight down de valley and when I get to de bottom ob de gut I scream for my fadder and brudders shoutin' and last ting I hear one of de men dat follow me say "dat not Diana, hu! What silly fools us is tink old woman run like dat," and den I fall down and when I wake up, I in my fader's house and de lamp burnin', and my mudder sittin' by me. Next mornin' I goes back to massa Bagster, and just about nine o'clock massa come back and he call me in to misiss' room, and he say, "Now Chloe, you sit down and tell me what happen last night." Den I tell him, and he look sad and he say, "You only see two men, follow you, dat cunnin' debil Lysander he stay behind, and when poor Diana get up from de bushes where she hidden, he follow her and she go to Mount Eternity, and

> when he get dere he find her dere dead, but *he no find de box*, and he so 'fraid dat he gib himself up to me and I send him to de jail in Jamestown. And de udder two runaways? I asks. Ah! said massa dey come to a bad end coming back over de ridge to try and get into Sandy Bay and one ob dem so tired he slip and break his neck, and de search party catch the other one, and he fight and dey shoot him." "Now, said massa I want you go and see Lysander in de prison, and you get him to tell de troof about what de do [sic] at Mt. 'Ternity." Well next day I goes to de prison and 'count if de pass Massa gib me dey let me see Lysander–and dis what he tell me. "When Diana come out to see us on de peak she tell me dat it no use our comin' for de jewel box in missis' room because she had sent it to Jamestown. Now we wanted dat box, 'cause we tink if we can hide it some place, we might get chance to sell some little bits to passengers when dey comes ashore in Jamestown and den we go and have a spree. Well, Diana go into house, and we wait little bit and when you and her comes out, I says "Diana want put us off de scent. I tink *she* got dat box." Den when you *two* go into bushes and only *one* come out I was shuah she got it and when you run, you no run like old 'ooman and I watch: den I see Diana come out and she look dis way and dat way and den she slip down Broad Bottom and up Blueman's Hill and back Mt. 'Ternity and den I not see her, but I look about and I find a grave which dey just dig for that black feller as die out at Lemon Valley and dere I see Dian sitting in it, and she look like dead and she say "Lysander, you my sistah's son and you kill me, you make me run and my heart break : you got to bury me here and I make de curse on any one dat move me for forty year," den she fall back and her jaw drop and she die, and I go straight back to massa and gib myself up." "Well," continued Chloe, "Massa Bagster he got disgusted with de Island and he sell his slaves, all but me, he gib me my freedom, and he and missus goes to England, where her daughter livin' there now." "But," she added, "de forty year am ober now and I tink if you like to look you find something good in Diana's grave, for Massah Bagster he never let anybody meddle with her body and dat same mornin' he find it, he cover it up and put up a gravestone over it. (*emphasis* in original)

This passage is extraordinarily rich and insightful and it contains the following features of interest:

- TH stopping ("last ting I hear", "and I tink if you like to look", "and dat same mornin'", "me and two or three udder gals"))
- /v/ stopping ([b]) ("dat cunnin' debil Lysander", "back to massa and gib myself up", "but she berry kind to me")
- consonant cluster reduction ("When I was 'bout fourteen years ole, I live with ole Massa Bagster", "she so strick")
- non-rhoticity ("you want nuffin moah", "you my sistah's son", "I was shuah she got it", "for ten minutes or mo' ")
- negator *no* ("he no find de box", "you no run like old 'ooman")
- negator *not* ("back Mt. 'Ternity and den I not see her")
- past *be* regularisation to *was* ("some of the slaves was a bad lot")

- present tense *be* regularisation with pivot form *is* ("some ob dem runaways is in the gumtrees", "below de peak, where de bushes is high")
- *–s* agreement with all persons ("passengers when dey comes ashore", "Next mornin' I goes back to massa Bagster", "he and missus goes to England")
- 3rd person singular present tense zero ("Diana want put us off de scent", "about nine o'clock massa come back and he call me in")
- absence of plural marking ("one dat move me for forty year")
- serial verbs ("Diana want put us off")
- absence of determiners ("Diana go into house")
- objective *us* for subjective *we* ("What silly fools us is")
- clipping of unstressed initial syllables ("before de 'Mancipation'")
- bare root extension ("a grave which dey just dig for that black feller", "he got disgusted with de Island and he sell his slaves")
- copula absence ("but she Ø berry kind to me", "from de bushes where she Ø hidden")

The passage also contains some unusual features: *am* for *are* ("de forty year am ober now"), or the verb *steal* without an object ("they come back here tonight and steal Ø") as well as archaisms (e.g. the preposition *afore* in "just afore sun down Diana she go out").

Another possible source of late 19th century StHE comes from an early issue of *The Mosquito*, a local gazette that ran for more than two years and a total of ten issues. The articles that featured in this newspaper are quite diverse, ranging from jokes and local news to philosophical treatises (depending how benevolent the reader is). There is plenty of 'local colour' and this is obviously am attempt to address as big an audience as possible by reporting on local events and characters (for marketing purposes, presumably). The issue published on July 28 1888 recounts a (quite possibly made up) verbatim conversation between two country labourers:

Billey	Good mornin Johny.
Johny	Mornin Billey, how de rain out you side de country.
Billey	Oh! my goody my boy dont tork, rain like any dorg out dare; de mud stick to you foot like any keow
Johny	Well, it mite be pootty bad out you way, but I dont tink it ken be wusseren out my way, I take my oaf de mud is pootty near two foot deep.
Billey	Go long man; who you stuffin long dat. It mite be pootty muddy out you way, but two feet is strechin it little bit too much; by golly you ken yarn like any dorg. I know betteren dat; it mite be bout one foot.

Johny	Well you mite not tork so bloomin plane to a feller corse I oney gess it you know. Howsomdever us wont fall out about dat. I say Billey wot you tink bout dat robry case?
Billey	Well! To tell you de troof, I doan know wot to tink bout it; but ef dat wus de man wat dun it, I tink he wus a stoopit feller, corse he mussy know he would bin git kitch some time or de yurrer.
Johny	You rite Billey; he wus a stoopit feller. You know a feller mite skape fur a little time, but he will git fine out in de long run; dem lor people cunnin like any dorg. You see how dat young feller got suck in de yurrer nite when he gorne parse dat drink troo de kort winder. I tell you man, you mus be werry kunnin how you do tings dese days, else you git suck in I tell you man.
Billey	You rite man; I wus suck in down de back way de yurrer day by sarsy young willin. I give him sixpence to buy sticker bakker an he never bring me no change; wait till I kitch him dats all; if I doan give him dat wollup wid my stick, I tell you I'll make him sore for munt. Boys in dese days, sarsy an steal like any dorg.
Johny	Yes! You jiss said it; boys in ower days had to behave demselfs, an if dey did'nt [sic], dey would git a jolly good wuckin' dat would make dem know dems place.
Billey	Oh! I furgit to ax you how you ole womin an de fambly getting on; I spose dem all foller de fashin long de cole.
Johny	By George, yes man, de ole womin an children corfin like any dorg, an it play de devil long feller's money to buy stuff from de Dokter furrum. How all you folks do.
Billey	Oh! dem is all potty well tank you, sep mysef, I trubble long de roomtisem you know, an dat sarve me wusseren any dorg. Well I mus say good nite as tis parse hapas fore an I gutter go long way you know.
Johny	Well good nite Billy boy, gimmy specks to de fambly, good nite.

Even though it is more than likely that local features are over-exaggerated and stereotyped (see above), this passage's "degree of vernacularity" seems to be high and comparatively reliable. Noteworthy features include:

- TH stopping ("how you do tings")
- TH fronting ("I take my oaf", "To tell you de troof")
- *you* as a second person singular possessive ("out you side de country")
- 3rd person singular present tense zero ("my boy dont tork)
- centralised onset in MOUTH ("like any keow")
- STRUT for NURSE ("I dont tink it ken be wusseren out my way", "dey would git a jolly good wuckin'", "an dat sarve me wusseren any dorg")

- no plural *–s* with nouns of measurement ("de mud is pootty near two foot deep")
- alveolar /n/ for *–ing* ("who you stuffin long dat")
- objective *us* for objective *we* ("us wont fall out about dat")
- /v~w/ interchange ("you mus be werry kunnin how you do tings")
- preterit *done* ("dat wus de man wat dun it") and *gone* ("dat young feller got suck in de yurrer nite when he gorne parse dat drink")
- *what* as a relative pronoun ("de man wat dun it")
- KIT for DRESS ("he will git fine", "wait till I kitch him dats all", "I furgit to ax you")
- intrusive /r/ ("dorg", "sarsy", "corfin")
- absence of copula and auxiliary verbs ("lor people Ø cunnin like any dorg", "de ole womin an children Ø corfin like any dorg")
- modal usage of *mussy* ("corse he mussy know he would bin git kitch")
- clipping of unstressed syllables ("a feller mite skape fur a little time", "gimmy specks to de fambly")
- consonant cluster reduction in a diagnostic pre-V context ("dat young feller got suckØ in de yurrer nite")
- adjective *sassy* ("by sarsy young willin")
- multiple negation ("he never bring me no change")
- no plural *–s* marking ("I'll make him sore for munt [= months]")
- third person plural possessive *them* ("make dem know dems place")
- objective *them* for subjective *they* ("dem is all potty well tank you")
- <aks> for *ask* ("I furgit to ax you")
- *long* meaning 'with' ("I spose dem all foller de fashin long de cole")

4.5 Miscellaneous observations from the 20th century

The 20th century, finally, provides insights into the local variety as well, mainly from travellers, journalists and visitors, but also by clerks and administration staff who stayed on the island for longer periods. For instance, there is a reference in the *St Helena Magazine* from January 1950, concerning the 100 men who went to England for work after WW II (see ch. 3). Their arrival in the UK aroused considerable interest, and the *Sunday Empire News* wrote that "They speak an English which sounds strange to us. It is the English of the eighteenth century larded with old-fashioned picturesque phrases."[4]

Cross (1980: 91) is more specific when he remarks that

[4] Interestingly, the editor of the *St Helena Magazine* felt the need to add a replying comment, namely that "the English as spoken in some of the rural districts of Sussex, Somerset and Yorkshire, in centuries' old phrase and pronunciation, is much more quaint than anything we have in St Helena."

> Spoken English possibly has more regional variations than any other language and the island's contribution is unique. There are many resemblances to the speech of the West Indians but there are inversions and oddities that are peculiar to St Helena. To be asked 'How you are then?' 'How is you be this morning?' is readily understood, but it is the use of familiar English words to mean something other than their normally accepted meaning that causes difficulty. To accept the polite, well-intentioned St Helenian's offer of 'a nice couple of mackerel' might result in the unsuspecting three or four dozen fish – a couple seems to be any number greater than two … By far the most interesting and distinctive pattern of speech is the frequent interchange of 'v' and 'w' in the manner of Dickens's Londoners. A government officer advised an English official 'Keep your serwant under wigilant superwision' and a tape recording of an islander intended for British radio listeners was scrapped when he repeated several times that he was the island's 'wet'. Some St Helenians have a slight 'th' difficulty similar to that of the Irish, so that Thorpe is rendered 'T'orp', but the characteristic colour of the dialect derives principally from a vigorous vocabulary which includes many words created for local use by local people.

Bain (1993: 31) notes:

> When we came out of Cardiff", said one of the deck stewards [of the RMS St Helena], "half the crew were suck." The distorted pronunciation of the letter 'I' is a characteristic of Saints' speech. Sixpence becomes suckspence. It is not altogether unlike what happens to the same letter in New Zealand where 'milk' is 'moolk' and 'tea' is 'toy'. Or nearly so. In a burst of passing affection, one old lady said to me, 'Give us a kuss, luv.'

Some of the features mentioned here are widely reported elsewhere (such as TH stopping and the /v~w/ interchange); others, however, show up here for the first time (KIT centralisation, or the co-occurrence of *is* and *be* in the same VP: "How is you be this morning?").

Another reliable source of 20th century StHE comes from Basil George's short stories (George 2002a, b). Basil George is a native Saint Helenian, who spent practically his entire life on the island and worked as a teacher at various local schools. He has a profound interest in local culture and the history of the islanders and instigated St Helena studies in the local curriculum. Upon his retirement, George started writing short stories, mainly for children ("The Pepper Tree", "The Banyan Tree"), in which he describes the island and its community. The main character in his stories is Nummes, a small boy from Jamestown, who experiences all kinds of adventures.

Direct speech is used as a main narrative device, and George took great care to use the local variety as closely as possible. The passages are too numerous and scattered for reproduction here, so I opt for a short list of features (complete with examples from the short stories):

- *you* as a second person singular possessive, instead of *your* ("Come here, look at you boy"; Pepper Tree (PT), p. 9; "you take you turn after Boji"; Banyan Tree (BT), p. 2; "let you mind take shape in you hands"; BT, p. 20)
- absence of copulas and auxiliaries ("the boy Ø holdin' a live scorpion"; PT, p. 10; ("I Ø sure I see him go outside after breakfast"; PT, p. 16; "I Ø fed up with that boy"; PT, p.16; "It Ø not safe under a tree, boy"; PT, p. 22; I Ø big enough to go by myself; BT, p. 2; my dad Ø in the army man; BT, p. 5)
- 3rd person singular present tense zero ("Gertie goØ get one shoe"; PT, p. 10; "you think money growØ on trees"; PT, p. 11; "he'll get it when he comeØ in"; PT, p. 16; "it be too hot if the air on you arm singeØ"; BT, p. 14; "the oven never goØ cold"; BT, p. 14)
- indeterminate *one* for 'a' ("Gertie go get one shoe"; PT, p. 10; "Gertie's boy bring one live scorpion into the house")
- serial verbs ("Gertie go get one shoe"; PT, p. 10)
- *go* as a future marker ("otherwise she go have trouble with him later on"; PT, p. 12)
- bare roots in preterit contexts ("I sure I see him go outside after breakfast"; PT, p. 16; "you wet my bes Sunday shoes I only buy las week from Camp Corker"; BT, p. 20)
- regularisation of past *be* with pivot *was* ("Where you was when the rocks come down?"; PT, p. 21)
- no word-order inversion in question-type sentences ("Where you was when the rocks come down?"; PT, p. 21)
- preverbal *bin* ("the boy could bin got kill"; PT, p. 21)
- invariant *be* ("it be too hot if the air on you arm singe"; BT, p. 14)
- negator *never* ("the oven never go cold"; BT, p. 14; "you never went swimming in you school pants?"; BT, p. 17; "why you never worry bout that?"; BT, p. 18)
- alveolar /n/ for *–ing* ("I dirty the washin"; PT, p. 11; "what he go swimmin in ?"; BT, p. 17))
- consonant cluster reduction in diagnostic pre-V or pre-P contexts ("the boy could bin got killØ"; PT, p. 21; "I buy the big size so they could las"; BT, p. 18)
- clipping of unstressed syllables ("why you never worry bout that?"; BT, p. 18)

Finally, there are also personal reminiscences and anecdotes on the part of Saints who indicate how distinctive StHE is, and that even native speakers of English fail to understand them (or even fail to realise that this is a variety of English!). We heard several times that visiting tourists struggled badly with understanding the locals. One interviewee, for instance, told me that he was driving a bus with tourists when he stopped to have a little chat with a friend who waited by the roadside. A tourist who sat immediately behind him said later on: "I have lived in England all my life and I have never felt so lost understanding somebody!"

Consequently then, the 20th century provides insight into StHE as well; though written for various purposes, these sources contain features and observations that are helpful for historical research and may be used to complement findings based on data I collected myself (and which will be presented in the next two chapters). Now, however, we are left with the difficult task of evaluating these data and contextualising them in the light of the findings presented in ch. 3.

4.6 Some more detailed sociolinguistic implications

This chapter has presented some first hypotheses on earlier StHE, based on written sources produced between the 1670s and the 1990s, thus spanning more than three centuries of island history. The purposes for writing are extremely diverse, ranging from the transcripts of slave testimonies to visitors' impressions, from personal letters to short stories for children. Apart from the sketchy nature of written sources (and all the problems outlined above), we also have to take into account that the various text types may influence the direct speech reported, and that the "degree of vernacularity" has to be assessed separately in each case (the *StHR*, for instance, almost certainly underreport local features, whereas texts such as the exchange between two country labourers from (1888) *The Mosquito* issue very likely exaggerate, distort and stereotype local features for humorous purposes). Crucially then, we must not take these features at face value and I will certainly not make the mistake of assuming that they are representative of StHE in general. They give us no indication as to how individuals really spoke and one is constantly left with the cumbersome task of assessing how valuable they are for our research.

Consequently, I would like to start by summarising the main findings of this chapter, based on the texts discussed and supported by the socio-historical examination given in ch. 3, and then go on to look at the reported features in more detail. How are we to interpret the sociolinguistic implications of our analysis of earlier StHE, and what can this tell us about the origins and development of the variety? It appears to me that two criteria are paramount: first of all, the island population witnessed a transition from ethnically, regionally and sociolinguistically diverse groups to a thoroughly mixed and relatively homogeneous community (recall the discussion in ch. 3, where it was shown that population mixing occurred between the 1740s and the 1870s, i.e., within five to six generations). Needless to say, sociodemographic developments of this kind have far-reaching sociolinguistic consequences. Until the 1730s, the local population was quite diverse. The documents sighted here provide further evidence that the slaves' linguistic backgrounds, or better: the varieties they spoke natively and brought to St Helena, may have included English- or Portuguese-based jargons and/or pidgins along with various West and South African as well as Asian languages.

Second, the early records attest to the fact that English was used widely in the community. The majority of the white population had English origins or descended from immigrants from England. English was the language used in court, in church, in the administration and for all official purposes, and the slaves had to defend themselves in court in English (even if it was to claim that their competence was not sufficient to partake in plotting a rebellion, which again indicates that the slaves had at least some knowledge of English). The documents discussed in this chapter reveal that practically all the slaves in the early period were proficient in English (there is thus no evidence whatsoever of *prima facie* language contact on the island in the 17th century). The dominant function of English in the colony's early years was to some extent politically motivated; we saw above that, for fear of rebellions and uprisings, the import of cheap labour was regulated until the 1790s. This effectively meant that slaves did not arrive in large numbers; in fact, when ships passed and called at St Helena with a cargo of slaves, it was common practice that a handful (or even only one) of them remained for the local markets, and these were often hand-picked by the governor. If it is true that the person in charge was instructed to choose slaves that spoke English, then the sociolinguistic context of the early years would certainly not have favoured large-scale language contact, making it extremely unlikely that StHE underwent pidginisation at an early stage.

The role of English was further strengthened by the fact that the community was not urbanised at the time, and that the planters lived in small farms and villages scattered all over the island. Slave ownership was never extensive, and the fact that the vast majority of the planters owned less than five slaves would certainly have meant that English was readily accessible, that it was used as a medium of communication between whites and blacks, and also that it functioned as a *lingua franca* among the slaves themselves when their first languages were not mutually intelligible. Of course, this is not to say that the slaves shifted to English quickly and that they acquired a native-like command within a generation or so; we saw above that they were socially stratified (just as the whites were) and that they displayed considerable variation from very early on, ranging from rudimentary (jargon-like) types to acrolectal varieties. What we can exclude, however, solely based on socio-historical and linguistic evidence, is that the conditions in the colony's early years led to pidginisation on a societal level.

However, this does not exclude *a priori* pidginisation and/or creolisation of StHE. We have to bear in mind that the situation was likely to change in the first half of the 18th century, namely when shiploads of slaves arrived from

Madagascar to develop the ambitious New Ground project (ch. 3). Indeed, the scenario may have changed radically after the almost simultaneous arrival of comparatively large groups of slaves (which effectively may have entailed sociolinguistic *swamping* and eradicated pre-existing *founder effects*; ch. 2). Accordingly, we must also focus on the impact of the slaves who came *en bloc* in 1717 and represented numbers large enough to change the sociolinguistic balance at the time, so that they could have affected the evolution of StHE.

Though information is scarce, there is reason to assume that many of the newly arriving slaves were Malagasy monolinguals. Crucially, Madagascar was not an English colony, there was no English-speaking population there[5] and it would have been extremely unlikely for slaves from that island to speak (some form of) English. Moreover, they were shipped from Madagascar to St Helena directly (perhaps with a short stop-over in South Africa), and the fact that they travelled in large groups (there were dozens of slaves on each ship, and more than one hundred and fifty on one occasion) makes it unlikely that they picked up or developed an English-based jargon on the ship, which would point in the direction of *Ship or Nautical English* (ch. 2); they by far outnumbered the ship's crew and would in all likelihood have continued to speak their native language. We may thus exclude the possibility that English-derived pidgins and/or creoles were brought to the island, simply because English did not pidginise and/or creolise in Madagascar.[6] Consequently, all this would have favoured the maintenance of Malagasy and sustained bilingualism on St Helena (there is no doubt that the Malagasy community maintained their language perhaps for as long as three to four generations, as witnessed by the reports of Malagasy-English bilingual interpreters in the 1760s). This situation led to renewed and intensified language contact, which raises the possibility that StHE emerged as a contact variety and underwent pidginisation and/or creolisation, though at a later stage.

Again, however, the sociolinguistic impact of the Malagasy-speaking slaves was weakened by the interplay of three factors. First, they were split up

---

[5] The linguistic landscape of Madagascar is described as follows: "The Malagasy language - spoken throughout Madagascar by the entire population - is the only one in the African region that belongs to the Malayo-Polynesian language family … [I]t shares a common origin with, and is most closely related to Maanyan, a language spoken in southeast Borneo. Both Malagasy and Maanyan bear a close affinity with the languages of the western Indonesian archipelago, such as Malay, Javanese, Balinese, and the Minangkabau language of Sumatra … Although different regional dialects of Malagasy exist, these are mutually intelligible." (http://countrystudies.us/madagascar/16.htm; accessed January 5 2006).

[6] The situation, however, may have been different in the case of slaves from St Iago and Angola, i.e., from former Portuguese colonies, who may have brought pidginised forms of Portuguese to St Helena (see Figure 3.3).

and sold singly or in small groups, so that they did not reside together in one plantation; second, they found themselves in a locale that was founded and established by others who had come before them, and these "founders" (in the widest sense, of course, including both black and white) still represented the majority of the local population; third, the presence of the Madagascar slaves coincided with a period of heavy population mixing, which intensified from the 1740s onwards (ch. 3). The breaking down of social and ethnic barriers and the integration of the community went hand in hand with the disappearance of languages other than English. This must have been a rapid process; by the 19th century, St Helena was "an exclusively English speaking colony" (Schulenburg & Schulenburg 1997: 7). Ethnic mixing and the loss of distinctive group identities based on origins and skin colour therefore accompanied (or made possible) the adoption of English, enshrining its role as the sole language of communication on the island. All this leads me to conclude that, although StHE developed in a bi- and/or multilingual context, in a setting that witnessed coexistence of various ethnic groups, each socially stratified, the most important reference variety on the island was (and always has been) English, which effectively served as a *lingua franca* at all times. There is ample room for speculation, however, as to whether, and to what extent, languages spoken by the slave populations influenced the development of a local English variety, and I will address this issue again when presenting my analysis of 20th century fieldwork data.

The second question of relevance concerns the extent to which the features of earlier StHE discussed above are diachronically representative and indicative of individual donor varieties. Can we make any guesses as to where these features were drawn from and how widespread and consistent they were? One method is to compare the various features, with due caution, of course, and check whether they are found in more than one source. This allows us to speculate on the historical continuity and (putative) presence of diagnostic features at earlier stages of the variety. The best way of doing this is listing the features chronologically and assessing whether they are found in more than one text or in more than one period. This type of comparative analysis seems most suitable for our purposes, particularly so since the manifestation of one and the same feature in non-related texts written by various authors is a strong indication of its presence in StHE indeed.

Tables 4.1 and 4.2 provide a summary of the findings presented in this chapter. They list the individual features and indicate when and where these made an appearance. Due to the paucity of data for the 18th century, the columns for the 17th and 18th centuries are collapsed and presented jointly. Moreover, the observed features are listed globally; no information is provided about their putative sources (which are often unclear anyway), the alleged speakers and (sub-)communities on the island and the context of the utterance, which means that the features that contributed to StHE's feature pool are presented in the most general way.

Starting with the phonology of earlier StHE, Table 4.1 lists the features that can be traced in the sources discussed, indicating in what century they are reported (giving the year of appearance in brackets). As expected, the early periods yield practically no phonological insights (and the column for the 17th and 18th century remains empty). The picture changes and the 19th century (i.e., the material from the ghost stories and newspapers) is most fruitful.

Table 4.1 A comparative analysis of phonological features in earlier StHE

	17th/18th c.	19th c.	20th c.
TH stopping		✓ (1851, 1888, 1892)	✓ (1980)
TH fronting		✓ (1888)	
/v~w/ interchange, pivot /w/		✓ (1851, 1888)	✓ (1980)
/v~w/ interchange, pivot /v/		✓ (1851)	
/v/ stopping ([b])		✓ (1892)	
/h/ insertion		✓ (1851)	
/h/ dropping		✓ (1851)	
consonant cluster reduction in diagnostic pre-V or pre-P contexts		✓ (1851, 1888, 1892)	✓ (1990s)
non-rhoticity		✓ (1892)	
KIT centralisation			✓ (1993)
STRUT for NURSE		✓ (1851, 1888)	
KIT for DRESS		✓ (1851, 1888)	
PEN~PIN merger		✓ (1888)	
happY tensing		✓ (1851)	
jod dropping		✓ (1851)	
alveolar /n/ for *–ing*		✓ (1851, 1888)	✓ (1990s)
clipping of unstressed syllables		✓ (1851, 1888)	✓ (1990s)

The three features that occur most regularly are: 1) alveolar /n/ for *–ing*; 2) the reduction of consonant clusters in diagnostic pre-V or pre-P contexts; and 3) the clipping of unstressed syllables. It is not surprising at all to find the first two features in this list; after all, they fall into the category of "vernacular universals" (Chambers 2004) and make an appearance in practically all varieties of English. The fact that they can be attributed to earlier StHE is not indicative of the origins and development of the variety as such, and it does not help us pinpoint structural affinities with other varieties (simply because all varieties have them). On the positive side, we may conclude that the reports are at least to some extent authentic and representative.

As for the other phonological features listed, we can distinguish between those showing up more than once (in un-related texts) and others where we have sporadic references only. In the first category, we find the /v~w/ interchange (even though it is not clear what the pivot is in this merging process) and TH stopping (particularly noticeable with voiceless dental fricatives); it is plausible to suggest that both of them were regular in earlier StHE. Other features make a more sporadic appearance but offer us more detailed insights into origins and ancestral effects. These include /v/ stopping (which is common in English-based pidgins and creoles, and also in Gullah and earlier AAE), KIT centralisation (a well-studied variable in SHemE; Gordon & Sudbury 2002), STRUT for NURSE (evident in "dat sarve me wusseren any dorg", which makes an appearance on Tristan da Cunha as well; Schreier 2003a: 209), KIT for DRESS (in words like 'get', 'again' or 'forget'), /h/ insertion and /h/ dropping (as in "for a hindependent Briton" and "gremlin on ard times", common in 19th century London English), or the PEN~PIN merger ("the gin'ral", reported in Southern US AmE as well). At first glance then, these features seem more helpful for a reconstruction of the evolutionary path of StHE; many of the features listed here can be attributed to the South of England (/h/-dropping, the /v~w/ interchange, etc.) or they have parallels in English-based contact varieties (/v/ stopping, consonant cluster reduction, clipping of unstressed syllables), which fairly precisely matches what was deduced from the community's social history.

What about the grammatical properties of earlier StHE? Table 4.2 lists the morphosyntactic features attested. The picture here is more complete since we saw that some of the earliest documents available contain insightful grammatical structures (such as extension of bare roots to preterit contexts, copula absence, or 3rd person singular present tense zero). Importantly, all these features are attested throughout, i.e., they make an appearance in 19th and 20th century documents as well (moreover in reliable ones, such as Basil George's short stories or the reported speech in *The Mosquito*). We find a similar pattern as with the phonological features, in that vernacular features are attested frequently and regularly (past *be* regularisation with pivot *was*, no plurals with mass nouns and measurements, *never* as a negator, *what* as a relative pronoun or objective *them* for subjective *they*, etc.). All these features are common and found in many (if not all) non-standard varieties of English around the world. Again, it is the rarer structures that yield insights into the contact history and typological affiliations of StHE; here I would mention the lack of plural *–s* suffixation, present *be* regularisation with pivot *is*, perfective *be*, pre-predicate *do* ("gits so beestlee toksikated, but doe I sa it myself I is a onnest man", common in East Anglian English), *a*-prefixing, extension of bare roots to preterit contexts, *go* and *by and by* as future markers, etc. Some of these features make several appearances, others only one (a modal-type *mussy* – "corse he *mussy* know he would bin git kitch", no word-order inversion in question-type sentences or existential *it*). We await the analysis of 20th century StHE to study the properties and history of these features in more detail.

Table 4.2 A comparative analysis of morphosyntactic features in earlier StHE

	17th /18th c.	19th c.	20th c.
no plural with nouns of measurement	✓ (1687)	✓ (1888, 1892)	
no plural –s marking	✓ (1695)	✓ (1888, 1892)	
past be regularisation with pivot was	✓ (1688)	✓ (1851, 1892)	✓ (1990s)
present be regularisation with pivot is	✓ (1697)	✓ (1851, 1892)	
present tense –s with all persons		✓ (1851)	
is + BE			✓ (1980)
3rd person singular present tense zero	✓ (1679)	✓ (1851, 1892)	✓ (1990s)
–ed past tense suffixation with strong verbs		✓ (1851)	
perfective be	✓ (1701)		
periphrastic/emphatic do	✓ (1679)	✓ (1851)	
pre-predicate do		✓ (1851)	
PRO drop	✓ (1679)		
me as first person singular subject pronoun	✓ (1695)		
us as first person plural subject pronoun		✓ (1888, 1892)	✓ (1980)
you as a second person singular possessive		✓ (1888)	✓ (1990s)
negator never	✓ (1695)	✓ (1888)	✓ (1990s)
negator no	✓ (1695)	✓ (1892)	
negator ain't		✓ (1851)	
multiple negation	✓ (1695)	✓ (1851, 1888, 1892)	✓ (1990s)
future by and by	✓ (1695)		
copula absence	✓ (1695)	✓ (1851, 1888, 1892)	✓ (1990s)
a-prefixing	✓ (1695)	✓ (1851, 1892)	
extension of bare roots to preterit contexts	✓ (1695, 1762)	✓ (1892)	✓ (1990s)
serial verbs	✓ (1679)	✓ (1892)	✓ (1990s)
completive don/done		✓ (1892)	
preverbal bin			✓ (1990s)
preterit done		✓ (1888)	
go as a future marker			✓ (1990s)
article absence	✓ (1695)	✓ (1892)	
indeterminate one for 'a'			✓ (1990s)
relative pronoun what		✓ (1851, 1888)	
existential it		✓ (1851)	
invariant be		✓ (1851)	✓ (1990s)
no word-order inversion in question-type sentences			✓ (1990s)
modal-type mussy		✓ (1888)	
third person plural possessive them		✓ (1888)	
them for they		✓ (1888)	

In conclusion, this chapter has located and discussed some preliminary evidence of earlier StHE. For this purpose, a variety of sources from a time span of more than three centuries was analysed; even though text types and writing purposes differ considerably (which, needless to say, has an impact on the sources' "degree of vernacularity"), I have been able to locate a good number of phonological and morphosyntactic features in the documents available. Some of these represent "vernacular universals", being of little diagnostic value (simply because they make an appearance in all varieties of English), whereas others are more specific, on occasion even allowing direct parallels to potential donor varieties (Southeast EngE, for instance). The data yield a puzzling picture, a testimony of the diffuse sociolinguistic scenario that gave rise to contemporary StHE; this is suitably exemplified by the negation system, for which no less than five different techniques can be traced (a standard-type system with *do* support, as well as the negators *no* ("me noe save speake English"), *never* ("Tobey says he Never di<>") or ain't ("I aint a goin to sa nuthin for dem fellers") and various manifestations of multiple negation ("he never bring me no change", "noe not I wont make one", etc., another of the "vernacular universals").) The coexistence (and ultimately: the competition) of various features is typically found in the early stages of a contact scenario and particularly common in a pre-focussed stage of a new variety (ch. 2); as for ancestry and evolution, the creole-like marker *no* indicates potential restructuring and quite likely originated in substratal effects that shaped the development of StHE's negation system (which, interestingly, is not paralleled in the case of mood and aspect, since slaves are often reported using modal verbs such as 'would', 'will' or 'shall' – if the reports are accurate, of course).

It is unfortunate that there are gaps and that the material discussed did not yield a more chronologically representative picture (this is particularly noticeable in the case of 17th and 18th century phonology). For the time being, we have no means of finding out whether the features in question were present or not in the sparsely recorded periods (i.e., the 1700s). In Wang's famous (1969: 21) words, "We cannot prove that the platypus does not lay eggs with photographs of a platypus NOT laying eggs." The simple absence of a feature is surely no justification for claiming that it was not in use, just as the first or last mention of a feature is no indication that this was the approximate date of its genesis or disappearance. We are simply bound by the data available to us and must take this into consideration at all times. It is my hope that a more extensive search in the Jamestown archives at a future stage can help us complete the picture presented here.

In any case, this chapter provided a sociolinguistic complement to the social history as outlined in ch. 3, and the linguistic data hold up to the premises formulated earlier on historical and sociodemographic information. We are now left with the task of completing our assessments by providing an in-depth analysis of a more representative data basis, and the next two chapters will show

how many of the historically attested features make an appearance in contemporary StHE as well.

5. Synchrony I: A descriptive profile of 20th century StHE

The goal of this chapter is to provide a descriptive analysis of the most prominent phonological and morphosyntactic features of early 20th century StHE. A detailed description is necessary for several reasons. First and foremost, StHE ranks among the 'lesser-known varieties of English' in that it is understudied and has found no or very little attention in the canon of World Englishes. Second, synchronic data put some 'meat on the socio-historical bone', so to speak, and are simply indispensable for analysis. A profile of 20th century StHE (based on natives of the island born before WWII) allows us to complement (ideally, to complete) the sociohistorical analysis and will thus add to (or challenge) the hypotheses on the origins and development of the variety based on social history (ch. 3) and earlier evidence (ch. 4) alone. Third, the status of StHE as the oldest variety of SHemE raises some important questions, e.g. how StHE fits in with other post-colonial varieties that have been documented more extensively (in the Caribbean and the Southern Hemisphere), whether it is typologically or structurally affiliated with English-based creoles elsewhere (Hancock 1991), what role StHE played in the formation of TdCE in the 1820s and '30s, etc (ch. 1). We can only address these issues in depth once we have a detailed phonological and syntactic profile of the variety.

However, the problem is how the findings should be presented. On the one hand, broad descriptions (of the type "StHE has KIT centralisation"; "*don* and *go* function as preverbal tense markers") are helpful in that they provide the information we need. A general overview of this kind has the advantage that it is economic, short and concise; it facilitates cross-comparison of varieties and has been adopted successfully in recent handbooks (Schneider et al. 2004 provide data for a total of 59 varieties of English world-wide; the CD that accompanies the handbook is an excellent research tool). On the other hand, this way of describing a variety has a number of setbacks also, particularly in what regards data selection and representativeness. A major shortcoming is that these accounts only provide qualitative descriptions and neglect the quantitative dimension (and can say little about the extralinguistic factors that govern it). If I adopted it for the profile of StHE, then this chapter would provide little, if any, information on variation between speakers, between different speech communities and few insights into changes in progress, thus virtually excluding the diachronic dimension as outlined in the previous chapter. When investigating a post-colonial variety with the aim of finding out whether it has undergone focussing or not, then the only option we have is working within a quantitative paradigm. A purely qualitative approach is simply too broad for this purpose and any attempt at uncovering the patterns and paradigms of variation would be unsubstantiated speculation. There is ample evidence of patterned variation and structured heterogeneity in the variationist sociolinguistics literature. All speakers vary in their language usage, no matter whether or not they speak a contact-derived variety that may or may not be in the process of focussing. Consequently, single speakers can never represent a variety in its entirety, no matter how 'vernacular', 'local' or 'typical' their speech is perceived by the researcher; it is simply not the case that all speakers of StHE have one particular feature, for instance 'remote *been*' or a centralised KIT vowel. Some certainly do, whereas others do not, some have it frequently, some rarely, some speakers may have a given feature in a lexical subset only, etc. The reasons are manifold (regional, social, ethnic, individual, …). There is no doubt that this kind of information is at least as important as a global phonological and morphosyntactic profile and researchers need to make every effort to provide such data so as not to portray an idealised and inaccurate image of homogeneity.

Of course, and here comes the major disadvantage, this is not an economic type of analysis at all. The emphasis here is on the trees, not on the forest. A large-scale quantitative analysis of selected variables is not only time- and space-consuming, it also runs the risk of providing information that is too detailed and specific, so that an accessible hands-on overview of phonological and morphosyntactic features is not provided (which is of great interest for a variety as understudied as StHE). The challenge, then, is to combine general and variationist viewpoints into a coherent analysis, i.e. to consider both qualitative *and* quantitative aspects when putting the puzzle pieces together. Both are necessary when interpreting the synchronic findings from a historical perspective and drawing a global picture of the forest while not losing sight of the trees. Ideally, then, this book should provide both an accurate descriptive profile of the variety and at the same time investigate variation within individuals and across speaker groups.

The approach adopted here is a compromise between the two approaches. On the one hand, information on 20th century StHE is provided for all of Wells' (1982) reference vowels (this design has also been adopted in Schneider et al.'s 2004 handbook). However, the technique was somewhat adapted for the present purpose. I decided to present findings not for one but for *four* individuals from different parts of the island. The reference vowel is presented for each of the speakers selected, and if there are various realisations then the word in which it occurs is indicated as well (simply to allow for co-articulation effects, change in progress, lexical diffusion, etc.). Of course, this does not exempt me from justifying my choice of representative speakers and there is always room to challenge the data on the premise that findings would have been different if an alternative set of informants had been chosen. I am the first to admit this. Nevertheless, one must bear in mind that a presentation of this kind allows for a more comprehensive view of variation within and across speakers. The quantitative dimension is integrated into the synchronic profile as well. To gain further insights into the external parameters that govern variation within StHE, I selected two variables, one phonological (consonant cluster reduction) and one morphosyntactic (copula absence), which were subjected to a detailed variationist analysis (to follow in ch. 6). The aim is to provide a portrait of variation within StHE and to scrutinise its 'envelope of variation' as accurately as possible. It is hoped that the two analyses complement each other in ways that are economical and concise for the needs of readers, publishers and the author alike, so that they provide an overview of StHE's distinctive properties and of its parameters of variation. Consequently, sections 5.2-3 present a profile of the segmental phonology and morphosyntax of StHE, and I start with a brief overview of fieldwork activities, methodology and principles of data collection.

5.1. Data and fieldwork

My wife and I spent about nine weeks on St Helena from July to early September 2003. Our aims of collecting data were twofold, both a synchronic field-based method and an archive-oriented one, which effectively meant that our work on the island consisted of two parts. For one, we jointly carried out ethnographic and sociolinguistic fieldwork, i.e. tape-recording interviews with locally-born islanders from various parts of St Helena (to obtain data of spoken contemporary StHE). Second, I spent many hours searching for historical material in the Jamestown Castle archives, unearthing whatever information I could on the historical development of the local variety and the community in which it evolved (these were presented and discussed in ch. 4).

Our fieldwork benefited from several fortunate circumstances. First and foremost, the fact that my wife had spent two years of secondary schooling on the island gave us a real head-start. She was familiar with the place and knew lots of Saints personally. Moreover, word got around quickly that I had spent time on Tristan da Cunha and the shared acquaintances as well as experiences of the life and times of people in the South Atlantic Ocean had a strong bonding effect, which provided ample room for chats and discussions. Second, the local family with whom my wife had stayed in the mid-1990s invited us to live with them, and they turned out to be the most helpful and friendly hosts. They truly made us feel at home on St Helena and assisted us in any way imaginable. They took us around to see the places of interest (of which there are many on this small island!), took us for picnics, went hiking with us and even organised a car so that we could travel around on our own to visit Saints in more isolated parts of the island. Moreover, they were supportive of my research project and volunteered to assist us in any possible way; they called family members and friends, telling them about the project and asking them whether they would like to have "a chat" with us, they gave important contact information for my research in the Castle archives, and they filled us in about the local history of the people. The fact that we found a quick way into the community – and that practically no ice had to be broken – made our fieldwork experience extremely rewarding and the project benefited tremendously from their interest and help.

A local 'pre-selected' and approached potential interview partners for us and we quickly became 'friends of a friend'. We thus had ideal working conditions and a wide set of networks from the start. We were most warmly welcomed by people we had never met before and there was an immediate point of reference and shared knowledge to open up a conversation. By and large, we were happy to chat with whoever was suggested by our 'host family' but asked that they met a number of criteria (local born, pre-specified age group, restricted outward mobility). We concentrated on people born on St Helena before WWII, who had spent most of their lives on the island. Moreover, we did our best to obtain a regionally representative sample and to conduct recordings with Saints representing distinct regions of St Helena. All in all, only one person turned us down (saying that he was too old to speak "posh English" and that he had no time to clear up his house); all the others were happy to meet us. As for time and place of interviews, we visited the people who had agreed to talk to us at their own convenience and in their own homes (with two exceptions: BB, who was interviewed in his cabin on board the RMS *St Helena*, and JC, who wanted to tell us about the "olden times" of Sandy Bay and chose a hill top where he could show us the area). All the Saints we interviewed were briefly informed about the aims of the project and were granted full anonymity. We agreed to start by asking some general questions about life in the early 20th century and their childhood reminiscences, which were promising topics. After that we let the interviewees decide on the course of the chat, and this led to discussions about topics as diverse as welfare on St Helena (or the lack of it), working conditions on Ascension Island, local ghost stories, military service during the war, German submarine attacks, the local economy, knitting and embroidery, cooking recipes, how to repair old boots, the flax industry, and many other things that make fieldwork such a rewardingly different experience. We never paid informants (a practice I have always objected to) but helped them out in whatever way we could (giving them a lift, making phone calls, getting prescriptions from the doctor, buying groceries, etc.). We visited all our informants before we left the island to say thank you again, which was greatly appreciated (and some asked about the results of our study, which I promised to send them at a later stage).

As for recording procedures, I opted for a recording device that was as non-intrusive as possible, as this had worked out well in earlier projects on Tristan da Cunha and in the North Carolina Appalachians. We used a portable SONY MiniDisc Recorder (MZ-R70) and a separate SONY ECM–R100 electret condenser microphone, which was placed on the table and recorded all the people present. All in all, we interviewed a total of 33 Saints, of which we selected a sub-sample of 20 for our analysis: ten men and ten women, born between 1911 and 1940 and representing all the regions on the island; Table 5.1 lists them by sex, birth date and place of residence and Map 5.1 indicates their places of residence.

Table 5.1 List of Saints interviewed (arranged by year of birth)

Male			Female		
Initials	*Year of Birth*	*Residence*	*Initials*	*Year of Birth*	*Residence*
JB	1911	Sunnyside, Ascension Island	LB	1916	Longwood
PF	1917	Blue Hill	MF	1916	Blue Hill
JJ	1920	Thompson's Hill	EP	1919	Sapper Way
GY	1921	Half Tree Hollow	GC	1920	Jamestown
ChC	1927	Sandy Bay	TH	1924	Longwood
BB	1927	Cleugh's Plain, Half Tree Hollow	DF	1925	Sandy Bay
LeG	1928	Levelwood	HF	1925	Deadwood
AH	1930	Levelwood	JM	1926	Blue Hill
GB	1935	Pounceys, St Paul	LiG	1935	Levelwood
CyC	1940	Jamestown	MP	1935	Blue Hill

Moreover, by meeting all these people, we built up and expanded our personal network as well, which soon included people from all walks of life: local journalists and radio broadcasters, historians, educationalists and teachers, artists, fishermen, builders, restaurant owners and waiters, old-age pensioners, clerks, etc., a kaleidoscope of the local community. The Saints are immensely outgoing and friendly people, and soon we were invited and taken out to local parties or events. Among others, we indulged in activities I can only describe as pure fun, far way from every-day life in academia: participating at the annual shooting tournament, parties and game evenings, tuna fishing, hiking to all parts of the island, swimming, playing golf, etc. Needless to say, we had a wonderful time on St Helena. We enjoyed the stay tremendously and our nine weeks on the island saw all the special experiences and cherishing memories only fieldwork can bring. We came to know the island and its inhabitants very well, became very fond of the local lifestyle but also learnt of the hardships and the worries about the future of the community.

Map 5.1 Places of residence of Saints interviewed

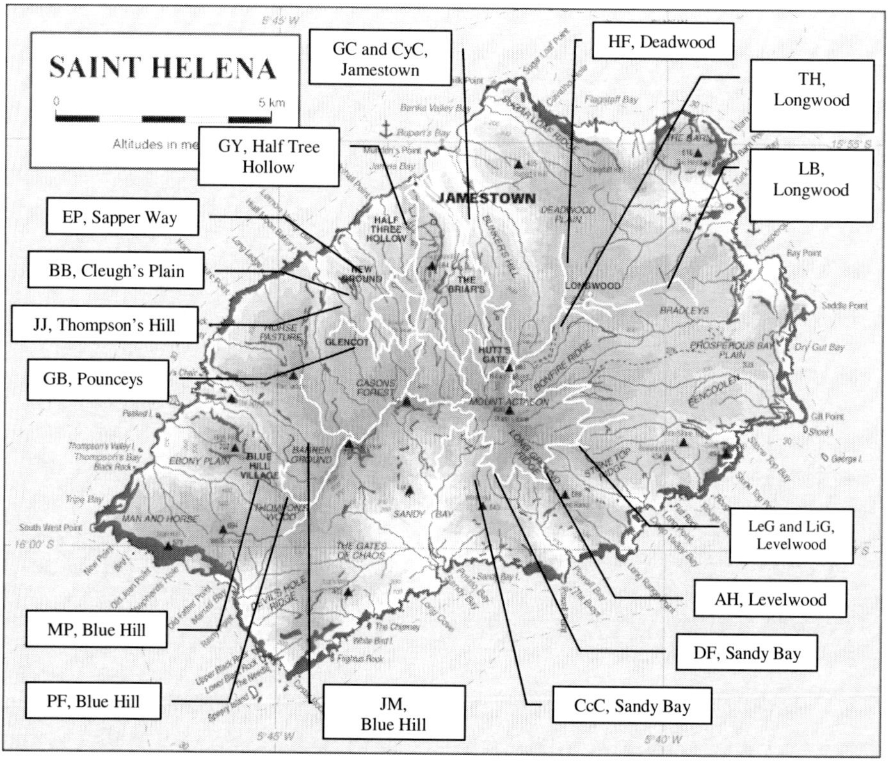

The historical research in the archives was successful as well. I became acquainted with RF, a clerk in the archives, and informed him about my work and the project I was engaged in. He was supportive in every possible way and granted me full, non-restricted access to all the documents, and I collected as much as I could in my limited time. The only problem I faced was the amount of the material I found. Whereas other researchers complain about the paucity of data, my problem was of a different kind. Apart from the massive *St Helena Records*, there were all kinds of manuscripts, maps, letters, newspapers, copies of books written about the island, reports on flora and fauna, population statistics, etc. I am still under the impression that a whole team of historians could spend a year in the archives without being able to sight the documents in their entirety. Consequently, I had to rely heavily on RF's memory and good advice. It was only thanks to his generous help that I managed to collect enough material for a data-based reconstruction of earlier StHE (ch. 4). However, I must stress that additional research is necessary (after all, I only had some nine weeks on the island to carry out the entire research project) and that additional material may refine the hypotheses put forward here or even challenge some of the conclusions (particularly if there is material for periods that are uncovered here, such as the late 17th century). Apart from Alexander Schulenburg's work (Schulenburg fc.), the Jamestown Castle archives are unexplored and I would encourage historical linguists to make use of this immensely interesting collection for their own research. What I can present here is than a first step, no more.

On a more general note, I was very surprised to find that the Saints became genuinely and openly interested in my research (this was quite unusual, at least judging from my previous experiences over the years and discussions I have had with colleagues engaged in similar fieldwork-based projects). Initially, people were a bit concerned and cautious (which is perfectly normal; after all, you do not find yourself in a position that often in which a complete stranger from a far-away university visits you in your home and tape-records your speech). Soon, however, people opened up and were happy to talk to us, often inviting others to join in and tell us good stories and old yarns, so that many an interview lasted for more than two hours (and even went on after the recorder had been switched off, or continued on another occasion and in another place). The people we talked to also ventured some theories of their own as to the origins of StHE and gave us plenty of information as to regional variation on the island (all of them were convinced that each village had its own speech ways indeed, and they even singled out specific features to us, such as an unrounded centralised LOT vowel; see below).

The public media heard of our project as well. Soon after our arrival, my wife was invited by a local radio host to appear on his weekly talk show and give her impressions of how she felt like being back on St Helena. The presenter became interested in my previous work on TdCE and invited me to join him in a special talk show with the topic "Is St Helenian English a Creole?", a question which, to his big disappointment, I felt I could not decisively answer at the time (but see ch. 7) . The interview was aired on *Radio St Helena* and the public responded immediately. People called or asked me in the street about my opinions and work, they informed me of their own speech ways and pointed out further sources and contacts. The *St Helena National Trust*, an independent, local, non-profit organisation established to "promote the appreciation, protection and enhancement of St Helena's unique environmental and cultural heritage"[1], invited me to give a lecture for its members and present some results of my research on the genesis and development of TdCE and the connection between StHE and TdCE. The local newspaper, the *St Helena Herald*, finally, ran two stories about the project and about South Atlantic English in general. This led to a fruitful, amiable atmosphere, in which our activities and some tentative first hypotheses were disseminated to the interested

[1] This quote is taken from the website http://www.sthelenanattrust.org/ (accessed March 7, 2007.

public and which allowed us to collect a massive amount of data during our stay on the island.

The less enjoyable part of analysis began back in the office. I digitised the entire database (approximately 28 hours of recorded speech of 33 Saints) and some of the interviews were transcribed orthographically (those with BB, ChC and EP), simply to closely listen in on some of the data and to start a corpus for analysis. These served as the basis for preliminary analyses and the formulation of some working hypotheses (ch. 1). I then proceeded to complete the socio-historical analysis, go through the hundreds of photocopies I had made in the Jamestown archive on St Helena and set out to complete the phonological and morphosyntactic analyses, which are presented now. The chapter ends with a summary and first assessment of the data presented, the practice adopted in ch. 4 already.

5.2 Segmental phonology

I first turn to the discussion of StHE's segmental phonology, describing the phonemes individually (using the lexical sets developed by Wells 1982). The adoption of a conventionalised reference set is most promising here, not only to ensure an accurate hands-on description of the variety but also for a cross-comparison with other forms of English, where this practice has been adopted successfully (most notably Wells 1982, but also Schneider et al. 2004, Schreier & Trudgill 2006).

However, as pointed out above, the inherent risk is that StHE (or any other variety) is portrayed as a homogeneous variety from which all variation is abstracted. To avoid this, I decided to report data for four individuals from different parts of the island: BB (male, born 1927, from Cleugh's Plain, Half Tree Hollow), JM (female, born 1926, from Head o'Wain, Blue Hill), LG (male, born 1928, from Levelwood), and ChC (male, born 1927, from Sandy Bay). The risk of over-generalisation always exists and there is no reason why these four speakers were selected from the sub-sample (other than that they had lived in their place of origin for most of their lives - with minor exceptions: BB, for instance, worked on Ascension for a few years - and that they had not moved around the island a lot; JM from Blue Hill, for instance, told us that she had not been to Sandy Bay - just four kilometres away over the ridge - in more than fifty years). However, the four speakers are by no means meant to represent 'authentic' speakers of their region (if regional varieties on St Helena exist, what still needs investigation; ch. 6). This method allows us to get at least some information about the amount of individual and/or regional variation on the island. This is central for any investigation of sociolinguistic focussing, while it at the same time has the advantages outlined above. I start with the vowels and then go on to discuss consonants.

5.2.1 Vowels

StHE joins the majority of varieties of English around the world in that it has a set of six *short vowels* (i.e., KIT, DRESS, TRAP, CLOTH; STRUT and FOOT are distinct). The realisations are as follows:

KIT /ɪ/
JM: [ɪ] (*livin'*), [ɪ̝] (*tins*, *big*), [ɪ̈] (*trips*, *pick*, *quick*)
BB: [ɪ] (*distillation*, *itchy*), [ɪ̝] (*tins*, *thing*), [ɪ̞] (*twist*, *syrup*, *fifty*)
LG: [ɪ] (*distric'*, *livin'*, *six*, *little*), [ɪ̟] (*difference*, *milk*), [ɪ] (*six*)
ChC: [ɪ] (*fish*, *bridge*), [i^{ə}] (*tins*), [ɪ] (*pigs*, *district*), [ɪ̈] (*mill*, *trips*, *fifty*)
StHE realisations of this vowel display considerable variation. While all four speakers display a stable KIT (in words such as *livin'*, *fish*, *little* or *itchy*), which resembles modern mainstream EngE, both KIT raising (in words such as *big* and *tin*) and KIT centralisation (*trip*, *pick*, *mill*) are found as well. It seems quite remarkable that both are found in the sub-sample of speakers analysed. ChC has a particularly close realisation ([i^{ə}]) with an off-glide, which is somewhat unusual. As in many South of England and American accents, some DRESS words have KIT rather than DRESS, namely when an alveolar consonant follows the vowel, /t/ in *get* or *kettle*, /d/ in *head*, or /n/ in *engine*. The word *till* very often has DRESS.

DRESS /ɛ/
JM: [ɛ] (*eleven*, *next*, *went*), [ɛ̝ ~ e̞] (*leg*)
BB: [ɛ] (*seven*, *twenty*, *went*), [ɛ̞] (*reference*), [e̞ˑ] (*leg*, *longleg*, *crafish*)
LG: [ɛ] (*fellow*, *asbestos*, *tell*, *friend*), [ɛ̝] (*seventy*), [iə] (*dead*)
ChC: [ɛ] (*twenty*, *rest*), [ɛ̝] (*leg*)
DRESS displays a considerable amount of variation also. All four speakers have a mid-close realisation ([ɛ]) and slightly raised realisations (most usually [ɛ̝ ~ e̞]). Raised variants ([e̞]) are common and particularly noticeable in voiced pre-velar environments (*leg*). LG has [iə] for the word *dead*, which, quite interestingly, is also found in one speaker (ChC) for KIT. In any case, one notes that lowering is absent.

TRAP /æ/
JM: [æ] (*back*), [æˑ^{ə}] (*jam*, *hand*), [ɛ^{ə}] (*glad*, *hand*), [ɛ̞] (*daddy*)
BB: [æ] (*family*, *flax*, *lantern*, *fancy*), [ɛ̞^{ə}] (*land*, *flax*, *Crasher*), [e̞] (*daddy*)
LG: [æ] (*gap*, *bag*, *gangs*), [æˑ^{ə}] (*land*, *flax*, *back*, *cracks*)
ChC: [æ] (*bank*, *ration*), [æ̝ˑ^{ə}] (*hand*)
A similar pattern is found in the most open of the short front vowels, TRAP. All four speakers have [æ] and this seems the most common realisation. The pattern is complicated, however, since raising and slight lengthening accompanied by

off-gliding are found as well ([ɛ̞ ~ æˑᵊ ~ æ̝ˑᵊ ~ ɛ̞ᵊ ~ ɛᵊ]). Glides are most common in pre-alveolar and pre-velar environments and before nasals. Generally speaking, though, TRAP raising is not as prominent as it is in most other accents of SHemE; [e̞] is found on occasion, but this vowel is more stable compared to the two other short front vowels.

FOOT /ʊ/

JM: [ʊ ~ ʊ̜] (*wood*; though the same word may also have [uˑ])
BB: [ʊ] (*took*, *bullock*)
LG: [ʊ ~ ʊ̜] (*roof*, *lookin'*)
ChC: [ʊ ~ ʊ̜] (*full*)

This vowel is in fact quite unremarkable in StHE. FOOT is commonly close-mid/close and fully back, though, as in many parts of the English-speaking world, unrounded and slightly centralised variants occur. This vowel may also feature in words such as *room*, *roof*, or *hoof*.

STRUT /ʌ/

JM: [ʌ] (*mummy*, *run*), [ɐ̟] (*up*, *lovey*), [ʊ] (*rub*)
BB: [ʌ] (*chuck*, *struggle*), [ʌ̟] (*cut*, *bundle*, *run*, *drums*)
LG: [ɐ] (*rubber*, *country*), [ɐ̟] (*rushes*, *tuck*, *mamma*)
ChC: [ʌ] (*much*, *bus*), [ʌ̟] (*dozen*, *jumpin'*), [ɐ] (*comin'*)

The most common realisation of STRUT is fully-mid back. All four speakers have fronting to [ɐ̟], however, and there is considerable variation here as well. It is quite interesting to find that JM on one occasion has [ʊ] (in *rub*). One could make a case in point that this is a remnant feature of an older five-vowel system, but I have no doubt that a quantitative analysis would show [ʌ] to be quasi-normative.

CLOTH /ɒ/

JM: [ɒ] (*clock*, *shot*), [ɑ] (*box*, *Scotland*, *forgot*, *knock*)
BB: [ɑ] (*contract*, *scotch*, *Thompson*, *hospital*, *bottle*), [oˑᵘ] (*long*), [ɔə] (*cost*)
LG: [ɒ] (*coffee*), [ɑ] (*doctor*, *hospital*, *top*), [ɔə] (*daughter*)
ChC: [ɑ] (*shop*, *Solomon*, *clock*), [ɔ̝] (*off*), [ɔ̝ə] (*gone*)

Unrounded [ɑ] variants are more common than rounded ones, and all four speakers have both. The realisation of CLOTH is complex since there are two more realisations. Raising to [ɔ̝] before labiodental fricatives (*off*) occurs (a feature widely attested in 19th century BrE, Wells 1982) and there is lengthening and slight off-gliding (as in [oˑᵘ], *long*) as well, which resembles varieties of English in the Caribbean. Perhaps the most diagnostic realisation is found in the speech of DF, born 1925, from Sandy Bay, who has a highly salient and unusual realisation, which I would somewhat hesitantly identify as [ɞː], i.e. as an open-mid central vowel that shows both unrounding and lengthening. My field notes indicate that this is found in other speakers as well (and it certainly is highly salient; visitors from Tristan da Cunha, for instance, consider it so prominent that they stereotype it, and the Saints themselves list this as a prime candidate for regional variation).

There is one more point of interest. Some words may have /ɔə/: *gone*, *daughter*, *cost*, etc., and it seems to me that this is indicative of a partial overlap with the THOUGHT/FORCE/NORTH/POOR sets, which are merged (see below).

As for the *long monophthongs* (FLEECE, GOOSE, NURSE, START, NORTH, FORCE, THOUGHT), the realisations are as follows:

FLEECE /iː/
JM: [iː] (*tea*, *teenager*, *weak*), [iˑᶤ] (*see*)
BB: [iː] (*see*, *people*, *clean*)
LG: [iː] (*tea*, *sweet*), [iˑ] *people*)
ChC: [iː] (*cheap*, *mean*, *see*)
This vowel is most commonly a long monophthongal [iː]; JM also has an off-glide [iˑᶤ] and slight diphthongisation, which is not frequent, however. Centralisation and backing do not occur, neither does breaking.

GOOSE /uː/
JM: [uː] (*two*, *blue*, *coolin'*)
BB: [uː] (*two*, *school*, *root*, *cool*, *booze*)
LG: [uː] (*do*, *afternoon*)
ChC: [uː] (*two*, *school*)
GOOSE is genuinely monophthongal for all four speakers: a fully back and close [uː] is quasi-normative and there is no trace of fronting (which has been well documented in many varieties of English around the world and the SHemE).

NURSE /ɜː/
JM: [ɜ̜ː] (*learn*, *servant*, *hers*, *girl*)
BB: [ɜˑ~ ɜː] (*first*, *work*), [ɜ̜ː] (*turkey*)
LG: [ɞː ~ ɞˑ] (*purpose*, *workin'*, *girl*)
ChC: [ɜ̜ː ~ ɜ̜ˑ] (*church*, *circle*)
NURSE is characterised by little lip rounding in StHE. The vowel is open-mid central and fronted or back variants are not found.

START /ɑː/
JM: [ɑː] (*far*, *start*, *star*); note *car* [kɔə]
BB: [ɑː] (*hard*, *farm*, *card*, *start*, *after*), [æ] (*plant*)
LG: [ɑː] (*farm*, *start*, *hard*); note *car* [kɔə]
ChC: [ɑː] (*park*, *hard*, *dance*), [ɑ̝ˑᵊ] (*parkway*, *start*); note *heart* [hɔət], *smart* [smɔət], also [mɔək̥] (*mark*)

START has a number of realisations in StHE. First of all, at least one speaker has both /ɑː/ and /æ/, the latter in pre-nasal environments (*dance*, *sample*, *demand*, *plant*, etc.). This pattern prevails elsewhere (IrE and AmE, for instance) but all in all, it is not common in StHE. All four speakers have a fully back [ɑː].

What is most remarkable, however, is that words such as *heart*, *car*, *smart*, or *mark* may have [ɔə] rather than /ɑː/. The incidence of START is thus complex and unusual and this is further evidence of a possible overlap with the THOUGHT/FORCE/NORTH/POOR set, which already made an appearance in the case of CLOTH above.

THOUGHT/FORCE/NORTH/POOR /oə/

JM: [oə] (*short*, *war*, *for*)
BB: [oə] (*Thorpe*, *for*, *foreman*, *sort*), [oɐ] (*store*)
LG: [oə] (*more*, *poor*, *war*, *short*, *walk*)
ChC: [oə] (*war*, *call*, *poor*, *Corker*, *chalk*), [uə] (*poor*)

One of the most striking features of the StHE vowel system is that the four vowel sets THOUGHT, FORCE, NORTH and POOR are closing diphthongs. They are generally merged, being pronounced [oə], with a rounded close-mid nucleus and with an off-glide /ə/, sometimes even /ɐ/. It occurs in all five lexical sets, so both the *First* and the *Second Force mergers* (Wells 1982) are completed. It is unusual that /oə/ is also extended to include lexical items from the CLOTH and START sets.

The analysis of the *rising/closing diphthongs* (FACE, PRICE, CHOICE, GOAT, and MOUTH) yields the following:

FACE /eɪ/

JM: [ɛɪ] (*lady*, *lace*, *say*), [ɛˑⁱ] (*bale*, *take*, *later*)
BB: [ɛɪ] (*day*, *take*, *plain*, *bail*, *break*), [ɛᴵ] (*eighteen*), [ɛ̞ˑ] (*came*, *bakehouse*)
LG: [ɛɪ] (*taste*), [ɛ̞ː] (*say*, *day*), [ɛˑⁱ] (*day*)
ChC: [ɛɪ] (*take*, *way*, *away*), [ɛᴵ] (*taker*), [ɛ̞ˑ] (*today*)

StHE FACE has what Wells (1982: 210-1) refers to as "long mid diphthonging", so the most common realisation is a diphthong. However, the nucleus may be lengthened and slightly raised, which means that the off-glide ([ɛˑⁱ]) is less prominent. Alternative realisations exist: Three speakers have a monophthong (most commonly [ɛ̞ˑ]), which differs from accents elsewhere (North of England, Scotland or Ireland) in that it is not as tense and may have a slight offglide [ɛˑᴵ]. It is certainly noteworthy that "diphthong shift" (Wells 1982: 256) to [aɪ] does not occur, which means that one of the hallmarks of AusE or Cockney is absent.

PRICE /aɪ/

JM: [ɑɨ ~ ɔ̝ɪ ~ ɔ̝ɨ] (*mine*, *times*, *library*), [əɪ] (*night*)

BB: [ɑɨ ~ ɔ̞ɨ] (*GIs, fibre, while, driver, sign, style, cider*), [ɐ̞ɪ] (*wife, inside, height*), [əɪ] (*right, like*)
LG: [ɑɨ ~ ɔ̞ɨ] (*buy, die, line*), [ɑi] (*time, island*), [əɪ ~ æ̝i] (*fight, arthritis*)
ChC: [ɑɨ ~ ɔ̞ɨ] (*side, fibre, buy*), [əɪ] (*quite, right*)

The most common realisation of StHE PRICE is [ɔ̞ɨ], with a back open-mid onset, though a more open [ɑ] is found as well. At least one speaker (BB) has [ɐ̞ɪ]. Consequently, in contrast with FACE, PRICE demonstrates diphthong shift since its nucleus has shifted to a rather back place of articulation (Wells 1982: 256). It displays some mild *glide weakening* as well ([ɨ]). Moreover, the nucleus is raised to a mid-central [ə ~ æ̝] when it precedes voiceless environments, the well-known 'Canadian raising' pattern (Chambers 1973).

CHOICE /oi/
JM: [o̞ɨ ~ oɨ] (*broidery, boyfriend*)
BB: [ɔ̞ɨ] (*boy, join, Joy*)
LG: [o̞ɨ ~ o̞ɨ] (*boy*)
ChC: [o̞ɨ ~ o̞i] (*boy*), [a̞ɨ] (*point*)

This vowel has a rather close first element, around [o̞ɨ]. The nucleus of CHOICE is thus raised and this diphthong has shifted too. Moreover, at least one speaker (ChC) has the archaic dialectal feature where PRICE occurs instead of CHOICE, e.g. *boil* which is pronounced like *bile*. This could represent a remnant variety of earlier British inputs, where it is well attested (Strang 1970: 112), but as in the case above, one should probably not interpret too much here since this realisation is rare and unusual in StHE.

GOAT /ou/
JM: [ɔu] (*go, old, own*), [o̞ː] (*home*)
BB: [ɔ̞u] (*stone, boat, goat*), [o̞ˑ ~ o̞ˑᶷ] (*home, go*)
LG: [ɔ̞u] (*clothes, stone*), [o̞ˑᶷ] (*ago*)
ChC: [ɔu] (*go, old*), [ɔ̝u] (*no, show*)

Though monophthongal [o̞ː] variants are found occasionally, GOAT is typically diphthongised ([ɔ̞u ~ ɔ̝u ~ ɔ̞u]). The onset is an open-mid and fully rounded [ɔ], and there are no traces of onset shift to /ʌ ~ œ ~ a/ or glide weakening. Even though StHE GOAT has to some extent partaken in long-mid diphthonging, the realisation of this vowel is conservative.

MOUTH /aʊ/
JM: [aʊ] (*now, out, cow*), [ɔʊ] (*about*)
BB: [o̞ʊ] (*about, out*), [ɑ̟ʊ] (*pound, house, out*)
LG: [ɑ̟ʊ] (*now, out, house*), [ɔʊ] (*about*)
ChC: [a̝ʊ] (*now, house, mountain*), [ɔʊ] (*out*)

The most usual pronunciation is [aʊ ~ ɑ̟ʊ ~ ɔʊ]. Interestingly, a back /ɔ/ onset features in function words (*out, about*), whereas the onset of lexical words tends to be somewhat more front (without shifting to TRAP or DRESS, however). Glide weakening is uncommon. There is an apparent asymmetry between front and back vowel pairs in that, in contrast to PRICE, there is no Canadian raising pattern in MOUTH (the same mismatch is reported in TdCE, Schreier & Trudgill 2006: 126, no doubt a legacy of the StHE-speaking co-founders of the Tristan da Cunha community).

As for the centring diphthongs (NEAR, SQUARE), finally, the analysis is as follows:

NEAR /iə/ ~ **SQUARE** /ɛə/
JM: generally merged; pivot [iə] (*where*, *parents*, *spare*, *care*); *there* may have [ɛə].
BB: generally merged; pivot [iə] (*fear*, *Fairy*, also *Claire*, *share*); *there* occasionally has [ɛə].
LG: merger uncommon ([iə] in *year*, [ɛə] in *barefoot*, *care*)
ChC: generally merged; pivot [iə] (*caretaker*, *share*, *Fairy*); *there* occasionally has [ɛə].
Three out of the four speakers have thus merged NEAR and SQUARE, even though a few exceptions remain (the word *there* is very often /dɛə/). Only one speaker keeps the two vowels separate on a regular basis.

Minor features of StHE's vowel system deserve attention also. First of all, the triphthongs (/aɪə/ and /aʊə/) behave differently in that only one of them (/aʊə/) may display smoothing (Wells 1982: 239), differing from modern BrE in that it has undergone backing and raising as well:

JM: no triphthong smoothing (*hour* [a̠̝ʊᵊ])
BB: /aɪə/ (as in *hire*) is [ɑ̝ʲə], /aʊə/ is a fully back [ɑː] or [ɔ̝ˑᵊ] (*flour*)
LG: smoothing ([ɔ̝ˑᵊ] *flour*)
ChC: no triphthong smoothing (*hour* [aʊᵊ])

Other features common in English accents around the world and found in StHE also are the weak vowel merger, /h/ dropping, happY tensing and Yod dropping. StHE, like all other SHemEs, has /ə/ in unstressed syllables in all or nearly all cases where southeast England has /ɪ/ (*David, market, wanted, walkin', hate it, like'im*, etc.), which means that pairs such as *abbot* and *rabbit* rhyme, both ending in /ət/, and that *trumpet* and *trump it* are indistinguishable. StHE thus has the "weak vowel merger" (Wells 1982: 167), which is also found in East Anglia and Ireland. "happY tensing" (Wells 1982: 595, 616) is common as well, so that words like *happy, money* have word-final /iː/ rather than /ɪ/ (however, JM has /ɪ/ in *broidery*).

As for Yod dropping, all four speakers have a strong tendency to drop /j/ before stressed syllables (*Tuesday*, *few*, *tune*, *leukaemia*), but it may occasionally be retained in *music* (ChC). Another interesting feature is the so-called PEN/PIN merger: KIT and DRESS are merged (pivot /ɪ/) when followed by a nasal: ChC, for intance, has /də mɪn/ (*the men*). LettER is occasionally /ɐ/, as in *bigger* [bigɐ].

5.2.2 Consonants

As for the consonants, we first note that StHE is genuinely non-rhotic. None of the speakers analysed pronounced /r/ in pre-consonantal (*farm*, *sort*) or pre-pausal environments, the only exception being BB, who says /gitɔ̞ᵊr/ *guitar* (and is /r/-ful in this lexical item only) when speaking about learning how to play this instrument on Ascension Island – from Americans stationed there. Interestingly, some speakers have linking and intrusive /r/ ("he went to South Africa /r/ eh", "after he saw /r/ it"), others do not, and this resembles SAfrE. The pronunciation of /r/ is an [ɹ] approximant, although it is occasionally post-alveolar and somewhat more retroflexed than elsewhere. By the same token, none of the four speakers has /h/ dropping in stressed content words (in unstressed function words, however, /h/ is commonly dropped, just as elsewhere, so this is not at all unusual). There is no trace of /h/ insertion either (which is fairly extensive in TdCE, Schreier 2003a: 211).

Another prominent (and much remarked on) feature of StHE is the */v~w/ interchange* (in *work*, *well*, *when*, *went*). StHE has a pre-stressed-syllable merger of /w/ and /v/, just like a number of other post-colonial English and 19th century southeastern England varieties (Trudgill, Schreier, Long & Williams 2004). Phonetically, the single consonant is realised as an approximant [β̞], a bilabial fricative, or, less often, [β] (which, as we argued in Trudgill et al. 2004, may explain why this merger is historically reported with both pivots /v/ and /w/, the approximant being perceived and reported as either). In any case, StHE does not have /ʍ/, the labio-velar approximant in *where*, *wheel*, etc. (which features prominently in ScE, IrE and (Otago) NZE). Interestingly, none of the four speakers has */v/ stopping* to [b]. This proto-typical Creole feature is thus absent in the speakers analysed. However, at least one of the other speakers in the corpus (EP, female, born 1919, from Sapper Way), has a bilabial stop in the word *fiver*, [fa̰ibə]).

Intervocalic /p/ and /k/ are often pre-glottalised: *people* [pi:ʔpɫ], *check* [tʃɛʔq]. Intervocalic /t/, on the other hand, (as in *better*, *letter*, *butter*) is nearly always a voiced flap. Since intervocalic /d/ (in *bidder*) is also a flap, the contrast between the two phonemes is neutralised in this position. By contrast, StHE has *pre-glottalisation* (Wells 1982: 260), i.e. a glottal stop before /p, t, k, tʃ/ in items such as *hopeless* [houʔpləs] or *match* [mæʔtʃ]. Another striking feature is that syllable-final /k/ is often uvular, particularly in pre-pausal environments and when following back vowels: *clock* [klɑq], *work* [ꞵ̞ɞq], *back* [bæˑᵊq].

Dental fricatives are uncommon in StHE. The most common realisation is *TH stopping* to /t/ and /d/, not only in function words such as *the*, *that*, *then*, which is also found in IrE and other varieties of English, but also in stressed lexical items (*think*, *through*, *cathedral*). Some speakers have a palatalised stop. *TH fronting* to /f/ and /v/, common in Cockney and also, in some environments, in AAE (Labov 1972), is uncommon by contrast (occasionally found in words such as *both*). A clear /l/ is usual in prevocalic position and after front vowels, but dark /l/ occurs after back vowels, displaying the usual type of allophony. None of the four speakers has *L vocalisation*.

A final characteristic of the consonantal system of StHE is the deletion of consonants from word-final clusters (so-called consonant cluster reduction, or CCR), which occurs frequently and affects both monomorphemic words (*post*, cask, *left*, etc.) and bimorphemic ones, where the final plosive represents an *-ed* tense suffix and thus carries morphological meaning (in *passed*, *laughed*, etc.). This process is highly diagnostic and will be analysed quantitatively in ch. 6. Word-initial unstressed syllables are commonly deleted. The clipping of unstressed syllables (which is common in Caribbean creoles; Holm 1989) occurs among others in words such as *assistant* (/sistn̩/), *accordion* /koədjən/, etc. Unstressed *-ing* is practically always [ɪn ~ ən].

5.3 Morphology and syntax

This section presents the synchronic-structural description of StHE morphosyntax, this time solely based on the data I collected on the island in 2003. Again, I would like to emphasise that this is by no means supposed to be an accurate representation of the variety. This section reports on the speech of more than 30 Saints and examples are drawn both from the recordings directly and from notes taken informally in the field. Listing features is always an abstraction and the result of a long and subjective selection process on the part of the researcher. No single Saint will have all the features presented below; it is erroneous to assume that they combine to characterise the morphosyntax of contemporary StHE.

In addition, a quantitative dimension of descriptive analysis is missing due to space and time restrictions. Analysing multiple features quantitatively or providing information as to how frequently they occur is simply not an option for a global overview (see above). This is an important point, particularly when we are looking into the manifestation of variation during focussing. For instance, we learn little of interest when I give examples of copula absence, other than that some of the Saints we interviewed for the project did have this feature indeed; by simply listing some examples from my corpus, I say nothing about the frequency with which this variable occurs and its conditioning factors remain unexplored as well. I try to avoid this problem whenever possible, namely by indicating whether the given feature is found in all or several speakers or in one individual only, by making some observations as to possible conditioning effects, etc.

Perhaps a note on transcription: no efforts were made to employ dialect writing conventions so as to represent the phonological characteristics of StHE or to make the examples look more 'authentic' in any way, the reason being that examples are easier to read and interpret when standard spelling conventions are employed. Moreover, using a different orthography poses a number of problems (consistency, to name but one). The description follows a top-down practice, starting from larger syntactic units (sentences) and moving to smaller ones (clauses, phrases). Here the features are loosely arranged by noun phrase (articles, pronouns, and nouns), verb phrase (negation, agreement patterns, tense-mood-aspect, etc.), and adjective phrase (comparatives and superlatives). Any potential overlap, such as when prepositional phrases affect NPs, is indicated and cross-referenced wherever possible. Each category is illustrated with examples from the entire database, though many are drawn from the speakers whose interviews were transcribed.

5.3.1 Basic sentence types

The word order of declarative sentences in StHE is SV(O), and this is maintained categorically throughout in subordinate clauses as well.

(1) I's retired now (SV)

(2) people grow pumpkins and cabbage (SVO)

The object may on rare occasions precede the verb, but this is for the purpose of focus or emphasis only.

(3) *Question*: So where you get water from in those days? *Answer*: Water us start to put in the place (OSVprepP) when we (S) start to build (V) the home (O) eh (TH, Longwood)

As for interrogative sentences, Yes-no questions are distinguished from declaratives by the fact that they have rising intonation (↗), which is a reliable marker of all types of questions in StHE (declarative sentences usually have falling intonation (↘), though at least one speaker (TH from Longwood) has high-rise intonation).

(4) She say what she go do now ↗ (JM, Blue Hill)

(5) but you can't see much now no but I t- sh- oh come here I show you . you see – you see up there ↗ (ChC, Sandy Bay)

(6) Y'all been see it ↗ (TH, Longwood)

(7) Perhaps you like to come back one day ↗ (PF, Blue Hill)

WH-question words are often monomorphemic, though compounds occur also. The former contain the classical WH-words *who*, *what*, *where*, *which*, *how* and *why*, with no notable difference from their equivalents in BrE or SHemE generally, whereas the latter include *what-thing*, *what-time*, widely attested in English-derived creoles (cf. section 5.4), but no combinations with *which* (*which-place*, etc.). The most likely explanation is that *which* as an interrogative or relative pronoun is generally rare in StHE (see below).

It is striking that StHE does not have word-order inversion in WH-questions. As a result, syntactic complexity is reduced and the order of S and V remains as in declaratives (which reinforces the use of high-rise patterns in intonation). Moreover, *do*-support is rare:

(8) Where you (S) was (V) stayin' then? (GB, Pounceys)

(9) Where you lef' you car? (TH, Longwood)

(10) You was on the island then? (CyC, Jamestown)

5.3.2 Clauses

To start with the relative clauses, it is striking that relative pronouns are on occasion missing, so that there is in fact zero relativisation.

(11) And they say those was the donkeys Ø belong to Scotland (DF, Sandy Bay)

When they are used, relative pronouns are very often *what* (with animate subjects) and *that* (with unanimate ones), though *that* can occur with animate subjects as well.

(12) I went with the car last time - you know the lady <u>what</u> do take over (EP, Sapper Way)

(13) you know the boys what I used to play with . they play for my weddin' (BB, Cleugh's Plain)

(14) lucky enough she don't have no children by the men that she married (EP, Sapper Way)

(15) all the people that you not see for a long time (TH, Longwood)

5.3.3 Adjective Phrase

StHE has two techniques of expressing comparatives and superlatives, an analytic one (*more/most ADJ*) and synthetic one (with *-er* and *-est* affixation). Typically, mono- and bisyllabic adjectives take affixation whereas adjectives with three and more syllables take *more* and *most*. However, and this seems to be a general trend in StHE, analytic techniques are much more common, and *more/most* is used with monosyllabic ADJ as well.

(16) people were more genuine than what they are today (EP, Sapper Way)

(17) They humaner now, they shoot 'em (BB, Cleugh's Plain)

On the other hand, the two techniques are also mixed, resulting in *more* co-occurring with an adjective that is affixed:

(18) It was a bit more better ... it wasn't as bad as this but it got worser (JJ, Thompson's Hill)

(19) Those days was more rough but more kind you know . more rough but more kinder (TH, Longwood)

5.3.4 Noun phrase

A prominent characteristic of NPs in StHE is that indefinite articles may on occasion be absent:

(20) they used to cut the head off the gunny bag and cut Ø hole in each side (TH, Longwood)

(21) I used to work for PanAmerican for Ø few years . for Ø few years (BB, Cleugh's Plain)

(22) she had to get Ø operation (BB, Cleugh's Plain)

(23) we used to have societies . they used to have Ø march every year (GC, Jamestown)

(24) that was in Mr Deason's time, that was Ø long long time ago (DF, Sandy Bay)

The same is possible for definite articles:

(25) that's the way we was brought up . all our people on Ø island (GC, Jamestown)

(26) ah that shop you talkin' about . was one lady there . Ms G . she had Ø shop there (DF, Sandy Bay)

(27) he had Ø generator to run the 'lectricity (GY, Half Tree Hollow)

On the other hand, definite articles are sometimes present in NPs where it is unusual for them to occur elsewhere:

(28) she was infected in the leg . all from <u>the</u> diabetes (TH, Longwood)

(29) they come out for <u>the</u> Christmas eh (TH, Longwood)

(30) So I went to <u>the</u> them (BB, Cleugh's Plain)

(31) I think it go be better cos <u>the</u> most of the old people live in town now (GY, Half Tree Hollow)

On occasion, indefinite articles are invariant in form. Hiatus strategies are reduced, so that allomorphs are not sensitive to context. For instance, there are cases when the following environment is not a conditioning factor (*a* before consonants and *an* before vowels). Consequently, *a* can occur before vocalic onsets as well:

(32) oh, I bought that at aØ auction (TH, Longwood)

The same applies for definite articles. Some speakers have invariant /də ~ dɐ/, which means that they do not vary according to the following segment as is the case elsewhere (/ði/ in pre-vocalic and /ðə/ in pre-consonantal environments).

Alternatively, we also find indeterminate *one*, i.e. the usage of *one* for an indefinite article:

(33) They say <u>one</u> iron gate there (JM, Blue Hill)

(34) You see that house yonder? Live one missus there name P. (ChC, Sandy Bay)

(35) Me and my hubby decide to give one window (TH, Longwood)

(36) After that I didn't go work no more cos I had one young baby (DF, Sandy Bay)

(37) You wan' one drop of Whiskey? (MH, Levelwood)

These and *those* are both used as demonstratives with a distal relationship, though *them* occurs frequently as well:

(38) When those dumplings float on the top (GC, Jamestown)

(39) And then there wasn't any machine then . so they had these oxen (PF, Blue Hill)

(40) I used to do deep water them days . for tuna and wahoo (BB, Cleugh's Plain)

(41) Drink was cheap them days (BB, Cleugh's Plain)

(42) He play for them small churches (BB, Cleugh's Plain)

The distinction between *this* and *that* is made in StHE as well:

(43) Yes we built this house sir . not this part here (GC, Jamestown)

(44) And then you walk down till you get to that house at Rupert's (GC, Jamestown)

As for pluralisation, nouns often take *-s* suffixation (with the exception of nouns of measure). *-s* is context-sensitive in that it is bisegmental after sibilants and dental fricatives.

(45) we gotta carry on our back see [laughs] carry on our backs . us make eh eight . maybe about uh four fellas eh eight or ten ten twenty fourty eh hooks (ChC, Sandy Bay)

(46) you pick the blackberries off the blackberry bushes (GC, Jamestown)

With agent nouns and animate subjects, the so-called associative plural *dem/n' dem* (suffixed to plural NPs) is also found:

(47) they stay over there my daddy n' dem you know (ChC, Sandy Bay)

Nouns of measurement, on the other hand, are rarely marked. Plural is not overtly marked and has to be interpreted using context.

(48) Her weddin' never cost no more than sixty seventy poundØ (BB, Cleugh's Plain)

(49) I stay there for over twelve monthØ (BB, Cleugh's Plain)

(50) I lost my husband nineteen yearØ ago (TH, Longwood)

(51) A bottle of brandy is over 10 poundØ now (DF, Sandy Bay)

However, and this makes pluralisation a complex issue, plural NPs are often not marked. The absence of plural markers is widespread in StHE and plural NPs (other than mass or count nouns) may take zero marking as well.

(52) cause there wasn't many houseØ you . you . you never had you own house cause you . ah . one or two houseØ was there (ChC, Sandy Bay)

Interestingly, even the place name *Falkland Islands* may lack plural *-s*:

(53) Down the Falkland IslandØ (DF, Sandy Bay)

Interestingly, some speakers (such as TH from Longwood) refer to the Chinese indentured labourers as /tʃaɪni/ ("I come off the /tʃaɪni/ breed"), so this is quite possibly a reanalysis and misinterpretation of *-s* suffixation, which is indicative of weakened pluralisation in StHE as well.

As for pronouns, subject personal pronouns are occasionally absent in StHE:

(54) Ø met with two girls on the train . trying to sleep had to keep wake (EP, Sapper Way)

(55) Ø don't get nothin' much only 14 pound a week (GC, Jamestown)

A personal pronoun that is non-specified and generic, such as *one* or *you*, may be absent as well:

(56) Oh yes, Ø gotta pay for you water now . Ø get nothing free . [laughs] Ø get nothing for free now (ChC, Sandy Bay)

(57) you know to the stripper see and then Ø come down fine and then after Ø have to go out in the field to spread out see (ChC, Sandy Bay)

When personal pronouns are present, then the singular forms match the general patterns found in most varieties of English around the world (*I* for first person singular, *you* for second and *he/she/it* for third). The plurals are different, however, the first person plural pronoun categorically being *us*:

(58) us come up Peak Hill way see (ChC, Sandy Bay)

(59) us had a very saucy school master (TH, Levelwood)

(60) not so long ago us wen' up by Cason's (DF, Sandy Bay)

(61) us useta pray for Christmas cos us got roast meat and potatoes and us got cakes, so many cakes on the table, see, us useta pray for those days to come (GC, Jamestown)

The second person plural pronoun is typically *you all/y'all*:

(62) But one thing I will tell y'all, thing was cheap them days (AH, Levelwood)

(63) So y'all be goin' back soon? (DF, Sandy Bay)

(64) So you had breakfas' before y'all come (TH, Longwood)

Table 5.2 summarises the subject personal pronouns in StHE.

Object personal pronouns resemble the paradigms found in most other varieties of English (*me* for first person singular, *you* for second and *him/her/it* for third). *Y'all* is the most common pronoun for second person plural objects (Table 5.3).

(65) You can't blame her and you can't blame him (GC, Jamestown)

(66) I always tell 'em I will see y'all before you see me (GC, Jamestown)

Table 5.2 StHE subject pronouns

Person	**Singular**	**Plural**
1st	I	us
2nd	you	y'all
3rd	he, she, it	they/them

Table 5.3 StHE object pronouns

Person	Singular	Plural
1st	me/us	us
2nd	you	y'all
3rd	him, her, it	them

There is a range of variants for possessive pronouns, illustrated by the following examples:

(67) he was a good boy he'd come home with his months pay . had a shirt with a pocket up here . and he say I got my pay (EP, Sapper Way)

(68) us used to put a bit of egg shell on top of the cake to mark it . to say that is my cake and that is you cake (GC, Jamestown)

(69) I have three granddaughters but this one is very very close - she says her mummy says I'm you mum (EP, Sapper Way)

(70) when you put you head down it scratch you head (AH, Levelwood)

(71) I had a friend . his name Eddy (TH, Longwood)

(72) my husband say no cos his sister say we had to pay our own passage (GC, Jamestown)

(73) we gotta carry on our back see (ChC, Sandy Bay)

(74) y'all been seein' anything like that in y'all's countries? (TH, Longwood)

(75) so you follow y'all's own way roun' yesterday? (GC, Jamestown)

(76) we used to take the cow grass, dry it, and take it down for they beds (JM, Blue Hill)

(77) that's they occupation (DF, Sandy Bay)

(78) those people on they way out now (AH, Levelwood)

(79) the old generation, they used to catch they own fish (PF, Blue Hill)

(80) at Bamboo Hedge they got they own piggery down there (PF, Blue Hill)

The first persons and third person singular are unremarkable. The second persons and third person plural, on the other hand, have (at least in part) merged with the subject pronouns: *you* functions at the same time as a subject and object pronoun as well as a possessive pronoun, and *they* is both subject and possessive pronoun. This usage is very common and found in all the speakers analysed. It is also interesting that the second possessive plural is *y'all's*, i.e. a pluralised form of the subjective and objective *y'all* that takes genitive *-s*. What is equally remarkable is that third person plural possessive *they* can be complemented by *own* (*they own*), for which I have no evidence in the other persons. Table 5.4 summarises these findings.

Table 5.4 StHE possessive pronouns

Person	Singular	Plural
1st	my/mine	our
2nd	you	y'alls
3rd	his, her, its	they/they own

The reflexive pronouns are merged as well. The second person singular is *youself* (perhaps for both numbers, though this cannot be verified in all cases) and the third singular masculine is *hisself*. The latter is widespread in varieties of English around the world (Kortmann & Szmrecsanyi 2004).

(81) he was all to hisself that's the sort of person he was (GC, Jamestown)

(82) cause they gotta do so many trips – that was saving the children going going you see that for youself (ChC, Sandy Bay)

On occasion, reflexives may be reinforced by *own self* (*my own self*, *they own self*, etc.), possibly a marker of personal involvement and a narrative intensifier, which has also been reported in Caribbean English, e.g. on the Bahamas, in Earlier AAE (Schneider, p.c. Dec 17 2007) and is very common on Tristan da Cunha as well (Schreier 2003a):

(83) I don't know if she think I was only hittin' on my own self or what (GB, Pounceys)

Indefinite pronouns are *some* and *any*:

(84) Some is sweet and some is acid (GC, Jamestown)

(85) I ain't done see any much around here (BB, Cleugh's Plain)

As for quantifiers, there is variation between the standard types *many* and *a lot of* as well as *heaps of*, *a (nice) couple of* (with the meaning 'quite a few'), and *plenty (of)*:

(86) I used to do a lot of fishing when I was young (PG, Blue Hill)

(87) oh yes, he had heaps of sweets and they was so cheap them days eh (TH, Longwood)

(88) I take a couple of tourists round (GB, Pounceys)

(89) nice couple of Tristans been here (GC, Jamestown)

(90) Us got so many cakes on the table (GC, Jamestown)

(91) No it wasn't many . only was a few (DF, Sandy Bay)

(92) He was a big fellow . plenty of people been workin' for him (AH, Levelwood)

A final characteristic of the StHE noun phrase is that the possessive noun phrase constructions often lack genitive *-s*, which is reduced to zero (or simply absent) in the following examples:

(93) I go town, do my mummyØ shoppin' (JM, Blue Hill)

(94) us used to go up Brian IsaacØ Shop (TH, Longwood)

(95) many a personØ downfall is drink (GC, Jamestown)

StHE also has an unusual adverbial, *mussy*, which may also function in ways similar to a modal verb (see below). The semantics of this marker is not always clear, but there are cases where this is quite likely a contracted form (with consonant cluster reduction) of *must be*, referring to points in time and duration or else places and locations:

(96) I went to London in 1984 . mussy 1985 (GB, Pounceys)

(97) Rock Rose – mussy the only old building there now (AH, Levelwood)

(98) They had some wind turbines . oh mussy some six or seven years ago (GY, Half Tree Hollow)

(99) That place do be cram . about a hundred mussy (ChC, Sandy Bay)

As for auxiliaries, *has* occurs with plural NPs in present perfect:

(100) Him and I has always been very close (EP, Sapper Way)

(101) Hard work people has been through (TH, Longwood)

(102) Did you ride donkeys too? (DS) Has been, has been (DF, Sandy Bay)

5.3.5 Prepositional phrase

First of all, prepositions such as *to*, *at*, etc. are more often than not absent, particularly with locatives:

(103) I went Ø Ascension (BB, Cleuth's Plain)

(104) now I wasn' goin' Ø school (JM, Blue Hill)

(105) oh yeah he won't come back Ø St Helena . no he made his home over there now (EP, Sapper Way)

(106) I don't go much Ø town dear (TH, Longwood)

(107) I never like to go Ø country to stay (GC, Jamestown)

On the other hand, the usage of locative, spatial and temporal attributives *-way*, *-side*, and *-time* is very common in StHE; these are always post-posed to the NP or PrepP they modify, as in the following examples.

(108) That's Sandy Bay-side (GB, Pounceys)

(109) They jus' have one gang Blue Hill-side (AH, Levelwood)

(110) I was born over White Gate-way (GB, Pounceys)

(111) You go down Woods-way and then you go down (MH, Levelwood)

(112) so he'll bring you up with the car take you up Black Gate-way (TH, Longwood)

(113) and winter-time eh you soaking wet 'fore you got there (ChC, Sandy Bay)

(114) us only used to get a bit of meat at Christmas-time and festival-time (GC, Jamestown)

(115) only in the last part November-time (GB, Pounceys)

(116) I go down there every Saturday afternoon . ah and I go say us go down half pas' three-time you know (ChC, Sandy Bay)

On rare occasions *at* is used in the context of *to*, as in:

(117) I thought she'd be a bit of company for me . listen at the radio or listen at this (EP, Sapper Way)

The archaic form *yonder* is frequently used with distal meaning; it can either precede or follow an NP or occur in the context of *that*:

(118) right there where the house is . yonder red roof (ChC, Sandy Bay)

(119) see that hill that be on the side . it all up top yonder (ChC, Sandy Bay)

(120) today I work here with all the Yanks . tomorrow I work over yonder (AH, Levelwood)

5.3.6 Verb phrase

To start with existential constructions, the existential is often *it* or simply absent:

(121) yes, it was a mill up there (DF, Sandy Bay)

(122) it was some places down there you come up the hill like that see you know but it was nothing to it hey (ChC, Sandy Bay)

(123) Ø was never that amount over there, only was a few (DF, Sandy Bay)

(124) Ø wasn't no fridges like they have today (GB, Pounceys)

(125) Ø wasn't much money those days (GC, Jamestown)

(126) don't know when they get it finish cos Ø a lot of hard rock there see (GY, Half Tree Hollow)

Infinitives may lack *to*:

(127) now they want me Ø do that (BB, Cleugh's Plain)

As for verbal morphology, affixation is generally rare in StHE. This means that third person singular present tense is very often zero:

(128) Phyllis workØ down the Education (DF, Sandy Bay)

(129) what what makeØ it good what makeØ it . not everybody doØ it (BB, Cleugh's Plain)

(130) he doØn't write now . sometimes he sendØ me a card at Christmas but very seldom (EP, Sapper Way)

(131) sometimes the bus carryØ twenty-five eh (TH, Longwood)

By the same token, *-ed* past tense affixation of regular verbs is frequently absent also (this is one of the two features subjected to a quantitative analysis in ch. 6):

(132) I never walkØ around much them days (CC, Sandy Bay)

(133) She passØ it over and I grabØ it as fast as I could (BB, Cleugh's Plain)

Mussy co-occurs with infinitives and even with modal verbs (such as *can* or *could*). Future research will show whether this is indicative of semantic bleaching and grammaticalisation, but for the time being, this is certainly a possibility. The following examples suggest that StHE *mussy* resembles modal verbs:

(134) Mr Solomon had the mills see . you mussy hear about it hey (ChC, Sandy Bay)

(135) They mussy take that down and buil' the house (DF, Sandy Bay)

(136) You mussy hear some histories about people on St Helena eh (TH, Longwood)

(137) We mussy couldn't get it here (LG, Levelwood)

(138) You mussy can smell the rubbin' stuff (HF, Longwood)

Another striking feature of the StHE verb phrase is invariant *be* (which is also found in regional BrE and AAE). This usage may have a habitual meaning, as in:

(139) the Jack o' Lanterns generally be round there too, up top the mountain (ChC, Sandy Bay)

(140) it don't be pain like 'fore days … it don't be real pain (DF, Sandy Bay)

(141) it don't be nothing much for them . get 14 pound a week for it, you see (GC, Jamestown)

(142) see that hill that be on the side . it all up top yonder (ChC, Sandy Bay)

(143) see up there now all up there see the donkeys be go up on top then eh (ChC, Sandy Bay)

(144) when you start feedin' one pen all the rest be shoutin' for they food (GB, Pounceys)

However, there are also contexts where the meaning is non-habitual or where there is future reference:

(145) He don't be well now (DF, Sandy Bay)

(146) He be home this September (EP, Sapper Way)

(147) Next Tuesday week I be goin' day centre (TH, Longwood)

(148) They say they be leavin' on the first' of September (MF, Blue Hill)

Futurity may alternatively be expressed by *will* (and, with negative polarity, *won't*), or even *go*:

(149) one thing I'll tell y'all the pay was very small (AH, Levelwood)

(150) I don't know if they'll send me any money again this year (EP, Sapper Way)

(151) teen shillings today won't get you breakfas' (GC, Jamestown)

(152) if you pick up sweet potatoes, if it's one kilo, two kilos, it go be expensive (GB, Pounceys)

(153) yeah, the weather nice up here, but you don't know what it go be Sandy Bay (PY, Kunjee Field)

(154) no, if he go use the kitchen from 6 to 7 you can go in from 8 (GB, Pounceys)

(155) I jus' go show you something before you go home (PF, Blue Hill)

(156) in two weeks time I go be 82 (GY, Half Tree Hollow)

Will semantically resembles the modal *would* in:

(157) he will insult his bes' frien' when he drinkin' (GC, Jamestown)

StHE also has what one might call *redundant tense marking*. Preterits or participles may occur instead of bare infinitives, with negatives, *to* and even with quasi-modals (e.g. *used to*), as in:

(158) my daddy used to got the flax (DF, Sandy Bay)

(159) I didn't thought I could do flowers … I didn't got into doin' flowers (EP, Sapper Way)

(160) I tell her if I wasn't too old I like to went down Falklands . my daughter was wan' me to come down there (DF, Sandy Bay)

(161) he did all the work to got the machinery in the truck (AH, Levelwood)

(162) and afterwards, they decide to got a bike and then he used to ride the bike (GC, Jamestown)

(163) I didn't went out nowhere eh (TH, Longwood)

The StHE negation system is particularly rich and complex. On the one hand, there is a standard negation type that takes *do* support, as in:

(164) we didn't have imported eggs . imported chickens like we get now (EP, Sapper Way)

(165) so nevertheless he got this job down Solomon's office so he didn't go back to secondary school (EP, Sapper Way)

(166) ah . you didn't keep goin' (CyC, Jamestown)

(167) I don't know if you know anything about it (PF, Blue Hill)

However, StHE has alternative techniques as well; for one, like many varieties of English around the world, it has merged *am not*, *is not* and *are not* to *ain't*. *Ain't* may also occur in combination with preverbal markers such as *done* (see below):

(168) No way, I ain't goin' in for that (CyC, Jamestown)

(169) They ain't plannin' that (BB, Cleugh's Plain)

(170) He ain't done examine you (LeG, Levelwood)

Moreover, we find a number of alternative negative operators, such as *never*, *not* or *no* (all of which occur in preverbal positions):

(171) But after members never join so the societies went down . there was no more money (GC, Jamestown)

(172) pity that now you never see that 'fore you go you know (ChC, Sandy Bay)

(173) "Jessie, they say to me, Jessie, you no eat no food" (JM, Blue Hill)

(174) I got more pictures but I not got them close by (GC, Jamestown)

(175) No, we not really see any foreign ships (PF, Blue Hill)

Multiple negation is frequent as well:

(176) Nothin' no come (AH, Levelwood)

(177) I a young girl only then, don't know nothin' and nowhere none to help me nothin' (JM, Blue Hill)

(178) Now I say I won't get nothin' . I no get nothin' (AH, Levelwood)

Another striking characteristic of the StHE verb phrase is that *was* occasionally co-occurs with *want* (i.e. *was want/was wanna*), as in:

(179) If you was wan' one beer . one shillin' now that's in the old currency before this currency change (AH, Levelwood)

(180) My daughter was wan' me to come there (DF, Sandy Bay)

(181) They all come look for something cos everybody was wan' something eh . everybody was wan' something (TH, Longwood)

(182) Nobody was wanna go on them endemic walks you know (GB, Pounceys)

(183) They was wan' somebody to work in the galley (GY, Half Tree Hollow)

For to, finally, may occur instead of 'in order to V':

(184) it will stay there until the sun come for to pick up you know (ChC, Sandy Bay)

5.3.7 *Tense, mood, aspect*

In present tense, *do* (mostly in the form of unstressed /də/) is often used as a marker of emphasis or habituality:

(185) When I do kill I send half a pound to Cape Town (BB, Cleugh's Plain)

(186) that's what all of us do query (PF, Blue Hill)

(187) yeah no I went with the car last time - you know the lady what do take over (EP, Sapper Way)

(188) they do grow a lot of vegetables in those days - you had to grow it (GB, Pounceys)

Done very often functions as a preterit of *do*:

(189) I never done no lace that day (JM, Blue Hill)

(190) no, never find out who done it (TH, Longwood)

(191) the last tow tests they done . they done on the 26th of March (BB, Cleugh's Plain)

(192) so they wanna know what I done . so I tell 'em (GB, Pounceys)

As pointed out already, weak verbs very rarely take *-ed* suffixation and rely on context:

(193) I workØ for the GIs that was just after the war in 1947 (ChC, Sandy Bay)

(194) My husband liveØ in Jamestown all his life and I liveØ in Jamestown all my life (GC, Jamestown)

This also applies to passive sentences, as in:

(195) I got two grandsons in Germany . one nameØ Gary and the other nameØ Steve (DF, Sandy Bay)

(196) And one dressØ in pink (JM, Blue Hill)

For the time being, it is unclear whether this is a phonological process (namely the reduction – or simplification – of a cluster of consonants through the deletion of a final stop) or, alternatively, a grammatical one (namely that past tense is not expressed via suffixation, mirroring the process of bare root extension).

Generally speaking, one can say that overt past tense marking is rare in StHE. Irregular verbs typically undergo bare root extension, so that infinitives come to be used with past tense reference as well:

(197) I <u>make</u> so many trips to get the wood in (JM, Blue Hill)

(198) When it was wet we gotta take shelter an' when the rain <u>go</u> off we start again (DF, Sandy Bay)

(199) I <u>leave</u> school when I was fourteen (DF, Sandy Bay)

(200) that's the way it <u>go</u> . that's the way it was . that's the way us had to do it (ChC, Sandy Bay)

(201) the lady who jus' <u>ring</u> ask if y'all gonna come visit (TH, Longwood)

(202) rent first and then lucky they <u>sell</u> it to us (GB, Pounceys)

(203) some people got the whole house <u>light</u> up (GY, Half Tree Hollow)

Pre-verbal *been* expresses present perfect and often carries a sense of remoteness:

(204) quite a few <u>been</u> droppin' out cos they pass on (TH, Longwood)

(205) I <u>been</u> on the ships you know. to visit . but I never <u>been</u> travel (TH, Longwood)

(206) you went somewhere where I not <u>been</u> (DF, Sandy Bay)

(207) some people <u>been</u> on the old RMS ever since (GY, Half Tree Hollow)

(208) he say "Albert" he say "I <u>been</u> lookin' you record up" (AH, Levelwood)

(209) he <u>been</u> to Ascension when 16 and he still there (GC, Jamestown)g

Completive *done* is very frequent in StHE:

(210) I <u>done</u> beat him now, I seventy-five see (LeG, Levelwood)

(211) I <u>done</u> scotch up there myself see … I <u>done</u> scotch down the mill too (ChC, Sandy Bay)

(212) the birthday's <u>done</u> gone now see (TH, Longwood)

(213) they dead'n <u>done</u> gone a long time now (ChC, Sandy Bay)

(214) he tell me he say you friend, they <u>done</u> kill him (HF, Longwood)

(215) so she was <u>done</u> tell my mummy (JM, Blue Hill)

Pre-verbal *been* occurs with regular frequency also, very often carrying a meaning of remoteness and anteriority:

(216) I scotch, I sort, but I not <u>been</u> bale (BB, Cleugh's Plain, talking about his work in the flax industry)

(217) I <u>been</u> ride up on a donkey up this road here, up Peak Hill, when the [school] treats was on the plain (GC, Jamestown)

(218) if he <u>been</u> stick to his police job he been up there Derek Thomas' (GC, Jamestown)

Unstressed preverbal *do* and *did* are in use as well:

(219) whatever my boss <u>do</u> start me . I's try my bes' to do it (BB, Cleugh's Plain)

(220) I <u>did</u> like it down there pretty good (AH, Levelwood)

(221) he <u>did</u> really like . he <u>did</u> love it (TH, Longwood)

(222) I know some weeks they <u>did</u> give out the numbers what used to come here (GB, Pounceys)

(223) but a foreign ship <u>did</u> get here cos it blew up our *Darkdale* (PF, Blue Hill)

Note also *do be*, which is maybe used for special emphasis or as an expression of emotional involvement:

(224) that place do be terrible now (BB, Cleugh's Plain)

(225) that place do be cram . about a hundred (ChC, Sandy Bay)

Aspect markers can also co-occur in the same VP. Most common are the combinations *done* + *been*:

(226) if you done been down there Collie Williams I don't know if you know him (ChC, Sandy Bay)

a-prefixing, on the other hand, is extremely uncommon, and I found only one example in my corpus:

(227) you see that house up there? He's a-livin' there (AH, Levelwood)

Functions of modality (irrealis, etc.) are often expressed by *would*:

(228) I would take you a fine [?] day and explain to y'all (ChC, Sandy Bay)

(229) they would buy for people with plenty chickens (EP, Sapper Way)

(230) those who had big families, they would give more bread than I would give with only two of us (TH, Longwood)

(231) my brother Sidney ask if I would like to come England (TH, Longwood)

(232) the girl ask me what I would pay back St Helena (BB, Cleugh's Plain)

(233) I put myself in the picture how I would do it (GB, Pounceys)

(234) they had these big stones on the roofs and the ropes tyin' them down so the wind wouldn't blow the roofs off (GC, Jamestown)

On the other hand, *may*, *might*, *could* and *couldn't* take this (or at least a similar) function as well:

(235) then us all put it in a basket and then we raffle it . what she bring, somebody else may draw out (TH, Longwood)

(236) I may stay up there cos I want a bit of stuff (BB, Cleugh's Plain)

(237) there might be a possibility to cut down the electricity see (GY, Half Tree Hollow)

(238) we didn't have imported eggs . imported chickens like we get now . people had it on the island . were their own and they could sell or give you one (EP, Sapper Way)

(239) I could've been gone but my husband say no (GC, Jamestown)

(240) he couldn't have the bread cos he used to want the bread . he was the baby (GC, Jamestown)

Double modals are not frequent but occur as well:

(241) what I bring you may can draw out (TH, Longwood)

Go may also occur instead of *would*. In the following example, ChC from Sandy Bay recalls the hard work in the flax plantations in the 1940s and '50s and describes how flax was collected and produced in the factory buildings:

(242) then you gotta you got it uh and then uh the people gotta roll it up like hanks like you know . just like ha- . and then the dray go take it in for the scotcher . scotcher in the same place (ChC, Sandy Bay)

The same usage is found in the following example, where GC recounts where her husband used to hide his money:

(243) and never worry over money . as soon as he come he go say to me you find my money down the side of my drawer (GC, Jamestown)

Deontic and epistemic modality are often expressed with *must* (for present tense) and *had to* (past tense), or even, though this is very unusual, *must have (to)*:

(244) whatever they want you to do you must do it maybe pipelines fittin' in compressors trucks all like that (AH, Levelwood)

(245) St Andrew's School . that's where Valerie must be now (DF, Sandy Bay)

(246) every Sunday us had to go church . every Sunday . had to go . you couldn't say no you not goin' (GC, Jamestown)

(247) in those days children had to walk to school (GB, Pounceys)

(248) after the electricity come here you won't see nothing and . and . I reckon it must be true you know (ChC, Sandy Bay)

(249) when you boil that you put salt or anything you boil of a pig - you must have to add a bit of salt in you food (BB, Cleugh's Plain)

(250) so if you want one pound . to bring back with you you must have to save every shillin' that you work for you can't afford one beer (AH, Levelwood)

Present tense progressives are typically expressed by *-ing*. On occasion, however, this suffix may be zero.

(251) you legs was painØ? (TH, Longwood)

(252) they got some Ascension and they tell me they's workØ very successful (GY, Half Tree Hollow)

Concord and agreement patterns have undergone large-scale regularisation in StHE (ch. 2). Standard usage of *are* with second singular and plural persons and *am* with first person singular is found on occasion, as in:

(253) after coming back from England . ah Jehovahs Witness people come about here . I accept them we're all people (EP, Sapper Way)

Notwithstanding, a standard usage of *am* and *are* is uncommon. Present tense *be* is practically always levelled with the pivot *is*, so that first person and second person singulars and all the plural pronouns and NPs agree with *is*:

(254) I's quite happy (TH, Longwood)

(255) He come to me and he tell me "tell me I's sixty years ol'" (DF, Sandy Bay)

(256) I's certain he don't wanna go (GC, Jamestown)

(257) I think they's divorce (DF, Sandy Bay)

(258) though things is much easier people grumble more than those days (GY, Half Tree Hollow)

(259) galvanised windows is all right (GY, Half Tree Hollow)

(260) When there's holidays you don't get nothin' (GC, Jamestown)

We find the same patterns in the past tense. Past *be* has undergone an equally extensive process of levelling towards pivot *was*, so that second person singulars as well as all the plural persons and plural existentials agree with the first and third singular persons.

(261) when we was young children, young'uns (TH, Longwood)

(262) but the blackberry is not plentiful like when we was children you know (GB, Pounceys)

(263) they was doin' that road up for quite a while (DF, Sandy Bay)

(264) now, they wasn't want me to do this, my parents (JM, Blue Hill)

(265) people was quite happy dem days, I fancy (ChC, Sandy Bay)

(266) there was no motor cars like today (GC, Jamestown)

(267) those days Ø wasn't no outboard engines like there is now (GY, Half Tree Hollow)

On the other hand, in view of the extensive levelling of present and past *be* to *is* and *was*, it is remarkable to find levelling to *were* and to *weren't* as well, though the following sentences are infrequent:

(268) when I were in Eng- he weren't born (EP, Sapper Way)

(269) actually when I were young that was our main diet (PF, Blue Hill)

(270) lunch time half an hour that's all . oh yes that were the worst you know (ChC, Sandy Bay)

Present *be* is typically levelled to *is*. More frequently, though, copulas are absent when following personal subject pronouns, NPs, adjectives, locatives (LOC), Verb + *-ing* and *gonna*, as in the following examples:

(271) I Ø on treatment for sugar you know (DF, Sandy Bay)

(272) I Ø happy . I got nothin' to grumble about (GY, Half Tree Hollow)

(273) tomorrow night he Ø on the station up there (GC, Jamestown)

(274) us Ø like school children to 'em (AH, Levelwood)

(275) they Ø keepin' him in the hospital now (EP, Sapper Way)

(276) of course the roads Ø much better nowadays (GY, Half Tree Hollow)

(277) my house Ø in Cleugh's Plain (BB, Cleugh's Plain)

(278) people Ø leavin' the island on every ship . yeah the population Ø goin' down quickly since we got the citizenship (PF, Blue Hill)

The rate of copula absence is extremely high in StHE and will be analysed in more detail in the following chapter (particularly since this variable allows us to speculate about the variety's contact history).

Finally, serial verbs are common in StHE, particularly when the first V is dynamic:

(279) so these two went tell the senior officer what I say (BB, Cleugh's Plain)

(280) so you hear talk about it? (PF, Blue Hill)

(281) they also got people to help look after the old people (GY, Half Tree Hollow)

We already saw that *go* co-occurs with verbs, particularly when *go* has an active meaning:

(282) sometimes I go look for something it lookin's at me (DF, Sandy Bay)

(283) nobody like go for that today (GB, Pounceys)

It is somewhat unusual that a locative may be placed between two verbs, as in:

(284) My hubby used to go Ladder Hill work (TH, Longwood)

(285) After I got married I come Green Hill stay (DF, Sandy Bay)

(286) When I first come Half Tree Hollow live (GY, Half Tree Hollow)

Finally, and to conclude the analysis of the verb phrase, StHE also has the (now) archaic feature of perfective *be*, which means that *be* is used instead of *have* in present perfect. This is further evidence of present *be* levelling to *is*, since *have* corresponds with *is*. The auxiliary in the following sentences, for instance, most likely underwent a path of *have* > *are* > *is*:

(287) So you jus' see how times is changed (PF, Blue Hill)

(288) St Helena is really changed a lot since these days (PF, Blue Hill)

5.3.8 *Morphosyntax: Summary and some first assessments*

The morphosyntactic profile of 20th century StHE has provided a number of important insights. For instance, it is striking that grammatical complexity is reduced, for example: there is no word order inversion in question-type sentences ("Where she is?"), analytic techniques are more commonly used than synthetic ones for comparatives and superlatives, there is a strong trend to merge pronouns (so that *you* is used as a possessive pronoun as well), there is no environment-conditioned constraint on allomorphy (so that the indefinite article *a* is invariant and used in pre-vocalic contexts as well), etc.

One can establish parallels between the features found in StHE and varieties elsewhere, which is of course an important piece of evidence for typological classification. Even though this is by no means intended to be exhaustive (a general overview of all the features is not possible for the reasons outlined, the assignment to a single variety may not be clear-cut due to extensive overlap between the donors, independent developments, etc.), one finds quite a few similarities with non-standard varieties of English around the world. Though the following observations must be handled with care, I would suggest that quite a few of these features can be traced to the British Isles (and better still: to different parts of the British Isles). Such a list would include the adoption of *what* and *that* as relative pronouns, extensive levelling of past *be* with pivot form *was*, no pluralisation of nouns of measure, *them* as a demonstrative, mergers of reflexive pronouns (e.g. *hisself*), invariant *be*, *ain't* as merger for *am not*, *is not* and *are not*, *never* as a negator ("she *never* talk to him las' week"), double modals ("it *may can* draw you out"), or present tense *be* regularisation with pivot form *is* ("*I's* quite happy here"), all of which are documented in regional varieties of southern EngE. StHE also has a number of features that are now archaic or obsolete in the British Isles, such as: *yonder* as a locative, perfective *be*, or *for to* 'in order to'.

By the same token, a good number of the morphosyntactic features are predominant in English-based creoles: absence of definite and indefinite articles before NPs ("that was Ø long time ago", "our people on Ø island"), indeterminate *one* ("live *one* missus there"), absence of morphologically encoded pluralisation, absence of subject personal pronouns, *plenty* as a quantifier, absence of genitive *-s* with noun phrase constructions, absence of prepositions and the usage of locative, temporal and spatial attributives (*-side*, *-time*, etc.), absence of existentials or existential *it*, a very strong tendency to avoid morphological tense marking (i.e., lack of *-s* or *-ed* suffixation) and reliance on pre-verbal markers instead (*done*, *been*, *used to*, etc.), *go* as a future marker ("you don't know what the weather *go be* like on the other side of the island"), completive *done*, *no* and *not* as negators ("you *no* eat *no* food"), bare root extension of irregular verbs (*ring*, *sing*, *sell*, *light*, *make* etc. as preterits and participles), copula absence, and serial verbs.

Diagnostic and rare (possibly even endemic) features that may have arisen through independent developments on the island are: *they own* as a third person plural possessive pronoun, usage of *mussy* with VPs ("you *mussy* hear about that"), preterits instead of bare infinitives with quasi-modals *used to* or in other contexts ("I like to *went* down Falklands", "my daddy used to *got* the flax"), or the *was want* construction ("she *was want* one beer", "the thing is they never *was wanna* do that").

A more detailed assessment, with a consideration and contextualisation of the historical findings, will follow in ch. 7 below. For now, I conclude that the morphoyntax of StHE is characterised by mixing and diversity. It is not possible to single out one donor, and there is no doubt that StHE must have evolved out of contact between diverse varieties, drawing features from several coexisting dialects and/or languages or developing its distinctive characteristics out of interaction between them.

5.4 Summary

This chapter has provided a general overview of the most salient features of 20th century StHE, as found in the speech of Saints born before WWII. The most important implications are discussed in ch. 7 below and will not be recapitulated here. For now, I emphasise that a comparison of the features does not yield a coherent picture at all. First of all, the parallels with varieties of English elsewhere are striking. For instance, StHE aligns with the major SHemEs in that it has the weak vowel merger and in that the short front vowels are raised and typically close; it resembles AmE by the fact that yod dropping is widespread; it has a set of six short vowels and the well-established *Canadian raising* pattern of FACE diphthong onsets before voiceless environments (but not in MOUTH, which seems diagnostic). Like SAfrE, it has a fully back START vowel and it has a strong tendency to merge NEAR and SQUARE, just like NZE. The transmission and maintenance of (now) archaic and obsolete BrE features manifests itself in features such as the /v~w/ merger, PRICE for CHOICE in words like *boil*, etc. On the other hand, the segmental phonology of StHE also has features that are difficult (or even impossible) to explain by the variety's British ancestry alone. Proto-typical creole features also make an appearance, such as consonant cluster reduction, [b] instead of /v/ in *fiver*, etc. This points to a language contact history and suggests that the sociolinguistic scenario that gave rise to StHE was much more complex than one of simple dialect contact and koinéisation. It would be a serious mistake to try and explain shared features causally (i.e. by attempting to establish relationships between these varieties), and they quite possibly represent a shared legacy of earlier forms of post-colonial English and are thus best regarded as remnants.

This is further supported by the morphosyntactic analysis. StHE does not align itself with (non-standard) BrE varieties on a number of accounts, to mention but a few: the extensive usage of preverbal tense markers (*done*, *been*, *go*, *do*, etc.), the tendency to avoid suffixation of verbs for present and past tense, the extensive amount of bare root extension (so that infinitives of strong and semi-weak verbs are very often used as preterits and/or participles as well), the lack of grammatical complexity and the uniformity and syntactic pre-eminence of SVO word order (the subject precedes the verb even in question-type sentences: Where *she is*?), serial verbs, copula absence, etc.

Consequently, we are in a much better position to tackle some of the questions raised in ch. 1. We have outlined the social history and complemented the analysis with linguistic data, both from historical attestations (ch. 4) and my own evaluation of spoken data from 20th century StHE. What is missing still is a quantitative angle. As argued in ch. 2, sociolinguists cannot – and should not – investigate focussing and norm emergence from a purely qualitative perspective. The detailed intricacies of language variation, i.e. the language-internal and extralinguistic conditioning parameters, remain hidden, yet they are of crucial importance for processes of creolisation and new-dialect formation. Consequently, then, the next chapter provides a quantitative analysis of two selected features, consonant cluster reduction and copula absence. This will provide insights into questions relating to focussing and regional variation, which are then discussed and evaluated in the final chapter.

6. Synchrony II: A variationist analysis of 20th century StHE

> "Because the way they dress they used to identify what district they come from. Even the way they speak eh: one day one woman say to me - I say to myself I should have wound her up - I was friends with her daughter at school and we got talking. She said 'you come from Blue Hill, I can hear the way you talk.' I told myself that's great, I should tell her I come from Longwood!" (MP, Blue Hill)

The people on St Helena are convinced that they can tell the origins of a native Saint just by the way he or she speaks. During our fieldwork activities, the topic of regional variation on the island came up a number of times (as illustrated by the quote above, drawn from one of our interviews) and several interviewees pointed out that sociolinguistic variation correlated with socio-cultural parameters (such as food, dress, religion, or life-style). For instance, we were told that one could tell someone from Levelwood by the bright colours they typically wear, the people from Sandy Bay by the way they like hot and spicy food, and we received more comments of this type. Indeed, as ch. 3 has shown, St Helena may be small but its topography (slopes, steep cliffs, gorges, and deep valleys) would force the island's population(s) to live in regionally separated settlements. Once the local populaces stabilise and cross-island migration ceases (which was the case in the second half of the 18th century, see above), it is plausible to assume that, given the distinct sociolinguistic set-ups and local settler ecologies, each village would in time develop distinct endonormative sub-varieties by drawing from their specific feature pools (ch. 2). This, in theory at least, might lead to the emergence of different dialects in distinct mini-speech communities living in close proximity yet in mountainous terrain. The differences would then increase due to limited contacts with people from other parts of the island (i.e. from the early 1800s onwards). This is confirmed by the Saints themselves; the case of JM (a resident of Blue Hill, who had not been over the ridge to Sandy Bay in more than 50 years) was presented in ch. 5; by the same token, LG from Levelwood told us that when he was young there was little contact with people from Longwood, a mere 2 kilometres away across the gorge. Youngsters going out with someone from Levelwood were hunted by men and adolescents from Longwood and beaten with stones, for instance.

The discussion of settlement patterns and the fanning out of population movements from Jamestown across the island would certainly legitimise speculations of this kind, particularly when we recall the distinct ratios of whites and blacks and the social transformation and urbanisation in the early

19th century. The question, then, is simply whether we should continue to speak of StHE as such (suggesting it is a more or less stable variety) or whether it is not justified to speak about St Helenian English*es* instead, i.e., to take into consideration that there might exist regionally distinctive forms of the variety. The latter might open up new perspectives on a number of theoretical issues discussed in ch. 2, i.e., whether StHE has undergone focussing or not (is it possible that focussing occurred in some parts of the island only, but not everywhere?), local contact settings, population ecologies and the locally differing sociolinguistic outcomes (was there pidginisation on the plantations 'up country' but not in Jamestown?) or the legacy of founder effects, which may have been most persistent in socially and topographically isolated communities.

This chapter completes the qualitative description provided in ch. 5. Though limited in scope (I can only concentrate on two variables for space limitations), it provides some first insights as to whether StHE is subject to systematic regional variation or not. The aim is to provide an in-depth analysis of quantitative differentiation, which could then allow us to identify donors (in the best case: how they interacted and which of them was most influential) and thus arrive at a better understanding of diversification within the variety. The two variables selected for this purpose are *consonant cluster reduction* (CCR, as in 'she wen' home', 'he lef' it where it was and never touch' it') and *copula absence* (the absence of copulative verbs in declaratives, e.g. 'she Ø really angry now'). The two features have the advantage that they have been studied in great detail in the literature, so this allows us to contextualise the status of StHE and further assess the amount and impact of language contact when it formed. They are studied in a sub-sample of the StHE speakers interviewed (7 men and 7 women from all over the island; details in Table 6.1).

Table 6.1 Sub-sample of 14 StHE speakers analysed for CCR and copula absence

Male			**Female**		
Initials	*Year of Birth*	*Residence*	*Initials*	*Year of Birth*	*Residence*
PF	1917	Blue Hill	EP	1919	Sapper Way
GY	1921	Half Tree Hollow	GC	1920	Jamestown
ChC	1927	Sandy Bay	TH	1924	Longwood
BB	1927	Cleugh's Plain, Half Tree Hollow	DF	1925	Sandy Bay
LeG	1928	Levelwood	HF	1925	Deadwood
AH	1930	Levelwood	JM	1926	Blue Hill
GB	1935	Pounceys, St Paul	MP	1935	Blue Hill

I analysed internal constraints (e.g. preceding phonetic and grammatical environment) for all 14 speakers. One of them was removed from the analysis of regionality effects (GB lived in an isolated hamlet, right between Half Tree Hollow and Blue Hill, and I felt it would be problematic to assign him to either of the two localities). This explains why the analysis of regional variation with regard to these two features (Tables 6.3 and 6.8) is based on a slightly lower number of tokens.

The order of data presentation is as follows: I first provide some general information on the variable, i.e. its manifestation and conditioning, complete with a description where it is found and what explanations have been offered to account for it. Then the findings from the corpus are presented and evaluated. In conclusion, the main results are summarised and discussed, with reference to the findings presented in chs. 4 and 5.

6.1 Consonant cluster reduction

The first variable studied in this context is *consonant cluster reduction* (CCR), also referred to as "word-final stop deletion" (Guy 1980), which is a process of phonological reduction that operates on the final segment of syllable-coda consonant clusters. English belongs to the typologically unusual languages with phonotactic systems that admit more than one consonant in syllable onsets and/or codas (the nucleus always being a vowel, however). Up to three consonants can occur in the onset (e.g. /spr-/ in *spring* or /skr-/ in *scratch*) and up to four in the coda (e.g. /-mpst/ in *glimpsed*; though this is of course bisyllabic). CCR affects cluster-final plosives (e.g. /t/ in *fast*, or /k/ in *flask*) and operates in English universally; it is found in all speakers (regardless of whether they are mono-, bi- or multilingual, though this is an important criterion to determine how often the process occurs; see below), in all regional, social and ethnic varieties and in all speech styles (casual, careful, formal). It has been particularly well researched in varieties of AmE (for instance in Tejano English, Bailey 1994, Santa Ana 1996; Appalachian English, Wolfram & Christian 1976; Philadelphia English, Guy 1980; Lumbee English, Torbert 2001), but also in York/UK English (Tagliamonte & Temple 2005), Indian English (Khan 1991), mesolectal JamCrE (Patrick 1991) and NZE (Holmes & Bell 1994; Schreier 2003b).

The variable was analysed in detail in Schreier (2005), so I keep this part of the study as short as possible and focus on some of the most relevant questions for the purpose of this book. Even though some issues have not been settled to the satisfaction of all researchers (most notably the amount of clusters that may undergo reduction and the nature and strength of conditioning factors such as preceding segment), the general consensus is that a combination of phonetic and morphosyntactic factors has an impact on the variable application of CCR. The findings postulated in the pioneering studies of Labov, Cohen, Lewis & Robins (1968), Wolfram (1969) and Fasold (1972) have been confirmed with remarkable consistency in the vast majority of varieties studied. Monomorphemic clusters (e.g. /-st/, /-sk/ and /-nd/ in *past*, *desk* or *find*) are subject to reduction more frequently than bimorphemic clusters, where the final cluster element represents a morpheme in its own right (past tense formation of English regular verbs involves *-ed* suffixation, which leads to bimorphemic clusters, e.g., /vd/ in *lived*, /st/ in *passed*, or /zd/ in *praised*, unless, of course, the cluster segment that precedes the suffix is an alveolar plosive, in which case the *-ed* is bisegmental, e.g. in *nodded* or *patted*). Clusters are more robust when the final consonant carries morphological meaning. The second factor concerns the nature of the immediately following phonetic environment: Consonants have an enhancing effect on CCR, whereas vowels and pauses impede it. Therefore, both the morphemic status of the final cluster element and the cluster's phonetic environment affect the variable nature of CCR, and this has been confirmed in practically all varieties in which the process has been studied. Such is the regularity of CCR in English around the world that it has been labelled the "showcase variable for variationist sociolinguistics" (Patrick 1991: 171) or even "the paradigm case of systematic variability in social dialectology" (Wolfram et al 2000: 17).

On the other hand, while all varieties of English variably reduce syllable-coda clusters to at least some extent, they differ in how frequently the process applies and in the factors that condition its application (I have argued elsewhere that this is a particularly diagnostic tool to differentiate varieties of English around the world; Schreier 2005, fc.). For instance, varieties such as AAE or Hispanic varieties of English have comparatively higher CCR percentages than varieties such as (White) NZE or York/UK English. When there is coexistence of varieties, then the variety that most heavily originated under contact conditions has the highest CCR levels, which sets it apart from the (English) inputs from which it in part derives. This is most plausibly explained as a hold-over effect of language contact processes and direct phonotactic transfer (discussion in Wolfram et al. 2000). Consequently, the question here is how high CCR levels are in StHE and how similar or dissimilar the variety is with regard to other contact-derived varieties of English elsewhere.

6.1.1 Methodology

The methodological criteria applied here differ slightly from those of other studies. The main motive for the procedure adopted was that it allowed me to control for a number of important factors that are not consistently addressed in other studies, namely: the roles of stress, total cluster length, and general word length. For instance, consonant clusters in polysyllabic words with stress on the first syllable are more likely to undergo reduction than consonant clusters in monosyllabic words, or in polysyllabic words with stress on the last syllable (e.g., /-nt/ in a word like *applicant* is more likely and more often reduced than the same cluster in *tent* or *extent*, Guy 1980: 9). Some studies mention the possibility of such an effect in their data (e.g. Holmes & Bell 1994), yet few actually take it into account.

Data extraction and selection criteria were as follows. In order to get a sample size as representative as possible to allow for a quantitative and variationist analysis, I extracted a total of 100 tokens for each of the 14 speakers. All word-final plosives that were preceded by one consonant (bisegmental CC, *last*) were extracted and classified as potential candidates for reduction (clusters consisting of more than two consonants, as in CCC# *danced* or CCCC# *glimpsed*, were not considered). Data extraction procedures included all CCs in monosyllabic items, e.g. *rest*, *laughed*, and also CCs in polysyllabic words on condition that stress fell on the last syllable. This meant that I counted and analysed reduction levels of final CCs in *extend*, *aghast*, but did not consider those in *mutant*, *breakfast* or *different*. I tabulated words like *strict* and *land*, but ignored *district* and *Zealand*. No more than six words in a particular environment were tabulated so as to control for type-token relations. Moreover, I did not consider unstressed function words that could be subject to lexicalised reduction, particularly the unstressed adverb *just* and the verbs *want to*/*wanna* or contracted forms of *not* (*didn'*, *wasn'*). High-frequency items (e.g. *and*) were not considered either, for the reason that they are more likely to undergo reduction (Neu 1980: 53).

Moreover, following Wolfram (1969), Fasold (1972) and Guy (1980), I did not tabulate word-final plosives when followed by homorganic stops, e.g. 'The parcel was sen*t t*o my mother' or 'I've seen that kid knocke*d d*own many times', as a following alveolar plosive makes it "impossible to perceive from the tape recordings whether the final stop [of a CC] was absent or present" (Wolfram 1969: 58). By the same token, this decision had consequences for the analyses of some of the data: CCs followed by dental fricatives could not be included (e.g. 'I *sent them* home') since /ð/ and /θ/ were very often realised as stops (ch. 5), which resulted in the same masking effect.

6.1.2 Results and analysis

First of all, one notes that StHE has a prominent tendency to reduce CCs. The overall percentage of reduction is 86.5% (n=1.300), which is much higher than what is found in varieties of White BrE, AmE and NZE, for instance (around 25-35%, but note that slightly different data extraction procedures were applied). As for the effects of the following phonetic segment and the morphemic status of the cluster, Table 6.2 and Figure 6.1 provide a break-down by immediately following linguistic environments (C, P or V) and the morphemic status of a cluster-final stop. The following segment constraint is in line with general constraints: a following consonant enhances CCR more than pauses and vowels (C > P > V), so StHE is not at all unusual here.

Table 6.2 Internal effects on CCR in StHE

	Pre-C		Pre-P		Pre-V	
	mono	***bi***	***mono***	***bi***	***mono***	***bi***
Total	559	123	173	31	386	128
Reduced	521	123	146	29	275	115
CCR %	**93.2**	**100**	**84.4**	**93.5**	**73.8**	**89.8**

Figure 6.1 Internal effects on CCR in StHE

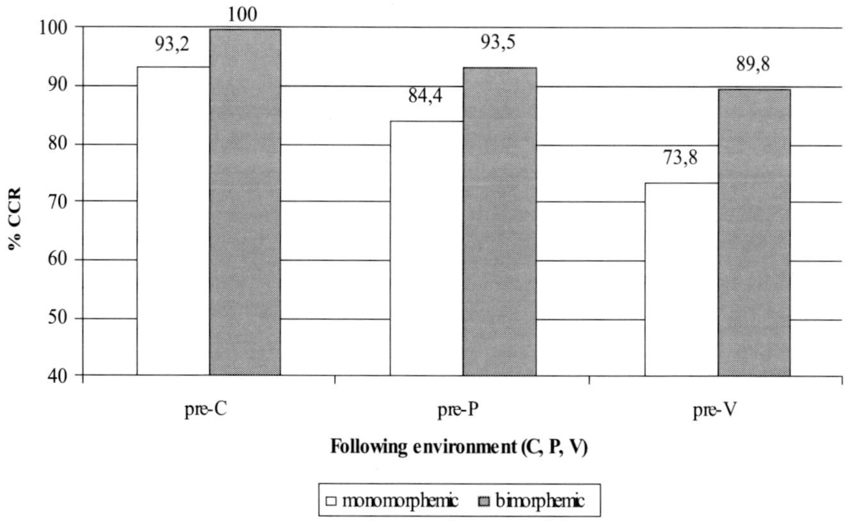

CCR is categorical in pre-consonantal environments and only slightly lower when followed by pauses or vowels (albeit the effect is weaker in StHE, no doubt due to the high tendency to reduce final clusters). A pattern that is not expected, however, is that the effect of segment clusters' morphemic status exerts a 'reverse' effect. Bimorphemic clusters have in fact higher reduction rates than monomorphemic clusters, and this in all three environments. StHE thus diverges from the common pattern in a highly consistent way. CCR in StHE is unusual on at least two accounts. First, in what regards its frequency, which is extremely high when compared with other varieties, and second, in its internal conditioning, namely in that a final *-ed* suffix is more commonly absent than a non-morphemic cluster-final plosive.

Table 6.3 Regional CCR variation in StHE

		Pre-C		**Pre-P**		**Pre-V**	
		mono	***bi***	***mono***	***bi***	***mono***	***bi***
Levelwood (AH, LG)	Total	78	22	29	4	43	24
	Reduced	75	22	26	4	36	24
	CCR (%)	**96.2**	**100.0**	**89.7**	**100.0**	**83.7**	**100.0**
Sandy Bay (CC, DF)	Total	94	16	25	1	51	13
	Reduced	87	16	21	1	42	13
	CCR (%)	**92.6**	**100.0**	**84.0**	**100.0**	**82.4**	**100.0**
Blue Hill (JM, MP, PF)	Total	111	31	42	10	76	30
	Reduced	102	31	33	9	55	25
	CCR (%)	**91.9**	**100.0**	**78.6**	**90.0**	**72.4**	**83.3**
Longwood (HS, TH)	Total	78	17	19	9	52	25
	Reduced	76	17	18	9	43	22
	CCR (%)	**97.4**	**100.0**	**94.7**	**100.0**	**82.7**	**88.0**
Half Tree Hollow (BB, GY)	Total	81	20	22	3	62	12
	Reduced	77	20	19	3	44	11
	CCR (%)	**95.1**	**100.0**	**86.4**	**100.0**	**71.0**	**91.2**
Jamestown (EP, GC)	Total	79	7	24	2	70	18
	Reduced	68	7	20	1	41	14
	CCR (%)	**86.1**	**100.0**	**83.3**	**50.0**	**58.6**	**77.8**

The next question concerns regional variation, i.e. whether there is locally varying usage of this variables in speakers from different parts of the island. Table 6.3 and Figure 6.2 present the results for individuals grouped together by region. There is quite a bit of regional variation with regard to this variable. The global reduction rates range from 75.5% (Jamestown; 151/200), 87.0% (Half

Tree Hollow; 174/200), 88.3% (Blue Hill; 255/300), 90.0% (Sandy Bay; 180/200), 92.5% (Longwood 185/200) to 93.5% (Levelwood; 187/200). As expected, they are high in all the localities: StHE speakers from Jamestown have the lowest CCR levels (75.5%), whereas the differences are minimal for the other five regions. If we lump these together in a group 'country', then the combined percentage is 88.6% (975/1100). There is thus regional variation with regard to this feature, but the most important factor seems to be rural vs. urban, with minimal local differences 'up country'.

A second point is of interest also. As noted, the most diagnostic environment for CCR is pre-vocalic and bisegmental, since these two criteria have an inhibiting influence on the process. We already saw in Figure 6.1 that the common pattern is reversed. Figure 6.2 shows that the six regions align very concisely in pre-C and also in pre-P monomorphemic environments. As for pre-V, however, differences increase and CCR is lowest in the Jamestown speakers (with a notable drop in pre-P bimorphemic environments, which may be explained by the low token number). However, despite the fact that clusters are intact in Saint Helenians from Jamestown, they still display the unusual preference of reducing clusters that are bimorphemic more frequently than monomorphemic ones.

Figure 6.2 Regional CCR variation in StHE

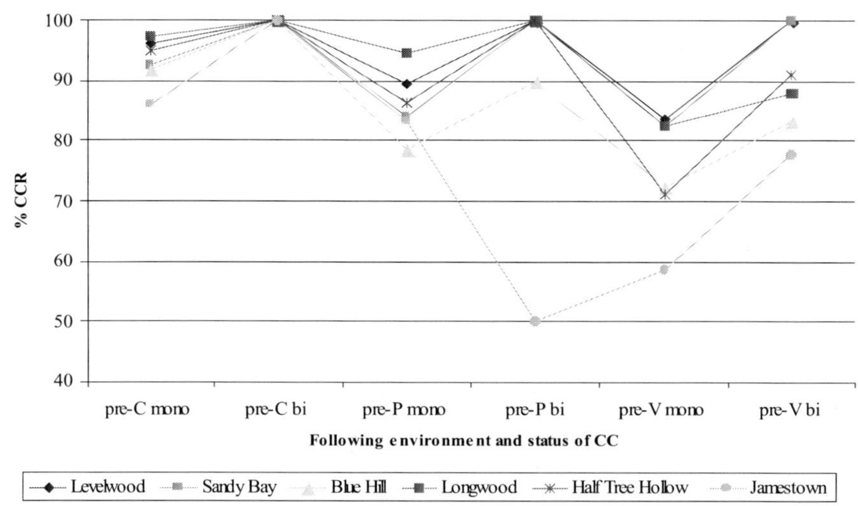

While a descriptive analysis provides valuable insights into the general patterning of variables, it is limited in that it fails to provide the envelope of variation, i.e., to display the permutations and interactive effects of potential constraints. What is missing is an informed and statistically sensitive analysis of the data that brings to light the strength of the effects interacting in language variation. With this effect, the data were subjected to a VARBRUL analysis. VARBRUL is a probabilistic-based multivariate regression analysis that weighs the strength and relative impact of pre-specified linguistic and/or social factors. It conducts a binomial analysis and produces factor weights between 0 and 1; a weighting higher than .5 indicates a favouring and below .5 an inhibiting effect. It also produces a Chi square per cell score that yields the relative 'goodness-of-fit', a low score indicating a better fit than a high one (Young & Bayley 1996).

Table 6.4 VARBRUL factor weights for CCR in StHE

	Clusters reduced	Total N	%	Factor weight
Following phonetic environment				
_C	644	682	94.4	**.68**
_P	175	204	85.8	**.45**
_V	390	514	75.9	**.29**
Cluster type				
monomorphemic	942	1118	84.3	**.44**
bimorphemic	267	282	94.7	**.72**
Regionality				
Levelwood	187	200	93.5	**.65**
Longwood	186	200	92,5	**.62**
Sandy Bay	180	200	90.0	**.55**
Blue Hill	265	300	88.3	**.42**
Half Tree Hollow	174	200	87.0	**.49**
Jamestown	151	200	75.5	**.31**

The factors selected for analysis were following phonological environment and status of the cluster (as internal factors) and regionality and settlement (as a language-external one). Table 6.4 provides the VARBRUL factor weightings for CCR in StHE (with the factor groups *following phonetic environment*, *cluster type* and *regionality*). A step-up/step-down procedure yielded that all the factor groups were significant. As expected, given the high percentages, the following environment was highly significant (C > P > V) and it is noteworthy (and unusual in World English) that CCR in bimorphemic clusters would have a factor weight of .72, as opposed to .44 for monomorphemic ones. Regionality, finally, had a significant effect as well, with Jamestown having a factor weight of .31 and the rural locations ranging between .42 and .65. The chi-square/cell was low in the one level analysis.

6.1.3 *Summary and a short assessment*

How should we interpret the CCR findings and what is their relevance for the status of StHE? A more extensive and detailed analysis follows in the final chapter, so it suffices to just briefly summarise the main findings here.

First of all, CCR in StHE is extremely high (86.5%). I have shown in Schreier (2005: 198ff.) that contact between systems with similar amounts of CCR does *not* lead to an increase in this variable. This, for instance, explains the similarities with regard to this feature between White BrE, AmE and NZE (Tagliamonte & Temple 2005; Guy 1980; Holmes & Bell 1994), both in total frequency and internal conditioning. In contrast, "[p]honotactic transfer and change [including CCR; DS] is most likely to occur in contact between language varieties with distinct phonotactic systems" (Schreier 2005: 201). Consequently, then, high CCR levels must be an indicator of extensive language contact and the legacy of language varieties with phonotactic systems that do not admit consonant clusters, having CV syllable structures. Second, the *mono>bi* constraint is found in practically all the varieties of English around the world where this variable has been researched so far; nearly everywhere, monomorphemic clusters are more likely to undergo CCR. It is therefore extremely unusual to find a consistent *bi>mono* patterning, which points to an unusual set of internal constraints. This is extremely diagnostic and we have to check for possible explanations for the evolution of StHE. Third, CCR variation is regionally-indicative. Though the differences between several of the regions investigated are small, the general pattern is that speakers from 'up country' have this feature more frequently (and in all environments) than those from Jamestown, so there is definitely evidence of an 'urban-rural' split with regard to this feature.

6.2 *Present tense concord/copula absence*

The second variable studied in this context is present tense concord, with particular focus on copula absence in "'the cows Ø runnin' around', 'she Ø one happy grandmother'. The absence of *am*, *is* and *are* in verb phrases has been amply studied in contact-derived varieties of English in the US and in the Caribbean as well: White Southern AmE (Wolfram 1974; Feagin 1979), AAE (Labov 1972a; Fasold 1972; Baugh 1980; Bailey & Maynor 1985), varieties transplanted to Canada and the Caribbean (Poplack & Sankoff 1987; Walker 2000, 2001) and creole varieties of English, such as Guyanese Creole or Gullah (Holm 1984; Rickford 1987; Winford 1992, 1993; Weldon 2003a, b; Walker & Meyerhoff 2006). Moreover, it was one of the features most intensely debated in the recently (re-) emerging debate on the origins and development of AAE (Rickford 1998; Poplack 2000; Poplack & Tagliamonte 2001; Wolfram &

Thomas 2002). For instance, it has been claimed that he copula is at "the center of the debate over the putative creole ancestory [sic] of Black English" and has "figured prominently in the discussion of African influence on the process of creolization" (Winford 1993: 155). There are a number of reasons why this variable is important in contact linguistics. First of all, it occurs at very low frequencies in varieties of White BrE or AmE (around 2-4%), whereas it is found in significantly higher rates in English-derived creoles. It has been argued (e.g. by Rickford 1998) that British inputs can not account for frequency of copula absence, which is interpreted as evidence of substratum or transfer effects from the non-lexifiers. Secondly, whether a copula is present or absent is constrained by the linguistic environment in which it occurs. It is found mostly with *gonna* and progressives in White varieties ("I don't know whether I Ø gonna come or not", "the kids Ø jumping up and down like crazy"). Contact varieties behave quite differently; in English-derived creoles, for instance, the copula can also be (variably) absent when preceded by a personal pronoun, a noun phrase or an adjective. The presence (or rather: the absence) of copulas in contact-derived varieties thus differs significantly from that of the English superstrates, which makes it a particularly diagnostic variable for the research of contact-induced language change and transfer (and explains why it has such canonic status in contact linguistics).

A second (and perhaps equally diagnostic) factor is that varieties of English differ in their systems of present tense concord (of which copula absence is only a part, of course). When colonies witness heterogeneous settler ecologies (from several social strata or distinct regions of origin), then the inputs in contact are not homogeneous and correlate with all sorts of extralinguistic parameters; the theoretical implications have been described in ch. 2. Consequently, then, we may also gain valuable insights from analysing how the copula is realised, whether StHE has a (more or less) standard-type patterning (*am* for first person singular; *is* for third person singular; *are* for all other persons) or whether it has adopted an alternative system. The question, quite simply, is whether StHE has a present tense concord system that resembles British inputs (standard or non-standard) or whether it aligns itself with contact-derived varieties (e.g. Caribbean creoles) where change induced by language contact phenomena is undisputed. In this sense, the analysis of copula absence and presence in StHE allows to speculate on what copula systems were brought to the island and how they interacted and developed when the morpho-syntactic properties of StHE evolved.

6.2.1 Methodology

Most (recent) studies on copula absence agree on a general set of extraction procedures and 'don't count cases', and these are summarised most concisely in

Blake (1997). Though somewhat biased to phonological and morphosyntactic properties of AmE varieties, Blake maintains that copulas in the following environments do not lend themselves to analysis and should not be extracted: a) past tense; b) syntactic prominence, e.g. clause-final position; c) emphatic stress and emphasis; d) examples of finite *be*; e) a following environment that is homorganically similar or identical (/s/ or /r/); f) question type sentences formed through word-order inversion; g) *am*, both as a full and contracted form; h) when the copula co-occurs with so-called WIT forms (*what*, *it*, *that*); and i) existential constructions. These environments are illustrated as follows (all examples drawn from my 2003 StHE corpus):

a) "people *were* more genuine than what they are today" (EP, Sapper Way)
b) "phone down the house he . Keith I don't know what he *is*" (CC, Sandy Bay); "oh yeah, heavy dough it *is*" (BB, Cleugh's Plain)
c) "some people never believe it but that *IS* the truth" (MP, Blue Hill)
d) "it always *be* foggy up there" (KY, Kunjee Field)
e) "a lot of youngsters go from St Helena now - to get married *it's so* cheap see" (BB, Cleughs Plain)
f) "you know what dynamite *is* eh?" (AH, Levelwood); "you know where Hutt's Gate *is*?" (TH, Levelwood); "*is* y'all goin' home next ship?" (GC, Jamestown)
g) "I'*m* still around" (EP, Jamestown); "I'*m* here today" (JM, Blue Hill)
h) "so *that's* my transfer I do put under that you see" (EP, Sapper Way) "yeah when *it's* something like that yes" (CC, Sandy Bay)
i) "and *there's* a taper or scotcher see you got the scotcher up there" (CC, Sandy Bay)

The question is how (and whether) to apply these criteria for the analysis of StHE. It certainly makes sense to adopt the 'non-count' cases that are based on problems with coding, such as homorganic environments, where the variable cannot be identified beyond doubt. It is more problematic to adopt the criteria that were formulated on the basis of copula presence/absence in varieties of AmE specifically, such as AAE. Can we apply them to StHE *strictu sensu* or should they be adapted somehow? If an alternative set is preferable, then which of the criteria should be selected? Two examples illustrate this well. First person singulars are particularly salient, since in AAE and other varieties of AmE, the copula is categorically present here; consequently, one does not gain information on copula absence by including this environment in the analysis (the same goes for past tense *was* and *were*). On the other hand, *am*, *was* and *were* are variably absent in Gullah and English-derived Caribbean creoles (Shilling 1980; Holm 1988; Winford 2000; Rickford 1998, 2000; Walker 1999), which has given rise to extensive discussions, at times heated debates.

Consequently, then, we have to know something about the present tense concord in StHE before we can select the extraction procedures

I decided to proceed as follows: I selected two speakers (JM from Blue Hill and ChC from Sandy Bay) and extracted a full set of tokens for each of them. These were subjected to analysis and the pioneering results were taken into consideration for the adoption of extraction procedures for the other speakers. For instance, I found that first person singular *am* was commonly absent and decided to extract this environment as well. I consequently extracted tokens from allomorphs of present tense *be* where the copula could be variably absent, and this included the first person singulars. Plural *are* is realised as *is* ("the horses is out in the field"), which was tabulated also. However, I decided against extracting copulas from negative contexts, particularly when there was a merged form. As we saw in the previous chapter, StHE, like many varieties of English around the world, generally tends to merge the copula with *not* to *ain't*. These were not extracted; in the words of Blake (1997: 70), "variable rule outcome may be skewed by the exclusion of *ain't*, whose linguistic status [is] not yet resolved." Consequently, the 'don't count' criteria adopted were: syntactic prominence, e.g. clause-final position; emphatic stress and emphasis; finite *be*; a following environment that is homorganically similar or identical (/s/ or /r/); question type sentences formed through word-order inversion; co-occurrence with so-called WIT forms (*what*, *it*, *that*); and existential constructions.

All the copulas that fit the criteria outlined were extracted for each speaker, and the aim was to collect a total of 50-60 tokens for each of the 13 speakers in the sub-sample. Due to the set-up of the interview (mostly personal narratives and reminiscences of the 'old days'), the target could not be reached for three speakers, for which only about 40 present tense copulas could be extracted. The total of copulas extracted and analysed was 741. The tokens were coded by grammatical person and number (first singular, third singular, first plural, etc.) and by preceding grammatical environment (pronoun or noun phrase) and following grammatical environment (*gonna*, verb+*ing*, locative, adjective phrase, noun phrase). The latter constraint has to be handled with care in varieties that have undergone creolisation since it is common for the verbal complement to have an impact on the copula. For instance, it has been suggested that predicate adjectives may trigger copula absence strongly in Caribbean varieties and it is not clear whether and to what extent this is diagnostic here. Researchers such as Baugh (1980) and Holm (1984) have taken the point of view that higher absence rates before adjectival phrases characterise mesolectal varieties and are thus reliable evidence of creole status, whereas others (Mufwene 1992; Winford 2000; Weldon 2003a) have argued against these claims.

Finally, following the discussion in Rickford (1999a: 63-87), I adopted the so-called "straight deletion" methodology, in which a copula was counted as present no matter whether it was realised fully (*am*, *is*) or contracted (*'m*, *'s*). While the analysis of contraction may allow for more specific and detailed insights into patterns of variation within the variety, particularly of language-internal conditioning, it is of lesser importance to one of the central aims of the study, namely to compare StHE with other varieties and assessing its status in the canon of English around the world.

6.2.2 Results and analysis

The first question concerns how often the copula is absent in StHE. 569 out of 741 present tense copulas were absent (a total percentage of 76.8%), only 172 were present. There is no doubt that StHE has a strong trend for copulas to be absent.

The second point concerns language-internal conditioning and the effects of grammatical and phonological environments. An important point here is the effect of copula type, i.e., whether the *am*, *is* and *are* allomorphs are equally likely to be absent or not, and, when they are present, whether they are realised in a standard-type pattern (*am* – first person singular; *is* – third person singular; *are* – all other persons) or in an alternative paradigm. Table 6.5 summarises the findings for the three forms. *Am*, *are* and *is* are frequently absent (which was expected, given that the global absence rate is so high) but they are not equally sensitive to this process: there is a quantitative difference in global absence levels (*am* 87.1%, *are* 77.4%, and *is* 72.8%). It is particularly noteworthy that the first person singular environments are most likely to have copula absence; this is commonly reported in English-based Caribbean creoles (but not in AAE; see above) and I will return to this point below.

Table 6.5 Copula absence in StHE (am, is, are)

	Copula *am* (1st person sing)	Copula *is* (3rd person singular)	Copula *are* (all other persons)
am	9	0	0
is	6	93	50
are	0	0	14
zero	101	249	219
Total	116	342	283
Copula absence (%)	**87.1%**	**72.8%**	**77.4%**

A second finding is that StHE does not have a standard type of present tense concord. Quite to the contrary, *is* is by far the most frequent form in the

23.2% of cases when the copula is present. Indeed, *is* features in all three environments and it effectively competes with – even outdoes – the other two. *Am* and *are* make an appearance but are no more than minority features, restricted to the distribution in standard varieties (**I are* or **we am* do not occur). *Is* instead of *am* features in 40.0% of all cases (6/15) and instead of *are* in 78.1% (50/64). *Is* is therefore the most frequently used allomorph (with the exception of first person singular) and sentences such as 'I's living in Levelwood' or 'the boats is back early', though relatively infrequent, are attested. When the copula is present, then it is most likely *is*, regardless of grammatical person.

Two more potentially important factors are the preceding and following grammatical environments. Table 6.6 summarises the effects of preceding pronouns (PRO_) and nouns (NP_), showing that copulas are more likely to be absent after subject pronouns (81.2%) than after nouns and noun phrases (67.2%).

Table 6.6 Copula absence by preceding grammatical environment in StHE

	PRO_ (I, she, us, etc.)	NP_ (St Helena, the ship, etc.)
Copula present	95	77
Copula absent	411	158
Total	506	235
Copula absence (%)	**81.2%**	**67.2%**

The grammatical environment that follows the copula is insightful too. Table 6.7 indicates that the variable displays context-sensitivity, ranging from 50.0% absence (_NP) to 95.0% (_gonna). Here the hierarchy is:
_gonna > _V+*ing* > _loc > _adj > _ NP

Table 6.7 Copula absence in StHE by following environment

	_NP	_loc	_adj	_V+ing	_gonna
Copula present	32	25	98	16	1
Copula absent	32	134	155	228	19
Total	64	159	253	244	20
Copula absence (%)	**50.0**	**84.3**	**61.3**	**93.4**	**95.0**

The final point to consider is the potential for regional differentiation. Table 6.8 summarises the results for StHE speakers grouped by region (in identical fashion to the analysis of CCR above). There is regional variation in the six island regions (Jamestown, Half Tree Hollow, Longwood, Levelwood, Sandy Bay and Blue Hill), though copula absence is practically on a par in the latter four (ranging between 79.4% and 83.6%). Half Tree Hollow follows with 71.3% and again it is the Jamestown speakers that have the lowest percentage (63.6%). If, in analogy to the analysis of CCR, we split the speakers into two groups, then the average for those 'up country' is 79.3%, considerably higher than the 63.6% for the Jamestown speakers.

Table 6.8 Regional variation in StHE (Copula absence)

		_NP	_loc	_adj	_V+ing	_gonna	Total
Levelwood (AH, LG)	Total	8	16	40	41	5	110
	absent	6	15	30	39	5	95
	%	**75**	**93.8**	**75.0**	**95.1**	**100.0**	**83.6**
Sandy Bay (CC, DF)	Total	5	32	40	27	4	108
	absent	3	29	26	26	4	88
	%	**60.0**	**90.6**	**65.0**	**96.3**	**100**	**81.5**
Blue Hill (JM, MP, PF)	Total	12	26	34	58	5	135
	absent	7	20	21	53	5	106
	%	**58.3**	**76.9**	**61.8**	**91.4**	**100**	**78.5**
Longwood (HS, TH)	Total	11	30	34	25	2	102
	absent	5	26	26	22	2	81
	%	**45.5**	**86.7**	**76.5**	**88.0**	**100.0**	**79.4**
Half Tree Hollow (BB, GY)	Total	10	14	50	40	1	115
	absent	4	12	26	39	1	82
	%	**40.0**	**85.7**	**52.0**	**97.5**	**100**	**71.3**
Jamestown (EP, GC)	Total	15	28	32	32	3	110
	absent	6	21	11	31	1	70
	%	**40.0**	**75.0**	**34.4**	**96.9**	**33.3**	**63.6**

Table 6.9 summarises the results for copula absence in StHE. A chi-square test was conducted separately for each of the factor groups (preceding grammatical environment, following grammatical environment, copula type and regionality). All the probabilities for copula absence calculated from observed and expected frequencies through chi-square were significant at the $p < .0001$ or $< .01$ levels: Preceding grammatical environment $p < 0.0001$, Following grammatical environment $p <.0001$, Copula type $p < .01$, Regionality $p < .01$. When locations were analysed separately and split up into urban vs. rural, then p was < 0.001.

Table 6.9 Copula absence in StHE: Summary

	Copula absent	Total N	%
Preceding grammatical environment			
PRO_	411	506	81.2
NP_	158	235	67.2
Following grammatical environment			
_gonna	19	20	95.0
_V+*ing*	228	244	93.4
_loc	134	159	84.3
_adj	155	253	61.3
_ NP	32	64	50.0
Copula type			
am	101	116	87.1
are	219	283	77.4
is	249	342	72.8
Regionality			
Levelwood	92	110	83.6
Longwood	81	102	79.4
Sandy Bay	88	108	81.5
Blue Hill	106	135	78.5
Half Tree Hollow	82	115	71.3
Jamestown	70	110	63.6
Urban (Jamestown only)	70	110	63.3
Rural (all others)	452	570	79.3

6.2.3 Summary and a short assessment

An in-depth study of copula absence provides a number of insights. First of all, we note that it is a particularly prominent feature of StHE: the copula is much more likely to be absent than present (the ratio being 3-1). The global copula absence rates are high by comparison. This is (yet) another quantitative difference with varieties of BrE where it is practically inexistent (other than when preceded by gonna and V+*ing*, but even here the copula is mostly present). It is also much higher than what is reported for varieties of White SAmE. One of the most detailed studies (Wolfram & Thomas 2002) reports that in rural Hyde County, North Carolina, *is* absence is insignificant (less than 1%) and *are* absence amounts to 8.0% (p. 81); the total percentage is 4.4% (not counting *am*, which is categorically present). This is very low indeed when compared to 76.8% in StHE. We can only interpret this as a further indication that there are striking differences between StHE and White BrE and AmE, so the British inputs were not the sole determinants of the evolutionary path of StHE.

Quite to the contrary, we find that StHE bears resemblances with varieties shaped in conditions of extensive language contact: AAE. Wolfram & Thomas (2002), using 'straight deletion' methodology and a similar set of criteria as employed here, report 59.4% copula absence for *are* (N=244) and 21.1% for *is* (N=565), which resembles the StHE findings quite closely. The parallels in AAE throughout the US are evident, at least with regard to this feature: *am* is categorically present, *are* is more likely to be absent than *is*, preceding pronouns favour absence over NPs, and the following environments *gonna* and V+*ing* have an enhancing effect on copula absence whereas NPs or adjectives do not (New York, Labov 1972a; Washington DC, Fasold 1972; California, Rickford, Ball, Blake, Jackson & Martin 1991; Mississippi, Wolfram 1974; Texas, Bailey & Maynor 1985, 1987; North Carolina, Wolfram & Thomas 2002; Hazen 2000). Whereas StHE aligns itself quantitatively with AAE (though still having higher levels of copula absence), there is one important difference: 1st person singular *am* is very often absent in StHE (in fact, we saw in Table 6.5 that *am* copulas are even more likely to be absent than *are* and *is*, which was not expected). This is found in English-based creoles throughout the Caribbean (discussion in Kortmann & Szmrecsanyi 2004) and thus an important piece of information in our effort to classify the typological status of this variety. Consequently, we note that copula absence in StHE is very high. It displays a couple of common characteristics (preceding environment effects; *are* > *is*; following environment effects: the commonly attested hierarchy, whereby *gonna* favours copula absence more than verb+*ing*, locatives, adjectival phrases and noun phrases). At the same time, copula absence operates generally across the present tense paradigm, thus affecting all three forms of the copula (*am*, *are*, *is*, in this order).

The second point of importance concerns cases where the copula is realised (23.2%; 172/741). Table 6.5 showed that the allomorph used most often is in fact *is*, which effectively makes an appearance with first person singulars ("I's quite happy now"), second singulars and all the plural persons, both with pronouns and NPs ("if you's up there…", "the children is very naughty"). Consequently, then, we are dealing with a levelling process (ch. 2), so that *am* and *are* are levelled out of the local present tense concord system. The pivot form adopted for the levelled paradigm is *is*. This is most likely interpreted as evidence of convergence and mixing of two systems. Copula absence in StHE may be the legacy of jargons and/or pidgins brought to the island (or alternatively originate as a contact phenomenon), and *is* with all persons in present tense was quite likely drawn from one or several of the British donors. The latter has been reported in a range of English varieties around the world; to name but a few: Southern EngE (Cheshire 1982), York/UK English (Tagliamonte 1998), AAE (Rickford 1999), AusE (Eisikovits 1991) and TdCE (Schreier 2003). This resembles the scenario found in Black BahE, where there is "only the form *is*, with *am* and *are* very seldom appearing and then sometimes appearing inappropriately" (Shilling 1980: 136). Reaser (2004), on the other hand, finds that "categorical levelling is not universal in Bahamian varieties as only 8.2% (31/379) of *are* copula [sic] are levelled to *is* … and there are no examples (0/141) of *am* being levelled to *is*" (Reaser 2004: 17). This may point to regional variation on the Bahamas or else to language change in progress, and I will return to this point in the next chapter. For now, however, we note that StHE copula absence is extremely diagnostic, both in its absolute frequency and internal conditioning.

The final issue regards the potential for regional variation on St Helena. Copula absence mirrors the CCR findings, in that the speakers from various regions across the island differentiate themselves in how often they have copula absence. However, the differences are minimal and non-significant for at least four of the locations (Levelwood, Sandy Bay, Blue Hill, Longwood). When lumping together the findings for the 'up country' speakers, we again have evidence of an 'urban-rural' divide. StHE speakers from Jamestown are much more likely to have copula verbs present.

Consequently, then, the two variables studied provide insights of regional variation on the island (both displaying similar trends). They also provide valuable insights into the degree of variety-specific differentiation and parallels with other varieties of English around the world. We now need to do go on and evaluate the quantitative analysis in the light of the qualitative description provided in ch. 5 and check how these findings fit in with the historical reconstruction based on sociodemographic, social and sociolinguistic principles (chs. 3 and 4). In other words, we are ready for the conclusion.

7. Summary and conclusion

Insular speech communities live in self-contained areas, often under linguistically self-focused and sociologically endocentric conditions. More than elsewhere, their socio-cultural characteristics are shaped by geophysical seclusion from other settlements and speaker groups (and consequently: from other language varieties). These living conditions favour the development of local norms and the emergence of distinctive, 'new' varieties, which is evidenced by the fact that dozens of post-colonial varieties have developed on islands in all of the major oceans (such as FIE, Sudbury 2001, and TdCE in the South Atlantic, Schreier 2002b, 2003a; Bonin/Ogasawara English in the Pacific, Long 2007; numerous English-based Creoles in the Caribbean, Aceto & Williams 2003; etc.). As argued in ch. 2, insular communities offer an ideal test setting for studying processes of contact-induced language change, sociolinguistic diversification and parallel developments of language(s) in isolation. They provide an excellent opportunity for studying how 'new' varieties come into being in distinct settings and contact scenarios, how and from where they draw their characteristic features, whether they undergo similar and/or parallel developments, etc.

English is particularly suitable in this context: the Empire's colonisation activities occurred (relatively) recently, and practically all insular varieties of English around the world have developed over the last three centuries only. They are thus characterised by *shallow time depth*, a crucial factor in linguistic and sociolinguistic analysis. Thus, the fact that post-colonial Englishes are 'young' varieties (and still evolving; cf. Schneider 2003) allows us to *in situ* investigate the interplay and contribution of diachronic factors such as settlement history, sociohistorical immigration patterns, sociodemographic fluctuation and population turnover, and to study and analyse their sociolinguistic consequences. Crucially, such research depends both on synchronic and historical data and it is paramount to locate and evaluate as much earlier evidence as possible. Both sources should ideally complement each other in order to fully uncover and reconstruct contact-induced, sociolinguistic processes that underlie new-dialect formation and give rise to 'new' varieties. All these factors make StHE an ideal research site.

I am left with the task of summarising and assessing the general findings of this book. The discussion of a theoretical framework of contact linguistics (ch. 2) presented some possible outcomes of dialect and language contact that may have given risen to StHE. Chs. 3 and 4 provided the sociohistorical background of the community and its variety and some evidence of what StHE may have looked like between the early 17th and late 19th centuries. Chs. 5 and 6, finally, gave a phonological and morphosyntactic profile of the variety accompanied by a quantitative analysis of two selected variables. Ch. 7 now discusses and reassesses the results in the light of the theoretical and sociohistorical framework, addressing the origins of StHE (how did it form and who formed it?) and its typological status vis-à-vis other varieties of English around the world. These issues are discussed in turn, though there is considerable overlap between them, as we shall see.

7.1 Where does St Helenian English come from?

The social development of the community strongly suggests that StHE is *not* a product if the 17th century. Though colonised in the late 1650s and continuously inhabited since the Dutch interregnum, the social conditions on St Helena in the first 50 years did not favour stability at all. Practically all the founders moved away, being dissatisfied with the social conditions on the island and their dependence on the EIC; they had effectively no opportunity to make a decent living, partly because they had to repay their passage (effectively working as indentured labourers), partly because they were not allowed to acquire additional property or slaves (in contrast to the Company's representatives). Nearly all of them left as soon as possible, moving on to other colonies in India or returning to the UK, or even fleeing the island clandestinely and loosing everything they had. The *StHR* as well as the 1715 census of the population leave no doubt about this. Only one planter registered in the 1670s was still on the island some 45 years later. Consequently, in what regards the white populace, there were far-reaching fluctuations and migratory movements, an extreme population turnover that would simply not provide stable conditions necessary for new-dialect formation (ch. 2). Founder effects à la Mufwene (1996) are thus highly unlikely. By the same token, there is little evidence for a swamping scenario (Lass 1990), since in- and out-migration went hand in hand, the local population being replenished and 'stocked up' to counter an ongoing loss of the workforce that threatened the colonial enterprise. This means that the disappearance of the founders was countered by the gradual arrival of new settlers, so that we have to consider what one might best refer to as "pseudo founder effects", which is an additional complication in a scenario that is quite complicated already. The EIC continued to recruit settlers throughout the first half of the 18th century and there is strong evidence to assume that many of them came from the Greater London area and the English Southeast in general. In other words, the later waves of immigrants came from the same regions as the founders of the colony, but at a later period in settlement history. Consequently, there is no doubt that the British input component to StHE derives to a large extent from Southeastern EnglE; however, it is not the legacy of the founders but rather that of the subsequently arriving settlers, who incidentally hailed from the same region. This sets the clock forward by half a century. When looking at the British heritage of StHE, we thus have to focus on the late 17th (or more likely: the early 18th century), i.e. the period when the permanent white population of St Helena was born in the UK, and not on the mid-17th century. This would explain why StHE picked up a number of 18th century innovations in BrE (START backing and long-mid diphthonging of FACE and GOAT, for instance). There is little doubt that, sociolinguistically speaking, StHE is younger than it appears.

Another influential group was non-white: the slaves and their descendants. Ch. 3 has traced some important issues concerning their origins and the possible patterns of accommodation or accessibility of the English target. Indeed, Gargen's (1665) report attests to the presence of slaves on St Helena. The majority was in the possession of the Company and the fact that orders were given to acquire slaves on St Iago, en route to St Helena, points to the Caboverde Islands as a place of origin. Later sources indicate that (some form of) Portuguese was spoken on the island some twenty years later, though we have practically no first-hand information to assess its status (a Portuguese-based creole perhaps? Recall the verbatim report of "me noe save speake English" in the StHR from December 1695). We know even less about the language backgrounds of the slaves who arrived from West Africa or the Indian subcontinent. Notwithstanding, we can draw several conclusions. First of all, the slaves on St Helena in the 17th century were not a socio-culturally and sociolinguistically homogeneous group. They were brought from several destinations, some arriving with the first wave of white settlers, others successively later. Some arrived in small groups of two or three, others individually, hand-picked by the governor as a toll or passage fee from passing ships. Whereas great care was taken in the 1670s and 1680s to control the black population for fear of a rebellion, a later reassessment of the economic situation led to an increasing import of slaves from the early 1700s onwards. This meant that they became available to a larger section of the white population, who until then had complained bitterly about EIC policies that favoured the local government. As a consequence, 'up country' planters had the possibility to acquire slaves as well, though the 1815 census indicates that this never happened on a large scale and that it was not comparable with plantation scenarios elsewhere (e.g. in the Caribbean). According to the sources consulted, the existing population caused considerable problems, and ch. 3 has documented the alleged rebellions, threats and random acts of aggression, which meant not only that the slaves were dissatisfied with their conditions but also that some of them sought active means to end them. Thus, there was a constant sense of distrust, at times open violence, murder, torture and executions, and quite a few slaves attempted to flee the island.

The situation changed in the early 18th century. There was an increasing demand for slaves for a number of projects around the island and a specific preference for Madagascar, since good experience had been made with slaves from there. If the following entry from the *St Helena Consultations* is correct, then some of the first slaves on St Helena came from Madagascar:

> Old Will aged 100 years and hath faithfully served the Company ever since the English had this Island under the command of 21 Governors and when he came to this Island he brought 3 Yams, 9 head of Cattle and 2 Turtle Doves from Madagascar. (*Consultations*, 1735)

Slaves from Madagascar were regarded as quiet, reasonable and reliable, and this was in obvious contrast to the slaves from West Africa. With regard to this, it is noteworthy that cultural anthropologists such as Keenan (1974, 1976) have shown that the Malagasy value indirectness and reject direct confrontation. This is expressed in the ritual *kabary* speech event, which is a ceremonial dialogue between two men (women are not allowed) and often involves some sort of mutual criticism, which is delivered via proverbs, allusions and innuendo. This may help explaining why slaves from this particular locale were held in such high esteem by the St Helena government, their reputation being non-confrontational, diligent and subservient.

As a consequence, more than one hundred slaves, mostly men (though there were some women as well), arrived in 1717 for the New Ground project. The island had never seen such a massive influx of slaves before. At first sight, this could be taken to imply that the arrival of such a large number had a swamping effect on the black population, since the local slaves were outnumbered practically overnight. Moreover, the arriving group was fairly homogeneous and entirely Malagasy-speaking, which means that the language situation of the slave population changed dramatically. Whereas there is evidence that earlier slaves had competence in English (as witnessed by the fact that governors selected slaves as a passage fee who had some command of English and that instructions were given to choose English-speaking slaves for an exploratory trip of Tristan da Cunha in 1684), it seems clear that the majority of the newly arriving slaves did *not* speak English (or if they did, then it would be no more than a rudimentary jargon learnt on board ship). It must be emphasised that they were brought in directly from a place that had no colonial ties with England and that they did not spend time elsewhere. Thus, the arrival of a substantial group of slaves from Madagascar coincides with the beginning stabilisation of the white community, and this is further evidence that the beginnings of contemporary StHE should be traced to the 1720-1750 period.

A third point to consider in our attempt to reconstruct the evolutionary path of StHE is the degree of interaction between the British planters and the Madagascar slaves. It appears that they were in close contact for a number of reasons. For one, the planter-slave ratio was low and the vast majority of planters had no more than a handful of slaves. Moreover, they interchanged their slaves freely and many planters made a stable income from renting their slaves out to the EIC; Company slaves worked up country, where they must have come into contact with the planters' slaves, and slaves generally had to take their share in communal work, such as road maintenance or land clearing, where they would have come into frequent face-to-face contact with whites. Another criterion that would have led to frequent interaction was the common practice of letting out children (of little use to the EIC) to settlers, often on contract for several years, an opportunity that was taken up readily. If single black children were hired out to white planting families, spending several years with them, then they would have acquired English quickly and used on a daily basis, perhaps also when their contracts were up and they returned to the Company. This was further reinforced by the efforts to give some of the black children education and schooling (Evans 1994). Consequently, the slave population was quite mobile when compared with conditions elsewhere; a social integration of this kind, coupled with small-scale ownership, would have favoured access and a general functioning in an English-speaking environment, arguably leading to rapid language shift and attrition.

A final point to consider is the sociodemographic development of the population in the 18th century. Ch. 3 showed that stability occurred in the 1730s only, which is also when the population grew due to local reproduction rather than immigration or (slave) import. Notwithstanding occasional escape attempts (which became less frequent from the early 18th century onwards), the majority of the slaves remained on the island. In some respects, it is no exaggeration to say that the black population was more permanent than the white one, since we know of individuals like Old Will or Black Oliver, who were island residents for the best parts of their lives and died at an old age. In this context, we must especially focus on black women and their children (who are crucial in new-dialect formation and/or creolisation; ch. 2). A crucial point is that they were the community members who were most likely to stay on the island (I have not found a single report of an escape attempt by women, for instance), thus playing a most prominent role in the evolution of the variety.

To sum up, StHE formed in a sociolinguistic environment that was diverse and heterogeneous. Its most influential founders came from the British Southeast and Madagascar (with little, often insignificant, input from other groups). These groups were interacting on a regular basis, though they were socially stratified, being either employees of the EIC or free or indentured planters; they carried different social statuses in the general community as well as in their local sub-communities (indentured labourers vs. free planters, government and administrative staff vs. soldiers, free blacks vs. slaves, Company slaves vs. planter slaves); some were transient (army personnel, practically all of the planters in the 17th century), others permanent (mostly the slaves, whites only from the 1720s onwards). In terms of linguistic development, we have evidence that several varieties were spoken: English, Portuguese, French, Malagasy, plus a number of non-identifiable Indian and African languages. Consequently, I in part agree with Wilson & Mesthrie (2004: 1006) in their assessment that "present-day St Helena English is the result of the contact between regional varieties of Southern British English, many of them 'non-standard', and the rudimentary pidgin English ('slave fort English') that some slaves must have brought to the island." While their identification of StHE's British heritage is certainly correct, the other inputs that contributed significantly to language evolution on St Helena were much more than mere 'slave fort English' and I hope this book has shown that the scenario is much more complex than that. Moreover, whereas the white population has always been English-speaking (or shifted to English quickly, e.g. the French Huguenots), the slaves maintained their languages while speaking English at an early stage of settlement history. Slave testimonies from the 1680s and 1690s suggest that slaves had at least some rudimentary knowledge of English (though they were very likely to continue using their own native languages amongst themselves). There was only one occasion of a slave being acquitted because his command of English was judged too basic for partaking in a task as complex as planning a rebellion. By contrast, the trial against Black Oliver's son is evidence that the slave community was stratified very early on (the distinction between slaves and freemen may have been an important factor here) and that the blacks displayed diversity in English, just as the whites did. The most likely interpretation is that those immersed in and highly respected by the white community (such as house slaves or black freemen, particularly Oliver's family) were more acrolectal whereas farm slaves housed with planter families up country were more basilectal. In any case, all this strongly suggests that English has served as a lingua franca in a multilingual environment from the earliest stages of the community onwards.

At what stage did English win out and when did the usage of other languages cease, so that other languages fell out of use? I would argue that three factors play a role here. First of all, the overall sociodemographic development of the population; Figure 3.1 showed that the whites were in the majority throughout the 17th century. The balance tipped in favour of the blacks around 1720, but by the mid-18th century, the ratio was only about 60-40. The situation changed from the 1750s onwards (reaching a total 80-20 ratio in 1780), but this was also the period of extensive population mixing. Ethnic mixing continued and intensified over the next century since Governor Charles Elliot noted in 1868 that "there can be no position on the face of the earth where it would be more difficult to discriminate between the various strains of blood of which the body of the population is composed than here in St Helena" (quoted in Gosse 1938).

A second factor is the total socio-economic dependence on the UK. The island was ruled by the EIC until 1834 and then transferred into a Crown colony, which meant that it was controlled by the Foreign Office. St Helena has always depended on aides from the UK and never been economically viable, despite all the efforts to start a successful business enterprise on the island. This meant not only that government officials and staff were present on the island at all times (providing an accessible English target), but also that St Helena has always oriented itself towards its British heritage. The St Helenians adopted and maintained English customs and institutions, public holidays, such as Guy Fawkes Day or Queen's Day, and English role models in architecture and landscaping. In the words of Turner and Hopkins (1996: 5), "Saint Helenians are, and always have been, British", and Cross (1980: 11) states that

> St Helena is one of the last remaining British colonial possessions and it is part of its charm that it is so obviously just that. The fact that it is British cannot be mistaken ... The islanders' dress, the groceries they buy from Solomon's or Benjamin's, the Guides, the cricket and football clubs, the Women's Institutes, the whole way of life is British but subtly transformed by climate, terrain and racial characteristics.

The British apparel of the community was commented on much earlier, for instance by Charles Darwin:

> The English, or rather Welsh character of the scenery, is kept up by the numerous cottages and small white houses; some buried at the bottom of the deepest valleys, and others mounted on the crests of lofty hills. (Darwin 1839)

William Dampier, the famous explorer and naturalist, visited the island in June 1691 and noted:

> While we stay'd here, many of the seamen got sweethearts ... several other of our men, were over head and ears in love with the St Hellena [sic] maids, who tho' they were born there, yet very earnestly desired to be released from that prison, which they have no other way to compass, but by marrying seamen, or passengers that touch here. The young women born here, are but one remove from English, being the daughters of such. (quoted in Gosse 1938: 104)

Captain Daniel Beeckman, on visit on June 9 1715, wrote that all the white inhabitants were "English" and that they owned a large number of slaves. Moreover, it struck him that the local feeling was very much one of dependence on the mother country and one of a colonial outpost, not of an independent colony: "They all have a great desire to see England, which they call home, though many of them never saw it, nor can have any true idea thereof" (quoted in Gosse 1938: 139). This is further confirmed by the StHR; an entry dated July 7 1715 reads:

> If your Honours would please to send English farthings and halfe pence they would certainly doe much better than Pice and have been more agreeable to the English people, for all the St. Helenians account themselves so, though three quarters of them never saw England.

The dependence on - and general orientation towards - Great Britain is therefore an important factor as well. I fully agree with Schulenburg & Schulenburg (1997: 9) who write that "[w]hile the ascription and self-ascription of an English or British identity to St Helena's population was first restricted to the island's white settlers, it gradually came to encompass the island's entire population. Today, there are no divisions in terms of colour or ethnic identity." This does of course not mean that acculturation was complete and that all African roots disappeared without a trace. As late as in the 1980s, one would find comments such as

> It is strange that despite the apparently civilised way of life of the people and the strength of Christianity there are still many islanders who also believe in magic and the occult, particularly the power of the evil eye. A man will visit the doctor complaining of a 'chicken in my leg' and will proceed to say who wished this calamity on him ... In some districts a visiting dance band from town has been known to refuse to play because among those present there has been one notorious for the possession of his dark power. (Cross 1980: 99)

Similarly, in other important domains such as home or food, non-British influences are strong. The Saints' diet consists of hot and spicy dishes, curries, plo (a traditional rice dish), rice (until recently: yams) and not potatoes (though these could be grown easily), which attests to a non-British heritage and is the sociocultural legacy of the black founding populations. Nevertheless, and this seems undisputed, the focus and dependence on Great Britain has at all times been strong and unquestioned, and this is without doubt a most important factor in our attempt to retrace the evolution of StHE.

Third, blacks were taught (some) trades and received job training (though they were not allowed in domains where they were seen as competition for the white, e.g. in carpentry). Some slaves were held in such a high esteem that it was demanded they were returned to the island after escape attempts. Ch. 3 discussed the case of the slave by the name of Grewer, who was described as "a stonelayer and a very useful man" (*Letters to England*, December 18 1760). The Governor himself called Grewer "a serviceable man ... very artful and designing". Blacks thus moved up the social scale and were employed in positions earlier held by whites only. There are also reports of black overseers as of the mid-18th century:

> Four Madagascar slaves attempt to run off in Sam Alexander's Fishing Boat in Sandy Bay – not knowing how to manage a boat the sea drove them on shore

> on the beach. Their excuse they did not like to be under *a Black* overseer. (*Consultations* April 18, 1768; emphasis in original)

Consequently, the combination of all these factors (socio-economic dependency on the UK and identity as a British outpost, continuous presence of native speakers of British English, job training for slaves, comparatively good integration of the black community, long-term socio-demographic stability between whites and blacks, low settler-slave ratio) reinforced the importance of English as a means of communication in the black population, speeding up language shift. We know that this process must have been completed by the end of the 19th century, since Grant (1879: 10) talks about the "Inhabitants, who are of European, Asiatic and African origin, and whose only language is English."

This leads me to argue that there were three major phases in the formation of StHE: a *founding phase*, characterised by high social fluctuation, socio-ethnic diversity as well as multidialectalism and -lingualism (from 1658 until the 1720s); a *consolidation phase*, which saw population stability, reduced in-migration and the beginnings of sociolinguistic norm formation (from the 1720s to the 1770s); and a *focussing phase*, which saw the completion of language shift, the emergence of a monolingual and fairly homogeneous population in which an endonormative StHE variety had emerged (from the 1770s to the mid-19th century). The founding phase would have seen coexistence of multiple inputs and the emerging feature pool that contained all the features from which StHE could have selected (ch. 2). This was a non-focussed, unstable heterogeneous conglomerate of more than a dozen transplanted varieties, with high levels of intra- and inter-speaker variation. The consolidation phase was characterised by beginning stability and sociodemographic non-fluctuation. The St Helenian population grew due to local reproduction and not via continuing immigration or import (of slaves), which means that children, prime agents in new-dialect formation and creolisation soon were in a majority, outnumbering the adult population. This is the stage where initial mixing and levelling were most likely to occur and where the initial diffuseness and variability began to decrease. The focussing phase of StHE, finally, went hand in hand with ethnic mixing. Ethnic divisions (fragile earlier on anyway) came down for good and most children had parents of mixed ethnicity (which continued throughout the 19th century; see above). This phase was one of focussing, emerging homogeneity and endonormativity, and (though this cannot be verified) probably also of the completion of language shift. Table 7.1 summarises the evolutionary path suggested for StHE.

Social factors and the external history of the variety were paramount for the development of a distinctive local StHE variety. Demography was particularly important, providing the 'right' social setting in which language-internal mechanisms (mixing, levelling, etc.) operated. This shows how intimately intertwined language-external and intralinguistic factors are and that it is a combination of processes that ultimately accounts for the complexity of contact-induced language change.

Table 7.1 The evolutionary path of StHE

Phase	***Processes involved***	***Period***
FOUNDING PHASE	Social fluctuation Frequent in-, out-migration Linguistic diversity Competition of inputs Initial feature pool formed	1658-1720s
CONSOLIDATION PHASE	Population stabilises Migration less common Local reproduction Ethnic boundaries blurred Sociolinguistic Mixing and levelling Incipient normativity	1720s-1770s
FOCUSSING PHASE	Continuing stability Homogeneity Ethnic mixing continues Endonormativity Language shift completed Focussing completed	1770s-1850s

This leads me to the second aim of this book, the variety's typological status. StHE did not exist some 300 years ago and it now has parallels and differences with other varieties. This means that it must have undergone processes similar to those operating elsewhere. What is does this mean for the status of StHE and how are we to place the variety in the canon of English around the world?

7.2 *The typological status of Helenian English*

In a way, it would be easy, perhaps even tempting, to classify StHE as an English-based Creole. From a sociohistorical point of view, it is undisputed that the variety has had an extensive contact history, that it formed from multiple inputs, English being the most influential one, and that it emerged in a socio-ethnic melting pot. All of these factors are prerequisites for creolisation and have given rise to English-based creoles elsewhere. StHE thus meets all the *social* criteria for such a classification.

A linguistically-founded argument for StHE being a Creole is that it shares (some) diagnostic features with varieties for which such a status seems undisputed. For instance, the analysis of CCR in ch. 6 showed that StHE has an extremely rare tendency to reduce bimorphemic clusters (final segment *–ed*) more frequently than monomorphemic ones (*passed* > *past*). This is exceptional; the only other variety in which a *bi* > *mono* constraint has been documented for is (mesolectal) JamCrE (Patrick 1991, 1999). Patrick explains this by the interaction of two processes, namely a) a strong (grammatical) trend towards non-marking of regular verbs for past tense (an extreme simplification of the verbal paradigm: a dropping of irregular and/or marked features that carry a high cognitive load and have little functional significance, such as tense suffixes), and b) a strong tendency toward cluster-final plosive deletion due to direct phonotactic transfer of syllable types without clusters (particularly CV(C)). The only donor that could have had such an impact on a focussing form of StHE is Malagasy, which does *not* admit clusters. Indeed, Richardson (1885: xiv) finds that "Malagasy does not allow the free combination of consonants common in European languages, and many of our words appear to the natives extremely harsh. The allowable combinations of consonants are very few, and the tendency of the language is to use short open syllables; at the close of a word no exception is allowed to this rule." By the same token, Domenichini-Ramiaramananan (1976: 27), in her descriptive summary of Malagasy, notes that

> la langue classique viellie ne connaît normalement ni groupes de consonnes, ni syllabes fermées, ce qui explique, dans les emprunts à des langues les connaissant, le fréquent développement de voyelles épenthétiques. ["The classical ancient language normally has neither groups of consonants nor closed syllables, which explains, in borrowings into other languages, the frequent development of epenthetic vowels"; translation DS]

Her observations on syllable patterns merit attention also (ibid.):

> Si l'on ne retient, en somme, que les unités perçues comme «racines primaires», la langue classique connaît des monosyllabes, des dissylabes, des trissylabes et des quadrisyllabes, les premiers et les derniers étant d'un nombre très nettement inférieur à celui des autres, et les seconds plus nombreux que les troisièmes. ["If we only consider, in sum, the unities we perceive as "primary roots", the classical language has monosyllables, disyllables, tri-syllables and quadri-syllables, the first and the last being clearly inferior by number to the others, and the second ones being more frequent than the third"; translation DS)

She lists a total of 12 types of syllable structures: CV, V, VV, CVV (monosyllabic), CV-CV, V-CV, V-CVV, VV-CV, CVV-CV, VC-CV, CVC-CV, CCV-CV (bisyllabic). Only one of them admits a group of consonants (and this in initial position only!), so this is clearly a minority type. Consequently, Malagasy phonotactics does not close syllables; syllable-final consonants are not found at all, let alone final consonant clusters. One plausible explanation for why we would find this particular CCR pattern in StHE could be (substratum) influence from Malagasy (i.e. transfer of other syllable types and restructuring of English phonotactics, indicative of simplification), though incomplete accommodation as a consequence of L2 learning, resulting in fossilisation, is equally likely. The most plausible explanation, in my view, is that a combination of these two factors (substratum influence and processes triggered by L2 learning) accounts for the adoption and persistence of this highly diagnostic constraint.

Consequently, the fact that we should find this pattern in two varieties, one of which is commonly regarded as a Creole, would suggest that StHE must have the same status. This seems uncontroversial (though we need more data and more detailed feature analyses to justify such a classification). The close resemblance with regard to the feature under discussion is particularly remarkable since there are no direct connections between the two varieties; in fact, there are very few links in general between St Helena and the Caribbean (the South Atlantic was not integrated into the triangular trade system, being too geographically distant from the "middle passage"). JamCrE and StHE had different inputs and formed from distinct feature pools, which means that they independently developed an identical pattern (that was notably absent in the British inputs). This sheds light on parallel processes of restructuring and simplification in (English) creolisation, a question that I would like to pursue in future research.

Additional support for claims of StHE being an English-based Creole comes from the analysis of copula absence. This is commonly regarded as a legacy of language contact: "At the same time, most linguists agree that copula absence is a widespread trait of English-based creole and pidgin languages spoken in the African diaspora" (Wolfram & Thomas 2002: 78); "An interesting question raised by this hypothesis [that different varieties, such as AAVE and English-based creoles, have innovated zero copula independently of each other] is why zero copula has arisen less frequently outside of situations of language contact" (Walker & Meyerhoff 2006: 148). This point was made with reference to AAE: "The very fact that copula absence is widespread both in AAVE and in mesolectal creoles, but not in white Englishes outside of the American South (where it can be argued that whites adopted the speech patterns of blacks) strongly suggests that at least some of the predecessors of modern AAVE arose from a restructuring process similar to that which produced the English-based creoles" (Rickford 1998: 189) and "many West African languages and the deep, or basilectal, varieties of Creole English in the Caribbean regularly have no copula before adjectives, so this could be one model for copula absence in [AAE]." (Rickford & Rickford 2000: 155).

This is supported further when we take a general look at copula absence in English around the world. Using the *Handbook of Varieties of English* (Schneider et al. 2004) as a research tool, a high percentage of copula absence is indicative of large-scale language contact, making an appearance in nearly all English-based creoles. The authors use a taxonomic classification of features classed into three groups: (A) 'Feature(s) pervasive/very frequent'; (B) 'Feature(s) occur sometimes, in some groups/in some environments'; and (C) 'Feature(s) not documented: no positive evidence, does not apply or no information available'. Varieties classed as (C) include White varieties of American, British, South African, Australian and New Zealand English, (B) Appalachian English, Chicano English, Cameroon English, Isolated Se. American English, and Norfuk (Norfolk), and (A) Aboriginal English, Australian Creoles, Bahamian English, Belizean Creole, Bislama (Vanuatu), Butler English (India), Cameroon Pidgin English, Earlier AAE, Ghananian Pidgin, English Gullah, Hawaiian Creoles, Jamaican Creole, Malaysian English, Nigerian Pidgin English, Singapore English, Solomon Islands Pijin, Tok Pisin, Trinidadian Creole, and Urban AAVE (Figure 7.1, adapted from Schneider, Kortmann et al. 2004). The high levels of copula absence (total percentage: 76.8%) mean that StHE must be listed under category (A), so that it ranks alongside Creole varieties.

Figure 7.1 Copula absence in varieties of English around the world

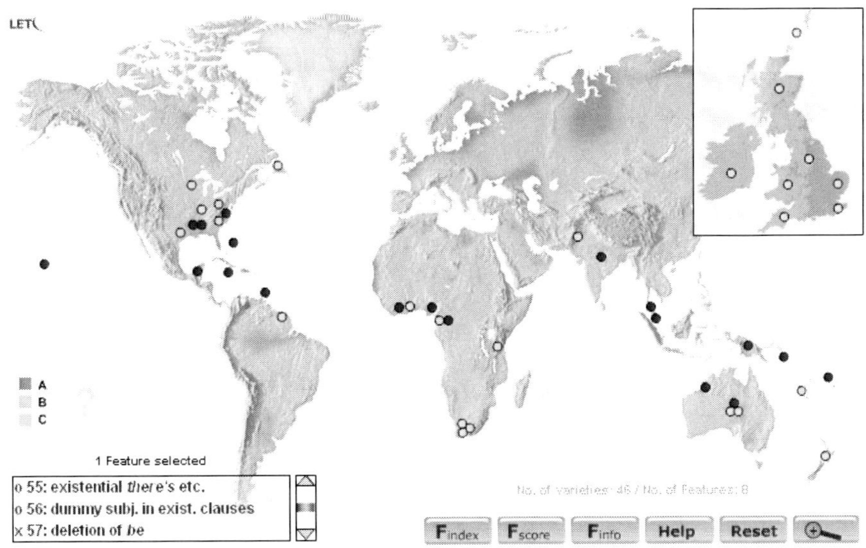

A final argument in favour of StHE being a creole is by nature comparative. Even though there exists no checklist of creole features (let alone a creole prototype; discussion below), a comparative analysis of morphosyntactic structures and lexical items yields important insights genetic affiliations, historical linguistics and language typology. This was common practice in the 19th century (to show genetic relationships between Indo-European languages; Lehmann 1992) and has been used since the 1960s for pidgin and creole languages around the world as well (Hancock 1969, 1987; Clark 1979; Holm 1986, 1992; Kautzsch & Schneider 2000). The most promising approach, and the one adopted here, is to use a feature list that is at the same time comparative and representative, one that has been used in similar research projects and provides a reliable yardstick for analysis. One of the most recent and encompassing attempts is Baker & Huber (2001), who built on and expanded their earlier research (Baker 1987, 1993 composed a list of earliest attestations of lexical features in Pacific pidgins and creoles, and Huber 1999 applied a similar technique in his study of Atlantic creoles and West African Pidgin Englishes). Their article "expands our earliest attestations approach in a systematic compilation of data from seven Atlantic and six Pacific varieties and by investigating the nature of the world-wide features and their role in the origin and diffusion of restructured Englishes" (159). Consequently, I apply the item-by-item discussion for the Creole features as compiled by Baker & Huber (2001) and follow their practice of classifying them into "Atlantic", "Pacific" or "World-wide". This approach allows me to investigate putative creolisation of StHE in more detail and to trace whether and to what extent it has affinities with English-based creoles in the Caribbean. Table 7.2 lists the 20th century StHE features classified as "Atlantic" by Baker & Huber (2001), Table 7.3 those listed as "World-wide".

Perhaps a word about the methodology adopted: I took lists of diagnostic features with me on St Helena (among those the feature list developed by Baker & Huber 2001) and searched for evidence both in the archives and in the field. Quite a few of the illustrative examples below come from my own corpus (some presented in section 5.2 already). Moreover, to provide a picture as complete as possible, I went through the entire list with Basil George, the author of the St Helenian short stories (cf. ch. 4), who had an intimate knowledge of the island and the community. He invited us to go hiking and climbing with him, showed us around St Helena and told us many an interesting story and anecdote about the Saints and their social history (quite a few of which were showcase examples of oral history, not found in history books). Basil George developed an interest in our project from the start and volunteered his help. When going through the list with him, I gave him possible examples of how these features could be used, which prompted him to provide examples of his own (which were then noted by myself). I asked him to judge whether the feature seemed acceptable to him or not (making a distinction between "frequent", "common" and "acceptable"), whether he thought it was widespread or not, or to offer any other piece of information he considered important. The features below, then, are all drawn from Baker & Huber's extensive (2001) study. They make an appearance in my own data (in which case the informant is labelled, just as in the morphosyntactic profile above) or are confirmed by Basil George. If features analysed by Baker & Huber (2001) do not show up in Tables 7.2 and 3, then they made no appearance in my own data or did not sound familiar to Basil George.

20th century StHE has a total of 30 features labelled "Atlantic" (total in Baker & Huber 2001: 173) and 50 classified as "World-wide" (total: 75). By contrast, only a handful of "Pacific" lexical items are found in StHE (*by-and by* 'future'; *bullock* 'cattle, beef'; *close up* 'near by'; and *sing out* 'shout', which is also found in TdCE). A substantial number of features located and analysed in 13 English-derived contact varieties by Baker & Huber (2001) are therefore found in StHE as well. When adding the total numbers and comparing them across the varieties, then StHE clearly ranks among the English-based Creoles, as Table 7.4 shows (adapted from Baker & Huber 2001: 171). The table breaks down the features in two categories, *Atlantic and Pacific features (combined)* and *World-wide features*, and arranges the 14 varieties by total number of features reported. By the same token, it is striking to find that StHE has comparatively few features from the "Atlantic" and "Pacific" categories. This was somewhat expected for the Pacific features (given the geographical distance, the different histories of genesis and evolution as well as the fact that StHE is much older), and, given what we know about St Helena's social history, it is not surprising for the Atlantic features either. This is entirely in line with conclusions from the community's social history (ch. 3): there were no connections with the Pacific areas (though there was substantial impact from communities in the Indian Ocean) and limited contact with the Caribbean (St Helena not being a major port of call for the triangular slave trade; though many ships arrived en route from or for South Africa and the Indian subcontinent, their stay was short-term only). Similarly, direct input from West African pidgins was small, and whatever little influence there may have been in the early years of the colony was likely to be swamped by later waves of immigrants (so that putative founder effects were eradicated).

Notwithstanding, a different picture emerges when we consider the "World-wide" features as a separate category. Here, StHE ranks among the top five (behind Krio and West African Pidgin English: 63 each; JamCrE: 52.5[1]; and Eastern Australian Pidgins: 51.5), well ahead of most of the English-based contact varieties studied by Baker & Huber (2001).

---

[1] I should add that Baker & Huber rate marginal attestations with a 0.5 score. This explains the totals arrived at for some of the varieties they study.

Table 7.2 "Atlantic" creole features in StHE

all you (2nd plural) = commonly y'all	"if y'all make arrangement" (ChC, Sandy Bay)
bad mouth (V)	BG: Common
bang 'hit'	BG: 'to bang a child', 'he got a good banging/lashing'
belong	"those was the donkeys belong to Scotland" (DF, Sandy Bay); (very often with the meaning 'family-wise'): "I gotta son belong to P, you see" (EH, Jamestown); "the baby belong to the guy what is accused" (CY, Kunjee Field)
how come? 'why?'	BG: Frequent
for V (modal)	BG: Acceptable
for true 'truly'	BG: Acceptable
fullup 'be full, fill'	"the people in Jamestown is fullup, they don't want any" (PF, Blue Hill)
brother, fella, pa = term of endearment (but apparently not buddy)	"everything OK brother?" (SF; Half Tree Hollow) - Very common in my data
chaw 'eat; food'	BG: Common
dem$_1$ (demonstrative)	"he play for them small churches" (BB, Cleugh's Plain)
dem$_2$ (post-posed nominative plural)	"Larry dem never catch nothing" (BB, Cleugh's Plain)
dem$_3$ (pre-posed nominative plural)	BG: Acceptable
completive done	"I done beat him now" (CY, Kunjee Field)
cabin 'bed'	BG: Acceptable
live used as locative copula	BG: Acceptable
look 'see, find, visit'	"So you went look him in the hospital, yeah" (BB, Cleugh's Plain); "y'all supposed to come look her" (TH, Longwood)
married for 'marry'	BG: Acceptable
no more 'merely'	BG: Fairly certain, but not sure
nuf(nuf) 'plenty' (> 'enough')	BG: "we had nuf sports now"
palaver 'dispute, discourse'	BG: Acceptable
say as complementiser	BG: Acceptable
shall 'future'	BG: Acceptable
tief 'V, steal'	BG: Acceptable
titty 'little girl, sister'	BG: Infrequent, survives as nickname ("Titty Maggott")
ugly 'evil'	BG: Acceptable
WH make 'why'	BG: Acceptable
WH matter 'why'	BG: "What matter he come look me?"
WH sort 'what kind of'	"You know what sort fish wahoo is" (ChC, Sandy Bay)

Table 7.3 "World-wide" creole features in StHE

all about 'everywhere'	"I bring him up off the bottle, and he used to follow me all about" (HF, Longwood); "people used to work in the fields all about" (TH, Longwood)
be$_1$ 'predicative copula'	BG: Frequent
be$_2$ 'future reference'	"yeah, I be there tomorrow" (BG); " I be lookin' out for him 10 o'clock" (EP, Sapper Way)
be$_3$ 'habitual reference'	"it always be hot in Jamestown" (AF, Levelwood); "up on top, that's where the fog normally be" (KY, Cunjee Field)
been 'remote anterior'	"I been break my leg when I was 18" (HF, Blue Hill)
before times / before days 'formerly'	"before-days when we bake we use to have to make our own yeast" (BB, Cleugh's Plain); "children used to sat in schools till they was 15 before-days" (GB, Pounceys); also common: "in the olden days"
by-and-by 'ADV, soon'	BG: "by-and-by I go do something"
capsize 'spill, pour out'	BG: Common
catch 'get, obtain, reach'	"in that time you only catch the water off the roof" (DF, Sandy Bay)
comeout 'go out' (reanalysis)	BG: Acceptable
COPULA absence$_1$ 'equative'	BG: Frequent
COPULA absence$_2$ 'predicative'	"St Helena Ø not what it used to be" (AH, Levelwood)
da(t) 'definite article'	"was that shop there" (JB, Sunnyside)
dead 'die'	"Kenny dead a couple weeks ago" (BB, Cleugh's Plain), but die 'present, future tense' ("she so sick she die soon", JM, Blue Hill)
dem '3rd plural'	BG: Frequent
falldown 'fall' (reanalysis)	BG: Acceptable
fashion 'manner'	BG: Common
V finish 'completive'	BG: Acceptable (but not common)
for 'infinitive'	BG: Acceptable
go 'future'	"that's it, I go retire today", "you know what the weather go be there" (PY, Kunjee Field)
got 'have'	"they got a small business between them" (EP, Sapper Way); "nowadays the people got them on the pastures" (GB, Pounceys)
he 'possessive'	BG: Acceptable
lick 'flog', but more common 'beat, hit'	"before days I used to lick it on him" (GC, Jamestown); also 'to beat in competition', e.g. in fishing; "I lick him proper" (BG)

little bit 'slightly'	BG: Common
long 'with'	"I pick up a job long Mr Thornton", "come go long me, come fishin' " (BB, Cleugh's Plain)
make 'causative / imperative'	BG: Acceptable
make haste 'hurry'	BG: Common
me 'possessive'	BG: Frequent
moon 'month'	"many moons ago" (BB, Cleugh's Plain)
more better 'better'	"it was a bit more better then" (JJ, Thompson's Hill)
mos' 'almost'	"you buy one cabbage, they mos' a pound" (ChC, Sandy Bay)
never 'negative – completive'	"the old man was different – he never drink, he never smoke" (GC, Jamestown)
no-good 'bad'	"he a no-good person" (BG)
number one 'best, chief'	BG: Common
one 'definite article'	"when you get the hanks out the fiber see you throw it over one engine see you throw it in there see" (ChC, Sandy Bay)
one time 'at once'	BG: Acceptable
picaninny 'small child'	BG: Common
plenty N 'a lot of'	"you know plenty girls in there don't do broidery" (JM, Blue Hill); "they would buy for people with plenty chickens" (EP, Sapper Way); "building that house take plenty of tone" (LG, Levelwood)
sabby 'know'	BG: "he got no sabby" = 'no sense'
-side 'locative suffix'	"That's Sandy Bay-side" (GB, Pounceys)
sitdown 'sit'	"the old people was crafty, they never let that happen; they sitdown and peel the pears and cut them down" (GC, Jamestown); "every night me and my husband used to sitdown by the table" (GC, Jamestown)
standup 'stand' (reanalysis)	BG: Acceptable
stop 'locative V'	"so the girl come stop with me for a while" (EP, Sapper Way)
suppose 'if'	BG: "suppose you go town, can you give me a lif'?"
throwaway 'throw' (reanalysis)	BG: Common
too much ADJ / V / N 'a lot'	BG: Acceptable
WH for 'why'	"what for she left already?" (AF, Levelwood)
WH place 'where'	"what place y'all stop?" (CF, Blue Hill)
WH thing 'what'	BG: Common
WH time 'when'	"what time y'all leave Cape Town?" (BB, Cleugh's Plain)

The analysis and cross-comparison of these features shows that StHE bears lexico-structural resemblances with English-based creoles. This strongly suggests that language contact processes contributed towards the shaping and evolution of the variety.

Table 7.4 StHE in comparison with English-derived contact varieties around the world

Variety	Atlantic and Pacific features (combined)	World-wide features	Total (n=302)
Jamaican	129	52.5	181.5
Krio	115	63	178
West African Pidgin English	87	63	150
St. Kitts	96	38	134
Sranan	89	44.5	133.5
Bajan	81	36	117
Gullah	80	42	122
Eastern Australian Pidgins	50.5	51.5	102
Melanesian Pidgin English	47	42	89
St Helenian English	**34**	**50**	**84**
Hawai'ian Pidgin English	13.5	49.5	63
Chinese Pidgin English	9	48	57
Pitcairn	14.5	20	34.5
Kiribati	6	27	33

All these findings invite the implication that StHE should be classified as a Creole. Is this the end of the story then? Unfortunately not; there are a number of complicating factors we need to take into account as well. First of all, language varieties have no DNA or unmistakable finger prints that would allow for error-proof matching and identification. Every contact-derived variety has its own history and as a consequence, the rich landscape of contact-derived, restructured or 'new' Englishes around the globe emerged in distinct (and indistinguishably characteristic) social contexts. This somewhat stands in the way of a global comparison of linguistic features. In the words of Thomason (1997: 73), "identifying creoles by means of a laundry list of grammatical features has proved to be an elusive goal: there are no features that are exclusive to, nor universal in, languages generally thought to be creoles." Mufwene (1991) maintains that creoles vary among themselves in the way they combine and share this stock of features and Schneider (1990: 79) adds that "there is no set of distinctive criteria that unequivocally establishes the category of creole languages or serves to identify any of its members." Moreover, features typically associated with creoles were selected (though not necessarily preserved intact!) from their lexifiers, i.e. from the non-standard, working-class varieties (mostly of southern EnglE) that fed into the local feature pool(s).

Creoles are structurally related both to their lexifiers and to their substrate languages, an observation that has led (Mufwene 2001) to call them "mixed languages". StHE drew a substantial set of features from its non-standard EnglE inputs, which were influential elsewhere too. Can this then really be used as diagnostic evidence that StHE is a creole, or would this not rather stress the importance of the lexifiers?

The dilemma is of course that if creole languages were considered to represent a category that is typologically and structurally different from others, then they should have a set of features that sets them apart on linguistic grounds. All varieties classified as creoles should have these features and the existence of a given creole feature X would be a *conditio sine qua non* for assessing the typological status or membership in this particular category. What would (or should) these features be? Some candidates have been proposed (by Bickerton 1981, for example), or more recently, by McWhorter (1998, 2005), who argued that a creole prototype would have 1) no inflectional morphology (at least not more than three inflectional affixes), 2) no tone on monosyllabic items, and 3) no semantically opaque word formation. Every language with these three features is a creole, McWhorter argues, and every creole must have these three features.

Without going into too much detail, I would like to point out that this hypothesis has been criticised for different reasons. First of all, some languages have all three features though they did not develop in sociohistorical contexts that give rise to creolisation (colonial possessions, slavery, ethnic mixing, etc.). Varieties such as Manding, Sooninke, Magoua French (Wittmann 1999) and Riau Indonesian (Gil 1994, 2006) thus pose a challenge to McWhorter's claims. Moreover, there exist creoles that have features they should not have if the creole protoype hypothesis is correct (Berbice Dutch Creole has inflectional morphology, Papiamentu distinguishes tone, for example). Similar problems arise with claims of simplification (ch. 2), e.g. McWhorter's famous claim that "the world's simplest grammars are Creole grammars" (i.e. that any creole language will necessarily be less complex than a 'non-Creole' one). Gil (2006) counter-argues that Riau Indonesian is precisely such a language, being in fact simpler than Saramaccan, which is central to the creole prototype hypothesis. The problems in defining creoles based on their features are so far-reaching that some creolists have questioned whether it is of value at all for linguistic theory. Chaudenson (1992, 2003) or Mufwene (2001) take the position that Creole languages are no different from any other language on structural grounds and that it is preferable to view *Creole* as a sociohistorical concept (not a linguistic one), approaching and defining it via language-external factors such as population displacement and slavery conditions. Ch. 2 showed that the concept of creole exceptionalism was discussed prominently by Thomason & Kaufman (1988), who claimed that creole languages were an instance of non-genetic language change due to catastrophic social conditions and a consequence of language shift without normal transmission. Others have questioned this, arguing that the processes that underlie the evolution of creole languages are in no way different from universal patterns of language change (see e.g. Mufwene 2001; Chaudenson 1992, 2003; Croft 2000; Wittmann 1983, 2001).

To cut a long story short and return to StHE, the problem is that a set of diagnostic (or unique) creole features has not been identified so far. Features that are said to be true of all (or most) creole languages are in fact true of all isolating language types (many of which are not creoles: Mandarin Chinese, Thai, or the Kwa languages of West Africa). If we do not know what typical creole features are and what features a creole needs to have in order to be classified as such, if creoles do not share their features universally, then it is practically impossible to make such a decision. The fact that StHE shares a certain number of features with varieties that were restructured in other places can tell us a lot about the degree of similarity, of course, but it obscures the fact that the common traits may in fact derive from the English lexifiers, particularly Southeastern EnglE varieties. These represented the majority of English inputs nearly everywhere and provided the bulk of the superstrates that fed into the local feature pool(s). The similarities may thus also point to a British ancestral heritage.

Moreover, a closer look at the StHE features presented in the descriptive profiles in ch. 4 reveals how complex genetic affiliations with other varieties of English around the world really are. The segmental phonology of StHE (vowel summary in Table 7.5), for instance, bears a striking resemblance with systems that are not considered creoles at all, such as AusE or NZE (if anything, these are koinés, since they evolved via dialect contact and new-dialect formation in a context where a direct British input was at all times strong; cf. ch. 2). A prominent example here is the realisation of StHE KIT, which mirrors variants found in other SHemEs, where raising (AusE) or centralisation (SAfrE, NZE) are well-documented, or *Canadian Raising*, i.e. a split allophony that occurs "in nearly every form of non-creolised, mixed, colonial English outside Australasia and South Africa" (Trudgill 1986: 160), including the Englishes of White Bahamians, White Bermudans, White SAmE, e.g. in Charleston, South Carolina (Kurath & McDavid 1961) or in the English Fens (Britain 1991, 1997). The descriptive profile has shown that StHE affiliates strongly with other varieties of English around the world (spoken in the British Isles, particularly in the Southeast, throughout the Southern Hemisphere, etc.). The short front vowels, first of all, have similar qualities as those reported elsewhere, particularly in the major SHemE varieties. KIT, DRESS and TRAP all display variation and their places of articulation tend to be closer rather than more open. The common trend in all four speakers analysed is one of raising, though we await results from a quantitative analysis to gain more detailed insights here (which will be subject to further research). Impressionistically, however, DRESS and TRAP seem to be more open than their counterparts in varieties such as FIE, SAfrE or AusE.

Also, DRESS and TRAP seem to vary less than the highest of the short front vowels: KIT displays stable, raised and centralised variants (and the four speakers analysed have all three realisations, which indicates considerable variation).

Table 7.5 The segmental phonology of StHE: Vowel summary

Reference vowel	***JM*** (Blue Hill)	***BB*** (Cleugh's Plain)	***LG*** (Levelwood)	***ChC*** (Sandy Bay)
KIT	[ɪ ~ ɪ̝ ~ ɪ̈]	[ɪ ~ ɪ̝ ~ ɪ̞]	[ɪ ~ ɪ̝ ~ ɪ̈]	[ɪ ~ ɪ̝ ~ iᵊ ~ ɪ̈]
DRESS	[ɛ ~ ɛ̝ ~ e̞]	[ɛ ~ ɛ̝ ~ e̞ˑ]	[ɛ ~ ɛ̝ ~ iə]	[ɛ ~ ɛ̝]
TRAP	[æ ~ æˑᵊ ~ ɛᵊ ~ ɛ̝]	[æ ~ ɛ̝ᵊ ~ e̞]	[æ ~ æˑᵊ]	[æ ~ æ̝ˑᵊ]
FOOT	[ʊ ~ uˑ]	[ʊ]	[ʊ]	[ʊ]
STRUT	[ʌ ~ ɐ̝ ~ ʊ]	[ʌ ~ ʌ̝]	[ɐ ~ ɐ̝]	[ʌ ~ ʌ̝ ~ ɐ]
CLOTH	[ɒ ~ ɑ]	[ɑ ~ oˑᶷ ~ ɔə]	[ɒ ~ ɑ ~ ɔə]	[ɑ ~ ɔ̝ ~ ɔ̝ə]
FLEECE	[iː ~ iˑⁱ]	[iː]	[iː ~ iˑ]	[iː]
NURSE	[ɜ̝ː]	[ɜˑ ~ ɜː ~ ɜ̝ː]	[ɵː ~ ɵˑ]	[ɜ̝ː ~ ɜ̝ˑ]
GOOSE	[uː]	[uː]	[uː]	[uː]
START	[ɑː ~ ɔə]	[ɑː]	[ɑː ~ ɑ̝ˑᵊ ~ ɔə]	[ɑː ~ ɔə]
THOUGHT/FORCE/ NORTH/POOR	[oə]	[oə ~ oɐ]	[oə]	[oə ~ uə]
FACE	[ɛɪ ~ ɛˑⁱ]	[ɛɪ ~ ɛᶦ ~ ɛ̝ˑ]	[ɛɪ ~ ɛ̝ː ~ ɛˑⁱ]	[ɛɪ ~ ɛᶦ ~ ɛ̝ˑ]
PRICE	[ɔ̝i ~ əɪ]	[ɔ̝i ~ ɐɪ ~ əɪ]	[ɔ̝i ~ əɪ ~ ɑi ~ æi]	[ɔ̝i ~ əɪ]
CHOICE	[o̞i ~ oi]	[ɔ̝i ~ ɐɪ]	[ɔi ~ o̞i]	[ɔ̝i ~ o̞i ~ ai]
GOAT	[ɔ̝ː ~ ɔu]	[ɔ̝ˑ ~ ɔ̝u]	[ɔ̝u ~ o̞ː]	[ɔu ~ ɔ̝u]
MOUTH	[aʊ ~ ɔʊ]	[o̞ʊ ~ ɑ̝ʊ]	[ɑ̝ʊ ~ ɔʊ]	[a̝ʊ ~ ɔʊ]
NEAR ~ SQUARE	merged [iə]	merged [iə]	not merged	merged [iə]
triphthong smoothing	-	✓ /aʊə/	✓ /aʊə/	-
weak vowel merger	✓	✓	✓	✓
happY tensing	✓	✓	✓	✓
Yod dropping	✓	✓	✓	✓

As for the back vowels, CLOTH displays a similar amount of variation: raising is common (in words such as off, froth, etc., which was common in 19th century EnglE) and /ɔə/ occurs as well. Three out of four speakers show an overlap with the THOUGHT/FORCE/NORTH/POOR set (this is also found in some of the

START words), which is a highly characteristic local development. FOOT and STRUT, finally, are distinct so that StHE has six short vowels and is in line with the vast majority of English varieties around the world. The front vowels show raising tendencies (and are subject to centralisation, in the case of KIT), a pattern of variation also found in CLOTH.

The long monophthongs, in contrast, are conservative. FLEECE and GOOSE are close and mostly monophthongal (though two speakers have sporadic – but slight – off-glides in FLEECE). Tendencies toward fronting or breaking are practically absent. NURSE unrounding is common (particularly in the case of LG from Levelwood) and lip-rounding, very frequent in SAfrE, is not found. One of the most striking features is that THOUGHT, FORCE, NORTH and POOR have undergone merging (pivot /ɔə/), and START is [ɑː], even though words like car, smart, mark have /ɔə/, which is indicative of an overlap of the START, CLOTH and THOUGHT/FORCE/NORTH/POOR sets, an unusual pattern that – to the best of my knowledge – has not been reported elsewhere. It is also noteworthy that the so-called "START backing innovation" (dated to the early 1800s by Wells, 1982: 234) is the norm, and a fully back [ɑː] is most common in all the lexical sets where it would occur in southeastern EnglE, e.g. start, last, path, strongly resembling SAfrE. As for the diphthongs, both FACE and GOAT display "long-mid diphthonging" (Wells 1982: 210); conservative monophthongs, though rare, are reported as well. PRICE and CHOICE have backed and raised onsets (/ɔ̝ ~ ɑ/ for PRICE, /o̝/ for CHOICE), which means that they have partaken in the "diphthong shift" which is common in "Cockney, also the local accents of much of the south of England and the midlands, together with those of Australia and New Zealand" (Wells 1982: 256). The backed and raised onset in PRICE resembles Cockney and working-class AusE. PRICE, on the other hand, has *Canadian raising* while MOUTH has not (which is unusual). *Glide weakening* is not prominent either. Quite remarkably, FACE, MOUTH, and GOAT remain stable and have not shifted in line with the other two diphthongs, being quite conservative in that they have fully back (MOUTH, GOAT) or open-mid front onsets (FACE). As for minor vowel features, StHE has the NEAR ~ SQUARE merger (attested in NZE), happY tensing (common in accents of English around the world), as well as Yod dropping and the weak vowel merger (normative in SHemE).

The analysis of consonants yields a picture of similar complexity. For instance, it is somewhat unexpected to find that 20th century StHE is non-rhotic. In the formative phase, the 18th century, most of the putative British inputs would still have been /r/-ful. Rhoticity was obviously not selected in StHE, and there are several possibilities to explain this. First of all, it is of course possible that the earlier speculations were wrong, that is to say, that (non-rhotic) 19th century inputs were more influential than the socio-historical evidence would suggest. This, however, would have meant that large numbers of settlers must have arrived in the late 18th century to swamp the founding populations; these are not attested and it is more plausible to argue in favour of a contact-based explanation. It is quite possible that the English varieties transplanted to St Helena were already in the process of change, so that rhoticity was vulnerable and levelled out (cf. ch. 2), /r/ being a minority form in pre-consonantal and syllable-final environments.

Alternatively, language contact with Malagasy may have been an important factor here as well, resembling explanations given for the same process in earlier AAE. Feagin (1979) has argued that contact with CV(C) syllable structures from African substrates may have had a reinforcing effect on the ongoing trend towards non-rhoticity in the gradually emerging (perhaps even focussing) variety of AAE. This seems a promising explanation in our scenario as well, particularly since other transfer effects make an appearance. We saw that TH stopping is very common in StHE, as it is in African Englishes, practically all contact-derived varieties of English and ESL varieties around the world. Furthermore, unstressed syllables are mostly clipped and there are extremely high rates of CCR, which cannot be explained via dialect contact (Schreier 2005; cf. ch. 6), etc.

The consonantal system of StHE shows that Southern EngE varieties were particularly influential. Typical northern features are absent (e.g. /ʍ/, the labio-velar approximant that is so common in ScE), whereas some historically attested southern features have survived well into the 20th century, e.g. the /v~w/ interchange (Trudgill et al. 2004). A further affiliation with BrE, notably with EAE, is that StHE has *pre-glottalisation* (Wells 1982: 260), i.e. a glottal stop before /p, t, k, tʃ/. By contrast, a particularly puzzling finding is the uvular quality of /k/, which is reported in the Caribbean, Indian English and also in Pacific Creoles.

Consequently, what do we make out of all this when deciding whether StHE is a Creole or not? Though such a typological assessment is complex and difficult, I think that, when taking everything into consideration, it is not exaggerated to say that StHE is an English-based creole after all. The parallels, both in linguistic features and in social history, are striking and far-reaching. By the same token, we must make a more fine-grained distinction and differentiate. Varieties classified as "Creole" are by no means a monolithic and homogeneous class, as has become clear in the discussion above. This was already pointed out by Schneider (1990), who demonstrated that a set of typical creole features associated with "creoleness" (Görlach 1986: 333) makes an appearance in all the Caribbean Englishes, though there is large-scale variation as to how many of them each variety has and how these features are combined: "The idea that the notion of creoleness may be not absolute but graded to some extent is not new but is frequently ignored" (Schneider 1990: 83). He analysed the occurrence of 24 contact-derived features commonly found in English-based creoles (*preverbal markers*: completive, future, habitual, progressive, anterior, anterior irrealis; *copula forms*: pre-adjectival, -locative, -nominal and topicalisation;

syntactic structures: negation of anterior and future, complementiser se; *morphology of nouns*: possessives, no pluralisation with numerals, non-redundant pluralisation, gerunds; and *pronoun morphology*: subject-object distinction in 1st person plural, 3rd person singular masculine and feminine, subject-possessive distinction in 3rd person plural, number distinction in the 2nd person, gender distinction in 3rd person singular) and found a massive difference in how often varieties would have these features and how they would combine them. In the words of Mufwene (1986: 137), "la mesure de créolité varie d'un créole à l'autre et … ces langues ne partagent pas toutes les charactéristiques associés au prototype créole" ([the measure of creoleness varies from creole to creole and … these languages do not partake in all the characteristics associated with the creole prototype; translation DS]). Saban English had only one of these features and Caymans Islands English a mere 5 (which led Schneider to classify it as a "semi-creole"; cf. ch. 2). The other 12 varieties fell under the category 'creole', though there was considerable variation. Barbadian English had 14 features (mostly in the verb phrase, but also absence of plural marking and simplification of pronouns), St Kitts and Nevis, Trinidadian and Bahamian English 16 and 17, respectively ("without concentrations in any of the grammatical subsystems", Schneider 1990: 97). The highest overall frequencies were found in Gullah, Guyanese Creole and Providencia English; they are "almost perfect creoles, in that they have almost all the features associated with this language type" (Schneider ibid.). Perhaps the real question is not whether or not a variety such as StHE is a creole or not, but where we should place on a continuum of creoleness. This seems more promising since, to quote Schneider (1990) again, "[t]he facts and outcomes of language contact and mixture are more complicated than can be reflected in simple terminologies and classifications. In linguistic matters, more and less are frequently more appropriate responses than simply yes and no" (106).

In sum, StHE affiliates with many varieties of English around the world in that a common stock of features and parallels are found (cf. Appendices III and IV). Some of these varieties are creoles, others not, and a substantial part of phonological and morphosyntactic properties was drawn from the English varieties transplanted to St Helena. I would thus subscribe to Hancock's (1991: 17) claim that a close analysis of StHE is important "firstly because of the many similarities with island dialects elsewhere, and secondly because of its implications for the study of nautical English, and for its relationship to creolised forms of that language", adding perhaps that the complexity of these relationships makes any water-tight classification problematic. I would suggest (in adaptation of Schneider's 1990's "cline of creoleness" approach) that, on a continuum of contact-derived English varieties ranging from more or less 'pure' dialect contact scenarios (as in FIE) to heavily restructured language-contact derived ones (e.g. Saramaccan), StHE would be placed somewhere in the middle. Taking into account that creoles vary among each other and that some creoles are simply more 'creole' than others (simply because they have more features typically associated with creoles), the most plausible (yet also the most careful) option is to place StHE somewhere to the left side on the cline from non-creole to creole, perhaps on a par with varieties such as St Kitts/Nevis and Bahamian English. However, we must not ignore its resemblance to varieties of EnglE, out of which it developed substantially.

7.3 Regional variation

The final point I would like to take up concerns the question whether regionality is a parameter of variation on the island, i.e., whether there exist different regionally characteristic varieties of StHE. If this was the case, then some of the processes described in ch. 2 may have operated simultaneously, leading to diverse contact scenarios and feature pools across the island (for instance, language contact being pre-eminent in the Sandy Bay area, dialect contact in Jamestown, etc.). The quantitative analysis of two selected features in ch. 6 has shown that there are some differences indeed and that Saints from different parts of the island vary in how often they use a sociolinguistic variable or not. Both CCR and copula absence rates are very high (a legacy of language contact; see above), but we found that the locations 'up country' (Levelwood, Sandy Bay, Longwood, Blue Hill, Sandy Bay, Half Tree Hollow) do not vary much, resembling each other quite strongly. There is an obvious contrast with Jamestown, where both variants, though still used fairly frequently, are less frequent than elsewhere on the island. This is evidence of a rural/urban divide on St Helena and that StHE speakers from Jamestown are more standard (at least with regard to the two variables studied, but I am sure this would be supported with other features). Ch. 3 has provided socio-historical explanation for this pattern of variation; the concentration of white army personnel and administrative staff was particularly high in the capital, since this was where the fort and EIC headquarters were situated, since Jamestown Valley provided a small harbour and safe access to the sea, etc. The whites were thus always in a majority here, at all times outnumbering the company and house slaves. The situation 'up country' was different, since the slaves represented a majority in some of the regions from very early on (most notably in Sandy Bay, where larger plantations were economically viable).

At first glance, one might interpret this as evidence that, throughout the 18th century, there existed locally different contact conditions and that the British input to the Jamestown population was stronger than elsewhere on the island. This explanation is tempting but it only goes half way, since we need to bear in mind two points. First of all, the capital was more transient and less stable than communities elsewhere (soldiers had a fixed-term contract, administrative personnel was withdrawn or sent on to other colonial possessions controlled by the EIC; etc.), so Jamestown did not have a single homogeneous stock of British settlers who could have contributed to the feature pool. Second, the place served as a community centre of St Helena, since this was where goods were bartered or sold, where the slave market was, etc. and there are ample records of the country population flocking to town when ships were at anchor. Thus, Jamestown had an important function for the island community throughout the 18th century; this was where one would meet, acquire goods, exchange news and gossip, and so on.

Figure 7.2 Map of Jamestown, 1764

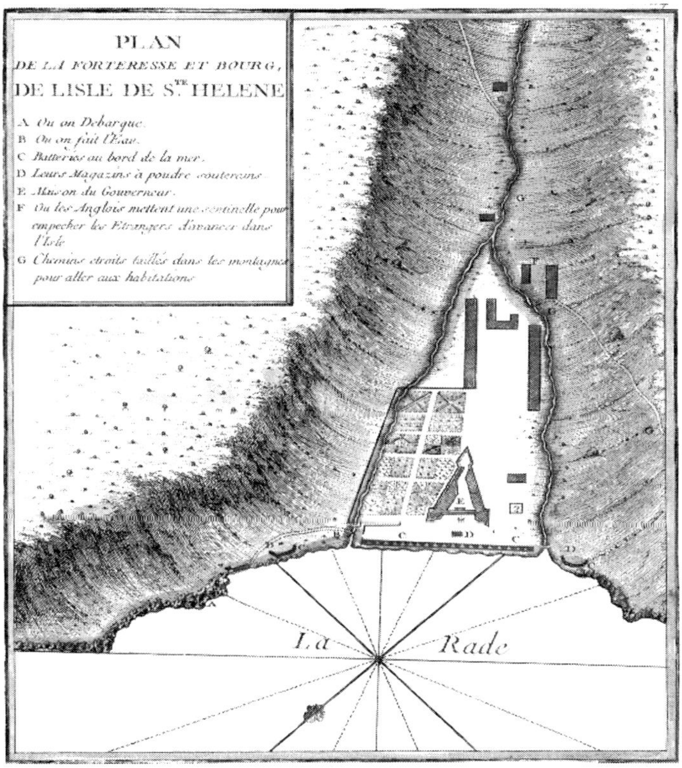

When did this change, i.e., at what stage was there a sizable permanent population in Jamestown? A map, the 'Plan de la forteresse et bourg de Lisle de S.te Helene', produced by the French cartographer J.N. Bellin in 1764, depicts Jamestown in the mid-18th century (Figure 7.2). We note a stream of water running through the valley, bifurcating in close proximity to the sea. Nearby, there are two longish buildings, no doubt army barracks, as well as three smaller ones (sheds or stables?). Near the defence walls and harbour area, there is the fort as well as the orchards and gardens of the garrison. Bellin's map indicates that Jamestown in the 1760s was a military fort and nothing else; there were no huts or houses for the general population, though there were roads to other parts of the island, the beginnings of a transport system and a local infrastructure.

Edward S. Blake, Lieutenant in the Bombay Artillery, illustrates a completely different place in 1830. His 'View of James's Town: Saint Helena' (Figure 7.3)[2] shows that, apart from the existing military infrastructure (fortifications, observatories, army barracks, etc.), there are now public roads, a town hall (10), a church (11), a prison (12), and a churchyard (13), a general hospital, as well as rows of terraced houses for the residents (see the close-up details in Figure 7.4).

Figure 7.3 Excerpt from Edward S. Blake's 'View of James's Town', 1830

Other than topography, this place bears little resemblance with what we see in Figure 7.1. What was a fort in the 1760s is a town in 1830. A complete infrastructure was built; there are housing facilities for a permanent population, a hospital and a town hall, people in the street, etc. Figures 7.2-4 show that the early 1800s were a period of increasing urbanisation, when Saints flocked to town in hope of a better living. This had repercussions for the social set-up of

[2] The two documents are taken from the *St Helena Virtual Library*, a website located at http://www.bweaver.nom.sh/#maps (last accessed April 24 2008).

the community since it reinforced the division between rich and poor on the island. Financial means were necessary for buying (former) Company land in Jamestown in order to build shops and terraced houses, a considerable obstacle since many families had barely enough to survive. The poverty of the rural population has been commented on frequently (e.g., by Charles Darwin in 1836, who also mentioned that some of the richer families emigrated, particularly following the political changes in the 1820s). Consequently, Jamestown became the wealthiest community on the island, whereas 'up country' impoverished and people lived in dire straits and despair. Whoever could afford it moved to town, and whoever did not remained (or moved) 'up country', struggling to make a living there. This affected blacks, whites and coloureds alike and may have reinforced ethnic mixing with all its correlating sociolinguistic effects.

Figure 7.4 Close-up detail from Edward S. Blake's 'View of James's Town', 1830

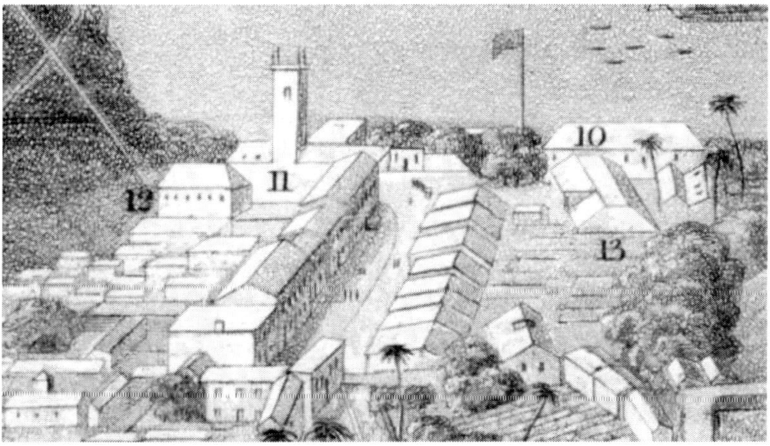

The data presented in ch. 6 thus complement the external history of St Helena and invite the implication that regional variation does indeed exist, though it is one along rural/urban lines and probably not one of regionality alone. I thus am sceptical as to whether there is a distinctive endonormative variety of, say, 'Blue Hill StHE', which can be kept apart from StHE as spoken in other parts of the island. However, I have no hesitation at all to admit that Jamestown StHE is different to varieties 'up country'; this is suggested both by an informed analysis of the island's social history and a quantitative analysis of sociolinguistic variation. Whereas urban/rural is an important criterion for regional variation on StHE, I cannot support alleged claims of different dialects outside Jamestown.

7.4 Outlook and future research

I hope that this book has answered some of the questions that surround the origins and evolution of StHE. It has argued that, though the colony was established in the late 1650s, the initial phase was irrelevant for the formation of the local variety. The roots of StHE can be traced to the 18th century, with focussing and stabilisation starting to operate as late as in the 1720s. Moreover, the variety evolved in a melting pot in which all kinds of contact-induced processes co-occurred: accommodation, dialect contact, language learning and attrition, language contact, jargonisation and pidginisation, language shift and focussing, to name but some. Given the colony's time depth, the sociolinguistic complexity of the community (communities) makes it extremely difficult to pinpoint the processes that were instrumental in shaping StHE. On occasion, information is simply missing, then again, we lack first-hand evidence of crucial inputs, and from a general perspective, it is practically impossible to keep the various processes apart or to determine how they interact and reinforce each other (or cancel each other out). This is beyond doubt the main reason why it should be so difficult to assess the typological status of StHE. Whereas StHE shares qualitative and quantitative similarities with English-derived creoles in the Caribbean (JamCrE or BahE, for example), it also affiliates with non-standard varieties of BrE or the SHemEs. The parallels are notably strong in segmental phonology, particularly in the vowel system. Finally, social changes such as urbanisation in the early 18th century gave rise to regional variation that has persisted well into the 20th century.

Consequently, then, what questions are left open? For instance, what this book has not shown (and not been able to show) is what other parameters of variation are at work, most notably social variation and ongoing change in the community. I was careful to select data from speakers that allowed for a comparative analysis (working-class membership being paramount) and only recorded Saints born in the early 1900s. I have thus little information about present-day StHE and can say very little about the factors that affect variation and change in the early 21st century. Such work clearly needs to be done, particularly so since the St Helenian society is socially stratified (not only confined to Jamestown, by the way, since wealthier Saints have recently started to build property 'up country' and to commute). On the other hand, the last 50 years have seen increasing population movements on the island and the Saints are now much more mobile than they used to be. The local infrastructure has improved a lot, safe roads connect all parts of the island now and there is a public transport system as well. One imminent consequence is that Jamestown is now even more important for the island, since this is where people work and where they commute to, where entertainment is sought, where the big shops are, etc.; the local micro-industries, on the other hand, decline. A recent development is that schools and pubs close down for good. Until the 1980s, most settlements on St Helena had their own schools, playgroups and entertainment facilities, their corner shops, pubs and meeting places. After the opening of Prince Andrew School in 1976, the authorities followed an education policy to make schooling compulsory there for children from all over the island. Consequently, this led to an amount of every-day mobility in the younger generation of Saints that their parents had not experienced before, and it remains to be seen how this affects the future of the variety.

The Saints and StHE face other challenges as well. The return of full citizenship in 1999 has affected the community deeply and many young families have taken the opportunity of migrating to the UK and starting a new life there. This deals a heavy blow to the island. It is mostly the elderly and poor Saints who remain and the total workforce decreases dramatically (somewhat resembling the situation after WW II, when Saints moved to Ascension Island for work, the difference being of course that they then had limited work contracts and returned after a set period of time). One way out of this dilemma is opening up the island and establishing new business enterprises, such as tourism. Plans have been underway for years now to build an airport on St Helena, complete with hotel and golf course. This may bring much-needed financial benefits but will have a massive impact on the Saints' every-day lives (and is bitterly fought over). If it came to this, that is if tourists spent their holidays on the island or if British families were to move to St Helena for good, then the sociolinguistic scenario would change significantly. It is unclear to what extent this would affect the future trajectory of StHE.

Consequently, it is my hope that this book has furthered our understanding of what StHE is like and why it became the way it is. At the same time, I hope that there will be follow-up projects and that opportunities for further research are taken up at some stage. StHE may have lost some of its mystery, we now have information as to where it came from and who formed it, what evolutionary path it took, etc., but in a way this can and should be no more than a modest beginning. There is a lot left to study about this truly noteworthy variety of English around the world.

Appendix I: A List of Passengers ordered on Board the Two Shipps for St Hellena 1673 (the *European* and the *John and Alexander*)

Capt. Antho: **Beale**, Elinor his wife, Richard his sonne, Mary his daughter, and seaven Serv'ts - 11
Wm. **Gates**, Bridget his wife, William & John their Children, Eliz. Palmir their Serv't - 5
James **Easting**, Anne his wife, Thomas and James their Children, Anne their Serv't - 5
John **Walls**, Bridget his wife, Dorothy Draper Serv't - 3
John **Greentree**, Mary his wife, Elizabeth, Anne & Jane their Children, one Maid Serv't one Black - 7
Mr Wm. **Swindell** Minister, Jno. Wharmly his Serv't - 2
Tho. **Smouet**, Anne his wife, Elizabeth their Child, Ric. Walett, Alice Walett - 5
Richard **Mattby** Armo. - 1
Tho: **Collins** - 1
Rob't. **Tamps**, Ann his wife - 2
Wm. **Young**, Eliz. his wife, John, Richard, Robert, Phillip their Children, Two Maid Servants - 9
John **Fuller**, Ann his wife, one Child - 3
Rich: **Swallow**, Marga: his wife, Margaret, Martha their Children, Abyas Betts. single woman, Two Negro Serv'ts - 7
Fran: **Rutter**, Marg: **Griffin**, Sarah **Butler** 3
Twelve Negro serv'ts of the Compa. - 12
Francis **Rangham**, Anne his wife, Samuell, Mary, Francis their Children, Mary Bennet, Mary Plowright - 7
John **Coulson**, Grace his wife, Nathaniell, Elizabeth, Martha their Children, Wm Dufton, Abigail Cox, one negro - 8
John **Younge**, Sarah his wife, John & Barbara their Children, Elizabeth Lewis Serv't - 5
Fran: **Moon** Chyrurgion, Marg: his wife, Francis, Ephrath, Mary their Children, Anne Perry, Sarah Tremor, Richard Hall Serv'ts - 8
John **Amps**, John **Starling**, one maid Serv't - 3
John **Keneday**, Elizabeth his wife, Sarah **Gray** - 3

Total 110 – Whites 94, Blacks 16

(Source: *India Office Library and Records*, E/3/88, p.88; reproduced online at: http://website.lineone.net/~sthelena/1673.htm)

Appendix II: Facsimile excerpt from the St Helena Records (1679), a declaration with all the marks and signatures of the settlers at that time

We whose Names are under written do declare yt we are willing to contribute as much as will come to or parts towards ye buying of a burying cloth, a Bear, & ye repair of ye Church, in wittness whereof we have hereunto set or hands

March 30th 1679.

William Bowman

The mark of John Greentree.

The mark of John Coleson

Tho Smoult

John Loftin

John Firth

John Boston

Benjamin Seale

Appendix III: Common StHE features found in other varieties of English, as compared with the *Handbook of English Varieties around the World* (based on Kortmann, Schneider et. al. 2004)

		A - Feature is widespread	B - Feature occurs sometimes
KIT	/ɪ/	default	
Raised/fronted	/i/	Aboriginal English	Australian English
		Australian Creoles	Cajun English
		Black South African English	Cape Flats English
		British Creole	Chicano English
		Cameroon Pidgin English	East Anglian English
		East African English	Indian English
		Ghanaian English	Jamaican Creole
		Ghanaian Pidgin English	Newfoundland English
		Hawaian Creole	St. Helena English
		Jamaican English	Trinidadian Creole (Acro-/ Mesolect)
		Malaysian English	
		Nigerian English (Southern)	
		Nigerian Pidgin	
		Philippines English	
		Singapore English	
		Surinam Creole	
Centralized	/ə/	Cape Flats English	Australian English
		Maori English	Channel Island English
		NZ English	Indian South African English
		Orkney and Shetland	Jamaican English
		St. Helena English	North America, Philadelphia
			North America, The Inland North
			Northern English
			South African English
			Southern AmE
			Trinidadian Creole (Acro-/ Mesolect)
			Trinidadian Creole (Basilect)
With off-glide	/ɪə, iə/	Southern AmE	AAVE
			Standard American English
			Urban South AmE

		A - Feature is widespread	B - Feature occurs sometimes
DRESS	/ɛ/	default	
Half-close	/e/	Australian Creoles	Black South African English
		Australian English	British Creole
		Bislama	Cameroon English
		Cameroon Pidgin English	Channel Island English
		Cape Flats English	East Anglian English
		East African English	Indian English
		Indian South African English	Malaysian English
		NZ English	Maori English
		Pakistan English	Orkney and Shetland
		Solomon Islands Pijin	
		South African English	
		St. Helena English	
		Tok Pisin	
TRAP	/æ/	default	
Raised	/e, ɛ/	Australian Creoles	Aboriginal English
		Black South African English	Bahamian English
		Cape Flats English	Chicano English
		Fijian English	East Anglian English
		Hawaian Creole	Indian English
		Maori English	Indian South African English
		Nigerian English (Northern)	Irish English
		NZ English	Malaysian English
		Singapore English	Newfoundland English
		South African English	North America, NYC
			North America, Philadelphia
			North America, The Inland North
			Orkney and Shetland
			Southern AmE
			Welsh English
With off-glide	/æə,	AAVE	Australian English
	æɛ/	Southern AmE	Chicano English
			East Anglian English

		A - Feature is widespread	B - Feature occurs sometimes
			New England English
			Newfoundland English
			North America, NYC
			North America, Philadelphia
			North America, The Inland North
			St. Helena English
			Standard American English
			Trinidadian Creole (Acro-/ Mesolect)
			Urban South AmE
FOOT	/ʊ/	default	
Unrounded		n/a	
Centralised		n/a	
STRUT	/ʌ/	default	
Central	/ə,ɐ/	Bislama	AAVE
		Chicano English	Black South African English
		East African English	British Creole
		Fijian English	East Anglian English
		Hawaian Creole	Ghanaian English
		Irish English	Ghanaian Pidgin English
		Maori English	Indian English
		NZ English	Newfoundland English
		Singapore English	North America, NYC
		Solomon Islands Pijin	North America, Philadelphia
		Southern AmE	North America, The Inland North
		Standard American English	North America, The West and Midwest
		Tok Pisin	Northern English
		Welsh English	South African English
			Trinidadian Creole (Acro-/ Mesolect)
			Trinidadian Creole (Basilect)
			Urban South AmE
High-back	/ʊ/	Northern English	Chicano English
			Irish English
			Nigerian English (Northern)

		A - Feature is widespread	**B - Feature occurs sometimes**
			Orkney and Shetland
			Welsh English
CLOTH	/ɒ/	default	
Back unrounded	/ɑ/	AAVE	Canadian English
		Aboriginal English	East Anglian English
		British Creole	Indian English
		Chicano English	Irish English
		Liberian Settler English	Newfoundland English
		New England English	North America, The Inland North
		North America, The West and Midwest	Southern AmE
		Trinidadian Creole (Basilect)	Standard American English
			Trinidadian Creole (Acro-/ Mesolect)
Front unrounded	/a/	Australian Creoles	Chicano English
		British Creole	St. Helena English
		Cajun	
		Newfoundland English	
		RP	
FLEECE	/iː/	default	
Centralizing off-glide	/iə/	-	North America, The West and Midwest
			North America, NYC
			Newfoundland English
			AAVE
			Trinidadian Creole (Acro-/ Mesolect)
			Irish English
			Welsh English
GOOSE	/uː/	default	
NURSE	/ɜː/	default	
Lip rounding	/ɞː/	n/a	
(Possibly lex.	/ʌr/	Cajun	Gullah

		A - Feature is widespread	B - Feature occurs sometimes
cond.)		Liberian Settler English	Hawaiian Creole
		Welsh English	Indian English
		Pakistan English	Irish English
			New England English
			Newfoundland English
			Nigerian English (Northern)
			Southern AmE
			St. Helena English
START	/ɑː/	default	
Front, raised	/æː/		Newfoundland English
			Irish English
	/oə/	n/a	
THOUGHT/ FORCE/ NORTH/POOR			
THOUGHT		Orkney and Shetland	AAVE
with offglide,		RP	Australian English
e.g. [ɔə, ʊə]		Southern AmE	Cape Flats English
			Maori English
			North America, NYC
			North America, Philadelphia
			NZ English
			St. Helena English
			Standard American English
			Urban South AmE
			Welsh English
FORCE		AAVE	Australian English
ingliding, e.g.		Jamaican Creole	Bislama
[ɔə(r), oə(r),		Northern America, NYC	Cajun
oa]		Standard American English	Canadian English
			Chicano English
			Maori English
			Newfoundland English
			Northern English

		A - Feature is widespread	**B - Feature occurs sometimes**
			NZ English
			Solomon Islands Pijin
			Southern AmE
			Tok Pisin
			Welsh English
NORTH with		Northern America, NYC	Australian English
offglide, e.g.		RP	Chicano English
[ɔə, oa]		St. Helena English	Maori English
			New England English
			Newfoundland English
			Northern English
			NZ English
			Southern AmE
			Welsh English
POOR		n/a	
FACE	/ei:/	default	
Lower onset	/ɛɪ,	Cape Flats English	AAVE
	æɪ/	East Anglian English	Australian English
		Maori English	Black South African English
		NZ English	British Creole
		Southern AmE	Chicano English
		Urban South AmE	Ghanaian English
			Ghanaian Pidgin English
			Newfoundland English
			North America, NYC
			South African English
Monophthongal		Aboriginal English	AAVE
		Australian Creoles	Black South African English
		Barbadian English	Cape Flats English
		Bislama	Chicano English
		British Creole	East Anglian English
		Cajun English	Ghanaian English
		Cameroon English	Newfoundland English
		Cameroon Pidgin English	North America, The Inland North

		A - Feature is widespread	B - Feature occurs sometimes
		East African English	North America, The West and Midwest
		Fijian English	Northern English
		Ghanaian Pidgin English	Pakistan English
		Gullah	Standard American English
		Hawaian Creole	
		Indian English	
		Irish English	
		Jamaican English	
		Liberian Settler English	
		Malaysian English	
		Nigerian English (Northern)	
		Nigerian English (Southern)	
		Nigerian Pidgin	
		Orkney and Shetland	
		Singapore English	
		Solomon Islands Pijin	
		Surinam Creole	
		Tok Pisin	
		Trinidadian Creole (Acro-/ Mesolect)	
		Trinidadian Creole (Basilect)	
		Welsh English	
PRICE	/aɪ/	default	
Backed onset	/ɔɪ, ɑɪ/	Maori English	Aboriginal English
		Nigerian English (Southern)	Australian English
		NZ English	Channel Island English
			Gullah
			Irish English
			Newfoundland English
			North America, NYC
			Southern AmE
			St. Helena English
Raised/central	/əɪ, ɜɪ/	Welsh English	AAVE
onset		Orkney and Shetland	Canadian English

		A - Feature is widespread	B - Feature occurs sometimes
			Cape Flats English
			Irish English
			New England English
			Newfoundland English
			North America, Philadelphia
			North America, The Inland North
			North America, The West and Midwest
			Southern AmE
			Trinidadian Creole (Acro-/ Mesolect)
			Trinidadian Creole (Basilect)
CHOICE	/ɔi/	default	
Raised	/oi/	n/a	
GOAT	/ou/		
Monophthongal	/oː/	Aboriginal English	AAVE
		Australian Creoles	Hawaian Creole
		Barbadian English	Indian South African English
		Bislama	Irish English
		Black South African English	New England English
		British Creole	Newfoundland English
		Cajun English	North America, The Inland North
		Cameroon English	North America, The West and Midwest
		Cameroon Pidgin English	Northern English
		Chicano English	Standard American English
		East African English	
		Fijian English	
		Ghanaian English	
		Ghanaian Pidgin English	
		Gullah	
		Indian English	
		Jamaican English	
		Liberian Settler English	
		Malaysian English	
		Nigerian English (Northern)	

		A - Feature is widespread	B - Feature occurs sometimes
		Nigerian English (Southern)	
		Nigerian Pidgin	
		Orkney and Shetland	
		Pakistan English	
		Philippines English	
		RP	
		Singapore English	
		Solomon Islands Pijin	
		Surinam Creole	
		Tok Pisin	
		Trinidadian Creole (Acro-/ Mesolect)	
		Trinidadian Creole (Basilect)	
		Welsh English	
MOUTH	/aʊ,	default	
	ɑʊ/		
Raised, backed	/ʌu,	Barbadian English	Canadian English
onset	ɔʊ/	Black South African English	Cape Flats English
		British Creole	Jamaican Creole
		Chicano English	Jamaican English
		Gullah	Newfoundland English
		Liberian Settler English	Orkney and Shetland
		Trinidadian Creole (Acro-/ Mesolect)	St. Helena English
		Trinidadian Creole (Basilect)	
Homophony of		East Anglian English	Black South African English
NEAR and		Jamaican Creole	British Creole
SQUARE		Jamaican English	Cameroon English
		Maori English	Indian English
		NZ English	Irish English
		St. Helena English	Newfoundland English
		Surinam Creole	Northern English
		Trinidadian Creole (Acro-/ Mesolect)	Southern AmE
		Trinidadian Creole (Basilect)	
[-INV/AUX] in		Aboriginal English	Isolated Se. American English
wh-questions		Appalachian English	Scottish English

		A - Feature is widespread	B - Feature occurs sometimes
		Australian Creoles	
		Australian Vernacular	
		Bahamian English	
		Belizean Creole	
		Bislama (Vanuatu)	
		Butler English (India)	
		Cameroon Pidgin English	
		Chicano English	
		Colloquial American English	
		Earlier AAVE	
		East African English	
		Ghananian Pidgin English	
		Gullah	
		Hawaiian Creoles	
		Indian South African English	
		Irish English	
		Jamaican Creole	
		Malaysian English	
		Newfoundland English	
		Nigerian Pidgin English	
		Non-Standard Australian English	
		Norfuk (Norfolk)	
		Northern English	
		Ozarks English	
		Pakistan English	
		Singapore English	
		Solomon Islands Pijin	
		Surinamese Creoles	
		Tok Pisin (Papua Guinea)	
		Trinidadian Creole	
		Urban AAVE	
[-INV] in		Aboriginal English	Earlier AAVE
yes/no-questions		Appalachian English	Isolated Se. American English
		Australian Creoles	Scottish English
		Australian Vernacular	Standard Ghanaian English
		Bahamian English	
		Belizean Creole	
		Bislama (Vanuatu)	
		Black South African English	
		Butler English (India)	

		A - Feature is widespread	B - Feature occurs sometimes
		Cameroon English	
		Cameroon Pidgin English	
		Chicano English	
		Colloquial American English	
		East African English	
		Ghananian Pidgin English	
		Gullah	
		Hawaiian Creoles	
		Indian South African English	
		Irish English	
		Jamaican Creole	
		Malaysian English	
		Newfoundland English	
		Nigerian Pidgin English	
		Non-Standard Australian English	
		Norfuk (Norfolk)	
		Northern English	
		NZ English	
		Ozarks English	
		Pakistan English	
		Singapore English	
		Solomon Islands Pijin	
		Surinamese Creoles	
		Tok Pisin (Papua Guinea)	
		Trinidadian Creole	
		Urban AAVE	
		Welsh English	
Relativization:		Appalachian English	Aboriginal English
Gapping in subj.		Australian Creoles	Australian Vernacular
Position		Belizean Creole	Cameroon English
		Gullah	Chicano English
		Hawaiian Creoles	Earlier AAVE
		Irish English	East Anglian English
		Isolated Se. Am. English	Nigerian Pidgin English
		Jamaican Creole	Non-Standard Australian English
		Newfoundland English	South-Eastern English
		Norfuk (Norfolk)	
		Northern English	

		A - Feature is widespread	B - Feature occurs sometimes
		NZ English	
		Solomon Islands Pijin	
		South-Western English	
		Tok Pisin (Papua Guinea)	
		Urban AAVE	
Relative particle		Bahamian English	Aboriginal English
what		Belizean Creole	Appalachian English
		Black South African English	Cameroon English
		Cameroon Pidgin English	Isolated Se. American English
		Colloquial American English	Newfoundland English
		Earlier AAVE	Non-Standard Australian English
		East Anglian English	NZ English
		Gullah	South-Eastern English
		Indian South African English	South-Western English
		Jamaican Creole	Welsh English
		Northern English	
		Ozarks English	
		Trinidadian Creole	
that/what in		Australian Vernacular	Aboriginal English
non-restrictive		Bahamian English	Appalachian English
contexts		Belizean Creole	Chicano English
		Cameroon English	Isolated Se. American English
		Colloquial American English	Non-Standard Australian English
		Jamaican Creole	Northern English
		Newfoundland English	NZ English
		Urban AAVE	Pakistan English
		White South African English	Scottish English
			South-Eastern English
			South-Western English
			Welsh English
Double		Australian Vernacular	Aboriginal English
comp./superl.		Cameroon English	Appalachian English
		Chicano English	Bahamian English
		East Anglian English	Butler English (India)
		Gullah	Earlier AAVE
		Indian South African English	Ghananian Pidgin English

		A - Feature is widespread	B - Feature occurs sometimes
		Irish English	Hawaiian Creoles
		Isolated Se. Am. English	Nigerian Pidgin English
		Jamaican Creole	Non-Standard Australian English
		Malaysian English	Scottish English
		Newfoundland English	Singapore English
		Northern English	South-Eastern English
		NZ English	South-Western English
		Ozarks English	Standard Ghanaian English
		Pakistan English	Welsh English
		Trinidadian Creole	
		Urban AAVE	
		White South American English	
Irregular use of		Aboriginal English	Appalachian English
articles		Australian Creoles	Bahamian English
		Belizean Creole	Chicano English
		Black South African English	East Anglian English
		Butler English (India)	Gullah
		Cameroon English	Newfoundland English
		East African English	Non-Standard Australian English
		Ghananian Pidgin English	Scottish English
		Hawaiian Creoles	South-Western English
		Indian South African English	Standard Ghanaian English
		Irish English	Urban AAVE
		Isolated Se. Am. English	Welsh English
		Jamaican Creole	
		Malaysian English	
		Nigerian Pidgin English	
		Northern English	
		Orkney and Shetland	
		Pakistan English	
		Singapore English	
		Trinidadian Creole	
Demonstrative		Aboriginal English	Belizean Creole
them		Appalachian English	Butler English (India)
		Australian Creoles	Chicano English
		Australian Vernacular	Hawaiian Creoles
		Colloquial American English	Non-Standard Australian

		A - Feature is widespread	B - Feature occurs sometimes
			English
		Earlier AAVE	NZ English
		East Anglian English	
		Gullah	
		Irish English	
		Isolated Se. Am. English	
		Jamaican Creole	
		Newfoundland English	
		Norfuk (Norfolk)	
		Northern English	
		Ozarks English	
		Scottish English	
		Solomon Islands Pijin	
		South-Eastern English	
		South-Western English	
		Trinidadian Creole	
		Urban AAVE	
		Welsh English	
Absence of		Aboriginal English	Appalachian English
plural marking		Australian Creoles	Cameroon English
(after measurem.		Australian Vernacular	Chicano English
nouns)		Bahamian English	Earlier AAVE
		Belizean Creole	Non-Standard Australian English
		Bislama (Vanuatu)	NZ English
		Butler English (India)	Pakistan English
		East African English	Singapore English
		East Anglian English	South-Eastern English
		Gullah	South-Western English
		Hawaiian Creoles	Welsh English
		Irish English	
		Isolated Se. Am. English	
		Jamaican Creole	
		Newfoundland English	
		Nigerian Pidgin English	
		Northern English	
		Orkney and Shetland	
		Ozarks English	
		Scottish English	
		Solomon Islands Pijin	

		A - Feature is widespread	B - Feature occurs sometimes
		Surinamese Creoles	
		Tok Pisin (Papua Guinea)	
		Trinidadian Creole	
		Urban AAVE	
Non-standard *us*		Australian Vernacular	Aboriginal English
		Belizean Creole	Earlier AAVE
		Hawaiian Creoles	Isolated Se. American English
		Irish English	Non-Standard Australian English
		Newfoundland English	Northern English
		NZ English	Scottish English
		Urban AAVE	South-Eastern English
			South-Western English
Special 2nd		Aboriginal English	Earlier AAVE
pers. pl. pron.		Appalachian English	East Anglian English
		Australian Creoles	Scottish English
		Australian Vernacular	
		Bahamian English	
		Belizean Creole	
		Bislama (Vanuatu)	
		Black South African English	
		Cameroon English	
		Cameroon Pidgin English	
		Chicano English	
		Colloquial American English	
		Gullah	
		Hawaiian Creoles	
		Indian South African English	
		Irish English	
		Isolated Se. Am. English	
		Jamaican Creole	
		Newfoundland English	
		Nigerian Pidgin English	
		Non-Standard Australian English	
		Norfuk (Norfolk)	
		Northern English	
		NZ English	
		Ozarks English	

		A - Feature is widespread	B - Feature occurs sometimes
		Solomon Islands Pijin	
		Surinamese Creoles	
		Tok Pisin (Papua Guinea)	
		Trinidadian Creole	
		Urban AAVE	
Regularized		Aboriginal English	Appalachian English
reflexives		Australian Creoles	Australian Vernacular
		Belizean Creole	Bahamian English
		Cameroon English	Butler English (India)
		East Anglian English	Chicano English
		Gullah	Colloquial American English
		Irish English	Earlier AAVE
		Isolated Se. Am. English	Non-Standard Australian English
		Jamaican Creole	Pakistan English
		Newfoundland English	South-Eastern English
		Nigerian Pidgin English	South-Western English
		Northern English	White South African English
		Ozarks English	
		Scottish English	
		Trinidadian Creole	
		Urban AAVE	
Dummy subj. in		Aboriginal English	Australian Creoles
exist. clauses		Appalachian English	Cameroon English
		Bahamian English	Newfoundland English
		Belizean Creole	Norfuk (Norfolk)
		Bislama (Vanuatu)	Singapore English
		Colloquial American English	
		Earlier AAVE	
		East Anglian English	
		Gullah	
		Hawaiian Creoles	
		Isolated Se. Am. English	
		Orkney and Shetland	
		Ozarks English	
		Trinidadian Creole	
		Urban AAVE	
Pres. tense no		Aboriginal English	Bahamian English
3rd sg. -s		Australian Creoles	Cameroon English

		A - Feature is widespread	B - Feature occurs sometimes
		Belizean Creole	Earlier AAVE
		Bislama (Vanuatu)	Standard Ghanaian English
		Butler English (India)	
		Cameroon Pidgin English	
		Chicano English	
		Colloquial American English	
		East Anglian English	
		Ghananian Pidgin English	
		Gullah	
		Hawaiian Creoles	
		Jamaican Creole	
		Newfoundland English	
		Nigerian Pidgin English	
		Norfuk (Norfolk)	
		Ozarks English	
		Singapore English	
		Solomon Islands Pijin	
		Tok Pisin (Papua Guinea)	
		Trinidadian Creole	
		Urban AAVE	
Zero past tense		Aboriginal English	Black South African English
		Australian Creoles	Butler English (India)
		Bahamian English	Cameroon English
		Belizean Creole	Chicano English
		Bislama (Vanuatu)	Colloquial American English
		East African English	Earlier AAVE
		Ghananian Pidgin English	Ozarks English
		Gullah	Pakistan English
		Hawaiian Creoles	Standard Ghanaian English
		Jamaican Creole	Urban AAVE
		Malaysian English	
		Newfoundland English	
		Nigerian Pidgin English	
		Norfuk (Norfolk)	
		Singapore English	
		Solomon Islands Pijin	
		Tok Pisin (Papua Guinea)	
		Trinidadian Creole	
Habitual *be*		Earlier AAVE	Earlier AAVE
		Bahamian English	Newfoundland English

		A - Feature is widespread	**B - Feature occurs sometimes**
		Gullah	Cameroon English
		Cameroon Pidgin English	Australian Creoles
		Indian South African English	Aboriginal English
		Butler English (India)	Irish English
ain't as negated		Appalachian English	Australian Vernacular
be		Bahamian English	Chicano English
		Cameroon English	Irish English
		Colloquial American English	Newfoundland English
		Earlier AAVE	South-Eastern English
		East Anglian English	South-Western English
		Gullah	Welsh English
		Isolated Se. Am. English	
		Ozarks English	
		Trinidadian Creole	
		Urban AAVE	
never as pre-		Aboriginal English	Bahamian English
verbal negator		Appalachian English	Earlier AAVE
(only available		Australian Creoles	Gullah
for past tense)		Australian Vernacular	Isolated Se. Am. English
		Belizean Creole	Malaysian English
		Black South African English	Non-Standard Australian English
		Cameroon English	Scottish English
		Cameroon Pidgin English	South-Eastern English
		Chicano English	South-Western English
		Colloquial American English	Urban AAVE
		East Anglian English	
		Ghananian Pidgin English	
		Hawaiian Creoles	
		Indian South African English	
		Irish English	
		Jamaican Creole	
		Newfoundland English	
		Nigerian Pidgin English	
		Norfuk (Norfolk)	
		Northern English	
		NZ English	
		Ozarks English	
		Pakistan English	

		A - Feature is widespread	B - Feature occurs sometimes
		Singapore English	
		Solomon Islands Pijin	
		Standard Ganaian English	
		Trinidadian Creole	
		Welsh English	
		White South African English	
no as pre-verbal		Australian Creoles	Bahamian English
negator		Belizean Creole	Norfuk (Norfolk)
		Bislama (Vanuatu)	
		Butler English (India)	
		Cameroon Pidgin English	
		Ghananian Pidgin English	
		Hawaiian Creoles	
		Jamaican Creole	
		Nigerian Pidgin English	
		Solomon Islands Pijin	
		Surinamese Creoles	
		Tok Pisin (Papua Guinea)	
		Trinidadian Creole	
Multiple		Aboriginal English	Australian Creoles
negation		Appalachian English	Chicano English
		Australian Vernacular	Non-Standard Australian English
		Bahamian English	Scottish English
		Belizean Creole	South-Eastern English
		Black South African English	South-Western English
		Butler English (India)	Standard Ghanaian English
		Cameroon English	
		Cameroon Pidgin English	
		Colloquial American English	
		Earlier AAVE	
		East Anglian English	
		Ghananian Pidgin English	
		Gullah	
		Hawaiian Creoles	
		Indian South African English	
		Irish English	
		Isolated Se. Am. English	
		Jamaican Creole	

		A - Feature is widespread	**B - Feature occurs sometimes**
		Newfoundland English	
		Northern English	
		NZ English	
		Ozarks English	
		Surinamese Creoles	
		Trinidadian Creole	
		Urban AAVE	
		Welsh English	
Unsplit *for to*		Cameroon English	Appalachian English
		Irish English	Chicano English
		Isolated Se. Am. English	Earlier AAVE
		Newfoundland English	Northern English
		Ozarks English	Orkney and Shetland
			Scottish English
			South-Eastern English
			South-Western English
			Urban AAVE
			Welsh English
Habitual *do*		Cameroon English	Aboriginal English
		Cameroon Pidgin English	Earlier AAVE
		Ghananian Pidgin English	Newfoundland English
		Gullah	Pakistan English
		Irish English	South-Western English
		Trinidadian Creole	
		Welsh English	
Levelling of		Aboriginal English	Australian Creoles
preterite and		Appalachian English	Cameroon English
past participle		Australian Vernaculars	Chicano English
verb forms:		Bahamian English	Colloquial American English
unmarked forms		Belizean Creole	Earlier AAVE
		Cameroon Pidgin English	Gullah
		East Anglian English	Non-Standard Australian English
		Irish English	Ozarks English
		Isolated Se. Am. English	South-Eastern English
		Jamaican Creole	South-Western English
		Newfoundland English	
		Nigerian Pidgin English	

		A - Feature is widespread	B - Feature occurs sometimes
		Northern English	
		NZ English	
		Orkney and Shetland	
		Scottish English	
		Singapore English	
		Urban AAVE	
Completive/		Appalachian English	Cameroon English
perfect *done*		Bahamian English	Earlier AAVE
		Belizean Creole	
		Cameroon Pidgin English	
		Gullah	
		Isolated Se. Am. English	
		Jamaican Creole	
		Nigerian Pidgin English	
		Norfuk (Norfolk)	
		Ozarks English	
		Trinidadian Creole	
		Urban AAVE	
been as past		Aboriginal English	Bahamian English
tense marker		Australian Creoles	Butler English (India)
		Belizean Creole	Cameroon English
		Bislama (Vanuatu)	Earlier AAVE
		Cameroon Pidgin English	Hawaiian Creole
		Gullah	Newfoundland English
		Jamaican Creole	Norfuk (Norfolk)
		Nigerian Pidgin English	Urban AAVE
		Solomon Islands Pijin	
		Surinamese Creoles	
		Tok Pisin (Papua Guinea)	
		Trinidadian Creole	
a-prefixing		Appalachian English	Cameroon English
		East Anglian English	Earlier AAVE
		Isolated Se. Am. English	South-Eastern English
		Newfoundland English	South-Western English
		Ozarks English	Welsh English
Double modals		Appalachian English	Earlier AAVE
		Colloquial American English	Gullah

		A - Feature is widespread	B - Feature occurs sometimes
		Isolated Se. Am. English	Hawaiian Creoles
		Jamaican Creole	Nigerian Pidgin English
		Ozarks English	Northern English
		Urban AAVE	Scottish English
was/were		Aboriginal English	Belizean Creole
generalization		Appalachian English	Butler English (India)
		Australian Creoles	Cameroon English
		Bahamian English	Chicano English
		Colloquial American English	NZ English
		Earlier AAVE	Scottish English
		East Anglian English	South-Eastern English
		Gullah	
		Hawaiian Creoles	
		Indian South African English	
		Irish English	
		Isolated Se. Am. English	
		Jamaican Creole	
		Newfoundland English	
		Northern English	
		Ozarks English	
		Trinidadian Creole	
		Urban AAVE	
		Welsh English	
Deletion of *be*		Aboriginal English	Appalachian English
		Australian Creoles	Cameroon English
		Bahamian English	Chicano English
		Belizean Creole	Isolated Se. American English
		Bislama (Vanuatu)	Norfuk (Norfolk)
		Butler English (India)	
		Cameroon Pidgin English	
		Earlier AAVE	
		Ghananian Pidgin English	
		Gullah	
		Hawaiian Creoles	
		Jamaican Creole	
		Malaysian English	
		Nigerian Pidgin English	
		Singapore English	
		Solomon Islands Pijin	

		A - Feature is widespread	B - Feature occurs sometimes
		Tok Pisin (Papua Guinea)	
		Trinidadian Creole	
		Urban AAVE	
Serial verbs		Aboriginal English	Chicano English
		Australian Creoles	Earlier AAVE
		Belizean Creole	Urban AAVE
		Bislama (Vanuatu)	Singapore English
		Butler English (India)	Norfuk (Norfolk)
		Cameroon English	
		Ghananian Pidgin English	
		Gullah	
		Hawaiian Creoles	
		Jamaican Creole	
		Nigerian Pidgin English	
		Non-Standard Australian English	
		Solomon Islands Pijin	
		Surinamese Creoles	
		Tok Pisin (Papua Guinea)	
		Trinidadian Creole	

Appendix IV: Less frequent StHE features found in other varieties of English, as compared with the *Handbook of English Varieties around the World* (based on Kortmann, Schneider et. al. 2004)

Omission of articles			
Butler English (India)	-	(p. 1034)	
Fiji English	"especially before proper nouns", "more common in written than spoken Fiji English"	(p. 776)	
Ghanaian English	often, sometimes	(p. 860)	
Gullah	-	(p. 362)	
Nigerian English	"notable tendency towards the omission of articles"	(p. 820)	not in index
Singapore English	"general absence of articles in the noun phrase"	(p. 1061)	not in index
Indeterminate *one*			
Aboriginal English	"often reported"	(p. 671)	
Belize and other central American varieties	*wan*, basilects and mesolects	(p. 541)	
Eastern Caribbean English-derived language varietes (e.g. Anguilla)	more vernacular than *a*	(p. 447)	
Fiji English	general	(p. 775)	
Ghanian Pidgin English	*wan*, "occasionally"	(p. 870)	
Indian South African English	"alternative form of the indefinite article *a*"	(p. 985)	
Jamaican Creole	*wan*, general	(p. 433)	
Miskito Coast Creole English	*wan*, "attested in"	(p. 661)	
Nigerian English	"other types of variability in article usage"	(p. 820)	
Nigerian Pidgin English	*won*, general	(p. 845)	
Torres Strait Creole	*wan*, optional	(p. 661)	
***these* and *those* with distal relationship**	n/a		
Associative plurals			
AAVE	-	(p. 333)	
Appalachian English	-	(p. 261)	
Cape Flats English	-	(p. 997-998)	

Gullah	"common usage"	(p. 359/362)	
Indian South African English	-	(p. 985-986)	
Jamaican Creole	-	(p. 436)	
Newfoundland English	"frequent use"	(p. 311)	
Vernacular Liberian English (basilect)	-	(p. 888)	
Absence of subject. pers. pron.			
Australian Vernacular English	"wider variety of ellipses in clause-initial position than is acceptable in more standard styles"	(p. 637)	
Butler English (India)	"reported to be much more widespread ... than in StE"	(p. 1139)	
Chicano English	"occasionally"	(p. 382)	
Colloquial Singapore English	"often left unexpressed"	(p. 1062)	
Indian South African English	"reported to be much more widespread ... than in StE"	(p. 1139)	
Malaysian English	"reported to be much more widespread ... than in StE"	(p. 1139)	
Solomon Islands Pijin	"third person pro-drop language"	(p. 711)	
Vernacular Indian English	-	(p. 1026)	
Vernacular Newfoundland English	"extremely common"	(p. 312)	
West African Pidgin	"reported to be much more widespread ... than in StE"	(p. 1139)	
you all/ y'all			
Eastern Caribbean	*you-aal* is less common than *aal-you*	(p. 1113)	
Appalachian English	"*You'uns* is the traditional periphrastic form that has been losing ground to *you all* (less often to *y'all*) for at least three generations"	(p. 261-262)	
Earlier AAVE	among others	(p. 351)	
Gullah	more common than *unu/una*	(p. 359)	
Indian South African English	"regular use"	(p. 986)	
Newfoundland English	"a number of competing variants"	(p. 314)	
Rural and ethnic varieties in the Southeast	"feature is present"	(p. 298)	
Urban AAVE	"quite common"	(p. 333)	

Possessive *you*			
Anglophone Eastern Caribbean varieties	*yu*	(p. 445)	
British Creole	*yuh*	(p. 204)	
Kriol and Torres Strait Creole	*yu*	(p. 664)	
Liberian Settler English	*you*	(p. 889)	not in index
Surinamese Creoles	*yu*	(p. 508)	
Possessive *y'alls*			
Gullah	-	(p. 363)	
Indian South African English	"regular use"	(p. 986)	
Liberian Settler English	without -s	(p. 889)	not in index
Urban AAVE	without -*s*	(p. 333)	
Possessive *they*			
Afro-Bahamian English	"documented"	(p. 1113)	
Earlier AAVE	*their* occurs as well	(p. 351)	
Gullah	*deh*, "attested"	(p. 363)	
Liberian Settler English	-	(p. 889)	not in index
Urban AAVE	"quite robust"	(p. 333)	
Possessive *they own*	n/a		
Reflexives with *own self*			
Appalachian English		(p. 263)	
Earlier AAVE		(p. 351)	
***couple of* 'quite a few'**	n/a		
plenty			
Bislama	*plande* 'many'	(p. 685)	
Fiji English	"common quantifier"	(p. 776)	
Hawaiian Creoles	*pleni/plenny* 'many'	(p. 764)	
Solomon Islands Pijin	*plande* 'lots of'	(p. 705)	
Tok Pisin (Papua Guinea)	*planti* 'many'	(p. 733)	
Absence of genitive -*s*			
Bahamian English	"reveals strong ethnic division"	(p. 399)	

	"almost categorically absent from even mesolectal AfBahE"		
Belizean Creole	optional	(p. 521)	
British Creole	"the possessive*'s* may appear variably"	(p. 204)	
Butler English (India)	"rarely used"	(p. 1035)	
Early AAVE	rare	(p. 351)	
East African English	"noun phrases are not always marked for number and case"	(p. 932)	
Jamaican Creole	"does not occur"	(p. 432)	
Liberian Settler English	some speakers	(p. 889)	
Nigerian Pidgin English	-	(p. 847)	
Norfolk Island-Pitcairn English	less in acrolectal speech	(p. 791)	
Urban AAVE	"relatively stable feature in AAVE wherever it is found in the US, though Rickford (1999: 271) suggests that it may be subject to age-grading since it is more frequent among younger speakers"	(p. 332-333)	
Preposition absence			
Aboriginal English	prep. often not required	(p. 675)	
Afro-Bahamian English	mesolect, "feature is infrequent"	(p. 405)	
Afro-Bahamian English	basilect, "feature is present"	(p. 405)	
Appalachian English	occasionally	(p. 275)	
Butler English (India)	-	(p. 1034)	
Cameroon Pidgin English	usually *fo*, but when it is "functioning as 'to', it can be omitted from a sentence without causing any change of meaning"	(p. 924)	
Creoles of Trinidad and Tobago	"to express movement to a goal, it is typical to leave out the prepositions *a*, *in*, and *tu*"	(p. 468)	
Gullah	"feature is present"	(p. 405)	
Jamaican Creole	"feature is present"	(p. 405)	
Newfoundland English	"*to* and *in* frequently absent after directional prepositions like *down, up, over*"	(p. 314)	
Nigerian Pidgin English	"Zero preposition between motion verb and destination"	(p. 852)	
NZ English (Southland)	occasionally	(p. 1123)	
Ozarks English	-	(p. 240)	
Usage of *-side, -way, -time*			

Indian South African English	"some uses"	(p. 987)	
yonder			
Orkney and Shetland	*yon,* "not exclusively", but "widely used and has come to signal foreignness and a special feeling of remoteness"	(p. 44)	
Appalachian English	*yan/yander,* "distinction beween proximate, intermediate, and distant is maintained"	(p. 264)	
English dialects in the North of England	*yon/yonder,* "traces of the three-term deictic system in Northern dialects"	(p. 119-120)	
Dummy subj. in exist. clauses: it			
Appalachian English	"more rarely"	(p. 278)	
Bahamian English	more frequent in AnBahE than in AfBahE	(p. 399)	
Cape Flats English	"may be used"	(p. 1000)	
Creoles of Trinidad and Tobago	*it ge(t), it ha(v)*	(p. 472)	
Earlier AAVE	"stable"	(p. 338)	
Gullah	infrequent	(p. 404)	
Newfoundland English	"somewhat less common"	(p. 312)	
Ozarks English	"leeched throughout the Midlands"	(p. 240)	
Rural AAVE	"stable"	(p. 338)	
Rural and ethnic varieties in the Southeast	"much more pervasive [than *they*]"	(p. 296)	
Southern EAVE	"stable"	(p. 338)	
Urban AAVE	"stable"	(p. 338)	
Dummy subj. in exist. clauses: zero			
Australian Vernacular English	"sometimes", subject and existential verb absent	(p. 637)	
Belizean Creole	with *ga, hav, iz*	(p. 540)	
Hawaiian Creole	with *get, had*	(p. 753)	
Malaysian English	with *got*	(p. 1081)	
mussy			
St Helena English		(p. 1010)	not in index
Gullah	*must be*	(p. 365)	not in index

Non-habitual *be* with future reference	n/a		
Futurity expressed by *go*			
Cameroon Pidgin English	general	(p. 922)	
Creoles of Trinidad and Tobago	-	(p. 474)	
Eastern Caribbean English-derived language varieties	"The general future tense marker in the Eastern Caribbean is *go* and sometimes *goin*, but these are not exclusive to the region"	(p. 441)	
Ghanian Pidgin English	-	(p. 867)	
Gullah	"extensive use of pre-verbal free morphemes", go/ga [ə]	(p. 358)	
Hawaiian Creole	"it can mark a future action", usually it denotes an unplanned action	(p. 750)	
Nigerian Pidgin English	irrealis marker, "normaly used to mark the future tense"	(p. 834)	
Suriname Creoles	reduced to *o*	(p. 1107)	
Torres Strait Creole	"optionally"	(p. 659)	
"used to got"/"didn't thought"	n/a		
***not* as pre-verbal negator**	n/a		
"was want/was wanna"	n/a		
done* as preterit of *do			
Appalachian English	also *did*	(p. 248)	
Colloquial American English	"irregular verbs typically occur in the three categories listed here"	(p. 223)	
East Anglian English	-	(p. 143)	
English dialects in the North of England	-	(p. 115)	
Newfoundland English	"extensive regularization of its irregular (i.e. "strong" or "mixed") past forms	(p. 307)	
NZ English	not all speakers	(p. 584)	
Rural and ethnic varieties in the	"Irregular verbs tend to fall well within the vernacular irrregular	(p. 290)	

Southeast	verb patterns set forth in Wolfram and Schilling-Estes (1998: 331)"		
South-Eastern English	-	(p. 180)	
South-Western English	-	(p. 170)	
Urban AAVE	-	(p. 330)	
Pre-verbal *been* for perfect tense	n/a with regard to perfect tense		
Unstressed pre-verbal *do* and *be*			
Cape Flats English	"reported in"	(p. 1135)	
English dialects in the Southwest	"periphrastic *do* is omnipresent with some speakers, while others do not have it in their language system at all"	(p. 171)	
Irish English	"common pattern", not clear whether unstressed or not	(p. 79)	
Welsh English	seems to be common	(p. 109-111)	
do be			
Irish English	"common pattern"	(p. 79)	
Co-occurence of aspect markers like *done been*	n/a		
***is* levelling**			
Rural AAVE	"feature is present"	(p. 335)	
Earlier AAVE	"feature is present"	(p. 335)	
Urban AAVE	"feature is infrequent"	(p. 335)	
Southern EAVE	"feature is infrequent"	(p. 335)	
Anglo-Bahamian	"feature is infrequent"	(p. 403)	
Afro-Bahamian (mesolect)	"feature is infrequent"	(p. 403)	
Afro-Bahamian (basilect)	"feature is present"	(p. 403)	
Jamaican Creole	"feature is present", "few standard copula forms in the basilect"	(p. 403)	
Gullah	"feature is present"	(p. 403)	

References

Aceto, Michael and Jeffrey K Williams, eds. 2003. *Contact Englishes of the Eastern Caribbean.* (Varieties of English Around the World Series G 30). Amsterdam and Philadelphia: John Benjamins.

Adendorff, Ralph. 2002. "Fanakalo: a pidgin in South Africa." In: Rajend Mesthrie, ed. *Language in South Africa.* Cambridge: Cambridge University Press, 179–99.

Altenhofen, Cléo Vilson. 1996. *Hunsrückisch in Rio Grande do Sul: Ein Beitrag zur Beschreibung einer deutschbrasilianischen Dialektvarietät im Kontakt mit dem Portugiesischen.* (Mainzer Studien zur Sprach- und Volksforschung 21). Stuttgart: Steiner.

Andersen, Henning. 1988. "Center and periphery: Adoption, diffusion and spread." In Jacek, Fisiak, ed. *Historical Dialectology: Regional and Social.* Berlin: Mouton de Gruyter, 39–83.

Anderwald, Lieselotte. 2001. "*Was/Were*-variation in Non-Standard British English today." *English World-Wide* 22: 1-21.

Anonymous (F. Duncan?). 1805. *A Description of the Island of St. Helena; Containing Observations on its Singular Structure and Formation; and an Account of its Climate, Natural History, and Inhabitants.* London: Phillips.

Arends, Jacques and Adrienne Bruyn. 1994. "Gradualist and developmental hypotheses." In Jacques Arends, Pieter Muysken, and Norval Smith, eds., 111–20.

———, Pieter Muysken, and Norval Smith. 1994. *Pidgins and Creoles: An Introduction.* Amsterdam and Philadelphia: John Benjamins.

Auer, Peter and Jürgen E. Schmidt, eds. fc. *Language and Space. An International Handbook of Linguistic Variation.* Berlin: Mouton de Gruyter.

———, Jacinta Arnhold, and Cintia Bueno Aniola. 2005. "Being 'Colono' and being 'Daitsch' in Rio Grande do Sul: Language choice and linguistic heterogeneity." *Calidoscópio: Universidade do vale do Rio dos Sinos* 3(3): 170–83.

Bailey, Guy. 1997. "When did Southern English begin?" In Edgar W. Schneider, ed. *Englishes Around the World: Studies in Honour of Manfred Görlach.* Amsterdam: John Benjamins, 255–75.

——— and Natalie Maynor. 1985. "The present tense of be in Southern Black folk speech." *American Speech* 60: 195–213

——— and ———. 1987. "Decreolization?" *Language in Society* 16: 449–73.

Bailey, Robert. 1994. "Consonant cluster reduction in Tejano English." *Language Variation and Change* 6: 303–27.

Bain, Kenneth. 1993. *St Helena: The Island, Her People and Their Ship.* York: Wilton.

Baker, Philip. 1987. "Historical developments in Chinese Pidgin English and the nature of the relationships between the various Pidgin Englishes of the Pacific region." *Journal of Pidgin and Creole Languages* 2: 163–207.

———. 1993. "Australian influence on Melanesian Pidgin English." *Te Reo* 36: 3–67.

———. 1995. "Motivation in Creole genesis." In Philip Baker, ed. *From Contact to Creole and Beyond.* (Westminster Creolistics Series). London: Battlebridge Press.

——— and Magnus Huber. 2001. "Atlantic, Pacific, and world-wide features in English lexicon contact languages." *English World-Wide* 22(2): 157–208.

Bakker, Peter. 1994. "Michif, the Cree-French mixed language of the Métis buffalo hunters in Canada." In Peter Bakker and Maarten Mous, eds. *Mixed Languages*. Amsterdam: IFOTT, 13–33.

———. 1997. *A Language of Our Own: The Genesis of Michif, the Mixed Cree-French Language of the Canadian Métis.* (Oxford Studies in Anthropological Linguistics 10). New York: Oxford University Press.

——— and Robert A. Papen. 1996. "Michif and other languages of the Canadian métis." In Stephen A. Wurm, Peter Mühlhäusler, and Darrell T. Tyron, eds. *Atlas of Languages of Intercultural Communication in the Pacific, Asia and the Americas.* Berlin: Mouton de Gruyter, 1171–83.

Bauer, Laurie. 2000. "The dialectal origins of New Zealand English." In Allan Bell and Koenraad Kuiper, eds. *New Zealand English.* (Varieties of English Around the World G25). Amsterdam and Philadelphia: John Benjamins, 40–52.

Baugh, Albert C. and Thomas Cable. 1951. *A History of the English Language.* London: Routledge.

Baugh, John. 1980. "A reexamination of the Black English copula." In William Labov, ed., 83–106.

Beatson, Anthony. 1816. *Tracts Relative to the Island of St. Helena; Written During a Residence of Five Years*. London: W. Bulmer & Co.

Beeckman, Daniel. 1973 [1718]. *A Voyage to and from the Island of Borneo.* Folkestone: Dawsons.

Bell, Allan. 1984. "Language style as audience design." *Language in Society* 13: 145–204.

Bernard, John R. 1981. "Australian Pronunciation." In Arthur Delbridge, John Bernard, David Blair, Pam Peters, and Susan Butler. *Macquarie Dictionary.* Sydney: Macquarie Library, 18–27.

———. 1989. "Quantitative aspects of the sounds of Australian English." In Peter Collins and David Blair, eds. *Australian English: The Language of a New Society*. St Lucia, Qld: University of Queensland Press, 187–204.

Bickerton, Derek. 1981. *Roots of Language*. Ann Arbor: Karoma Press.

Blair, David and Peter Collins, eds. 2001. *English in Australia.* (Varieties of English Around the World G26). Amsterdam and Philadelphia: John Benjamins.

Blake, Renée. 1997. "Defining the envelope of linguistic variation: The case of 'don't-count' forms in the copula analysis of African American Vernacular English." *Language Variation and Change* 9: 55–80.

——— and Meredith Josey. 2003. "The /ay/ diphthong in a Martha's Vineyard community: What can we say 40 years after Labov?" *Language in Society* 32: 451–85.

Blanc, Haim. 1968. "The Israeli Koine as an emergent national standard." In Joshua A. Fishman, Charles A. Ferguson, and Jyotirindra Das Gupta, eds. *Language Problems in Developing Nations*. New York: John Wiley and Sons, 237–51.

Booij, Geert. 2002. "The balance between storage and computation in the language faculty." Science Prestige Lecture given at the University of Canterbury, Christchurch, 30 July 2002.

Britain, David. 1991. "Dialect and Space: A Geolinguistic Study of Speech Variables in the Fens." Unpublished Ph.D. dissertation, University of Essex.

———. 1997. "Dialect Contact and Phonological Reallocation: 'Canadian Raising' in the English Fens." *Language in Society* 26: 15–46.

———. 2002. "Diffusion, levelling, simplification and reallocation in past tense BE in the English Fens." *Journal of Sociolinguistics* 6(1): 16–43.

——— and Peter Trudgill. 1999. "Migration, new dialect formation and sociolinguistic refunctionalisation: *reallocation* as an outcome of dialect contact." *Transactions of the Philological Society* 97: 245–56.

Broch, Ingvild and Ernst Håkon Jahr. 1984. *Russenorsk: Et pidgin språk i Norge*. Oslo: Novus.

Brooke, Thomas H. 1808. *A History of the Island of St Helena From Its Discovery by the Portuguese to the Year 1806*. London: Black, Parry and Kingsbury.

Campbell, Lyle. 1998. *Historical Linguistics: An Introduction*. Cambridge, MA: MIT Press.

——— and Alice C. Harris. 1995. *Historical Syntax in a Cross-Linguistic Perspective*. Cambridge: Cambridge University Press.

Chambers, J. K. 1973. "Canadian raising." *Canadian Journal of Linguistics* 18: 113–35.

———. 1992. "Dialect acquisition." *Language* 68: 673–705.

——. 1995. *Sociolinguistic Theory: Linguistic Variation and Its Social Significance.* Oxford: Blackwell.

——. 2004. "Dynamic typology and vernacular universals." In Bernd Kortmann, ed. *Dialectology Meets Typology*. Berlin/New York: Mouton de Gruyter, 127–45.

—— and Peter Trudgill. 1998. *Dialectology.* 2nd. ed. Cambridge: Cambridge University Press.

Chaudenson, Robert. 1992. *Des îles, des hommes, des langues: essais sur la créolisation linguistique et culturelle*. Paris: L'Harmattan.

——. 2003. *La créolisation: théorie, applications, implications*. Paris: L'Harmattan.

Cheshire, Jenny. 1982. *Variation in an English Dialect: A Sociolinguistic Study.* Cambridge: Cambridge University Press.

——, ed. 1991. *English Around the World: Sociolinguistic Perspectives.* Cambridge: Cambridge University Press.

Clark, Ross. 1979. "In search of Beach-la-Mar. Towards a history of Pacific Pidgin English." *Te Reo* 22: 3–64.

Collins, Peter and David Blair. 2001. "Language and identity in Australia." In David Blair and Peter Collins, eds. *English in Australia.* (Varieties of English Around the World G26). Amsterdam and Philadelphia: John Benjamins.

Corne, Chris. 1999. *From French to Creole: The Development of New Vernaculars in the French Colonial World.* London: University of Westminster Press.

Croft, William. 2000. *Explaining Language Change: An Evolutionary Approach*. London: Longman.

Cross, Tony. 1980. *St Helena, including Ascension Island and Tristan da Cunha*. Newton Abbot, Devon: David and Charles.

Crystal, David. 1991. *A Dictionary of Linguistics and Phonetics.* 3rd ed. Oxford: Blackwell.

——. 1997. *English as a Global Language*. Cambridge: Cambridge University Press.

Darwin, Charles. 1839. "Journal of researches into the natural history and geology of the countries visited during the voyage of H.M.S. "Beagle" round the world, under the command of Capt. Fitz Roy, R.N." [Chapter 21: From Mauritius to England].

de Rennefort, Sylvain. 1688. *Histoire des Indes Orientales*. Paris: A Seneuze.

Dickson, Vivienne. 1973. "St Helena Place-Names." *Names* 21: 205–19.

Dillard, Joey L. 1972. *Black English: Its Usage and History in the United States*. New York: Random House.

Domenichini-Ramiaramananan, Bakoly. 1977. *Le Malgache: Essai de description sommaire*. Paris: SELAF.

Domingue, Nicole. 1981. "Internal change in a transplanted language." *Studies in the Linguistic Sciences* 4(2): 151–59.

Eisikovits, Edina. 1991. "Variation in subject-verb agreement in inner Sydney English." In Cheshire, ed., 235–55.

Evans, Dorothy. 1994. *Schooling in the South Atlantic Islands 1661–1992*. Oswestry: Anthony Nelson.

Fasold, Ralph. 1972. *Tense Marking in Black English: A Linguistic and Social Analysis*. Arlington, VA: Center for Applied Linguistics.

Feagin, Crawford. 1979. *Variation and Change in Alabama English*. Washington, D.C.: Georgetown University Press.

———. 1991. "Preverbal done in Southern States English." In Peter Trudgill and J. K. Chambers, eds. *Dialects of English: Studies in Grammatical Variation*. London: Longman, 161–90.

Ferguson, Charles A. 1959. "The Arabic Koine." *Language* 35(4): 616–30.

Ferguson, Ronnie. 2003. "The Formation of the Dialect of Venice." *Forum for Modern Language Studies* 39: 450–64.

Fox, James A. 1983. "Simplified Input and Negotiation in Russenorsk." In Roger Anderson, ed. *Pidginization and Creolization as Language Acquisition*. Rowley, MA: Newbury House, 94–108.

Gambhir, Surendra Kumar. 1981. "The East Indian Speech Community in Guyana: A Sociolinguistic Study with Special Reference to Koiné Formation." Ph.D. dissertation, University of Pennsylvania.

Gargen, Henry. 1665. "A Description of the Island of St. Helena to whom itt may concerne: By mee Henry Gargen from ye year 1661 to ye yeare of our Lord: 1665." Ms.

George, Basil. 2002a. "The Pepper Tree." Self-published manuscript, illustrated. 24pp. 2nd edition.

———. 2002b. "The Banyan Tree." 2002. Self-published manuscript, illustrated. 24pp. 2nd edition.

Gil, David. 1994. "The Structure of Riau Indonesian." *Nordic Journal of Linguistics* 17: 179–200.

———. 2006. "Intonation and Thematic Roles in Riau Indonesian." In Chungmin Lee, Matthew Gordon, and Daniel Büring, eds. *Topic and Focus: Cross-Linguistic Perspectives on Meaning and Intonation*. (Studies in Linguistics and Philosophy 82). Dordrecht: Springer, 41–68.

Giles, Howard. 1973. "Accent mobility: a model and some data." *Anthropological Linguistics* 15, 87–105.

———, Justine Coupland, and Nikolas Coupland, eds. 1991. *Contexts of Accommodation: Developments in Applied Linguistics*. Cambridge: Cambridge University Press.

———, Donald M. Taylor, and Richard Y. Bourhis. 1973. "Towards a theory of interpersonal accommodation through speech: some Canadian data." *Language in Society* 2, 177–92.

Gill, Mrs. 1878. *Six Months in Ascension. An Unscientific Account of a Scientific Expedition*. London: John Murray.

Goodluck, Helen. 1991. *Language Acquisition: A Linguistic Introduction*. Oxford and Cambridge, MA: Blackwell.

Gordon, Elizabeth. 1998. "The Origins of New Zealand speech: The limits of recovering historical information from written records." *English World-Wide* 19: 61–86.

—— and Tony Deverson. 1998. *New Zealand English and English in New Zealand*. Auckland: New House.

—— and Andrea Sudbury. 2002. "The history of Southern Hemisphere Englishes." In Richard Watts and Peter Trudgill, eds. *Alternative Histories of English*. London: Routledge, 67–86.

——, Lyle Campbell, Jennifer Hay, Margaret Maclagan, Andrea Sudbury, and Peter Trudgill. 2004. *New Zealand English: Its Origins and Evolution*. Cambridge: Cambridge University Press.

Görlach, Manfred. 1986. "Middle English – a creole?" In Dieter Kastovsky and Aleksander Szwedek, eds. *Linguistics Across Historical and Geographical Boundaries: In Honour of Jacek Fisiak on the Occasion of his Fiftieth Birthday*. (Trends in Linguistics: Studies and Monographs 32). Berlin: Mouton de Gruyter, 329–44.

——. 1987. "Colonial lag? The alleged conservative character of American English and other 'colonial' varieties." *English World-Wide* 8: 41–60.

Gosse, Philip. 1938. *St Helena, 1502–1938*. London: Cassell.

Graddol, David, Dick Leith, and Joan Swann. 1996. *English: History, Diversity and Change*. London: Open University/Routledge.

Grant, Benjamin. 1879. *A Variety of Interesting and Statistical Information. Also a Photographic View*. St Helena: Grant.

——. 1881. *A Few Notes on St Helena*. St Helena: Grant.

Guy, Gregory. 1980. "Variation in the group and in the individual: The case of final stop deletion." In William Labov, ed., 1–36.

Hakluyt, Richard. 1600. *The Principal Navigations Voyages Traffiques & Discoveries of the English Nation*. London: Bishop, Newberie and Barker.

Hammarström, Göran. 1980. *Australian English: Its Origin and Status*. (Forum Phoneticum 19). Hamburg: Helmut Buske.

——. 1985. "On the origin of Australian English." *Beiträge zur Phonetik und Linguistik* 48: 369–72.

Hancock, Ian F. 1969. "A provisional comparison of the English-based Atlantic Creoles." *African Language Review* 8: 7–72.

——. 1987. "A preliminary classification of the anglophone Atlantic Creoles with syntactic data from thirty-three representative dialects." In Glenn G. Gilbert, ed. *Pidgin and Creole Languages. Essays in Memory of John E. Reinecke*. Honolulu: University of Hawai'i Press, 264–333.

———. 1991. "St. Helena English." In Francis Byrne and Thom Huebner, eds. *Development and Structures of Creole Languages: Essays in Honor of Derek Bickerton*. Amsterdam and Philadelphia: John Benjamins, 17–28.

Hartman Keiser, Steve. 2001. "Demystifying drift: explaining linguistic change across speech islands." Paper presented at the annual meeting of the *Linguistic Society of America*, Washington, D.C., 6–9 January 2001.

Hazen, Kirk. 2000. *Identity and Ethnicity in the Rural South: A Sociolinguistic View Through Past and Present Be* (Publications of the American Dialect Society No. 83). Durham, NC: Duke University Press.

Hickey, Raymond. 2003. "How do dialects get the features they have? On the process of new dialect formation." In Raymond Hickey, ed. *Motives for Language Change*. Cambridge: Cambridge University Press, 213–39.

———, ed. 2004. *Legacies of Colonial English: Studies in Transported Dialects*. Cambridge: Cambridge University Press.

Holm, John. 1984. "Variability of the copula in Black English and its creole kin." *American Speech* 59: 291–309.

———. 1986. "Substrate diffusion." In Pieter Muysken and Norval Smith, eds. *Substrata versus Universals in Creole Genesis*. London: University of Westminster Press, 259–78.

———. 1988. *Pidgins and Creoles*. Vol. 1: *Theory and Structure*. Cambridge: Cambridge University Press.

———. 1989. *Pidgins and Creoles*. Vol. 2: *Reference Survey*. Cambridge: Cambridge University Press.

———. 1992. "Atlantic meets Pacific: Lexicon common to the English-based pidgins and creoles." *Language Sciences* 14: 185–96.

———. 2000. *Introduction to Pidgins and Creoles*. Cambridge: Cambridge University Press.

———. 2004. *Languages in Contact: the Partial Restructuring of Vernaculars*. Cambridge: Cambridge University Press.

Holmes, Janet and Allan Bell. 1994. "Consonant cluster reduction in New Zealand English." *Wellington Working Papers in Linguistics* 6: 56–82.

Huber, Magnus. 1999. *Ghanaian Pidgin English in its West African context: A Sociohistorical and Structural Analysis*. (Varieties of English Around the World Series G 24). Amsterdam and Philadelphia: John Benjamins.

Hymes, Dell H, ed. 1971. *Pidginization and Creolization of Languages*. Cambridge: Cambridge University Press.

Jackson, Emily L. 1903. *St Helena: The Historic Island*. London: Ward, Lock and Co.

Janisch, Hudson Ralph. 1885. *Extracts from the St. Helena Records*. St. Helena: Grant.

Jenkins, Jennifer. 2003. *World Englishes. A Resource Book for Students*. London: Routledge.

Kautzsch, Alexander and Edgar W. Schneider. 2000. "Differential creolization: Some evidence from Earlier African American Vernacular English in South Carolina." In Ingrid Neumann-Holzschuh and Edgar W. Schneider, eds. *Degrees of Restructuring in Creole Languages*. Amsterdam and Philadelphia: John Benjamins, 247–74.

Keenan, Elinor. 1974. "Norm-makers, norm-breakers: uses of speech by men and women in a Malagasy community." In Richard Bauman and Joel Sherzer, eds. *Ethnography of Communication*. Cambridge: Cambridge University Press, 125–43.

——. 1976. "The universality of conversational postulates." *Language in Society* 5: 67–80.

Kerswill, Paul. 1994. "Babel in Buckinghamshire? Pre-school children acquiring accent features in the New Town of Milton Keynes." In Gunnel Melchers and Niels-Lennart Johannessen, eds. *Nonstandard Varieties of Language: Papers from the Stockholm Symposium*. Stockholm: Almquist and Wiksell, 64–84.

——. 1996. "Children, adolescents and language change." *Language Variation and Change* 8: 177–202.

——. 2001. "Koineization and accommodation." In J. K. Chambers, Peter Trudgill, and Natalie Schilling-Estes, eds. *The Handbook of Language Variation and Change*. Oxford, UK and Malden, MA: Blackwell, 669–702.

—— and Ann Williams. 1992. "Some principles of dialect contact: Evidence from the new town of Milton Keynes." In Irene Philippaki-Warburton and Richard Ingham, eds. *Reading Working Papers 1992*. University of Reading: Department of Linguistic Science, 68–90.

—— and ——. 2000. "Creating a new town koiné: children and language change in Milton Keynes." *Language in Society* 29: 65–115.

Khan, Farhat. 1991. "Final consonant cluster simplification in a variety of Indian English." In Jenny Cheshire, ed., 288–98.

Kortmann, Bernd and Benedikt Szmrecsanyi. 2004. "Global synopsis - morphological and syntactic variation in English." In Bernd Kortmann, Kate Burridge, Rajend Mesthrie, and Edgar Schneider, eds. *A Handbook of Varieties of English. A Multimedia Reference Tool.* Vol. 2: *Morphology and Syntax*. Berlin and New York: Mouton de Gruyter, 1122–82.

Kurath, Hans and Raven McDavid. 1961. *The Pronunciation of English in the Atlantic States; Based upon the Collections of the Linguistic Atlas of the Eastern United States*. Ann Arbor: University of Michigan Press.

Labov, William. 1972a. *Language in the Inner City. Studies in the Black English Vernacular*. Philadelphia: University of Pennsylvania Press.

——. 1972b. "The social motivation of a sound change." In William Labov, ed. *Sociolinguistic Patterns*. Philadelphia: University of Pennsylvania

Press, 1–42. [First published 1963. "The social motivation of a sound change." *Word* 19: 273–307.]

———, Paul Cohen, Clarence Robins, and John Lewis. 1968. "A Study of the Non-standard English of Negro and Puerto Rican Speakers in New York City" (final report, cooperative research project 3288). Washington, D.C.: Educational Research Information Center.

Lass, Roger. 1990. "Where do extraterritorial Englishes come from? Dialect input and recodification in transported Englishes." In Sylvia Adamson, Vivien Law, Nigel Vincent, and Susan Wright, eds. *Papers From the Fifth International Conference on English Historical Linguistics*. Amsterdam and Philadelphia: John Benjamins, 245–80.

Lawson, Philip. 1993. *The East India Company: A History*. London: Longman.

Le Page, Robert and Andrée Tabouret-Keller. 1985. *Acts of Identity*. Cambridge: Cambridge University Press.

Lehmann, Winfred P. 1992. *Historical Linguistics* (3rd ed.). London: Routledge.

Long, Daniel. 2007. *English on the Bonin (Ogasawara) Islands*. Durham: Duke University Press.

Mæhlum, Brit. 1992. "Dialect socialization in Longyearbyen, Svalbard (Spitsbergen): A fruitful chaos." In Ernst Håkon Jahr, ed. *Language Contact and Language Change*. Berlin: Mouton de Gruyter, 117–30.

Marckwardt, Albert H. 1958. *American English*. New York: Oxford University Press.

Markey, Thomas L. 1982. "Afrikaans: creole or non-creole?" *Zeitschrift für Dialektologie und Linguistik* 49: 169-207.

McCrum, Robert, William Cran, and Robert MacNeil. 1992. *The Story of English*. London: Faber and Faber.

McWhorter, John H. 1998. "Identifying the creole prototype: vindicating a typological class." *Language* 74(4): 788–818.

———. 2005. *Defining Creole*. Oxford: Oxford University Press.

Melliss, John C. 1875. *St. Helena: A Physical, Historical, and Topographical Description of the Island, Including Its Geology, Fauna, Flora, and Meteorology*. London: Reeve and Co.

Mesthrie, Rajend. 1989. "The Origins of Fanagalo." *Journal of Pidgin and Creole Languages* 4(2): 211–40.

———. 1993. "Koineization in the Bhojpuri-Hindi diaspora - with special reference to South Africa." *International Journal of the Sociology of Language* 99: 25-44.

Milroy, James and Lesley L. Milroy. 1995. *Authority in Language: Investigating Language Prescription and Standardization*. London: Routledge & Kegan Paul.

Mohan, Peggy. 1978. "Trinidad Bhojpuri: A Morphological Study." PhD dissertation, University of Michigan.

Montgomery, Michael. 1998. "Myth 9: In the Appalachians they speak like Shakespeare." In Laurie Bauer and Peter Trudgill, eds. *Language Myths*. London: Penguin Books, 66–76.

——. 2000. "Isolation as a linguistic construct." *Southern Journal of Linguistics* 24: 41–53.

——, Janet M. Fuller, and Sharon DeMarse. 1993. "'The Black Men Has Wives and Sweet Harts [and Third Person Plural -s] Jest like the White Men': Evidence for Verbal -s from Written Documents on Nineteenth-Century African American Speech." *Language Variation and Change* 5: 335–54.

Mufwene, Salikoko S. 1986. "Les langues créoles peuvent-elles être définies sans allusion à leur histoire?" *Études Créoles* 9: 135–50.

——. 1991. "Pidgins, Creoles, Typology, and Markedness." In Francis Byrne and Thom Huebner, eds. *Development and Structures of Creole Languages: Essays in Honor of Derek Bickerton*. Amsterdam and Philadelphia: John Benjamins, 123–43.

——. 1992. "Why grammars are not monolithic." In Diane Brentari, Gary Larson, and Lynn MacLeod, eds. *The Joy of Grammar: A Festschrift in Honor of James D. McCawley*. Amsterdam: John Benjamins, 225–50.

——. 1996. "The founder principle in creole genesis." *Diachronica* 13(1): 83–134.

——. 1999. "The founder principle revisited: Rethinking feature selection in North American English." Talk given at *Methods X: International Conference on Methods in Dialectology*, St. Johns, Newfoundland, Canada, 10–15 August 1999.

——. 2001. *The Ecology of Language Evolution*. Cambridge: Cambridge University Press.

Mühlhäusler, Peter. 1997. *Pidgin and Creole Linguistics*. London: Battlebridge Publications.

Myers-Scotton, Carol M. 2002. *Contact Linguistics: Bilingual Encounters and Grammatical Outcomes*. Oxford: Oxford University Press.

Neu, Helene. 1980. "Ranking of constraints on /t, d/ deletion in American English: A statistical analysis". In William Labov, ed. *Locating Language in Time and Space*. New York: Academic Press. 37–54.

Neumann-Holzschuh, Ingrid and Edgar W. Schneider, eds. 2000. *Degrees of Restructuring in Creole Languages*. Amsterdam and Philadelphia: John Benjamins,

Nida, Eugene A. and Harold W. Fehderau. 1970. "Indigenous pidgins and koïnés." *International Journal of American Linguistics* 36: 146–55.

Omdal, Helge. 1977. "Høyangermålet – en ny dialect." *Språklig Samling* 1: 7–9.

Papen, Robert. 2003. "Michif: One phonology or two?" In Yunhee Chung, Carrie Gillon, and Rachel Wojdak, eds. *University of British Columbia*

Working Papers in Linguistics. Vol. 12: *Proceedings of the Eighth Workshop on Structure and Constituency in Language of the Americas*. Vancouver: University of British Columbia, 47–58.

Patrick, Peter L. 1991. "Creoles at the intersection of variable processes: -t, d deletion and past marking in the Jamaican mesolect." *Language Variation and Change* 3: 171–89.

———. 1999. *Urban Jamaican Creole: Variation in the Mesolect*. (Varieties of English around the World G17). Amsterdam and Philadelphia: John Benjamins.

Payne, Arvilla C. 1976. "The acquisition of the phonological system of a second dialect." Ph.D. dissertation, University of Pennsylvania.

———. 1980. "Factors controlling the acquisition of the Philadelphia dialect by out-of-state children." In William Labov, ed., 143–78.

Plag, Ingo. 1993. *Sentential Complementation in Sranan. On the Formation of an English-based Creole Language*. Tübingen: Niemeyer.

Platt, John T. 1975. "The Singapore English speech continuum and its basilect 'Singlish' as a 'creoloid'." *Anthropological Linguistics* 17, 363–74.

Poplack, Shana, ed. 2000. *The English History of African American English*. Oxford: Blackwell Publishers.

——— and David Sankoff. 1987. "The Philadelphia story in the Spanish Caribbean." *American Speech* 64: 291–314.

——— and Sali Tagliamonte. 1989. "There's no tense like the present: Verbal -s inflection in Early Black English." *Language Variation and Change* 1: 47–84.

——— and ———. 1991. "African American English in the diaspora." *Language Variation and Change* 3: 301–39.

——— and ———. 2001. *African American English in the Diaspora*. Oxford: Blackwell Publishers.

Preston, Dennis and Roger W. Shuy, eds. 1979. *Variation in American English*. Washington, D.C.: United States Information Agency.

Reaser, Jeffrey. 2004. "A quantitative sociolinguistic analysis of Bahamian copula absence: morphosyntactic evidence from Abaco Island, The Bahamas." *Journal of Pidgin and Creole Languages* 19: 1–40.

Reinecke, John E. 1937. "Marginal Languages: A Sociological Survey of the Creole Languages and Trade Jargons." PhD dissertation, Yale University.

Richardson, J. Rev. 1885. *A New Malagasy-English Dictionary*. Antananrivo: The London Missionary Society.

Rickford, John R. 1987. *Dimensions of a Creole Continuum*. Stanford: Stanford University Press.

———. 1998. "The creole origins of African American vernacular English: Evidence from copula absence." In Salikoko Mufwene, John R. Rickford, Guy Bailey, and John Baugh, eds. *African-American English: Structure, History, and Use*. London: Routledge, 154–200.

———. 1999a. "Variation in the JC copula: New data and analysis." In John R. Rickford and Suzanne Romaine, eds. *Creole Genesis, Attitudes and Discourse: Studies Celebrating Charlene Sato*. Amsterdam: John Benjamins, 143–156.

———. 1999b. *African American Vernacular English: Features, Evolution and Educational Implications*. Cambridge: Blackwell.

——— and Russell John Rickford. 2000. *Spoken Soul: The Story of Black English*. New York: Wiley.

———, Arnetha Ball, Renée Blake, Raima Jackson and Nomi Martin. 1991. "Rappin' on the Copula Coffin: Theoretical and Methodological Issues in the Analysis of Copula Variation in African American Vernacular English." *Language Variation and Change* 3: 103-132.

Ritchie, William C. and Tej K. Bhatia, eds. 1999. *Handbook of Child Language Acquisition*. San Diego: Academic Press.

Roberge, Paul T. 2002. "Afrikaans: Considering Origins." In Rajend Mesthrie, ed. *Language in South Africa.* Cambridge: Cambridge University Press. 79–103.

Romaine, Suzanne. 1988. *Pidgin and Creole Languages*. London: Longman.

Samarin, William J. 1971. "Salient and substantive pidginization." In Dell H. Hymes, ed., 117–40.

Sands, Bonny and Tom Güldemann. fc. "What click languages can and can't tell us about language origins." In Botha, Rudie and Chris Knight, eds. *The Cradle of Language.* Vol. 2: *African Perspectives*. (Studies in the Evolution of Language). Oxford: Oxford University Press.

Sankoff, Gillian. 1979. "The genesis of language." In Kenneth C. Hill, ed. *The Genesis of Language.* Ann Arbor: Karema, 23–47.

Santa Ana, Otto. 1996. "Sonority and syllable structure in Chicano English." *Language Variation and Change* 8: 63–91.

Sapir, Edward. 1949. *Language: An Introduction to the Study of Speech*. New York: Harcourt Brace Jovanovich.

Schilling-Estes, Natalie. 1998. "Investigating 'self-conscious' speech: The performance register in Ocracoke English." *Language in Society* 27: 53–83.

———. 2002. "On the nature of isolated and post-isolated dialects: Innovation, variation and differentiation." *Journal of Sociolinguistics* 6(1): 64–85.

——— and Walt Wolfram. 1999. "Alternative models for dialect death: Dissipation vs. concentration." *Language* 75(3): 486–521.

Schneider, Edgar W. 1990. "The cline of creoleness in English-oriented creoles and semi-creoles of the Caribbean." *English World-Wide* 11, 79–113.

———. 2002. "Investigating variation and change in written documents." In Chambers, J. K., Peter Trudgill, and Natalie Schilling-Estes, eds. *The Handbook of Language Variation and Change*. Oxford, UK and Malden, MA: Blackwell, 67–96.

———. 2003. “The dynamics of New Englishes: From identity construction to dialect birth.” *Language* 79(2): 233–281.

———. 2007. *Postcolonial English: Varieties Around the World.* Cambridge: Cambridge University Press.

———, Bernd Kortmann, Clive Upton, Rajend Mesthrie, and Kate Burridge, eds. 2004. *A Handbook of Varieties of English. A Multimedia Reference Tool.* Vol. 1: *Phonology*. Berlin and New York: Mouton de Gruyter.

Scholtmeijer, Harm. 1992. *Het Nederlands van de Ijsselmeer Polders*. Kampen: Mondiss.

———. 1997. “Language in the Dutch Polders: why dialects did not mix.” Paper presented at the workshop ‘Migration as a factor in connection with convergence and divergence processes of dialects in Europe’, Heidelberg, Germany. 17–21 October 1997.

Schreier, Daniel. 2002a. “Past *be* in Tristan da Cunha: The rise and fall of categoricality in language change.” *American Speech* 77: 70–99.

———. 2002b. “*Terra incognita* in the Anglophone world: Tristan da Cunha, South Atlantic Ocean.” *English World-Wide* 23: 1–29.

———. 2003a. *Isolation and Language Change: Sociohistorical and Contemporary Evidence from Tristan da Cunha English.* Houndmills/Basingstoke and New York: Palgrave Macmillan.

———. 2003b. “Convergence and language shift in New Zealand: Consonant cluster reduction in 19th century Maori English.” *Journal of Sociolinguistics* 7(3): 378–91.

———. 2005. *Consonant Change in English Worldwide: Synchrony meets Diachrony.* (Palgrave Studies in Language History and Language Change 3). Houndmills/Basingstoke and New York: Palgrave Macmillan.

———. fc. 2009. “How Diagnostic are English universals?” In Markku Filppula, Juhani Klemola, and Heli Pitkänen, eds. *Vernacular Universals vs. Contact-Induced Language Change*. London: Routledge.

——— and Peter Trudgill. 2006. “The segmental phonology of 19th century Tristan da Cunha English: Convergence and local innovation.” *English Language and Linguistics* 10: 119–41.

———, Elizabeth Gordon, Jennifer Hay, and Margaret Maclagan. 2003. “The regional and sociolinguistic dimension of /hw-/ maintenance and loss in early 20th century New Zealand English.” *English World-Wide* 24: 245–269.

———, Peter Trudgill, Edgar Schneider, and Jeffrey P. Williams, eds. fc. *The Lesser-known Varieties of English: An Introduction.* Cambridge: Cambridge University Press.

Schulenburg, Alexander H. fc. *Transient Observations: St Helena Through Five Hundred Years of Colonial Discourse.* New York: Edwin Mellen Press.

Schulenburg, Helmut and Alexander Schulenburg. 1997. *St Helena, South Atlantic Ocean.* Allersberg: Jacob-Gilardi-Verlag.

Sebba, Mark. 1981. "Derivational regularities in a creole lexicon: The case of Sranan." *Linguistics* 19: 101–17.

———. 1997. *Contact Languages: Pidgins and Creoles*. London: Macmillan.

Shilling, Allison. 1980. "Bahamian English: A non-continuum?" In Richard Day, ed. *Issues in English Creoles*. Heidelberg: Julius Groos, 133–46.

Shorrocks, Graham. 1999. *A Grammar of the Dialect of the Bolton Area: Part 11, Morphology and Syntax.* (Bamberger Beiträge zur Englischen Sprachwissenschaft 42). Frankfurt: Peter Lang.

Siegel, Jeff. 1975. "Fiji Hindustani." *University of Hawaii Working Papers in Linguistics* 7(3): 127–44.

———. 1985. "Koines and koineisation." *Language in Society* 14: 357–78.

———. 1987. *Language Contact in a Plantation Environment.* Cambridge: Cambridge University Press.

———. 1997. "Mixing/leveling, and pidgin/creole development." In Arthur K. Spears and Donald Winford, eds. *The Structure and Status of Pidgins and Creole Languages*. Amsterdam: John Benjamins, 111–49.

Singler, John Victor. 1988. "The homogeneity of the substrate as a factor in pidgin/creole genesis." *Language* 64, 27–51.

Smith, Geoff P. 2003. *Growing up with Tok Pisin: Contact, Creolization, and Change in Papua New Guinea's National Language*. London, Battlebridge.

Sterndale, Robert A. 1899. "St Helena in Ye Olden Time and St Helena in the present time." Self-published ms.

Strang, Barbara. 1970. *A History of English*. London: Methuen.

Sudbury, Andrea. 2000. "Dialect contact and koinéisation in the Falkland Islands: Development of a southern hemisphere variety?" PhD dissertation, University of Essex.

———. 2001. "Falkland Islands English: A southern hemisphere variety?" *English World-Wide* 22:1, 55–80.

Tagliamonte, Sali. 1998. "*Was/were* variation across the generations. View from the city of York." *Language Variation and Change* 10: 153–91.

——— and Rosalind Temple. 2005. "New perspectives on an ol' variable: (t, d) in British English." *Language Variation and Change* 17(3): 281–302.

Thomason, Sarah G. 1997. "A typology of contact languages." In Arthur K. Spears and Donald Winford, eds. *The Structure and Status of Pidgins and Creoles*. Amsterdam: John Benjamins, 71–88.

———. 2001. *Language Contact: An Introduction*. Edinburgh: Edinburgh University Press.

——— and Terrence Kaufman. 1988. *Language Contact, Creolization, and Genetic Linguistics*. Los Angeles: University of California Press.

Todd, Loreto. 1990. *Pidgins and Creole.* 2nd ed. London: Routledge and Kegan Paul.

Torbert, Benjamin. 2001. "Tracing Native American language history through consonant cluster reduction: The case of Lumbee English." *American Speech* 76: 361–87.

Trudgill, Peter. 1986. *Dialects in Contact*. Oxford: Blackwell.

———. 1994. "Language contact and dialect contact in linguistic change." In Ulla Brit Kotsinas and John Helgander, eds. *Dialektkontakt, språkkontakt och språkörändring in Norden*. Stockholm: Stockholm University, 13–22.

———. 1995. *Sociolinguistics*. Harmondsworth: Penguin.

———. 1996. "Dual source pidgins and reverse creoles: northern perspectives on language contact." In Ingvild Broch and Ernst Håkon Jahr, eds. *Language Contact in the Arctic: Northern Pidgins and Contact Languages*. Berlin: Mouton de Gruyter, 5–14.

———. 1999. "A window on the past: 'colonial lag' and New Zealand evidence for the phonology of nineteenth century English." *American Speech* 74(3): 227–39.

———. 2000. *Sociolinguistic Variation and Change*. Edinburgh: Edinburgh University Press.

———. 2001. "On the irrelevance of prestige, stigma and identity in the development of New Zealand English phonology." *New Zealand English Journal* 15, 42–46.

———. 2004. *New Dialect Formation: The Inevitability of Colonial Englishes*. Edinburgh: Edinburgh University Press.

——— and Jean Hannah. 1982. *International English. A Guide to Varieties of Standard English*. London: Edward Arnold.

———, Gillian Lewis, and Margaret Maclagan. 2003. "Linguistic archaeology: The Scottish input to New Zealand English phonology." *Journal of English Linguistics* 31: 103–24.

———, Elizabeth Gordon, Gillian Lewis and Margaret Maclagan. 2000. "Determinism in new-dialect formation and the genesis of New Zealand English." *Journal of Linguistics* 36: 299–318.

———, Daniel Schreier, Daniel Long, and Jeffrey P. Williams. 2004. "On the reversibility of mergers: /w/, /v/ and evidence from lesser-known Englishes." *Folia Linguistica Historica* 24(1/2): 23–45.

Turner, George W. 1994. "English in Australia." In Robert Burchfield, ed. *The Cambridge History of the English Language*. Vol. 5: *English in Britain and Overseas: Origins and Development*. Cambridge: Cambridge University Press, 277–327.

Turner, Nicholas and Cathy Hopkins. 1996. "St Helena – The Lost County of England (First report by the Commission on Citizenship)."

Walker, James A. 2000. "Rephrasing the copula: contraction and zero in early African American English." In Shana Poplack, ed. *The English History of African American English*. Oxford: Blackwell Publishers. 35–72.

———. 2001. "Using the past to explain the present: tense and temporal reference in Early African American English." *Language Variation and Change* 13(1): 1–35.

——— and Miriam Meyerhoff. 2006. "Zero copula in the Eastern Caribbean: Evidence from Bequia." *American Speech* 81(2): 146–63.

Wang, William S.-Y. 1969. "Competing changes as a cause for residue." *Language* 45: 9–25.

Weaver, Barry. 1990. *A Guide to the Geology of St Helena*. Norman: University of Oklahoma Press.

Weldon, Tracy. 2003a. "Revisiting the Creolist Hypothesis: Copula Variability in Gullah and Southern Rural AAVE." *American Speech* 78(2): 171–91.

———. 2003b. "Copula variability in Gullah." *Language Variation and Change* 15(1): 37–72.

Wells, John C. 1982. *Accents of English*. 3 vols. Cambridge: Cambridge University Press.

Wilson, Sheila and Rajend Mesthrie. 2004. "St. Helena English: morphology and syntax." In Bernd Kortmann, Edgar W. Schneider, Rajend Mesthrie and Kate Burridge, eds. *A Handbook of Varieties of English. A Multimedia Reference Tool.* Vol. 2: *Morphology and Syntax*. Berlin and New York: Mouton de Gruyter, 1006–15.

Winford, Donald. 1992. "Back to the past: The BEV/creole connection revisited." *Language Variation and Change* 4: 311–357.

———. 1993. *Predication in Caribbean English Creoles*. Amsterdam: John Benjamins.

———. 2000. "Tense and aspect in Sranan and the creole prototype." In John McWhorter, ed. *Language Change and Language Contact in Pidgins and Creoles*. Amsterdam: John Benjamins, 383–442.

———. 2003. *Introduction to Contact Linguistics*. Oxford: Blackwell.

Wittmann, Henri. 1983. "Les réactions en chaîne en morphologie diachronique." *Actes du Colloque de la Société internationale de linguistique fonctionnelle* 10: 285–92.

———. 1999. "Prototype as a typological yardstick to creoleness." *The Creolist Archives Papers On-line*, Stockholms Universitet.

———. 2001. "Lexical diffusion and the glottogenetics of creole French." CreoList debate, parts I–VI, appendixes 1–9. *The Linguist List*, Eastern Michigan University and Wayne State University.

Wolfram, Walt. 1969. *A Sociolinguistic Description of Detroit Negro Speech*. Arlington, VA: Center for Applied Linguistics.

———. 1974. "The relationship of white Southern speech to Vernacular Black English." *Language* 50: 498–527.

——— and Donna Christian. 1976. *Appalachian Speech*. Arlington, VA: Center for Applied Linguistics.

——— and Erik R. Thomas. 2002. *The Development of African American English*. Oxford: Blackwell Publishers.

——— and Natalie Schilling-Estes. 1996. "Dialect change and maintenance in a post-insular island community." In Edgar Schneider, ed. *Focus on the USA*. Amsterdam and Philadelphia: John Benjamins, 103–48.

——— and ———. 2003. "Language change in 'conservative' dialects: The case of past tense *be* in Southern enclave communities." *American Speech* 78(2): 208–27.

——— and ———. 2004. "Remnant dialects in the coastal United States." In Raymond Hickey, ed., 172–202.

———, Becky Childs, and Benjamin Torbert. 2000. "Tracing language history through consonant cluster reduction: Comparative evidence from isolated dialects." *Southern Journal of Linguistics* 24: 17–40.

———, Kirk Hazen, and Natalie Schilling-Estes. 1999. *Dialect Change and Maintenance on the Outer Banks*. (Publication of the American Dialect Society (PADS) 80). Tuscaloosa: University of Alabama Press.

Wright, Laura. 2004. "Some data from slave speakers: the island of St Helena, 1695–1711." Paper presented at the Westminster Creolistics Workshop: Diachronic Studies and Theories of Creolisation, London UK, 15–17 April 2004.

Young, Richard and Robert Bailey. 1996. "VARBRUL analysis for second language acquisition research." In Robert Bailey and Dennis Preston, eds. *Second Language Acquisition and Linguistic Variation*. Amsterdam: John Benjamins, 253–306.

Index

O

P

Q

R

In the series *Varieties of English Around the World* the following titles have been published thus far or are scheduled for publication:

G36 **MURRAY, Thomas E. and Beth Lee SIMON (eds.):** Language Variation and Change in the American Midland. A New Look at 'Heartland' English. 2006. xii, 319 pp.

G35 **HICKEY, Raymond:** Dublin English. Evolution and change. 2005. x, 270 pp. (incl. CD-Rom).

G34 **MÜHLEISEN, Susanne and Bettina MIGGE (eds.):** Politeness and Face in Caribbean Creoles. 2005. viii, 293 pp.

G33 **LIM, Lisa (ed.):** Singapore English. A grammatical description. 2004. xiv, 174 pp.

G32 **HACKERT, Stephanie:** Urban Bahamian Creole. System and variation. 2004. xiv, 256 pp.

G31 **THOMPSON, Roger M.:** Filipino English and Taglish. Language switching from multiple perspectives. 2003. xiv, 288 pp.

G30 **ACETO, Michael and Jeffrey P. WILLIAMS (eds.):** Contact Englishes of the Eastern Caribbean. 2003. xx, 322 pp.

G29 **NELSON, Gerald, Sean WALLIS and Bas AARTS:** Exploring Natural Language. Working with the British Component of the International Corpus of English. 2002. xviii, 344 pp.

G28 **GÖRLACH, Manfred:** Still More Englishes. 2002. xiv, 240 pp.

G27 **LANEHART, Sonja L. (ed.):** Sociocultural and Historical Contexts of African American English. 2001. xviii, 373 pp.

G26 **BLAIR, David and Peter C. COLLINS (eds.):** English in Australia. 2001. vi, 368 pp.

G25 **BELL, Allan and Koenraad KUIPER (eds.):** New Zealand English. JB/Victoria UP, 2000. 368 pp.

G24 **HUBER, Magnus:** Ghanaian Pidgin English in its West African Context. A sociohistorical and structural analysis. 1999. xviii, 322 pp. (incl. CD-rom).

G23 **HUNDT, Marianne:** New Zealand English Grammar – Fact or Fiction? A corpus-based study in morphosyntactic variation. 1998. xvi, 212 pp.

G22 **GÖRLACH, Manfred:** Even More Englishes. Studies 1996–1997. With a foreword by John Spencer. 1998. x, 260 pp.

G21 **KALLEN, Jeffrey L. (ed.):** Focus on Ireland. 1997. xviii, 260 pp.

G20 **MACAULAY, Ronald K.S.:** Standards and Variation in Urban Speech. Examples from Lowland Scots. 1997. x, 201.

G19 **SCHNEIDER, Edgar W. (ed.):** Englishes around the World. Studies in honour of Manfred Görlach. Volume 2: Carribbean, Africa, Asia, Australasia. 1997. viii, 358 pp.

G18 **SCHNEIDER, Edgar W. (ed.):** Englishes around the World. Studies in honour of Manfred Görlach. Volume 1: General studies, British Isles, North America. 1997. vi, 329 pp.

G17 **PATRICK, Peter L.:** Urban Jamaican Creole. Variation in the Mesolect. 1999. xx, 329 pp.

G16 **SCHNEIDER, Edgar W. (ed.):** Focus on the USA. 1996. vi, 368 pp.

G15 **DE KLERK, Vivian (ed.):** Focus on South Africa. 1996. iv, 328 pp.

G14 **McCLURE, J. Derrick:** Scots and its Literature. 1996. vi, 218 pp.

G13 **GÖRLACH, Manfred:** More Englishes. New studies in varieties of English 1988–1994. 1995. 276 pp.

G12 **GLAUSER, Beat, Edgar W. SCHNEIDER and Manfred GÖRLACH:** A New Bibliography of Writings on Varieties of English, 1984–1992/93. 1993. 208 pp.

G11 **CLARKE, Sandra (ed.):** Focus on Canada. 1993. xii, 302 pp.

G10 **FISCHER, Andreas and Daniel AMMAN:** An Index to Dialect Maps of Great Britain. 1991. iv, 150 pp.

G9 **GÖRLACH, Manfred:** Englishes. Studies in varieties of English 1984–1988. 1991. 211 pp.

G8 **GÖRLACH, Manfred and John HOLM (eds.):** Focus on the Caribbean. 1986. viii, 209 pp.

G7 **PENFIELD, Joyce and Jack ORNSTEIN-GALICIA:** Chicano English. vii, 112 pp. *Out of print*

G6 **PETYT, K.M.:** 'Dialect' and 'Accent' in Industrial West Yorkshire. 1985. viii, 401 pp.

G5 **GÖRLACH, Manfred (ed.):** Focus on Scotland. iv, 241 pp. *Out of print*

G4 **VIERECK, Wolfgang (ed.):** Focus on: England and Wales. 1984. iv, 304 pp. (includes 40 maps).

G3 **VIERECK, Wolfgang, Edgar W. SCHNEIDER and Manfred GÖRLACH (comps.):** A Bibliography of Writings on Varieties of English, 1965–1983. 1984. iv, 319 pp.

G2 **DAY, Rita (ed.):** Issues in English Creoles. Papers from the 1975 Hawaii Conference. (Julius Groos) Heidelbergiii, 188 pp. *Out of print*

G1 **LANHAM, Len W. and C.A. MACDONALD:** The Standard in South African English and its Social History. (Julius Groos) Heidelberg96 pp. *Out of print*

T9 **MÜHLHÄUSLER, Peter, Thomas E. DUTTON and Suzanne ROMAINE:** Tok Pisin Texts. From the beginning to the present. 2003. x, 286 pp.

T8 **McCLURE, J. Derrick:** Doric. The dialect of North-East Scotland. 2002. vi, 222 pp.

T7 **MEHROTRA, Raja Ram:** Indian English. Texts and Interpretation. 1998. x, 148 pp.

T6 **WINER, Lise:** Trinidad and Tobago. 1993. xii, 368 pp.

T5 **WAKELIN, Martyn F.:** The Southwest of England. 1986. xii, 231 pp.

T4 **PLATT, John, Heidi WEBER and Mian Lian HO:** Singapore and Malaysia. 1983. iv, 138 pp.

T3 **MACAFEE, Caroline:** Glasgow. 1983. v, 167 pp.

T2 **HOLM, John:** Central American English. (Julius Groos) Heidelbergiv, 184 pp., + tape. *Out of print*

T1 **TODD, Loreto:** Cameroon. (Julius Groos) Heidelberg180 pp., 1 map. *Out of print*